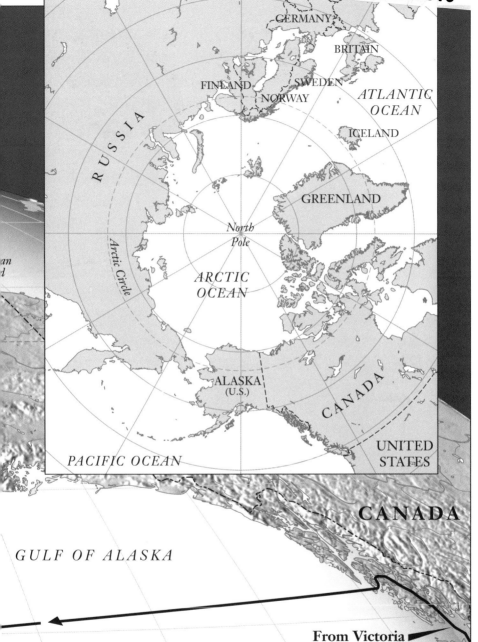

GERMANY

BRITAIN

FINLAND   SWEDEN   *ATLANTIC*
NORWAY   *OCEAN*

R U S S I A

ICELAND

GREENLAND

*North
Pole*

Arctic Circle

*ARCTIC
OCEAN*

ALASKA
(U.S.)

C A N A D A

UNITED
STATES

PACIFIC OCEAN

CANADA

GULF OF ALASKA

From Victoria ▶

────────────	*Karluk's* Northern Route
━ ━ ━ ━ ━ ━ ━	Drift of the *Karluk*
▪▪▪▪▪▪▪▪▪▪▪▪▪▪	Trek of Survivors to the Island
▪─▪─▪─▪─▪─▪─▪	Bartlett's Journey for Help

THE
ICE MASTER

THE
ICE MASTER

The Doomed 1913 Voyage of the KARLUK

JENNIFER NIVEN

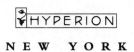

NEW YORK

For Penelope Niven and Jack Fain McJunkin, Jr.,

my mother and father.

And to the memory of the twenty-two men,

one woman, and two children

who stayed aboard the *Karluk*—

those who came back and those who did not.

A list of photo and map credits, constituting a continuation of the copyright page, appears on page 398.

Hyperion
77 W. 66th Street
New York, New York 10023-6298.

Library of Congress Cataloging-in-Publication Data
Niven, Jennifer.
The ice master : the doomed 1913 voyage of the Karluk / Jennifer Niven.—1st ed.
p. cm.
ISBN: 0-7868-6529-6
1. Karluk (Ship). 2. Canadian Artic Expedition (1913–1918). 3. Artic regions—
Discovery and exploration. I. Title.
G670 1913.K37N58 2000   00–061414
919.804—dc21   CIP

DESIGNED BY BTDNYC
PRODUCED BY K&N BOOKWORKS INCORPORATED
ENDPAPER MAP BY PAUL J. PUGLIESE

First Edition

1   3   5   7   9   10   8   6   4   2

It is good for the world to hear such stories sometimes. It makes the lives of Mallochs and Mamens live on after them.

—MRS. RUDOLPH MARTIN ANDERSON,

WIFE OF STEFANSSON'S

SECOND IN COMMAND, IN A LETTER TO WILLIAM McKINLAY,

OCTOBER 30, 1914

PROLOGUE

———— • ————

I am afraid that the task has taken complete charge of me.
—WILLIAM LAIRD McKINLAY

Williiam Laird McKinlay, a small, weak infant, was not expected to live very long. The doctors told his parents that he would be lucky to survive a year and that, if by some miracle the child should live longer, he would never make it to adulthood.

But William McKinlay did make it to adulthood. Against all odds, he was alive and well in 1913, a slight, attractive young man of twenty-four, fair-haired, articulate, with refined manners and a quick intellect. He had stopped growing at five feet four inches, earning the nickname "Wee Mac" from friends and family. It was a name he did not mind. He was, after all, lucky to be alive.

He didn't fully appreciate this fact until later in life after he joined Vilhjalmur Stefansson's ambitious Canadian Arctic Expedition in June 1913, signing on as magnetician and meteorologist. When McKinlay was an old man, he wrote, "The two years, 1913 and 1914, saw the last two expeditions to the polar regions of the old historic type in the wooden ships and before the days of radio and aeroplanes—the *Karluk* to the north and Shackleton's *Endurance* to the south. Both vessels met the same fate. Both stories tell of strenuous journeys of seven or eight hundreds of miles to bring rescue. The *Endurance* story ended happily and has been fully and faithfully recorded; the other ended tragically but has never been well and truthfully documented."

McKinlay spent most of the post-*Karluk* years of his life writing about and collecting material on the Canadian Arctic Expedition and Vilhjalmur

Stefansson. He was a man obsessed, determined to set the record straight, and to clear the name of Captain Robert A. Bartlett who, he believed, had saved his life. McKinlay finally published his version of the story in 1976 at the age of eighty-five. But for the next seven years, up until his death in 1983, he was actually working on a more forthright account of the 1913 Arctic expedition and Stefansson, its "leader." He never got to share that unfinished account with the world. Instead, his rough manuscript and papers were consigned to archives and libraries, read only by the random, interested researcher.

His notes are voluminous and amazingly detailed, many written in his neat yet shaky eighty-some-year-old hand. He had kept three diaries documenting his experiences in 1913 and 1914, one written expressly for the Canadian government, and the other two written only for himself. In these private journals, he recorded the full, tumultuous emotional experience of his journey. One of the journals was kept in pencil, written in a series of old student notebooks, and the other was an expanded version of this, painstakingly recopied by hand once he returned to civilization. He selected only statistics and the driest facts for the version he submitted to the government.

People who knew him describe a man haunted by the expedition. He himself wrote, "Not all the horrors of the Western Front, not the rubble of Arras, nor the hell of Ypres, nor all the mud of Flanders leading to Passchendale, could blot out the memories of that year in the Arctic."

Until his death at the age of ninety-two, McKinlay was not running from the disturbing memories of the past, but trying to recall them and present them to the world. The fact that this mission was never quite accomplished was one of the primary reasons I wanted to write this book. What could drive a man to devote sixty-some years of his life to recording the events of one year? Was it the horrors he witnessed? The memory of his tragically lost comrades? The debt he felt he owed to his hero, Captain Bartlett? Or that the only other point of view available for public consumption belonged to Stefansson, the man McKinlay held responsible for the *Karluk* tragedy?

Legendary Norwegian explorer Roald Amundsen went so far as to call Vilhjalmur Stefansson "the greatest humbug alive." There were some, in fact, who considered Stefansson a laughing stock for his alleged discovery of a race of "Blond Eskimo." His is the name that remains in the history books, however, while the men of his 1913–1914 expedition have been overlooked, lost, and essentially forgotten. McKinlay did his best to change this, but died before he could set the record straight. By tackling the subject myself, it is not my intention to dispute the good that Stefansson did in his lifetime or the valuable discoveries he made, nor do I intend to delve into Stefansson's pre- or post-*Karluk* careers, except as they relate to this particular expedition.

McKinlay's notes have been extremely helpful to me as I have attempted to reconstruct this fateful tale. His extreme patience with the mountains of material, as well as his great thoroughness, are impressive. But I have also made extensive use of diaries kept by seven other members of the expedition. I have included a note at the end of this book on my research, sources, and methodology.

The most important thing to me is that the people of the *Karluk* be allowed to speak on these pages in their own distinctive and passionate voices. In some places, they speak directly, and all dialogue that appears in quotes in this book comes verbatim from their own diaries or letters, or from interviews with the descendants and survivors. Likewise, any insight into the feelings or thoughts of these people comes from the feelings and thoughts explicitly expressed in their journals and descriptions of the Arctic conditions are either quoted directly or adapted from specific observations from journals and diaries of the men who experienced them.

I want you to know them by the names their comrades called them, and for that reason I have sacrificed formality in the following cases: first mate Alexander Anderson, known as "Sandy" to his shipmates, will also be known as "Sandy" here; Seaman Hugh Williams, who was only addressed by his nickname, "Clam," remains "Clam"; and the Inuit woman Kiruk is referred to by the name that the men of the *Karluk* affectionately called her—"Auntie." In addition, although "Inuit" is the proper term in this present day, during the time in which these men lived, the term "Eskimo" was used instead. To avoid confusion with the firsthand accounts from the time, I have chosen to use that word as well, even though it is now considered inaccurate.

McKinlay spent his life searching for answers and an understanding of what happened to him in the Arctic in 1913 and 1914. "If there is any explanation," he wrote at the end of his life, "I hope that someone may find it in the mass of material available and give it to the world."

That is what I have done my best to do.

CONTENTS

—— • ——

ABOARD THE *KARLUK*

———— • ————

THE CREW

Robert Abram Bartlett—*master (age 36)*

Alexander "Sandy" Anderson—*first officer (age 22)*

Charles Barker—*second officer (twenties)*

John Munro—*chief engineer (thirties)*

Robert Williamson—*second engineer (age 36)*

John Brady—*seaman (twenties)*

Edmund Lawrence Golightly (alias Archie King)—*seaman (twenties)*

T. Stanley Morris—*seaman (age 26)*

Hugh "Clam" Williams—*seaman (twenties)*

George Breddy—*fireman (early twenties)*

Fred Maurer—*fireman (age 21)*

Robert "Bob" Templeman—*cook and steward (early twenties)*

Ernest "Charlie" Chafe—*mess room boy/assistant steward (19–20)*

THE SCIENTIFIC STAFF

Vilhjalmur Stefansson—*commander (age 33)*

M. Henri Beuchat—*anthropologist (age 34)*

Diamond Jenness—*anthropologist (age 27)*

Alister Forbes Mackay—*surgeon (age 35)*

George Stewart Malloch—*geologist (age 33)*

Bjarne Mamen—*assistant topographer/forester (age 22)*

Burt McConnell—*secretary (age 24)*

William Laird McKinlay—*magnetician/meteorologist (age 24)*

James Murray—*oceanographer (age 46)*

George H. Wilkins—*photographer (age 24)*

THE ESKIMOS

Pauyuraq "Jerry"—*hunter (early twenties)*
Asecaq "Jimmy"—*hunter (early twenties)*
Kataktovik—*hunter (19)*
Kuraluk—*hunter (late twenties)*
Kiruk "Auntie"—*seamstress (late twenties)*
Helen—*age 8*
Mugpi—*age 3*

THE PASSENGERS

John Hadley—*carpenter (age 57)*
Nigeraurak—*ship's cat (not even a year old)*

THE
ICE MASTER

SEPTEMBER 29, 1924

———— • ————

We did not all come back.

—Captain Robert Bartlett

The island was a no-man's-land, little more than a mountainous slab of rock high above the Arctic Circle. Six miles of cliffs ran across it, four to seven hundred feet high. The only sliver of shoreline came at the northwestern point where the cliffs crumbled into piles of jagged rocks and gravel. The island was impossible to reach by ship or by plane, the winds raging about it, its shores surrounded by violent, raftering ice and fierce currents. So ferocious and unforgiving were the elements at Herald Island, in fact, that no one would ever live there, except for the polar bears, arctic foxes, and occasional birds that sought refuge on its rocky shores.

On September 29, 1924, however, eleven men stood silent, on the northwestern point of the island.

Captain Louis Lane and the passengers of the MS *Herman* had traveled to uninhabited Herald Island intending to claim it for the United States. Even though the island was essentially uninhabitable, men strove to possess it as they do all things, the first person to do so being Captain Kellett, R.N., who claimed it in 1849 for Great Britain in the name of Queen Victoria. And as far as Captain Lane and his men had known, they were to be the first human visitors to the island since Captain Calvin Hooper of the USS *Corwin,* forty-three years earlier.

Captain Lane had intended to land on September 27; but the tides were impenetrable, and he and his men had been unable to follow through. On September 28, they made it to land, planted the United States flag, and read a proclamation.

Their work accomplished, Captain Lane turned the ship toward the northwest. As they rounded the northwestern point of the island, however, he spotted something from the crow's nest—a shadow against the beach. Through the field glasses, the crew could make out the outline of a sled and several dark objects. The following morning, they dropped anchor half a mile offshore and once again landed on tiny Herald Island.

Eleven men went ashore that day. The bitter Arctic wind chilled them. It seemed more biting on this side of the island. It was barely October, and although winter had not yet set in with its full force, the weather was already savagely cold.

The outline they had seen was indeed a sled. Its skeletal frame, weathered and broken, lay shattered against the narrow beach. Strewn over the snow-covered ground surrounding the sled were over two dozen of the black objects, thick, rectangular tins: pemmican, that canned mixture of dried meat, fruit, and fat that was the staple of polar diets at the time. One man stooped to pick up a can. It was heavy and when he cracked it open he discovered its contents had never been touched.

The men took photographs before disturbing anything. And then they began to dig through the snow, searching for answers. Beneath all of that white, they uncovered the remains of a fire. From the pile of ashes that lay beneath, it was clear that a great many fires had been built in that very same spot, years and years ago. If this was any indication, the men who had built those fires had probably lived on the island for quite a long time.

Discarded on the gravel beach was a 30-30 Winchester automatic rifle with dozens of cartridges. It was an eerie souvenir, its stock weathered almost white, its barrel dark with rust, its magazine corroded and partially missing. And there, on the side, cut into the wood, two rusted initials were inscribed: "B.M."

Then someone stumbled across something that made these men draw back in horror—the crossed thighbones of a man. Just beyond, a bleached shoulder blade was discovered. The men kept digging. Soon they uncovered a decayed tent, its aged canvas torn and soiled from time and the elements, and underneath a sleeping bag of reindeer skin. Its folds hid other human bones, including a man's hand, perfectly intact, down to the tapered nail of the thumb, lacking only flesh to make it life-like.

And then someone held up a human jawbone. It was smooth and shrunken, bleached by the snow and wind. It was a strong jaw, with two of its wisdom teeth still imbedded. As one of the men described it: "A young man with a firm, capable jaw, cleft as to chin and with fine, regular teeth. A young man thus to die and leave his bones strewn to bleach on this wind-swept shore! With what hopes and ambitions had he sailed north— only to die, his deathplace all these years unknown and unmarked!"

It wasn't long before the men uncovered two more jawbones within feet of the first. They seemed to belong to older men. A hundred or so yards away, a fourth jawbone was discovered, the oldest yet. No skulls were found.

It was difficult to discern how long ago the men had come there, or how they had met their fates. Bear tracks encircled the camp, but close exami-nation of the bones revealed no teeth marks or signs of violent death. These four men, whoever they were, seemed to have died with all the ne-cessities of life at their fingertips. There was evidence of too much food for the men to have died of starvation. Even if they had run out of pem-mican, there was ammunition for both the 30-30 Winchester and a .22 Winchester automatic rifle. They also had an abundance of matches, two Primus stoves, and a beach strewn with driftwood.

They were probably suffering the effects of slow starvation and might also have been afflicted with scurvy. Only two or three teeth remained in each jawbone, and the men had most likely lost the rest of them while still alive. It must have been dreadful for them. If they had died of illness or the elements, however, it seemed odd that they would all perish at the same time. No one had been buried and the remains of their skeletons lay in similar positions, peaceful and undisturbed, as if the four men had just lain down to sleep.

The remaining discoveries gave few clues. Captain Lane and his men uncovered a silver watch, a pocket compass, snow glasses, field glasses, hunt-ing knives, a sled harness, three pocket knives (one engraved with the let-ter *M*), a thermometer tube, ice picks, axes, a shovel, a pair of snow shoes, a pair of skis, a can opener, a tin of tea, three enamel mugs, a silver spoon, two whiskey bottles, a candle, a nickel belt buckle, socks, mitts, caps, a sheepskin coat, rope, and the remains of a horsehair mattress.

The men searched the entire camp, digging beneath the snow and even into the earth, but no paper was found, no diaries and no documents. These men had not left behind any written record of their story. Captain Lane and his men could only speculate as to who they were and what had happened to them.

Back on board the ship, Captain Lane and the others set the four jaw-bones on a table, side by side. They tried to imagine what the men had looked like in life. Who were they before they gave up their living, breathing souls to this desolate place?

AUGUST 1913

———— • ————

The Chief of the Expedition will be careful not to endanger the lives of the party, and while neglecting no opportunity of furthering the aim of the Government, he will bear in mind the necessity of always providing for the safe return of the party. The safety of the ship itself is not so important.

—OFFICIAL JOURNAL,
CANADIAN ARCTIC EXPEDITION 1913–1918
(NORTHERN PARTY 1914–1918)

Captain Bob Bartlett stood in the crow's nest of the HMCS *Karluk* and damned the ship. She was stuck hard and fast and there was nothing he could do but narrow his eyes against the blinding white that surrounded them and survey the horizon, searching for any sign of passage through the thickening ice field.

Everyone had counted on another month of clear seas, not expecting traces of winter until September. But early on the evening of August 1, 1913, the drifting rafts of white were glimpsed just off the port bow. A few hours later, the ice was seen to starboard. In the distance, sweeping across the horizon, was a blinding band of unbroken white. Here and there, a loose floe of ice caught the sunlight and gleamed like a prism, a shimmering blue.

At first glance, Bartlett had condemned the *Karluk*. She was too slow and her hull was too weak. She would never have the power or strength to break through the ice they would inevitably face on their journey into the great, frozen Arctic. It was foolish to head north in such an ill-equipped, heavily loaded vessel, but expedition leader Vilhjalmur Stefansson had been impatient to be on his way.

They were going north in search of an undiscovered continent, which Stefansson wrongly suspected lay beneath the vast polar ice cap. They had set sail on June 17, 1913, a week later than planned. It was late in the season to be heading so far north, and they could do nothing but hope for clear seas and good weather.

This was to be the grandest and most elaborate Arctic expedition in history. It was also to be the most comprehensive scientific attack on the Arctic of all time, widely advertised as having the largest scientific staff ever taken on an expedition. Stefansson, the man who had dreamed it up, was well known for his unrelenting ambition and his grand ideas.

Yet the vessel Stefansson had chosen to take them north was a twenty-nine-year-old wooden whaler, which had been retired for years and which he had picked up for a bargain. At thirty-nine meters long and 251 tons, she was clearly an old ship whose day had passed. Originally built for the fishing industry in California—the word "karluk" means "fish"—the ship was not naturally equipped for ice breaking or sailing in the polar seas. In fact, before the purchase of the ship by the naval service, she had been condemned by a naval expert who stated that he did not find her a safe ship for freight carriage, much less ice breaking.

It was no matter to Stefansson, who purchased her for the irresistibly low price of ten thousand dollars. Also, he felt he knew the ship, having sailed on her briefly in 1908 and 1909. At the H.M.C. Dockyard in Esquimalt, British Columbia, the vessel underwent the first of many overhauls to prepare her for the voyage. On March 29, a lengthy list of repairs was submitted, including a new stern post, new water tanks, new sails, and a complete overhauling of the engines. Additional work was ordered in April, and again in May.

All the crucial decisions of the expedition had been made by the time Bartlett arrived in Esquimalt in June 1913. The *Karluk* had undergone extensive overhauling, but he immediately ordered four thousand dollars worth of additional repairs.

Her decks were cluttered and soiled, piled high with drums of coal oil and cartons of supplies and ropes and bags and large skin boats. Large, bulky sacks of supplies had been thrown onto random boxes and tools.

Underneath this wild disorganization, the ship's wood was stained, weathered, and warped in places, and the decks creaked when the men walked about.

Below deck was just as bad. The cabins were unpainted and crowded with junk and debris from previous trips, and cockroaches swarmed everywhere. The ship stank throughout of whale oil. She was far from the powerful Arctic ice vessel many of the men had expected. As chief engineer John Munro noted, her engine was nothing but "an old coffee pot."

The night before the *Karluk* was to sail from the Esquimalt Naval Yard, Bartlett sent a message to the deputy minister of the naval service, telling him that the ship would never be able to make the voyage. As far as he was concerned, the ship was "absolutely unsuitable to remain in winter ice."

But there was no other vessel to replace the *Karluk*. She was the cheapest and the readiest ship available, and as far as Vilhjalmur Stefansson was concerned, she would do just fine.

BEFORE THE TELEGRAM from Stefansson had arrived, Captain Bartlett had been trying to raise money and interest in an Antarctic expedition. His last true adventure had been the quest for the North Pole with Admiral Robert Peary in 1909, and Bartlett was restless to head either north or south to one of the polar regions. He missed the sea, the ice, the life aboard a ship. He was a man who never felt at home on land.

He had spent the spring of 1913 with the sealing fleet off Brigus Harbor, Newfoundland. It had been an unsuccessful run. Too many ships, too few seals. And the old itch had started: he badly wanted to go exploring again. So badly, in fact, that he would continue with the Stefansson trip despite his grave doubts about the *Karluk*.

Robert Abram Bartlett was born into a seafaring family in 1875. His mother wanted him to become a clergyman; at the age of fifteen he headed to the Methodist College in Saint John's, Newfoundland. He stuck it out for two years, but was utterly miserable and knew without a doubt that there was only one place where he belonged.

Bartlett was thirty-six years old when he was asked to be master of the *Karluk*. He had grown into a deep-chested, strongly built man with a ruddy complexion, a long, horselike face, and a distinct seaman's lurch. He seemed taller than five feet ten inches; his reddish hair was fading and unkempt and his blue eyes had a constant twinkle, as if he was always privately laughing at something.

Everything about him was powerful—his voice, his figure, his presence. He was famous for spouting profanities, both at his crew and in everyday conversation. He was the same on the ship and off, always, unfailingly, himself.

For all his rough appearance, Bartlett had a soft spot for beauty. He loved women, although he was a confirmed bachelor, and his heart truly belonged to his mother, whom he wrote every day, no matter where he was. He also loved music, and on ships he kept Shakespeare close at hand, as well as George Palmer's translation of the *Odyssey*, which he would quote from frequently. His constant companion, though, was Edward Fitzgerald's translation of the *Rubáiyát of Omar Khayyám*. Its pages were now frayed, and it was held together by surgeon's plaster to keep it from falling to pieces. That little book had gone with him on voyages to foreign ports while he was serving his years of apprenticeship to get his British master's certificate in 1905. The book had also been with him on both his trips with Peary aboard the *Roosevelt*, and to Europe after Peary's attempt at the North Pole. It had accompanied him on a hunting trip in the Arctic in 1910, and on numerous sealing trips.

From the beginning, he knew he was Stefansson's second choice for skipper. Whaling captain C. Theodore Pedersen had been the one hired first to pilot the *Karluk*, engage the crew, and see to the outfitting of the ship. But Pedersen resigned at the last minute, disgusted with Stefansson's questionable methods.

When Pedersen dropped out, it was Admiral Peary who recommended Bartlett. With a reputation as the world's greatest living ice master, Bartlett was a good second choice, and Stefansson was lucky to have him.

Bartlett had been at the helm of the ship *Roosevelt* in 1909, from which Peary launched his expedition to the North Pole. Peary had let Bartlett blaze the trail, but when it had come time to make the run for the Pole, the admiral had taken Bartlett aside, thanked him for his contribution, and asked the captain to see his team back to the ship. Peary took a photograph of Bartlett, against a blast of Arctic wind, standing the farthest north of any British citizen in history. Then Bartlett turned back at eighty-eight degrees north.

Bartlett took his leave with his usual staunch good cheer and watched his commander forge on toward the coveted North Pole. "Our parting was simple. He wished me good luck, told me to be careful of the new ice, and I told him I was sure he would make it."

Bartlett was gracious and uncomplaining, but it had been a bitter blow. For five years he had accompanied Peary on his quest for the Pole and they had never before gotten so close. Publicly, Bartlett later supported Peary's decision to take his manservant Matthew Henson to the Pole instead of Bartlett. The captain maintained, with apparent conviction, that Henson was the only choice to have gone, because Henson was a better dog driver than Bartlett.

The captain respected Peary above all men and would stand by him in the controversy surrounding his Pole discovery, including suggestions that Peary had never reached the Pole at all, and that he had chosen the African-American Henson so that he himself could be the only white man to reach the world's highest point. Bartlett had not been at Peary's side to witness his true and actual attainment of the Pole, but Peary's word was good enough for him. He was convinced the admiral had reached his goal, although today it is generally accepted that he did not.

Later, Bartlett said of him: "I thought Peary then—and I think him yet—the most wonderful man, the greatest, bravest, noblest man that ever lived."

STEFANSSON WAS A DIFFERENT animal altogether, and Bartlett knew he could never respect him as he did Peary. Stefansson arrived three days before the *Karluk* was scheduled to sail, in a flurry of flashbulbs and newspaper reporters. The first thing he did, before introducing himself to his crew and staff, was to hold a five-hour conference for the benefit of the press and the public. Elegant and intense, he had a way with people. His energy was contagious, so fiercely did he believe in what he was setting out to accomplish.

Stefansson's Nordic roots showed in his looks. He had commanding blue eyes; a high, impressive brow; and, at times, a formidable expression. He was not an imposing man or a man of great height or physical stature. To look at him, it was hard to believe he was the fierce Arctic explorer who boasted about living with the Eskimo and surviving in the Arctic wilderness. Yet he possessed extraordinary stamina, fueled by his great confidence in himself and in his work.

When he set out to organize the Canadian Arctic Expedition in the spring of 1913, thirty-three-year-old Stefansson was already famous, celebrated for his contributions to the world of anthropology and ethnology, particularly his studies of Eskimo life. He believed the Arctic was a "friendly" place where anyone with good sense could thrive. With this latest expedition, he would head into the northern regions above Canada. Stefansson was determined to be the one to discover the last, unknown continent by exploring the vast, unexplored region that lay beneath the ice between Alaska and the North Pole.

By 1913, the Northeast and Northwest Passages had long been found, and so had the Bering Strait. The Greenland ice cap had been crossed, and the North Pole was claimed for America by Peary. But the Arctic remained much of a mystery, and the majority of its highest frozen regions were still unexplored.

The American Museum of Natural History and the National Geographic Society had allotted $45,000 to the expedition. This sum was too little to carry out Stefansson's ambitious plans, so he traveled to Ottawa in February 1913 to seek additional assistance from the Canadian government, which offered to take over the operation completely. Without consulting the American Museum, the National Geographic Society, or his partner Dr. Rudolph Martin Anderson, Stefansson accepted the offer.

By orders of the Canadian government, the goals of the expedition were expanded, and two ships instead of one were to be employed, the *Karluk* and the *Alaska*. The expedition was also divided in two—a land-based Southern Party, functioning under the leadership of Dr. Anderson and sailing aboard the *Alaska,* and an ocean-based Northern Party, led by Stefansson on the *Karluk*. The scientists of the Southern Party would pursue anthropological studies and geographical surveys in the area around Coronation Gulf and the islands off the Canadian north coast. The staff of the Northern Party would search for the undiscovered, hidden continent in the great unknown high above Canada while also undertaking geographical, oceanographical, marine biological, geological, magnetical, anthropological, and terrestrial biological exploration.

In relinquishing its obligation to back the expedition, the National Geographic Society was emphatic on one point: the exploration, as financed by the Canadian government, must begin in May or June of 1913, otherwise the Society would once again have claim over the expedition and would send them north the following year. The Canadian government did not want to lose this grand venture, nor did Stefansson want to lose their generous backing. Thus, in April of 1913, Stefansson found himself short of time. He and his men would need to leave no later than June if they were to have a chance of safely traversing the ice-covered waters and beating the brutal Arctic winter. The plan was to head up the coast of Alaska to remote Herschel Island, where both Northern and Southern Parties would reconvene to sort out equipment and staff before continuing on into the far reaches of Canada. They hoped to reach Herschel Island by early August.

The need for haste governed every preparation, from refitting the ship to hiring the crew to provisioning the *Karluk* with enough supplies to sustain both the Northern and Southern Parties. Stefansson even damned and dismissed the required purity tests for pemmican, that standard of all polar diets, calling them suicidal delays. The important thing, above everything else, was to make that deadline.

In an early and ambitious statement, Stefansson boasted that he would hire only British subjects for his expedition. But in the end, the scientific staff would be an international one, some of the most distinguished men in their respective fields, gathered from New Zealand, Norway, Australia, France, Canada, Denmark, the United States, and Scotland. Of these, there were only two scientists of international renown who had polar experience.

Edinburgh native James Murray was a distinguished oceanographer and had served as biologist under Ernest Shackleton. He was a stout, dignified man of forty-six, robust and graying, with a well-trimmed mustache and a crisp way of speaking. He was authoritative, brilliant, and highly respected. He was also, as one of his colleagues observed, "exceedingly over-confident," due to his experience with the Shackleton expedition.

Upon signing on with Stefansson, Murray, in turn, put his leader in touch with a comrade from the Shackleton expedition, Alister Forbes Mackay. The hiring of Mackay was actually a favor to Shackleton, who was concerned about the doctor's reckless behavior and overindulgence in alcohol. Stefansson agreed to engage Dr. Mackay as surgeon to get him away from "the evil influences of civilization."

At thirty-five, Dr. Mackay was a legend, a veteran of Antarctica, having traveled with Shackleton on his famed *Nimrod* expedition of 1908-1909 and having made a name for himself on the seventh continent by being one of the first three men to locate the South Magnetic Pole, as well as a member of the first party to scale Mount Erebus, the world's southernmost volcano. In recognition of all he had accomplished on that expedition, he had been awarded the Polar Medal. They had even named an Antarctic glacier for him—Cape Mackay.

A darkly intense man, Dr. Mackay was, at times, impatient, surly, wry, and forthright. He had a mouth that wilted into a perpetual frown and the years melted away when he broke into one of his rare smiles. One of his colleagues once summed him up as a man who "looked ... as if he had been having a bad weekend." And he described himself, in typical dry humor, as "a man of... striking appearance. His keen, deep-set, hazel eyes peer out from shaggy brows, at times accentuating both a brooding calm and a boyish smile."

THEY SAILED AT SUNSET, 7:30 P.M., Tuesday, June 17. The ship was not—nor would it ever be—seaworthy, Bartlett argued, but Stefansson was unconcerned. On the evening of the second day out, the ship ran into driftwood and Bartlett ordered the engines stopped, cursing the ship up and down. On June 23, the steering gear gave out. It would break again and again. And then the engines stopped working.

Aside from Bartlett, the twenty-four men aboard ship were still high from weeks of living as the toast of Victoria, British Columbia. They had been given the keys to the city, had been celebrated and applauded for the great work they were setting out to do. As the culmination of a series of fetes, Stefansson, Bartlett, and Dr. Anderson had been the guests of honor at a special luncheon held at the impressive Empress Hotel. Dozens of dignitaries turned out to celebrate the three noted explorers.

From Esquimalt, the *Karluk* made her way north along the coast of Alaska, cruising through the famed Inside Passage from June 18 through June 23. The mood aboard ship was festive and frivolous as the men settled into shipboard life. While the crew worked, the scientists, for the most part, lay around deck and loafed. "And to think," one of them commented as they sprawled contentedly among the coal sacks, "that we get all this for nothing—the trip to Nome, tobacco, good grub and all the comforts of home. Not only that, but we are getting paid for all the time spent on board."

On July 2, they had entered the Bering Sea, where they were enveloped in fog and mist. A cautious Bartlett called for half-speed ahead. They were, at least, treated to endless sunlight, as murky as it appeared through the fog. There were only two or three hours of darkness now, and the sun rose every morning around 3:00. In spite of this, the temperature dipped to thirty-eight degrees Fahrenheit, and the men felt the cold acutely. It grew colder, the farther north they traveled, and they could no longer sit out on deck at night for very long.

On July 8, they dropped anchor off the shore of Nome where the *Karluk*'s engine and steering gear were repaired, and she took on water, coal, and provisions. At 4:00 on the morning of July 27, the *Karluk* crossed the Arctic Circle. Bartlett claimed, with a twinkle in his eye, that he could feel the bump. They had passed through the Bering Strait and were now entering the vast Arctic Ocean. They celebrated that night with a bottle of wine. Even the teetotalers—Bartlett, among them—celebrated the momentous event, although they abstained from anything stronger than lime juice.

The next morning had brought a thick fog and an unsettling wind from the northwest. The wind picked up rapidly and soon the *Karluk* was bucking the waves and taking on water. She was in the open, vulnerable and susceptible to each blast of wind and each swell of water. Her nose had dipped dangerously from time to time, and the forecastle deck was drenched. In no time, some of the cabins were badly flooded and most of the men fell terribly ill with seasickness. Many of the scientists retreated to their bunks, where they lay groaning and praying for it to end. Even Stefansson suffered from it, and disappeared into his cabin for some time.

Now, on August 1, a month and a half after her wildly celebrated departure from Esquimalt, the *Karluk* circled the edge of the ice pack, nosing her way sluggishly through the thickening fields of white. This ice was permanent, the enormous, free-floating rafts a fixed part of the Arctic horizon, yet always shifting and drifting. Each September as temperatures began to drop and winds increased, the ice would inevitably merge into a solid, impenetrable force. Toward the end of the season, the ice would grow violent, crashing and raftering, floe against floe, as they crushed everything that lay in their path, sometimes pushing one another into great ridges, which were as insurmountable and as high as mountains.

The *Karluk* could do only seven knots when pressed, under the best of conditions, and now she struggled to hold her own power against the growing pack. When it was obvious there was no way through, Captain Bob turned the ship around and headed south, damning her once more.

THE FIRST DAY OF AUGUST was a cold one, and the air had a distinctly different feel to it now—as if winter had already arrived. The snow fell, heavily, steadily, and for the men on deck it was the first taste of Arctic chill. William Laird McKinlay, dressed in his sheepskin corduroy coat and oilskins, spent an hour on the bridge helping to steer. He wore rubber boots, but these were painfully thin and of no use against the cold. He turned inside to his cabin and traded his regular clothes for a suit of fur. At last, he felt warm.

"Snow on the 1st of August!" he wrote with excitement. No one could believe the earliness of the season, but the dawning of an early winter made McKinlay's Arctic experience all the more real and thrilling. This kind of adventure was, after all, what he had come seeking.

He came from Clydebank, Scotland, a slightly impoverished, salt-of-the-earth neighborhood, inhabited by Glasgow's sturdy middle class. In April of 1913, young schoolmaster McKinlay had finished yet another workday, instructing students in mathematics and science at Shawlands Academy.

After the daily lessons, he left the sandstone walls of Shawlands for the evening and headed home to number 69 Montrose Street, where he lived with his parents, grandmother, brother, and three sisters.

He was the oldest at twenty-four, a true gentleman by nature, freshly hand-some, slight and fair, standing only five feet four inches. But he had a great determination, a firm, tenacious spirit, and was regarded a gracious young man who didn't give up easily and who liked getting his own way. "Wee Mac" was, as friends would later remark, a small man with an enormous per-sonality.

Before joining the faculty of Shawlands, McKinlay had completed his course work at the University of Glasgow. While there, he was recom-mended to the founder of the Scottish Oceanographical Laboratory to help calculate and catalog the sums and figures that had been taken on board the *Scotia* on a 1902–1904 Antarctic expedition.

While no explorer himself, McKinlay was intrigued by polar exploration and avidly followed the exploits and accomplishments of the heroes of the day. Despite the fact that news of fatal shipwrecks and lost exploring par-ties was disturbingly common and that in 1913, nearly two years after they had reached the South Pole, reports were still coming in about the tragic fate of Captain Robert Falcon Scott and his team, the world was swept up in the fervor of exploration.

In 1911, explorer Fridtjof Nansen observed: "Nowhere else have we won our way more slowly, nowhere else has every new step caused so much trouble, so many privations and sufferings, and certainly nowhere have the resulting discoveries promised fewer material advantages."

McKinlay, like other boys his age, had read with awe about these true-life adventure stories from his comfortable house in Clydebank. Of course, he knew the dangers of Arctic travel. He knew it hadn't been much im-proved or advanced since Leif Ericksson sailed his ship from Greenland to North America a thousand years ago. He knew the ice could trap or crush a ship until it sank without a trace. He knew a man could freeze to death or be attacked by a polar bear. He knew there were no radio transmissions or air travel over that part of the world. He knew if a ship was lost, it was lost.

But on an April evening in 1913 his doorbell had rung, announcing the arrival of a telegram. William McKinlay was not in the habit of receiving telegrams. With a curious and disbelieving eye he read: WOULD YOU BE WILLING TO JOIN AN ARCTIC EXPEDITION FOR THE NEXT FOUR YEARS?

It was signed Stefansson.

It was not a name he recognized. Indeed, McKinlay had never heard of Stefansson, but on the spur of the moment, without hesitation, he made up his mind. At last, he would be an explorer.

All of McKinlay's friends and family turned out to wish him well before he set sail for Canada from the docks of Glasgow. Just before he boarded, his local minister presented him with a Bible. Inside the flap, "Best wishes" was written, and the words "Psalms 121."

> *I will lift up mine eyes unto the hills, from whence cometh my help. My help cometh from the Lord, which made heaven and earth. The Lord is thy keeper: The Lord is thy shade upon thy right hand. The sun shall not smite thee by day, nor the moon by night. The Lord shall preserve thee from all evil: he shall preserve thy soul. The Lord shall preserve thy going out and thy coming in from this time forth, and even for evermore.*

ON AUGUST 2, the *Karluk* made another pass at the ice pack, but it was hopeless. She was not built for breaking the ice, and she hovered on the edge, in what appeared to be the only remaining open water, before Bartlett turned her again to the southwest.

Everyone gathered on deck to view with great excitement the first sighting of walrus and seals. The walrus were tremendous creatures, and massed together they gave, from a distance, the impression of a large, dirty ice cake.

The men also glimpsed their first polar bear, loping five hundred yards or so away from them on the ice. Bartlett called scientist Bjarne Mamen up to the crow's nest to get a better view of the animal. Together, they stood high above the ship and the ice, watching the magnificent creature as it lumbered along, so beautiful and unsuspecting. Mamen climbed back down to fetch Bartlett's rifle, then crouched in one of the whale boats on deck and aimed the gun.

"Shoot now," Bartlett called to him, but his first two shots were misses. The third, however, was a hit, and the bear dropped before rising to its feet and disappearing across the horizon. Mamen caught his breath from the thrill of it. His first polar bear, and although it wasn't a kill, he had at least made a hit.

Mamen was the last of the thirteen scientists hired for the expedition and the youngest. Stefansson was the only one who thought him qualified to be there, but Mamen was desperate to be taken on. Standing six feet two inches, with broad shoulders and a boyish face, the strapping young man was a ski champion in his native Christiania, Norway. The son of Christiania's leading funeral director, Mamen possessed all of the idealism and impatience of youth, tempered with a penetrating insight and sensitivity. But he had very little scientific experience.

He had heard about the expedition while working in the forests of Vancouver, and afterward he would not rest until he was hired. It meant he would be kept away from home for the next four years and also away from his sweetheart. They were recently engaged and Mamen loved her passionately; but he desperately wanted this job, so he fought for it. Unfortunately, his meager experience consisted only of a summer of photo topography on the Danish Spitzbergen Expedition. At the prospect of hiring him, one of Stefansson's colleagues remarked, "He appealed to me as a woeful scrub assistant but not worth burdening a party with.... I told Stefansson that his experience was of little value, that he could not do any responsible work and I did not think it worth while to take him."

Stefansson answered, "Poor boy he wants to go so much that I hate to turn him down." And that was that.

All but Stefansson were worried that Mamen would be a hindrance to the man he had been hired to assist, thirty-three-year-old George Malloch, who had a reputation as one of the most respected geologists in Canada. Malloch had been finishing a postgraduate course in geology at Yale when he received Stefansson's invitation. A ruggedly handsome man with a long-legged athlete's physique; a broad, striking face; and a sensuous mouth, Malloch was vain and temperamental, charming and good-natured. Before the ship was scheduled to sail, alarmed by the disorganization and poor leadership of Stefansson,

Malloch was urged by his superiors to resign from the expedition. He refused, making it clear that, through thick or thin, he was going to stick it out.

Malloch was promised at the outset that he would be provided with an
experienced geological and topographical assistant. Instead, Stefansson
hired Mamen just two days before the *Karluk* sailed.

Mamen's hero was fellow Norwegian Roald Amundsen, and he longed
to one day lead an expedition of his own, following in his hero's footsteps.
It was the reason he so desperately wanted the job as Stefansson's assistant
topographer. "I hope to get so much experience on this trip," he wrote in
his diary, "that I can qualify as leader of a small Norwegian expedition."

Stefansson had chosen several other members of his staff quickly and at
the last minute, not so much for their experience or qualifications, but because they were eager to go.

Physically, at least, Mamen was better qualified than anthropologist M.
Henri Beuchat, a sophisticated French gentleman with effeminate manners,
who had spent most of his career safely inside the offices of the *Revue de
Paris*, a prominent French magazine, and at the Laboratory of Anthropology
of the Museum of Natural History in Paris. Just thirty-four, his retiring, affected manner made him appear much older, and although scholarly and
brilliant, he had absolutely no experience in field work.

Stefansson's secretary, twenty-four-year-old American Burt McConnell,
also lacked practical experience and was the only member of the scientific
staff without a college or university degree. A good-looking young man
with plenty of ambition, he had hopped around from profession to profession, alternately trying his hand at railroad surveying, cashiering, clerking,
and mining, before being hired as Stefansson's personal secretary, stenographer, publicity agent, and assistant.

BARTLETT WAS JUST as unhappy with the choice of the crew as he was
with the choice of the ship. Selected out of desperation from along the western coast of Canada, one of the crewmen had only a pair of canvas trousers
to his name before signing on, two of the sailors were traveling under aliases,
two men smuggled liquor aboard even though it was forbidden, and the
cook, twenty-year-old Scotsman Robert "Bob" Templeman, was a con

firmed drug addict. He made no secret of it, carrying around a pocket-sized case that held his vials of drugs and hypodermic syringes. He was a nervous man to begin with, anxious, high-strung, and rail thin, and the drug abuse had added years to him. A pair of narrow, beady eyes darted above the thick mustache that hung from his gaunt face, and he chain-smoked feverishly.

There hadn't been time enough to search out the best candidates. Besides, the pay—ten British pounds per month—was meager. So the crew of the *Karluk* was, for the most part, made up of boys without any real experience or practical trade, attracted by the adventure the expedition promised and whatever money they could get.

Bartlett worried about their inexperience, their backgrounds, and their character. None, as far as he knew, had ever set foot on Arctic ice or snow. Not one of them had ever been trained in surviving the elements, and Stefansson, in a perpetual rush to accommodate the swift deadline of the Canadian government—disgracefully—had offered no such training.

One of the first things Bartlett did upon his arrival in Esquimalt was to fire the first officer for incompetence. Finding himself suddenly without a first mate, Bartlett promoted the second officer, in spite of his lack of experience and youth. He was a young Scot admired by staff and crew alike. Indeed, he was one of the only crewmen who seemed to stand apart, head and shoulders above the rest.

Alexander "Sandy" Anderson had barely earned his second mate's papers by the time he joined the *Karluk*. He was a slender young man, just twenty-two years old, with a sweet, boyish face, and a graceful manner, which won him friends easily. He had a beautiful singing voice, played the violin, and had a fondness for floppy, wide-brimmed hats. There wasn't anyone who didn't like Sandy.

His father's weekly income as a railway signalman was a meager thirty shillings a week, and young Sandy learned at an early age how to be enterprising and resourceful. The youngest of three boys, Sandy did not share his brothers' interest in formal education, and instead fixed his sights on taking an engineering apprenticeship.

In 1908, plagued by illness, he was instead led to an "open-air life" to cure his poor health. And so he took to the sea. He wasn't the only member of his family to have done so. Sandy's maternal grandfather had sailed on a whaling expedition to the Arctic and died there.

Apprenticed as a merchant seaman, Sandy later paid for his second mate's examination out of his own pocket in early 1913. He joined the SS *Lord Derby* as third mate, but when he arrived in Vancouver to join her company, he discovered she was in dry dock at the Esquimalt Naval Yard, undergoing repairs. Sandy hung about the shipyard, living on the *Lord Derby*, waiting for her to become seaworthy again. All repairs ceased, however, when the dock workers went on strike, and Sandy found himself stranded in Esquimalt without a ship or a job. He could continue to wait indefinitely for the *Lord Derby*, he could go ashore and try his luck, he could join the Dollar Line as some of his friends had done, or he could take a job as second mate on the ship *Karluk*.

Bartlett knew Sandy was young, but he had to follow maritime protocol by promoting the next in line. "I came here as 2nd mate at $80 a month & had only signed on for a couple of days when the skipper & mate had a row & the mate was discharged," Sandy wrote excitedly. "The old man appointed me chief officer on the spot ... although I have only a seconds ticket & haven't had that any time yet. At present ... the whole responsibility of getting her ready for sea [is] on my head & as we are booked to sail on Tuesday & ... behind in many ways I have my work cut out."

Bartlett had dismissed another member of the crew, this time one of the firemen who was put ashore when he refused to work. They had nicknamed him "the Suffragette" because he had stopped eating and working some weeks prior, and everyone agreed he should not have been hired to begin with. He was replaced by the youngest of the sailors, Fred Maurer.

Maurer had a quiet intensity about him, which came from his eyes. They were clear blue, penetrating, and piercing. Yet there was kindness in the gaze, and wisdom for such a young man. The rest of his features seemed to be a series of afterthoughts. He was husky and blond, with a firm, rugged jawline and an almost sheepish smile, as if he were perpetually trying to hold himself back and maintain a sense of control.

Just twenty years old, Maurer was a reserved, conscientious, churchgoing boy from New Philadelphia, Ohio, with "a thirst for excitement, plenty of determination, a saving sense of humor and a few cents in cash."

As a teenager, he had worked as many odd jobs as possible to save enough money to put himself through business college in Akron at the age of sixteen. Unfortunately, he had an intense dislike for school, and two years later, in 1911, Maurer and a boyhood friend headed to California. Arriving in San Francisco, the boys began looking for work and came across an advertisement in a newspaper: GREEN HANDS WANTED ON THE *BELVEDERE*.

The boys enlisted immediately, Maurer as deckhand, and it was while the expedition was wintering at Herschel Island that Maurer met Vilhjalmur Stefansson. The famed explorer made quite an impression on Maurer as he came aboard the *Belvedere* and regaled the crewmen with stories of his adventures.

When Maurer had finished his contract with the whaling ship at the end of 1912 and was once again on land, he stumbled across a newspaper article about Stefansson and his forthcoming Canadian Arctic Expedition. As soon as he returned to Ohio, Maurer lost no time in writing to Stefansson to volunteer his services.

Maurer's friends strongly advised him against going to the Arctic. His family, too, did not want him to go. Before he had left Ohio to join this new expedition, before he ventured far away from his loved ones and everything familiar, he decided to ask the fates if he was doing the right thing. "It was heads, I go; tails, I stay at home. I tossed the coin thrice, and twice the head turned up, and the fates decreed that I should go."

A SECOND BEAR was sighted on August 2, half an hour after the first was wounded, and this time each of the scientists was armed with a rifle, firing blindly away. Mamen watched as Bartlett stood at the bow and, in just two shots, brought the bear to its knees. It was a beautiful animal—seven feet, ten inches, from head to tail. The Eskimo hunters Stefansson had hired skinned the creature, and the skins were scraped and hung out on the rigging to dry, to be used later for clothing; the meat would be kept to feed both the men and the forty-some dogs on board, the pick of the finest dog breeder in Alaska.

That night, the *Karluk* forced her way into the heavy ice pack and bucked the ice until she was ground to a stop at midnight, surrounded by a solid field of white. There was nothing else to do but fill their tanks with fresh water from the nearby pools that had formed on the surface of the ice, and wait to be freed.

FOR THE NEXT SEVERAL DAYS, the *Karluk* sat trapped, just twenty-five miles from Point Barrow, Alaska. The staff and crew were restless and impatient to be on their way. No one knew what it meant, whether they would be stuck for the rest of the season, or whether it was only a minor setback. No one was more restless than Stefansson, and on August 3, he headed by dog sled to the Point Barrow trading station, Cape Smythe, where he hoped to hire more Eskimos and purchase more supplies.

That same day, the staff began amusing themselves by exploring the surrounding ice pack, going for long walks, playing European-style football, or trying their luck on skis. Mamen, who excelled in all sports, particularly skiing, was especially entertained by Beuchat's antics. The Frenchman was anything but athletic, and, his colleagues soon discovered, was quite clumsy. Beuchat raced about on the slippery ice, tumbling feet over ears, picking himself up and running on. Mamen warned him to be careful, told him he couldn't walk on ice as he did on the floor of a ship or on the ground, but the dignified anthropologist ignored his advice and promptly landed on his tail between two ice cakes, soaking himself to the bone.

McKinlay had dreamed of the moment when he would first set foot on the polar ice pack, and he was shaking with excitement as he stepped off the ship. He ran and danced with the rest of the men, leaping from one floe to another, scrambling to the tops of the ice hills, slipping and falling and sliding everywhere. It was exhilarating and liberating to be off the ship and running, momentarily free.

By August 5, however, the men of the *Karluk* were beginning to feel trapped and restless. Frolicking on the ice pack had lost its novelty. They had explored the ice, had reveled in their first taste of Arctic winter, but now they were ready to push forward. There was plenty of scientific and preparatory work to be done, but it was not enough to keep them from feeling claustrophobic. McKinlay made an attempt to retrieve his thermometers from the hold, but was unable to dig his way through the mountain of boxes to reach the instruments. He was anxious to begin working, but now it seemed he would have to wait until the stores could be rearranged and organized.

Later, young Mamen wrote in his diary, "… it begins to be monotonous and tedious to stay here, and I long to proceed north, but when? Who knows."

Then, miraculously, the ice drifted out on the sixth, and the *Karluk* broke free and steamed toward Cape Smythe. Their coveted freedom was short-lived, however. Suddenly, the tiller smashed and the steering gear broke; and they had to stop once again for repairs. It was maddening, this stopping and starting, and no matter how many times they fixed it, the steering gear never worked for long.

On one occasion, it had nearly led them to disaster, steering them toward a narrow passage between two enormous, treacherous reefs. The first mate, fortunately, saw the danger just in time and was able to alter her course, but otherwise the ship and all aboard would have been crushed against the rocks.

The engine, too, needed a good tightening up, because the rough seas had damaged it extensively. Bartlett was as vocal as ever about his displeasure at Stefansson's choice of vessel. "Our skipper has some strong things to say about the ship and her shortcomings," McKinlay observed. "It is unfortunate that he himself was not asked to buy the ship, as he might have made a better job of it."

Repairs made, they were on their way again two hours later, steaming within a mile of the beach of Cape Smythe before running up against more ice. Knocked about by the immense, churning floes, the ship took a beating.

ON THE EVENING of August 6, as the *Karluk* waited offshore of Cape Smythe, an Eskimo family came aboard. The father, Kuraluk, was rumored to be one of the greatest hunters in Alaska. He had been hired to hunt for the expedition while his wife, Kiruk, was commissioned by Stefansson as seamstress. She was a stout young woman, raw-boned and strong, and would sew the winter clothes and skin boots for the staff and crew. It was Eskimo tradition that when a married man was hired, his family came with him, so they had brought their two young children, eight-year-old Helen, and three-year-old Mugpi. Helen was a solemn child, serious and quiet, and Mugpi seemed a cheery little girl, all adorable curiosity and wide brown eyes.

Another Eskimo also came aboard that day. He was nineteen-year-old Claude Kataktovik, a widower with a baby daughter. He had left his daughter with his family when Stefansson invited him to join the expedition as a hunter, an opportunity he felt he could not refuse. After all, Stefansson had promised him a great deal of money for his services—twenty thousand dollars, according to Kataktovik, for a year's work. Stefansson also gave him twenty dollars and a rifle.

Signs of unrest stirred in the crew, who had not been outfitted with winter clothing, even though their orders had promised that they would be. Bring nothing, their orders had dictated. You will be taken care of. But they were still waiting and, it seemed, winter had already arrived. Meanwhile, the Eskimos were fitted out immediately and extensively by Stefansson, with mukluks—or boots made of animal skins—parkas, and sheepskin coats. Now some members of the crew were threatening mutiny if they weren't taken care of accordingly.

There had been trouble already between the crew and the first Eskimos hired by Stefansson—Pauyuraq and Asecaq, who went by "Jerry" and "Jimmy," respectively. In their early twenties, they spoke good English and had been assigned to bunk with the crew in the fo'c'sle. But the crew kicked them out and went together to Bartlett to voice their grievances. They were not going to room with any Eskimos, they said. In the end, of course, Bartlett got his way, and—in his presence, at least—not another word was said.

On the evening of August 6, Stefansson arrived shortly after the Eskimo family and Kataktovik with fifty-seven-year-old John "Jack" Hadley. He was an irascible-looking old salt, grizzled and weathered, with a trim white beard. His narrow eyes peered from a taut, finely lined face, burned by years in the sun and wind. He was an Englishman, from Canterbury, who had lived as a trapper, trader, and whaler in the far American north for over twenty years. No one on the staff or crew had any idea what his position was to be in the expedition, or what he had been hired to do, and Stefansson did not enlighten them on this matter. But Hadley immediately moved his belongings into Stefansson's cabin, which he was to share. Molly, his pet dog and traveling companion, moved in with the other dogs.

As the days wore on, the staff and crew received clues to the mystery of Hadley. He had a sharp tongue and he didn't mince words. He was forthright and ornery and growled when he talked.

He was on his way to a new trading post and seemed, from what they could tell, to be merely hitching a ride with the *Karluk*. He was an old friend of Stefansson's and had recently lost his Eskimo wife. In search of new surroundings, and a way to forget, he had decided to move on.

Hadley had a lifetime of experience, and he treated his shipmates to tales of being adrift on an ice floe for fifty-three days with only fourteen days provisions. When these ran out, he had survived by chewing his mukluks and sealskin coat. He had been a tramp in Australia, an officer in the Chilean Navy, and a soldier on a Chinese ship in the Chinese-Japanese War. He was also aboard the first United States revenue cutter to sail to the Arctic in 1889. Ernest Shackleton had three polar winters to his credit, Bartlett had spent four, Peary had endured nine, and Stefansson ten in all. But Hadley had survived at least twenty, and he was a good man to have around.

Later that night, after Hadley and the Eskimos had settled in, Stefansson stood by and watched as the staff and crew cleared the deck on the port side of the lab to make a house for the Eskimo family. Sandy gave the orders; the coal, lumber, and casks of goods were removed from the alleyway beside the lab, and the alleyway turned into a shelter. The work took hours, and the scientists were irritated by the way their leader stood on the sidelines and refused to help. Tempers flared. There weren't enough men to do the job, and they felt that the least Stefansson could have done was lend a hand.

Beuchat hated doing any kind of physical labor and snapped at Mamen, who called him a "pup." Mamen was not one to let things pass, and he would always speak his mind when he felt the need to defend himself or set someone straight. Now, he set Beuchat straight, calling him the "laziest man I have ever seen in all my life."

STEFANSSON HAD MADE his scientific staff pose for one last picture before they climbed aboard ship on June 17. The docks were lined with strangers, gathered to send the adventurers off. The entire Canadian Pacific Fleet had come to cheer them onward. Men of the fleet sounded their sirens, blew their whistles, dipped their flags, and hoisted good luck signals while the crowds of strangers—thousands of them—cheered and applauded.

For days, the scientists and crewmen had searched the docks for a cat to bring aboard as their mascot. According to maritime superstition, a feline presence aboard ship would bring them luck, but Stefansson put his foot down, saying that as soon as he hired sled dogs in Nome, the dogs would kill the cat. Just before pulling away from the dock, one of the engineers smuggled aboard a thin black kitten, which lived in the shipyard. They dubbed her Nigeraurak, or "Little Black One." Fireman Fred Maurer quickly came to think of her as his own.

On their first night at sea, geologist George Malloch had organized the members of the staff as lots were drawn for their quarters. Photographer George Wilkins and Chief Engineer John Munro would share the engineer's cabin; the decidedly unsociable Dr. Mackay ended up with a cabin to himself next door to Bartlett's cabin; and the remaining scientists drew the Cabin DeLuxe, as they called it, so named for its great size, at least four to five times larger than any of the other cabins. This cabin was to be shared by Malloch, Scottish school teacher McKinlay, the youthful and athletic Mamen, anthropologist Diamond Jenness, Stefansson's secretary Burt McConnell, and Beuchat, the well-mannered Frenchman.

From the beginning, the *Karluk's* crew and staff were divided. "Bloody scientists" was what the crew took to calling their more educated colleagues, with nothing but the most adamant disgust. Scientists and crew would live separately but in close quarters at the outset of the voyage, because the *Karluk* alone had to convey all men, equipment, and supplies as far as Nome, Alaska, where a second ship would be added to the Northern Party's expedition.

The crew's quarters were located in the bow of the ship. Fred Maurer's fellow fireman, or stoker, was a freckled, outspoken, cheeky Welshman named George Breddy. The A.B., or able-bodied, seamen were just as colorful, but the one who stood out most—and fit in least—was Hugh Williams, also from Wales. He was a tall, dark, sturdy fellow with a rough, handsome face; hooded eyes; a quiet humor; and a disarming smile. He had long ago earned the nickname "Clam" because he rarely spoke. While his comrades sat around and swore and cursed and bantered with one another, he would sit back quietly and observe them. He didn't swear and he didn't talk when he had nothing to say. When he did speak, it was with none of the profanity of his fellow crewmen.

Cook Robert Templeman and Ernest F. Chafe, the mess room boy and assistant steward, roomed in the steward's cabin, just next to the galley. Chafe, or "Charlie," as he was called, was the youngest crewman. Impressionable and athletic, he had a love of the outdoors and was an expert marksman. To prove it, he brought aboard the *Karluk* his most cherished possessions, two armloads of trophies and prizes he had won for marksmanship in his native Canada.

Second engineer Robert Williamson bunked with Sandy and the second mate, a Victoria, British Columbia, native who had been promoted when Sandy was made first officer. Meanwhile, the diminutive McKinlay took the upper bunk on the inside wall of the impressive Cabin DeLuxe, continually bumping his head against the berth or missing his footing and landing directly on the broad-shouldered, long-legged Malloch, who had the misfortune of sleeping below him. There were eight berths and the cabin itself was stacked full of boxes, books, magazines, and other paraphernalia. A major cleanup had to be performed before the men could sleep, and they spent a good while reorganizing and throwing things away.

The *Karluk* had soon left the Southern Party's *Alaska* behind, loaded with twice as many provisions as she could carry, and not long afterward, Stefansson purchased the *Mary Sachs*, a forty-one-ton gasoline schooner, to take the overflow of supplies. Not only was the expedition racking up more expenses than either the government or Stefansson had originally anticipated, it was beginning to look as impressive as it sounded. One of the scientists wrote, "The Canadian Arctic Expedition Navy now consists of the *Karluk, Alaska, Mary Sachs,* five whale boats (one with power), two other motor boats, three canoes, two dories, one dinghy and several skin boats."

ON AUGUST 8, Bartlett gave orders to push through the ice. They were expected to rendezvous with the Southern Party at Herschel Island in less than a week, and they hoped to reach the island in two or three days. Slivers of water, called "leads," occasionally opened in the ice around the ship, and the captain, navigating from the crow's nest, scanned the approaching ice for the farthest and most open of these, "at the same time trying to keep the ship on its course as straight as possible," observed mess room boy Chafe. The ice had loosened a bit, and the ship took advantage, steaming through to the east.

At times, the *Karluk* would pass between two mountainous ice floes that would scrape her on either side, creating such a violent shiver throughout the ship that the men expected her to be crushed. The lookout in the crow's nest—most often Bartlett, who was always on duty and never seemed to sleep—would send out continuous updates and commands: "Starboard—steady—Port—steady—go astern—go ahead." The commands were repeated by the officer on the bridge, and then from the man at the wheel, to confirm the path he was to follow.

Because of the perilous and unpredictable ice conditions, the ship could not rely upon her compass and traveled in a haphazard, vagabond path. When a floe crossed her bow, the men would direct her astern and ahead, in an attempt to break up the ice. Because she was forced to follow the spidery veins of open leads, the ship waltzed in a zigzag, moving two or three miles for every one advanced in the desired direction. The result was that the *Karluk*'s route was continually changing and the ship often went round in circles.

As the ice began to crush around the ship, the fine white cakes dissolving into powder, the men forgot their previous irritations. McKinlay, Mamen, and the others were drawn by the sight of it—the ice, alive and grinding against the ship, floes crashing against floes. The sound of it was a grisly, bone-chilling roar, continuous and deafening. The men were terrified, but fascinated. Afterward, when the din had faded to a distant rumble, there were signs of open water to the east of Point Barrow.

Stefansson immediately wanted to send members of the Southern Party ashore to await the *Mary Sachs* and the *Alaska,* which had traveled a separate route and had hopefully avoided the encroaching ice. McKinlay, James Murray, Wilkins, Jenness, and Beuchat should join their party as soon as possible, but it would be quite an undertaking. The equipment they would need for the journey would be cumbersome and the ice conditions were precarious at best. Bartlett and Hadley at once denounced the plan as "absurd & suicidal." Furthermore, they said, the *Karluk* would probably work her way free in a few days, and then she would be on her way again.

McKINLAY, AS A MEMBER of the Southern Party, wasn't even supposed to sail on the *Karluk*. In fact, in the haste of their departure, hardly anyone wound up on the ship where he was supposed to be stationed. The idea was that they would sort it all out at Herschel Island, where the *Karluk* was to rendezvous with the *Alaska* and the *Mary Sachs*. This confused, arbitrary strategy was symptomatic of how the whole expedition was run.

Because the *Karluk* had more passenger room, Beuchat, Jenness, Wilkins, Murray, and McKinlay sailed on her when they should have been on the *Alaska* with the rest of their party. Most of their scientific equipment, meanwhile, sailed aboard the *Alaska*.

For two weeks, they waited in Port Clarence while Stefansson remained in Nome, supervising the outfitting of the *Alaska*, the *Mary Sachs*, and his latest purchase, the thirteen-ton *North Star*.

The scientists had demanded a conference with Stefansson on July 10. They were alarmed by the disorganization of the supplies and their equipment. They could find guns, but could not find the ammunition. Several boxes of provisions were packed badly, and some of them were half empty. The men were provided with only one towel each, and the smaller members of the company—including McKinlay—had to make do with drawers and shirts that were too big for them. Stefansson had also purchased some secondhand parkas in Nome, which were horrible to look at, diseased and thin. He handed them to Dr. Mackay to disinfect, but the doctor pronounced the job impossible; so the men had to make do.

Stefansson seemed unconcerned about the chaos of the *Karluk*'s decks and the confused order of the supplies. "We'll sort it out at Herschel Island," became his favorite response.

The staff of his expedition was also astounded to learn that their private diaries would be property of the Canadian government and that their rights to grant interviews or supply news to the outside world had been signed away, without their knowledge, by Stefansson.

Stefansson, meanwhile, had drawn up contracts with three international newspapers, planning to send exclusive reports and articles for publication. He also sold all the newspaper, magazine, book, and photographic rights to the story of the expedition to the London *Chronicle* and the *New York Times*. In addition, he planned to write a book about the expedition and wanted to control all communications about the upcoming adventure, thus protecting his contracts.

At the conference, spokesman James Murray demanded to know the plans of the Northern Party, which had never been officially presented to any of the scientists. Stefansson bristled at their questions and, according to McKinlay, "seemed to resent our attitude in endeavouring to obtain details as to provisions for food, clothing, facilities for work, etc., & he went the length of telling Murray, when he asked what provision was being made for fur clothing, that the question was impertinent." Furthermore, Stefansson "told us that he thought our whole conduct in calling for a meeting seemed to imply a lack of confidence in our leader, and altogether failed to recognise that we all had an undeniable right to assure ourselves that every regard was being had for our protection."

It was only then that the men learned that Stefansson planned for the *Karluk* to proceed along the 141st meridian to search for new land. If no land was discovered, the Northern Party would form a base at Prince Patrick Island, which would leave the men free to explore the area from there. The ship and her crew would then return to Nome immediately for provisions.

Stefansson had said far more about his plans in press conferences than he had communicated to the men themselves. He also made a frightening prophecy—that the *Karluk* would no doubt be frozen in at some point and afterward would "certainly be crushed & sink."

Kenneth Chipman, botanist for the Southern Party, recorded an equally ominous fact in his diary: "V.S. in a signed statement has said that lives are secondary to attainment of objects and on several occasions has strongly intimated that he expected to put the *Karluk* into the ice. It is certain that if she goes into the ice she'll not come out...."

What's more, Stefansson claimed that not only were the lives secondary to the work, but that his men recognized this fact and agreed with it. This was untrue and stood in direct opposition to the instructions given to him by the Canadian government.

After the conference, several of the expedition members talked of resigning. Exasperated with Stefansson's tactics, they had no confidence in their leader and no enthusiasm for the prospect of working for him. Indeed, many of them were so disillusioned that they harbored little hope of getting any valuable work accomplished. Murray was so agitated that he threatened and intended to quit, and Dr. Anderson, of the Southern Party, even went so far as to hand in his resignation.

The following morning, Murray called a meeting of the Northern Party to discuss this possible loss of the *Karluk*. If Stefansson was to be believed, and if the *Karluk* really did have a chance of being crushed in the ice, Murray and the others felt they should plan ahead and know what was in store for them.

Murray and Dr. Mackay wrote a letter to Stefansson requesting the absolute assurance that there would be a base onshore, but their leader's reply to them was indefinite and vague.

After the disturbing and disheartening meeting with their leader, several of the men began to call him "His Lordship" behind his back. Chipman wrote: "Capt. Bartlett says he 'gave his best to Peary.' That is the spirit for Arctic work and to be able to give it to any man is inspiring. I wonder to what extent Stefansson is the man to whom I want to give mine."

THE *KARLUK* RAN AGROUND on August 10 in seventeen feet of water. McKinlay was in his cabin, typing some letters, when he heard a commotion from above and felt the *Karluk* lurch. He ran up to the deck to find her stalled, her engines still going full speed. They were about ten miles from the mouth of the Colville River, the bottom of which was covered in a glutinous mud. Twice she ran aground, and each time Bartlett reversed and re-reversed the engines until he managed to free her. But the ice thickened about her in the meantime, and once free from the shallows, she was trapped by the pack. For some time, she pushed the ice ahead of her, but was unable to break it. She would need more momentum than she was capable of to break through. As Mamen observed, the *Karluk* was a "poor ice breaker," and the ice was a "bad enemy."

Bartlett stood in the barrel for the entire day and cursed Stefansson and the ship. Mamen, as usual, kept him company. The two had become fast friends, despite the difference in their ages and backgrounds. In Mamen, Bartlett recognized a young man with great ambition and strength—bold, honest, and seemingly unafraid of anything.

Mamen, in return, admired the captain and his brilliant career, as well as his robust character. He was, thought Mamen, the only real man on board, unlike all of the crewmen, who were crass, and the scientists, who were lazy and useless. Beuchat did nothing but sleep all day. McConnell seemed capable of doing nothing but typing. According to Mamen, most of his colleagues "do indeed not know how to sew a button on their pants, much less how to darn a sock. It is disgusting to see such ignorant persons who can do only what they have been trained to do.... It is maddening to see people who always must have other people do everything for them."

It was rare for Bartlett to confide his frustrations or feelings in anyone, but as he cursed a blue streak, damning the broken-down ship that carried them and the leader who had purchased her and gotten them into this mess, Mamen was there to hear it. And he had to agree with him. Stefansson, for all his past glory and honors, was a rotten leader, from what he could see, and one needed look no further than his choice of vessel for proof. The *Karluk* was an old, weak ship. She should never have been made to do the work she was doing.

THE STAFF AND OFFICERS gathered nightly in the saloon for Victrola concerts. Each mess room—that of the scientists and of the crewmen—had a gramophone and there were over two hundred records aboard. They were mostly classical with some ragtime thrown in for variety. The Prologue from *Pagliacci* and Bach's "Air for G String" were special favorites with everyone, but they soon discovered that Bartlett had no patience for ragtime.

The members of the staff very quickly discovered that Mackay got an enormous kick out of singer Harry Lander's recording of the comic song "I've Something in the Bottle for the Morning." The doctor would rock with laughter as he listened to it and was such a hilarious sight that soon his shipmates played the record over and over again just to watch him.

Second mate Charles Barker was the only one who had any objections to this ritual. Personally, he found Harry Lander to be quite "coarse and vulgar" and did not at all approve of the nightly attention he was receiving in the saloon. Dr. Mackay silenced him in typical Mackay fashion, with caustic remarks, so that Barker, time and again, had no choice but to leave the room while Mackay enjoyed his favorite song.

The men began to run nightly bridge tournaments in the smoking room and, determined to find some diversion, cleared the amidships deck and set their sights on boxing. Mackay, thinking himself something of an expert—as he always did—taught them all they needed to know about the sport.

Many of the matches ended in draws, and none of them lasted for more than two two-minute rounds. It was Dr. Mackay versus Southern Party geologist J. J. O'Neill, however, who brought about "the trial." "Sheriff" Chipman, assisted by Burt McConnell, served the summons on O'Neill, charging him with assault and battery. The charges were simple—Mackay claimed that his thumb was sprained as a result of O'Neill hitting it repeatedly with his head. Mackay would not rest until O'Neill paid for his crime.

It was, of course, all in fun. As expected, O'Neill pled "not guilty," and the trial was soon under way. McKinlay, speaking for the doctor, stated that the defendant had "swung his head three times against his thumb, inflicting thereby grievous bodily injury." It was an absurd image, but even so, most of the witnesses called took the case extremely seriously, and defense counsel Burt McConnell, in particular, got so carried away by his newfound position of power that he forgot to see the humor in it. Instead, he conducted himself as if he were in a real courtroom.

When court was adjourned an hour later, Mackay consulted with the prosecution and suggested they drop the charges. Only a few seemed to possess a sense of humor great enough to recognize that it was a farce, and they did indeed end the trial; for the rest of the day, McKinlay regretted not being able to deliver his character assassinations of each witness, something that had taken him hours to prepare.

Bartlett often entertained the men with vivid stories. He also spent a notable amount of time cutting pictures from the illustrated papers and magazines they had on board, an activity that quite naturally piqued the interest of his shipmates. The editors of the ship's newsletter, the *Karluk Chronicle,* voiced the intense shipwide curiosity as to just where it was Bartlett was putting these clippings.

The ever-private Bartlett hated personal questions of any kind. "At the earnest request of the Editor, however," the *Chronicle* reported, "Capt. Bartlett will unbend just this once, and confess that he has the artists' love of the beautiful, and that the picture he clipped from the paper strongly reminded him of a young lady of whom he is very fond. He further states that it is nobody's d... business what pictures he cuts out, or what he does with them afterward."

Crew and staff had not yet learned to live in perfect harmony and their existences were quite separate—they lived, ate, worked, and relaxed at opposite ends of the ship. A few of the scientists—usually McKinlay, Mamen, and Malloch—did roll up their sleeves and pitch in now and then to help the crew tie up coal sacks, divide up boxes of provisions, and tidy and rearrange the deck.

Each day, the men rose early for breakfast, which ended promptly at 8:00, except on Sundays when they were allowed more flexibility. (Otherwise, it was breakfast at 7:30 A.M., dinner at 11:30 A.M., and tea at 5:30 P.M.) McKinlay, Mamen, Mackay, and the rest of them only wanted to sleep as long as possible. "Eat when you feel like it; sleep when you feel like it," Captain Bartlett had told them early on. "And have plenty of both for you never know how soon you will have neither."

They ate so much that Templeman attempted to close off his galley to the bloody scientists, some of whom—Beuchat being one of the prime suspects—were rude enough to devour everything in sight, without any consideration for the crewmen, who were forced to eat at sporadic hours, depending on their individual work schedules. Templeman was going to put a stop to it, if it was the last thing he did. McKinlay, because he often kept Sandy company on watch, was an exception and was thus permitted to eat whatever he wanted to. But as McKinlay noted in his journal, "From now on, 'scientists' has become a 'dirty word' with the crew!"

Mamen exercised religiously, and then would retreat to his bunk to pour over his books on polar exploration. Murray made depth soundings, and Malloch took latitude and longitudinal observations. McKinlay charted the daily temperature and studied navigation and nautical astronomy. Because he regularly joined Sandy on watch, the two had become friends and would often spend hours side by side, looking out onto the spectacular sea. There was usually nothing but gray mist and darkness and water to the far horizon.

One day in July, Sandy and McKinlay had fought to keep their balance as the waves climbed higher, until they loomed over their heads. Everything movable was being thrown about the deck and slamming into everything else. Later that night, McKinlay recorded in his journal how the salt of the sea had burned his lips and tongue, and how the bitter chill of the water stung his skin. Still, he was as exhilarated as he had ever been in his life. Because of the storm's violence, Sandy had lashed his friend to a stanchion to ride out the peak of it. The wind increased and the waves rose twenty feet high, slamming against the ship and dashing her sides and deck, immersing the engine room, and throwing the ship back the way she had come. It was cold on the bridge, and windy, but McKinlay found himself glowing all over.

McKinlay, like the others, had signed onto this voyage seeking the chance to do good work, to see more of the world, to aid in the furthering of science, and to find a bit of adventure. Like most of them, he was inexperienced in exploration. But the worries he might have had about his clumsiness and his naiveté were disappearing. He felt good and strong and healthy. The Arctic seemed to agree with him.

STEFANSSON WANTED to press onward at any cost. He was anxious about the signs of an early winter, impatient to be on his way. Bartlett, to the contrary, wanted to give the ship a rest, turn her back toward the coast, away from the ice, or simply let her drift for the winter. He knew they would not be able to make it much farther, even if the surrounding ice let up. It would be only a temporary reprieve, and soon after, he knew, there would be more ice waiting for them.

But Stefansson urged him forward, past the peak of Point Barrow, eastward along the northern Alaskan coast toward Herschel Island. He directed Bartlett to hug the shore so they could keep sight of land. They would be safe from the drifting ice as long as they did so, but the *Karluk* was so heav-ily loaded that she sat terribly low in the water and ran aground repeatedly.

Bartlett was, as Mamen observed, "a man who utilizes all chances to get ahead...." Stefansson demanded forward movement, and they could make no progress running aground. The *Karluk's* bow was too thin to forge through the ice, so finally Bartlett did what he had done in the past with Peary's ships—on August 12, he headed northward, following the open leads in the ice, all the while keeping her as much on course to Herschel Island as possible. "We steamed along through the open water," he wrote, "and because the ice near the shore was closely packed, we were driven far-ther off shore than I liked. We had to follow the open lanes, however, and go where they led." Apparently, Stefansson was sleeping when the decision was made to take the ship out into the pack.

Bartlett had good reasons for following the lanes of open water—aside from running aground, the ship was at risk from crushing ice pressure, which was always greater and more dangerous near land. But it turned out to be a controversial decision, which would alter their course irrevocably. They quickly lost sight of land. Every now and then, a lead would bring them back toward the coast, but then, once again, they would be led away from it.

It was a no-win situation. To stay close to land meant to sacrifice the chance to move forward, which Stefansson insisted upon doing. But to fol-low the open leads meant to separate the ship from the relative safety of the nearby land mass, and to risk being carried off course.

Both Stefansson and Bartlett were strong personalities who harbored their own strong opinions about what to do. Stefansson did not seem to under-stand—or care about—the deficiencies of his ship or the risks involved with pressing onward. A frustrated Bartlett, tired of running aground, steered the ship into the open water and ignored Stefansson's warnings.

Later on, looking back, Bartlett felt he had done what was best at the time, navigating the ship as he had done with the ships under Peary's com-mand. Stefansson had demanded they keep going, and Bartlett had com-plied the only way he could. Whether he would have done it over again, or whether or not it was the best decision is harder to say. It was a chance call based on his desire to get Stefansson where he wanted to go.

On August 11, Bartlett took a nap, his first sleep in two days. Afterward, he returned to the crow's nest to keep watch and continue his search for a passageway through the ice.

MAMEN SPENT THE MORNING of August 11 writing a letter to his beloved fiancée, Ellen, and then climbed up to the barrel to keep the captain company. They were treated to sunshine and snow that day, and in the afternoon the ship was able to buck the ice for several miles. The *Karluk* jumped and twisted as she rammed through the pack, and the crow's nest was shaking so violently that Mamen was sure they would be catapulted to the deck.

Finally, the *Karluk* rammed against the edge of a field of old, thick ice and was brought to a sudden halt. The young, or newer, ice was relatively easy to break, but the old ice was solid and impenetrable, especially for a ship like the *Karluk*.

The following day, Murray and Wilkins took out the umiak—a large, open wooden boat covered with walrus skins—and dropped Murray's dredge into a patch of open water, five fathoms deep. One of Murray's primary concerns as oceanographer was to study and document the sea life in different regions. The result from this dredging was a variety of interesting specimens, which Murray promptly spirited away to his makeshift laboratory, where he spent the rest of the day, cigarette dangling from his hand, studying them through his microscope.

Meanwhile, Mamen taught members of the staff and crew how to ski, and noted that most of his pupils were stiff as matches. Dr. Mackay and McKinlay were good students, but Beuchat, as expected, was awkward and extremely comical. Afterward, they held a football match on the ice, and although Mamen's team won, he injured his knee, the same one he had injured long ago in a skiing accident back home. Ever since that initial injury, it had been a little tender, and now it hurt like the devil. He turned in earlier than usual, worn out from the day and discouraged by the pain. He hated physical weakness of any kind, especially in himself.

———— • ————

ON AUGUST 13, with the mountains of Flaxman Island appearing off the ship's beam, the *Karluk* was listing to starboard at a worrisome degree, due to the overloading of coal in her starboard bunker. To protect the port bilges, which could easily be harmed, Bartlett had the men transfer a large part of the deck cargo to the port side to balance her out.

The following day was a wholly cheerless one for everyone on board. The only exception was the irascible old trapper Hadley, who was "playing guitar and singing so that we cannot hear ourselves think," wrote a disgusted Mamen. Mamen was already in a foul mood that day, his knee aching, the monotony of the ice draining him. The worst of it, though, was that August 14 was Ellen's birthday and the anniversary of their engagement. Mamen could not believe he was stuck in the ice, so very far way from her, going nowhere.

The following day dawned brighter, as it was Bartlett's thirty-seventh birthday. Freshly barbered and in a splendid humor, the captain was treated to a real celebration that evening. Templeman laid the mess room table with a white linen cloth, which alone created quite a sensation, and everyone gathered at 9:30 P.M. Templeman was an unambitious, rotten cook. But now everyone congratulated him on the feast he had prepared—cold roast beef; tongue; salads; and a variety of cakes, tarts, and fruit desserts. There was so much good food that he was unable to find room for all of it on the table.

There was lemonade and lime juice for the teetotalers—Bartlett, McKinlay, and Malloch—and whiskey for the rest. They raised their glasses and toasted the health of their captain, and afterward Stefansson gave him a box of cigars. These were passed around the table until all were puffing on them "as if we had been in the most fashionable restaurant in London or New York," wrote McKinlay.

After dinner Dr. Mackay sang a variety of Scottish songs, followed by Murray, and then McKinlay and Wilkins, who performed a duet. Hadley, of course, played the guitar and sang, Stefansson regaled them with stories, and secretary Burt McConnell gave a concert on the Victrola. Everyone's spirits seemed brighter, even the typically surly doctor's, whose mood was magically improved, as usual, by several drinks of whiskey. They turned in that night, close to 3:00 A.M., weary but refreshed, the celebration having given them a much-needed lift.

FOR DAYS AFTERWARD, they sat frozen into the ice pack, pelted by rain and wind. An oppressive, stifling fog rolled in, covering the ship in a blanket of mist, and Bartlett expected winter in full force at any time.

"The nights are beginning to show a little darkness which carries a warning of approaching winter," McKinlay worried. "Each morning now we rise, asking 'How is the weather today?'; each evening we lie down asking 'Will it come tomorrow?' It is here one learns what discipline means; the North is a hard school. What worries us most is that we may get no farther & may thus be deprived of opportunity to work; it is not prospect of danger, for there is none."

And then the rain changed to snow, which froze everything it fell upon, creating thick layers of frost. The temperature dropped and the pools of water on the nearby ice froze solid.

There were breathtaking evenings when the haloed moon shone silver in the dark blue sky and the stars burned brightly. McKinlay wanted to linger on deck; but there was a dangerous chill in the air, and it was too cold to stand for very long. But he gazed with wonder at the frost-covered rigging, the bejeweled mast and railings. The ship rose from the icy depths like a magical, majestic statue, her edges softened and blurred by the shimmering white and the starry frost that covered her. She looked, he decided, as if she were enchanted.

ALL ON BOARD WERE RESTLESS, especially their leader. Stefansson knew now that the chances of the *Karluk* breaking free and being able to continue on her journey were slim. "It is distressing to think that the winter already has come, and here we are, unable to go either back or forth, in the poorest part of the Arctic regions," wrote Mamen. "I am beginning to get restless and only long to go further north and then home, but … the chances are small, yes, infinitely small."

The outlook was black, and at Flaxman Island, the Southern Party began to wonder where their *Karluk* comrades were. They knew all too well the

Karluk's shortcomings and feared she would not be able to make it through the ice. Chipman wrote about Stefansson, "He may be good 'copy' but I wish he had paid more attention to the Expedition itself both publicly and personally."

THE KARLUK WAS DRIFTING now without power. She was trapped in a floe of old ice, easily half a mile wide, and suddenly found herself being carried with the current. Bartlett would not leave the crow's nest and thought that he could see in the distance signs that the ice was loosening. But he couldn't be sure anymore, and they were held fast in the viselike grip of the shifting ice pack.

Murray had never gotten over his dislike or distrust of Stefansson and had maintained a guarded distance from the leader ever since the July showdown in Nome where the scientists had confronted their leader. Now they were all stranded in the ice, and as far as Murray was concerned, it was Stefansson's fault. Stefansson was, in Murray's opinion, nothing more than "a self-seeking adventurer who deliberately intended to put the '*Karluk*' into the pack ice for the sake of notoriety and personal glorification." It would be the surest way for Stefansson to get his name in the papers, to be known as the gallant leader of a lost expedition.

DAY AFTER DAY, there was no change in the ice. The ship remained a prisoner, helpless to dictate her own course or break free. Bartlett noted Stefansson's restlessness, as did the members of the crew and staff. Stefansson was a man who hated sitting still. On August 22 he suddenly called the scientists who were supposed to be part of the Southern Party into his cabin and announced again that he intended to send them ashore. Murray, though, was quickly eliminated from the group, because his equipment was too heavy to make the trip. Then it was decided that McKinlay could just as well do his work on the *Karluk,* and Wilkins would also remain for similar reasons. That left Jenness and Beuchat, who had no equipment and no purpose for being on the ship, since their work was to live with and study the Eskimos.

The plan was for Jenness and Beuchat to head over the ice to Flaxman Island to seek word of the *Mary Sachs* and the *Alaska,* and then continue over the now solid ice by foot and dogsled to Herschel Island, if it turned out the Southern Party had gone ahead. Everyone pitched in to ready the expedition, but it was impossible to locate the equipment and stores they needed for travel because nothing was where it was supposed to be.

Even though the scientists had tried to establish some sense of order, the *Karluk's* stores were still a mess, without any sense of organization or supervision. Templeman always helped himself to whatever he needed from the food supplies and never bothered to document it. The expedition clothing worked in much the same way. It had never been officially issued to the men, as it should have been, upon their arrival to the ship. Instead, it had been handed out sporadically, first to some, then to others at a much later time, and anyone overlooked had to put in a request or help himself.

It was, thought McKinlay, indicative of the way the expedition was being run. The only clothing he had been issued thus far was a pair of mukluks and some slippers. His government-issued clothing was aboard the *Alaska,* as was the trunk containing his own clothing and personal items, which he had brought from home. "That was all right," he said, "in the ordinary course of affairs; but no thought has so far been taken of the change in prospects. I do not intend to ask for anything until I need it & then I shall demand it."

AUGUST 24 was the most promising morning they had seen for a long time. The ice showed signs of breaking, there was a sprawling open lead to the east, and the ship was abuzz with nervous excitement. The men were hopeful of getting free, but by the end of the day, the wind shifted to the west and killed all possibility of escape.

By the next morning, the ice had completely closed up again, and there was no sign of open water anywhere. Dr. Mackay had crafted an instrument that determined the speed and direction of the drift, and now they knew that the *Karluk* was drifting west at one mile per hour.

If they had been closer to shore, their prospects might have been better for breaking free. As it was, the snow was falling again, land was sighted far in the distance, and adverse winds blew in from the north. The *Karluk's* drift shifted daily, and by August 28, she was drifting southeast at a rate of twelve miles a day.

Meanwhile, unrest was brewing in the engine room over more than just the boiler tanks. Before being recommended for his post on the *Karluk,* Chief Engineer John Munro had been a junior officer on the British warship *Rainbow.* A Scot, he had emigrated to Canada and become a Canadian citizen. He was a towering man with a wide puttyish face, a rather soft chin, deep-set eyes, and a high forehead often in a crease when his brows were particularly furrowed, as they usually were.

Second Engineer Robert Williamson begrudged Munro his position as chief engineer. Munro was fond of shirking his work and putting much of it on Williamson, and Williamson soured at being ordered about by this man, whom he regarded as his inferior. Williamson was thirty-six years old, already weathered from over a decade of a seaman's life. Tall, brawny, and as sharply angled as a hawk, he had served in the North Atlantic, the Mediterranean, and the Baltic. On June 16, the day before the *Karluk* had sailed from Esquimalt, he introduced himself to Bartlett aboard a local streetcar and by the time the streetcar reached Esquimalt, he had a job as second engineer. Even with the last-minute hiring, he had hoped to join *Karluk* as chief engineer himself and had been bitterly disappointed over being given the second post.

STEFANSSON GAVE JENNESS and Beuchat final instructions for their journey, along with a check for two hundred dollars and a letter that gave them full authority to act independently of the expedition should the need arise. They were to attach themselves to the Southern Party as soon as possible, and Jenness was to telegraph any pertinent news to the *New York Times* on Stefansson's behalf.

Kataktovik broke the trail ahead of the two sleds, which were loaded with a large umiak, skins, and provisions for thirty days. Each sled was pulled by a team of seven dogs. The ice was still covered with snow, which made it difficult to pick out a good trail, and they hadn't gone far when the sleds became immersed in water and the umiak was damaged.

After dinner aboard the ship, Stefansson and Hadley set out to reach the party, to take a batch of letters to them to mail. When they overtook Jenness and the others, Stefansson was dismayed at their miserable and wet condition. They were soaked to the skin, the provisions were damaged from the rough journey, and the ice was in a treacherous state. Immediately, he ordered their return to the *Karluk*. They cached the stores on the ice to lighten the sleds and brought back only the most valuable of the equipment. It took twenty minutes to retrace what had taken them two hours to travel on the way out. Somewhere along the way, Beuchat took a tumble into the water and had to be carried back in the umiak.

BY LATE AUGUST it was clear that the men of the *Karluk* were trapped. The seventeen-degree-Fahrenheit temperature seemed even more bitterly cold. The imprisoned ship was drowning in snow. The wind blasted them from all directions, forever shifting and changing course. Inside the *Karluk,* they were warm, but the air was close and stale. The world around them was vast and wide—open sky, ice as far as the eye could see in all directions, nothing to obstruct their view of that boundless, frozen wonderland. But they began to feel claustrophobic. They felt smothered by the ice, as if it were not only compressing the sides of their ship, but constricting their throats, and the breath in their lungs.

"How long will this continue?" wrote McKinlay. "This ... inactivity is becoming unbearable. The ice even reflects the general state of affairs; there is not the slightest sign of movement in it. The small patches of open water have frozen up & all is as still & quiet as death. In the minds of all is the unuttered question, 'When will things change?' Will the change come soon? If not, ours will be a tame start; hard luck to be stuck thus early. But hope springs—."

THE WEATHER AND THE ICE conditions were growing worse every day. It was too late in the season, too late in the year to hope for a clear passage. Even Stefansson had to acknowledge this. There was no doubt in anyone's mind now that they would be imprisoned by the ice for the winter.

Everyone was aware of the hopelessness of the situation, but no one knew exactly what it meant for them or for the expedition, nor did they know what they could expect. They were not afraid, but the wait and the uncertainty were unsettling. On August 31, Bartlett and Mamen had a quiet talk on the ice about it all, just the two of them. Everyone else remained confined to the ship. The sky lit up briefly that night with the first auroral display they had seen. But it was very faint, just an ephemeral glimpse of color in all of that whiteness.

THE ESKIMOS UNDERSTOOD the gravity of their situation in a way that the scientists and crew did not. Borrowing a piece of writing paper from McKinlay, Kataktovik wrote a letter to a friend in Point Barrow, even though he had no idea if it would ever be mailed. He missed his home, and more than that, he was frightened. He asked his friend to pray for him, that he might get out of this safely.

"When will you prayer's to God & Jesus help to me," he said. "Please you tell my daughter's good her, & like to my daughter very much. Sometime I sorry & sometime happy to God & Jesus if you like to believe to God & Jesus. I like to believe to God & Jesus very much."

SEPTEMBER 1913

———— • ————

Goodbye, Stefansson. We did not then know that those of us who were left on your luckless ship were not to see you again.
—FRED MAURER, FIREMAN

Stefansson was growing more and more restless. Here and there, a lead would open in the ice around them, but the *Karluk* was held fast by the mile-and-a-half-wide floe that now entrapped her; the crew was helpless, unable to do anything but watch the open water and sit there. The ice was thickening, deepening, the whiteness stretching far across and extending far beneath the ocean's encrusted surface.

Stefansson hated being held prisoner by the ice. He could never sit still and he seldom slept. He worried that someone would beat him to his mysterious, undiscovered continent.

Meanwhile, Bartlett began rationing their coal oil and kerosene, which were already running low, because their full supply was stowed aboard the *Mary Sachs*. He called "lights out" now at midnight, to conserve fuel. The days were growing shorter and darker, and the lamp in the saloon was lit for the first time, signifying the advent of winter.

The captain also began to tighten the rationing of food, and the Eskimos went hunting for seal nearly every day, using the rifles Stefansson had issued them. Officers, scientists, and crewmen sometimes joined them, but Kuraluk was by far the best hunter and secured most of the seals himself. Seal hunting was by no means an exciting sport, and the Eskimos were the only ones who seemed to have the patience it required.

Kuraluk would settle behind a hummock of ice or take his kayak out into the open water and wait. He would sit, still as a statue, for eight hours at a time until a seal appeared out of a nearby watering hole. If the seal saw him, it was over. He had to be ready to shoot at any moment, even though his fingers were stiff and sore from the cold and lack of movement. But the seals were slippery creatures and surprisingly quick, and if he wasn't fast enough they would disappear before he could take another shot.

Sometimes hours passed without sighting anything, and sometimes the creatures were too far away to shoot. Seals were exceptionally curious, so whenever Kuraluk or the other Eskimos spied one in the distance, beyond range, they would let out a low whistle and watch as the inquisitive animal disappeared into the water and resurfaced just a few yards from them. Then came the shot, and if they were lucky, the seal was easy to retrieve. More often than not, the wounded animal slipped through their hands and the patient hunters came home empty-handed. At other times, Kuraluk and the others felt lucky enough to capture even one or two after a long day's work.

McKinlay, try as he might, could not seem to land even one seal. He was clumsy when it came to sports or hunting, and became the butt of jokes when he sat for twenty minutes on the ice one day and missed a seal that leapt up in front of him, simply because he was wiping his nose with his handkerchief. "Down went my 'hankie,' up went my rifle, but with a dive the seal was gone...."

Soon Templeman was replacing the salt meat they were accustomed to with seal meat at every meal. McKinlay, like most of the others, had never tasted seal, and Templeman, never having cooked it before, wasn't quite sure how to prepare it. It had a strong smell and a strong taste; but the liver and seal kidney pie were delicacies, and Templeman began serving the dishes once a week.

To pass the time, the men of the *Karluk* hunted, read, skated, slept, posed for Wilkins's camera, and watched the ice. They gave an orchestral concert one night, with Sandy on violin, Wilkins and McConnell on the harmonica, Hadley on mandolin, and Second Engineer Williamson playing the comb. Under Mamen's tutelage, they practiced their skiing and had a good laugh at Dr. Mackay, who insisted on wearing short pants, which became filled with snow every time he fell off his skis. Beuchat and Jenness studied the Eskimo language with Stefansson while Jimmy and Jerry shared traditional Eskimo folktales with everyone. Mackay, Chafe, Sandy, Munro, and Jenness engaged in a target-shooting competition with a pound of tobacco as the prize. But many of the staff members stayed in bed until dinnertime.

Despite their efforts to stay busy, it was a dreary, aimless existence. Templeman received a black eye from sailor John Brady; fireman Breddy received a scalding on the back of his head in an engine room accident; and Kataktovik suffered from a painful bout of venereal disease. Mamen, meanwhile, cursed his fellow scientists, thinking them the laziest men he had ever met. His knee was much better now and he was using every opportunity to exercise, to study, to write letters to Ellen that he hoped he would be able to send. He was also learning to use the sextant at Stefansson's request. Mamen might be asked to leave the ship soon and head for land, Stefansson told him, and he would need to know how to work the instrument.

THE SNOW CONTINUED TO FALL, the temperature plunged, the cabins dripped with water from evaporation, and the men held no hope whatsoever of being released from the ice. On September 10, there was an aching in Mamen's bones that meant a storm was coming. He often suffered from rheumatic pains in his arms and legs, which was the most accurate way he had ever found of predicting bad weather. "Soon," he wrote, "we will be enveloped in the darkness of the winter, so infinitely long."

At Bartlett's request, Murray had continued charting the ship's drift, and now it appeared that she was in the vicinity of Thetis Island, 140 miles or so east of Barrow, but still a good deal west of the desired goal, Herschel Island. They could just spot Thetis to the west.

On September 17, Stefansson sent Dr. Mackay and Jenness out on the ice to search for land to the south. Mamen saw them from the ship, obviously lost and wandering off in a northwesterly direction. He started after them, and when he was close enough, he shouted to them, asking in what direction they were headed.

"Due south," they replied.

"You must have a screw loose," he yelled and raced to catch up with them and set them on course. They returned after traveling six or eight miles, not having seen any sign of land.

Stefansson dispatched Mamen and the doctor again to look for land on September 19. Murray had estimated they were eighteen miles offshore of Beechey Point, sixteen miles east of Oliktok Point, on Alaska's northern coast. Mamen and Mackay walked for twelve miles in a westerly direction, and once again returned having seen nothing.

After supper that night, Stefansson sent for Mamen, Malloch, and McKinlay and met with them in his cabin. They were to leave the *Karluk,* he told them, and go ashore where they would be better able to conduct their work. Malloch and Mamen could expect to be on land for at least six weeks, mapping the coast, while McKinlay would make magnetic observations.

But Stefansson had even bigger plans. He was leaving the ship himself. He summoned Bartlett, Wilkins, Jenness, and McConnell to his cabin and told them of his news. He asked for the assistant steward, Chafe, to be present as well, since he would be in charge of outfitting the party. Stefansson would take Wilkins, Jenness, and McConnell with him. No one was more surprised about Stefansson's plans than Bartlett. It was a hunting trip, said Stefansson. They would also take Jimmy and Jerry, the first two Eskimo hunters he had hired. They would head southwest toward Thetis Island where they would hunt caribou up the Colville River to supplement their fresh meat supply.

Stefansson left the ship immediately after dinner on September 20. It seemed odd, noted McKinlay, to leave so late in the day. But Stefansson was anxious to be on his way. He took with him a bounty of food supplies and ammunition, guns, two sledges, and a dozen of the very best dogs, handpicked by himself and Hadley. They loaded the sleds with tents, candles, an alcohol stove, sugar, tea, matches, sleeping bags, skins, biscuits, rice, bacon, and pemmican. To each man traveling with him, Stefansson issued winter boots, socks, deerskin shirts, compasses, rifles, knives, and watches. As planned, his secretary Burt McConnell, anthropologist Diamond Jenness, photographer George Wilkins, and the hunters, Jimmy and Jerry, accompanied him.

Most of the crew and staff climbed down onto the ice to see the team off. Getting them ready to go had been quite a feat. As Mamen observed, it was like "Jerusalem's destruction; they didn't know what they had or what they should have." But, at last, they were equipped. Stefansson shook hands with all of the remaining scientists and crew and then was off across the ice, without a look back. He strode ahead, breaking the trail for the first sled while Jenness broke trail for the second, and Jimmy and Jerry drove the sleds.

Stefansson was only going hunting. He had said so himself. He would be back in a week or so. He would bring fresh meat for the winter. Bartlett knew that caribou were nearly extinct in the area. Stefansson himself had told them so, but he seemed to have forgotten that fact.

Before leaving, Stefansson had presented Bartlett with a letter that included detailed instructions for the men and the ship, should he be unable to return, and stated: "If the ice is strong enough I expect to cross thence to near Beechy Point to hunt caribou.... Should the *Karluk* during our absence be driven from her present position it will be well for you so soon as she has come to a stop again, and as soon as it appears safe to send a party ashore, to erect one or more beacons, giving information of the ship's location. If it becomes practicable, send off Malloch and Mamen for surveying purposes. McKinlay should accompany them for the purpose of establishing magnetic stations in connection with Malloch's survey.... Except for some especial reason, the Eskimo woman Kiruk should be kept sewing boots of the winter sea-ice type.... It is likely that we shall be back to the ship in ten days, if no accident happens."

Once Stefansson and his party disappeared over the snow and ice, into the vast, white landscape, the twenty-two men, one woman, and two children who had been left behind were helpless to do anything but wait for their return.

"Away 20 miles in the distance we see him and his party like small black specks against the everlasting white of the Alaskan hills," wrote Maurer. "They pass over the first ridge and out of sight. Goodbye, Stefansson."

TWO DAYS AFTER STEFANSSON and his group left the ship, a blizzard struck. It was the first big storm of the season, with winds reaching sixty miles an hour. The ship rolled and rocked, agonizing against the grip of the vise that held her. The men were trapped below. The gale was ferocious, wild, and terrifying.

Arctic weather varied from day to day, with dramatic differences in temperature. But now, winter had arrived early and with great hostility, and the wind, raw and cold, seemed to cut through the ship. The ice had begun raftering and crushing around them, forming enormous pressure ridges—twenty, forty, sixty feet tall—which threatened to impound the vessel. The *Karluk* sat in the midst of it all, still trapped in the same expanse of ice that had imprisoned her in Camden Bay, one hundred and fifty miles or so to the east of where she rested now. For weeks, they had drifted, but lately the floe sat still and unmoved, locked in the surrounding ice.

On September 23, McKinlay was in his cabin, talking to Mamen and Malloch. Suddenly, he had the unmistakable sense that the *Karluk* was moving again. The three scientists rushed up to the deck, but the winds forced them back inside. By this time, more of the men had gathered, each voicing the same sensation. Bartlett confirmed it. The ship was under way.

The gale had gathered such force that their ice floe had broken free. As the winds picked up, the ice carried the *Karluk,* and all of her passengers, westward, thirty miles a day, far away from Herschel Island toward the heart of the Arctic Ocean. The wind was swift and strong, the sky overcast and dark. They knew that if this continued Stefansson would have no chance of returning to the ship, since he would not be able to reach them. Nor did it then seem likely that they would have any chance of setting out to reach him and the rest of the original expedition.

FOR NEARLY A WEEK, they drifted sixty miles a day. The floe that carried them remained intact while all around them the ice was breaking up and the water was opening. The blizzard extinguished the stars, and day and night the men could not escape the thundering of the grinding, shattering ice. For now, the floe that held the *Karluk* protected her; but it could break apart at any moment, and she would be left to defend herself against churning, toppling floes of ice, and the jagged edges that lay hidden below the surface of the water "like the long, underwater arm that ripped the side out of the *Titanic*," wrote Bartlett. "Every moment the *Karluk* was in danger of being tossed up on one of these heavy floes and left stranded, to break up like a ship wrecked on a beach, or of being flung against the ice bodily like a ship thrown by wind and waves against a cliff."

The men slept fully dressed and with their eyes open. Beuchat, meanwhile, seemed to have gone "plumb crazy," according to Mamen. He stayed bundled in two heavy shirts, a skin vest, and a sheepskin coat and sat inside all the time, shivering. Whatever measures he took, he couldn't seem to get warm, and he was terrified of freezing in the unaccustomed cold.

Kuraluk's wife Kiruk began sewing fur clothing for the company. They piled the deck with provisions, and the underwear was placed in canvas bags where they could reach it at a moment's notice. The umiaks, which could be lowered to the ice if the time came to abandon ship, were filled with supplies, each with enough for eight people for twenty days. It was, wrote Bartlett, the worst experience he had been through in his long career at sea—worse than anything he had endured on the voyage of the *Roosevelt* with Peary. With the *Roosevelt,* at least, they had been blessed with a vessel that was built for breaking the ice and, too, they had had endless daylight. Now Bartlett had neither of these. He had winter, he had the encroaching polar darkness, and he had the *Karluk.*

Everyone received strict orders to remain on board; the ice conditions were too precarious and Bartlett would not risk leaving anyone behind. Everything that had been stored on the ice—provisions, equipment, dogs—was now brought back onto the ship.

It was a dreary time, and the spirits of the men plummeted. Mamen had been busy making preparations to go ashore as Stefansson had ordered, until Bartlett informed him that he, Malloch, and McKinlay would have to postpone their trip indefinitely until the ship stopped drifting.

ON SEPTEMBER 26, the *Karluk* began drifting east at nine miles a day, and hope returned. East was good. East was where they wanted to be. But on the twenty-eighth, she once again changed direction and began heading west. None of them—Bartlett, McKinlay, Malloch, Mamen—could determine their location, and there was much speculation as to their whereabouts. Murray took a depth sounding, and it was clear that, wherever they were, they were entering deeper water.

On September 29, the rugged Malloch managed to make his first observation since the storm began. The snow, the mist, and the northern lights had all made it impossible to get a reading on their position. But now he was able to determine that the *Karluk* was just ten miles from land.

Everyone on board was sewing in earnest now. McKinlay darned socks while the grumbling Mackay sewed pockets onto his pajama coat. Bartlett was mending a jacket, and Malloch was sewing strips of material onto his sheepskin trousers, something he had been doing for the past eight days. He bent over the pants, stretching his long legs in front of him, his handsome profile intent on his project, broad shoulders braced against the wall. He whistled while he worked, or sang at the top of his lungs. The odd dichotomy of it all—this overtly masculine man humbled by such work—made a funny picture and amused his cabin mates.

Beuchat, meanwhile, rested in bed for hours, shivering from the cold, and Mamen, at Bartlett's request, prepared to lead a small expedition in search of Stefansson. "All hope of the hunting party being able to pick us up has now been abandoned," wrote McKinlay. So they would go in search of Stefansson, taking him provisions. They planned to leave as soon as the wind died down.

Mamen was still eager to prove himself and was thrilled to have something useful to do with his time. He was also deeply honored by Bartlett's faith in him to find their leader. Bartlett's good opinion meant the world to him, and he wrote with great pride, "He knows what I am worth when it comes to showing courage and smartness in critical situations, otherwise he would not have given me the leadership of the coming relief expedition."

ON THE LAST DAY of the month, the temperature dropped to eight degrees Fahrenheit and the snow began to fall once more. The men were at last allowed out on the ice, and everyone took advantage of the opportunity to escape from their shipboard prison. Mamen stood in awe and watched the sunset at 4:30 that afternoon. He had never seen anything like it. "There is nothing so lovely and singularly beautiful as seeing the sun setting up in the cold north."

One thing was apparent. There was now absolutely no chance of Stefansson and his party making it back to the ship. At that very moment, in fact, they were miles away in Amauliktok, just off the mainland of Alaska, unaware that the *Karluk* had vanished.

BARTLETT, THIS TIME, did not confide in Mamen. Instead, he kept his suspicions to himself.

Stefansson had not gone on any hunting party. Bartlett knew it in his gut. Stefansson had abandoned ship. He had been anxious to be on his way, to continue his grand expedition. He could not sit still any longer. Whatever his motives, McConnell, Wilkins, Jenness, Jimmy, and Jerry were probably unaware. As far as any of them knew, they were on a hunting trip, and it didn't seem to occur to any of them that a secretary, a photographer, and an anthropologist made a strange hunting party. If it truly was a hunting trip, why was Hadley, the great trapper, not included? Or Chafe, the expert marksman? Why did Kuraluk, the best by far of the Eskimo hunters, remain on the *Karluk* while two other lesser hunters went in his place? If Stefansson were planning a simple hunting trip, surely he would have taken Kuraluk, who could have stood to be separated from his family for that short period of time. But if his intentions were indeed to be gone longer, better to take the two single Eskimos, knowing as he did the native tradition of families staying together when hired.

"A nice mess," Bartlett later wrote. "Stefansson, the leader, ashore and his whole blooming expedition floating around here in the ice out of sight of land. It certainly would have been embarrassing for Stefansson if the Premier of Canada had met him on the beach about that time and said, 'Sir, where's your expedition?' The only thing Stefansson could have answered would have been to have waved his arm out over the polar pack and said nonchalantly: 'They're out there waiting for me, sir,' which we were. We were waiting for him all right. We were stuck so hard and fast in that ice forty feet thick that all the motor trucks in Canada couldn't have pulled us out."

They had been abandoned. Because the ship could not be of use anymore, the staff and crew were not of use anymore, so they were left in the ice to fend for themselves. The men, woman, and children aboard the

Karluk were no longer Stefansson's concern. They belonged to Bartlett now. But he would say nothing to anyone. Let them think their leader hadn't deserted them. Let them think Stefansson had meant to come back.

AT NIGHT, the scientists gathered in the saloon and entertained themselves with ghost stories about the ships that had been frozen and trapped in that same region. There were so many that had drifted into the ice pack, before being carried helplessly away, never to be heard from again. In 1845, Sir John Franklin, with his two ships and 129 men, vanished without a trace. In 1881, George Washington De Long and his thirteen men on the ship *Jeannette* disappeared.

And there was another particularly eerie one. Seventy-five men, years ago, had reportedly escaped from their ship, only to become lost in the ice and the water. It was as if they had vanished into the air, leaving no trace of life behind. These stories made the blood freeze in their veins, and it was difficult to tell if Dr. Mackay was serious or not when he announced one evening that he, for one, had reconciled himself to leaving his bones out there on the ice, "never to see home again."

OCTOBER 1913

———— • ————

... we were drifting, drifting,—we knew not to what haven, in the silent, icy fastness of the North.

—ERNEST F. CHAFE, MESS ROOM BOY

Mamen spent a couple of hours each day up in the barrel, or crow's nest, keeping watch with Bartlett. It was a chance to be of use, to bond with the captain, and to escape the confinements of his cabin.

On October 3, Mamen and Bartlett could just make out land in the distance—Point Barrow, Alaska, five or so miles away. They were drifting swiftly to the west-northwest in gale force winds—still held captive in their ice floe—and the water was nine fathoms deep.

Mamen almost never got any time alone. The men in the Cabin DeLuxe had started calling themselves the "Four-Leaved Clover," an affectionate term, but one that, at times, implied too much togetherness, which was exactly the case. Mamen got a kick out of the good-natured Malloch, thought well of the more serious McKinlay, and, for all his irritation with the man, liked Beuchat. Still, it was close quarters. Either McKinlay was in there, reading and worrying, or Beuchat was complaining about something or other, or Malloch was singing at the top of his lungs, so loud that no one could think. But sometimes—on rare occasions—they would leave and Mamen would sneak into the cabin, hole up in his bunk, and enjoy some peace and quiet.

He spent a lot of time thinking of his friends and family back home, especially Ellen. Mostly, however, he studied. He read books by Amundsen and Nansen and some of the other explorers. The *Karluk* had an extensive polar library, everything from Robert Peary to Frederick Cook to Adolphus Greely—books on the Antarctic and the Arctic; reports of the steamer

Corwin and the United States revenue cutter *Bear;* narratives of journeys to the Northwest Passage, the Bering Sea, the heart of the polar ice pack.

The Norwegian Amundsen, of course, was Mamen's favorite, the man he wanted to become. For months now, he'd been scouring Amundsen's books, making mental notes on the expedition he wanted to lead himself one day. He thought of almost nothing else and lay in bed at night, studying and planning. He would spend the next three or four years with the *Karluk,* and afterward would return home to prepare for his own expedition. He and Ellen would marry, of course, but then he would have to leave her again, to pursue his dreams of exploration. "My dearest wish if I get safely out of this trip," he scrawled in his journal, "is to go home to Norway, scrape together enough money to enable me to get a small ship, and ... sail under the beautiful Norwegian flag."

Tonight was one of those nights Mamen always wished for, when Beuchat and Malloch and McKinlay weren't around. But tonight he did not study. His Amundsen books sat stacked nearby, closed and momentarily forgotten. Tonight he was reading something much more pressing—the ship and ice journals of George Washington De Long, who headed for the North Pole in July 1879 and never returned. De Long's diaries dated from 1879–1881 and were written in two volumes and eight hundred pages—not a quick read, nor an easy one, but compelling.

They had died out there—De Long and all thirteen of his men. In September of 1879, their ship the *Jeannette* became trapped in ice just east of Wrangel Island, an uninhabited scrap of land lying northeast of Siberia. She drifted for twenty-one months before going down, and De Long and his crew had set out across the ice toward Siberia in hopes of reaching civilization and safety, only they never made it. They died of cold and starvation before reaching land.

Years later, wreckage from their expedition was found off the coast of Greenland. De Long kept a journal to the very end, writing until the last days of his life. His final words were haunting. A man died almost daily, and De Long's last three entries read: "*October 28th, Friday.*—One hundred and thirty-eighth day. Iversen died during early morning. *October 29th, Saturday.*—One hundred and thirty-ninth day. Dressler died during night.

October 30th, Sunday.—One hundred and fortieth day. Boyd and Görtz died during night. Mr. Collins dying."

The journal stopped after that, and one could only guess what happened to him.

Mamen was transfixed by the journals, as horrific as they were. So, too, were McKinlay, Malloch, Mackay, Murray, and Beuchat. And for one good reason. The *Karluk* was following the same wayward drift as the *Jeannette*.

Dr. Mackay and Murray were the first to observe the similarities, and they led the long, increasingly obsessive late-night discussions about the comparable journeys of the two ships. Along with Beuchat and sometimes Malloch, they gathered almost nightly to pore over De Long's notes and charts. Whenever possible, Mamen avoided the conferences. They had a way of continuing for hours at a time, and Mamen had no patience with that. While the others were talking, he would sneak off to his bunk to get a little peace and quiet and some privacy. But secretly, when alone, he himself pored over the diaries of De Long, as worried as the others. Somehow it was easier for him to deal with the prospect of disaster on his own, by himself.

DAYS LATER, on October 7, Beuchat strode into the Cabin DeLuxe, eyes rolling, white as a ghost. "We are lost," he groaned, "we don't know where we are—everything is hopeless." And then he launched into a woeful monologue regarding Stefansson's mishandling of the expedition and of his absence.

Mamen looked at Beuchat over the leaves of Amundsen's book on the South Pole. The Frenchman was always so dramatic. Everyone knew he had no business being on this expedition—or any expedition for that matter. He was too weak-hearted, too squeamish, too spoiled. He wasn't able to do a thing for himself, and nice as he was—the perfect gentleman—he worried and complained all the time. He was impressionable, too, and Dr. Mackay and Murray had obviously been working on him.

Mamen couldn't help himself. He burst out laughing. They would probably get into another argument, but he didn't care.

McKinlay was next, wandering into the room, flustered and upset. McKinlay also avoided the late-night gatherings regarding the *Jeannette*, preferring, like Mamen, to study De Long in the privacy of his own bunk. McKinlay seldom vocalized his fears, but now he stood in the doorway of the Cabin DeLuxe, staring furiously at Mamen and Beuchat. "Stefansson," he said firmly, "read De Long's book about the voyage of the '*Jeannette*' a couple of days before he left the '*Karluk*'; he saw there that most ships, 99 percent of 100, in the ice north of Bering Strait are facing certain death, and for fear of losing his life he left the ship."

There it was, spoken aloud. The words no one dared speak. Everyone had wondered about Stefansson's departure. All of the scientists hosted their own theories on the matter. But no one had named it until now.

There were rumors that the plans of the expedition were not what the men had been "led to believe," according to McKinlay, and "that someone had been acting under false pretenses." Each day of their journey was a revelation for the men of the *Karluk* as they realized more clearly—and with increasing alarm—just how unprepared the expedition had been when they departed Esquimalt. Aside from the lack of proper fur clothing, there were no suitable tents or stoves, and much of the equipment was secondhand or in disrepair. Stefansson, they felt, would most certainly have to undergo an official enquiry when the expedition returned to civilization.

Stefansson surely knew the odds against the ship escaping from the ice this late in the season. He knew, as well as Bartlett, that there was no hope of breaking free until spring. If he stayed with the ship, he gave up all prospect of continuing on his great quest. But the very idea was incomprehensible. What kind of leader abandoned his men?

It was nothing Mamen hadn't lambasted Stefansson for in his own journal. But blaming Stefansson wouldn't help matters, nor would giving voice to suspicions that could never actually be proven. Mamen was disgusted with his comrades and their lack of restraint. Nothing good would ever come from talk like this, and it made him feel uneasy and unsettled.

"The Canadian Arctic Expedition will be a great fiasco, I see it now," he wrote in his diary. "It is not only the leader of the expedition who is to blame, but most of the members. I have never seen a bigger crowd of cowards in my life, they fear both for their lives and their limbs. Why should such people go to the Arctic, they should know what they risk, and when they see danger or dangers confronting them, they blame the leader and curse him up and down."

DR. MACKAY, for one, was planning to take charge of the situation. He and Murray, and to some extent Beuchat, did nothing to hide the fact that they were planning to abandon the ship and take themselves ashore. They charted the *Jeannette*'s route and compared it with the route of the *Karluk*. There had been no happy ending to De Long's expedition, and the doctor and Murray did not plan to entrust their own fates to a captain in whom they had no confidence—and they had no confidence in Bartlett. While the captain's long and celebrated reputation with Peary spoke for itself, Mackay and Murray thought much more of their own experience with Shackleton. They believed Bartlett to be simple, unimaginative, and impassive. They also felt he was showing a grave lack of concern for their situation, and it was maddening that he didn't seem to be doing anything to get them out of the ice. They felt far superior to him intellectually and in terms of their own polar experience. If anything, that one expedition with Shackleton had given them a sense of too much power and confidence— false confidence, but confidence nonetheless. Bartlett was no leader, as far as they could see. Shackleton was a leader, and having served under him, they considered themselves leaders by association.

Mackay, Murray, and Beuchat never mentioned their plans to McKinlay, but they invited Mamen to come with them. He was enraged at the suggestion of mutiny and he let them know it. His place was with the ship and with his captain. Afterward, he sought out Bartlett and told him that "as long as there are provisions ... and a deck on *Karluk*, I stay on board, unless I get orders to go."

Mackay confronted Bartlett with their plans to leave the ship. Bartlett, in his typically gruff way, dismissed the doctor. He did not want to waste his time with this kind of talk. Mackay demanded that Bartlett bring the ship's company together and lay his agenda before them. The doctor and the other scientists were unaware of Stefansson's instructions about what they were to do while wintering in the ice and were unaware of Bartlett's plans for getting them out of there and to safety. As far as they could see, he was doing nothing. They believed he had gotten them into the whole mess to begin with by following the open leads in the ice and steering the ship away from land. In their eyes, Bartlett was the reason they were now stuck in the ice pack, and it was his responsibility to get them out. Dr. Mackay and Murray also demanded that the captain inform them of his plan for the winter.

Bartlett, as usual, said nothing. He knew what the doctor was planning. He'd heard every word through the adjoining wall of their cabins. Mackay wanted Bartlett to hear everything, to know how disliked he was, and night after night, Bartlett had to listen to it. Generally not the most placid and even-tempered of men, the captain refrained from battle. He would not engage in a showdown with these men, would not give them the satisfaction or disrupt his ship. He had his crew to think of. He was in a precarious situation, left in charge of twenty-one men, one woman, and two children. Shouldered with a responsibility he never asked for or expected, he did not feel he could let himself respond to threats.

As far as Bartlett was concerned, there was nothing to discuss with these men, so there was no good reason to call a formal meeting. He was still hopeful that the ship would break free and, if not, that she would be prepared to last the winter held fast in the ice floe.

He did inform Mackay that anyone who required anything had only to ask for it, and if it was on the ship, the request would be taken care of. Afterwards, most of the staff felt satisfied with this, and for the time being at least, things seemed to smooth over.

Still, the worries remained, and everyone seemed suddenly aware of danger, discord, and trouble ahead, even if, for the moment, they stopped talking about it. To his journal, Mamen confided, "One stares death in the eyes every minute of the day. It is not only starvation but there are dangers lurking around you all the time, so you must keep the eyes wide open if you love your life."

WHENEVER BARTLETT SAID IT WAS SAFE, Mamen strapped on his skis and led the ski patrol out onto the ice surrounding the ship. When he could, Bartlett took a skiing lesson; Malloch and the doctor were also regular students. The captain and Malloch were both enthusiastic, if still a bit clumsy. Dr. Mackay, who always insisted on doing things his own way—even on skis—excelled in running and jumping.

They were usually the only living creatures out on the ice. It was an eerie world—vast, barren, and utterly still. White sky blended into the icescape, until you couldn't tell where one ended and one began. There was no sign of life but the ship and her men, the dogs, and the little black cat. Otherwise, the world was deafeningly silent and lifeless.

"I remember now how quiet the world appeared to be," wrote Fred Maurer. "The only noises were those made by the voices of men and the howling of the dogs; our engines were silent; the ice around us gave no sign of opening up, and there day after day and night after night we lay in helpless imprisonment."

On October 9 there was a near catastrophe when Bartlett and Mamen were out on their skis with Hadley's dog Molly. The ice broke about fifty yards ahead of the ship, forming a large lead, which grew rapidly into a dark chasm of water. The skiers barely had a chance to leap across the water before it widened, but poor Molly wasn't able to make the jump; and before either Bartlett or Mamen could go back for her, she was stranded on the other side.

Bartlett hurried back to the ship, hoping to seize this chance to put the *Karluk* back under her own power and pilot her through the passageway of water. It was the opportunity he had been searching for, ever since they had been carried away from land and leader in September. He would blast a way out of there if he had to.

There was only one problem—it was too dark. He would have to wait or risk driving her into the surrounding ice floes.

Bartlett's hopes were high the next morning as he climbed to the barrel to get a view of the extent of the open water. But the ship was shrouded in fog and it was impossible to see anything. The water closed up and the *Karluk* remained frozen in.

It wasn't the last time during the month that Bartlett was hopeful of breaking free of the ice. Time and again, a pathway opened and escape seemed promising. "We are still lying in the same ice floe as almost two months ago, but it has now begun to get frail; it won't take long, I think, before it breaks," wrote Mamen. But time and again, the hopes of the men were dashed. *Karluk,* it seemed, was undeniably trapped.

The ice was misleading. It was easy to feel safe when the ice was still and settled and the men were tucked safely inside the ship. Their frozen home gave them a false sense of security. The scenery, too, was unspeakably beautiful, and it was hard to believe that something so lovely could at the same time be so deadly. The sky was bright as a mirror at times, and there was only ice and snow "and a few openings and small water channels that shine and glitter" as far as the eye could see, observed Mamen.

The nighttime icescape was especially enchanting. Nearly every night, the sky came alive with a brilliant display of the aurora borealis. Even the jaded and cynical Mackay and Murray said the aurora—especially the vibrant colors—outshone anything they had ever witnessed in the Antarctic.

THE ICE WAS BREAKING UP. Floes shattered against floes in a terrifying inferno, causing cannonlike explosions as the ice threatened to crush the *Karluk.* For the first time, the men were afraid. "Opposing floes which had come together were being shattered one against another, piling higher & higher," wrote McKinlay. "Huge ice-blocks larger than houses were being tossed about like pebbles! What stupendous forces must have been at work with millions of tons of ice on either side trying to make way in opposite directions! As we watched this terrifying work of Nature, we noticed that the area of contention was creeping slowly but surely towards us, & we fell to wondering, with a shudder, what would be our lot.... To the East, West & South, are seething masses of ice battling for supremacy, grinding, crushing, groaning, roaring ice ...."

A special watch was kept because of ice conditions, and the men made preparations for a hasty departure from the ship by laying out provisions and equipment on the deck. Bartlett gave strict orders not to leave the ship. He made it clear that anyone who left was taking his life in his own hands and Bartlett would not be held accountable.

For the first time, the men began to have an inkling of what they were up against. The ship, their haven for the past two months, now suddenly seemed vulnerable. "So we are rapidly approaching the great, open, bottomless ocean," wrote Mamen in his journal. "It is indeed difficult to tell how long we will have a roof over our heads. If it continues this way it may be water rather than a roof, and that perhaps forever...."

SOMETIME IN MID-OCTOBER, Beuchat went in search of Mamen. Fearful of their situation, his conscience troubling him, stabbed by doubts thanks to all the talk from Mackay and Murray about Bartlett's ineptitude, Beuchat poured out his thoughts to the young topographer.

Murray and Mackay proposed to leave the ship and set out for land. They thought they could do better than the captain; they didn't have any faith in him and believed they could reach land on their own. If they stayed with the ship much longer, they might be lost. The Antarctic experience of both men spoke for them, especially Dr. Mackay, who had been a hero there. It was easy to be swayed by such talk from such confident and highly respected men. True, Bartlett had led Peary to the Pole, but that was a different time of year, a different ship, a different region. Mackay didn't want to wait any longer. He and Murray both felt now was the time to leave the ship and make their way to land. As far as either one could see, they were waiting for nothing. The ship was imprisoned, with no chance of being freed until spring, if she wasn't crushed long before that. There was no hope of continuing their work and fulfilling their duties, no hope of the *Karluk* sailing again under her own power.

Mamen told Beuchat it was lunacy to leave the *Karluk*. It was the wrong time of year, for one thing, with the days growing shorter and the weather growing colder and worsening day by day. The middle of January would be more reasonable—with the sun returning—but even then Mamen didn't believe in leaving the ship prematurely. "You must consider," Mamen told Beuchat, "that there are not only a few on board but 25 men all told, and if the crew sees that somebody leaves the ship, they will immediately assume that danger is threatening, and all will sneak away in the same manner! And with 29 dogs for 25 men this is no joke, and the distance is both long and full of danger."

———— • ————

THE WATER GREW DEEPER as the *Karluk* drifted slowly but steadily northward. By October 26, they reached 1,115 fathoms. At the beginning of the month, they had stood in a depth of nine.

Mamen needed to be working for his own peace of mind, so he and Malloch and McKinlay kept an eye on the temperature, studied the drift, charted the wind and weather conditions, and made latitudinal and longitudinal observations. They also worked in teams helping the crew and the Eskimos break ice to pack all around the ship. It was Bartlett's idea to form a cushion against the lateral pressure of the ice that trapped her. His hope was that this would keep the men warmer and well insulated while also helping the ship rise above the water so as to avoid being crushed. They cut the ice one meter round the *Karluk,* to help her rise, and banked her with snow blocks eighteen inches thick, reaching to the level of the poop deck.

Every day, Murray's dredge was lowered, and every day it was raised to examine the catch of Arctic sea life. When the dredge produced no results, Murray was crushed, but when he was successful his spirits improved dramatically. After a good catch, Murray would disappear into his cramped, makeshift laboratory, where he huddled in the cold, smoking furiously, gray hair falling in his eyes as he studied the specimens under his microscope. When he couldn't identify them, he still cataloged his findings, keeping meticulous notes in painstaking detail. Even his less educated comrades seemed to understand the significance of his work. If some of these creatures had indeed been seen by the human eye before, they were still unfamiliar. And Murray realized that he could have very well been the first to view—or, at the very least, to identify—some of these animals.

Malloch set up a theodolite on the ice so that every night when the weather was clear enough he could take sightings and keep track of the ship's position. He was also teaching himself how to make igloos. His colleagues discovered him out on the ice one day, making a shabby and badly constructed snow house. He was cheerful and determined as ever, having decided that he should know how to make an igloo, just in case the worst happened and they were forced to leave the ship.

Kataktovik, meanwhile, was teaching Beuchat, McKinlay, and Dr. Mackay to speak the Eskimo language. Every evening for half an hour, they would gather in his quarters in the lab for their lessons.

Beuchat was a brilliant linguist, and in his opinion it was the most difficult language of all to learn. Speaking Eskimo, for instance, was so much different from actually thinking Eskimo. And even with a wide grasp of the Eskimo dialect, it was hard to communicate with native speakers because so many Eskimo words, once translated into English and then back to Eskimo, became nonsense. "Dried apples" in English became "situk" in Eskimo, which meant "resembling an ear." "Salvation" in English became "pulling from a hole in the ice" in Eskimo. And the Twenty-third Psalm translated rather delightfully and alarmingly into: "The Lord is my great keeper; he does not want me. He shoots me down on the beach, & pushes me into the water."

In the evening, some of the men gathered in the saloon to play bridge and chess. Murray taught Mamen to play the latter. The young Norwegian had never played before but picked up the game quickly and began playing every night. In this temporary sanctum from the cold, the scientists and officers sat around the stove and lit their pipes and cigarettes from their treasured rations of tobacco and listened to the tunes of the phonograph. It was a cozy little retreat—a necessary one—and one all of the men came to count on in those long, bleak, darkening days.

In addition to their designated duties, the men—both staff and crew—were still hard at work sewing winter clothes. Stefansson had left them sorely ill-equipped for braving the cold, and Kiruk alone would not be able to outfit them; one woman would never be able to create an entire winter wardrobe for twenty-five people, and besides, her time was better spent making the winter boots. Under Kiruk's keen supervision, each man was given skins, cloth, and some blanketing to make an extra pair of socks and skin shirts. The crewmen were more experienced than their scientific counterparts in the field of embroidery. "Theirs may not be so very beautiful but I will guarantee that they will be solid; sailors know how to sew so it will last," observed Mamen.

At every sign of open water, Bartlett sent men out to hunt. The shortage of fresh meat aboard ship was a concern, and he knew all too well—and had seen firsthand—the devastating and sometimes fatal effects of a meat-free diet. So he sent Kuraluk and Kataktovik out looking for seal and for polar bear. The grizzled Hadley accompanied them, bound and determined to beat the "dirty Indians," as he called them, and bring back more game. Despite the fact that he had loved and married an Eskimo woman, the old man professed that he couldn't stand most Eskimos, made no pretense about his supposed deep-seated hatred of them, and was certainly not about to be out-hunted by a couple of them.

More often than not, the hunters came back empty-handed. Polar bears were often sighted in the distance, but the ice was usually too dangerous for the hunters to pursue them. Seals were easier to catch, but it was just as easy to lose one to the water, after they were killed. They sank like lead weights, straight to the bottom, and all the men had to show for their efforts was a waste of ammunition.

Miraculously, Hadley's dog Molly, the one who had been stranded when the ice broke on October 9, had returned to the ship by now, having wandered back one afternoon. Even the other dogs seemed happy to see her. The dogs themselves had been living loose on the ice for a couple of weeks, fighting with each other to the point of serious injury. They had a horrible way of ganging up on one member of the team, who was usually defended by his team partner, until both were brutally attacked by the rest of the pack. Mamen dubbed them "the lions" because they were so fierce.

One of the hounds, Bob, was fatally injured in a fight. He slunk away on the ice, accompanied by Mosse, his brother, and refused to come aboard. The dogs wouldn't let anyone near them and wouldn't take any nourishment. Several days later, Bob and Mosse returned to the ship, and the men took them aboard and made a bed for Bob on some dry bags. Mosse stayed with him. "It is awful not to be able to spend a bullet on him and thus end his life quickly," wrote Mamen, "instead of letting him lie in agony. It hurts me more than I can describe to see him lying there groaning and puffing, his body shivering incessantly."

When Bob died, Mosse still refused to leave him. He stayed by his side the rest of the night, wailing and howling. Inside their cabins, the men were chilled by his grieving cries, which reverberated, eerie and piercing, in the dead air.

As winter closed in, Bartlett ordered a new routine aboard the *Karluk,* with chief engineer Munro, second engineer Williamson, and firemen Maurer and Breddy working all day at drawing the fires and closing down the engine room to take the faulty engine apart and repair it once and for all: blowing down the boilers, as they called it. Munro and Williamson also installed a new tank for melting ice in the galley. Munro could be quite a diligent worker while Bartlett was watching. He said all the right things, worked with enthusiasm, and took charge of what needed to be done. As soon as Bartlett turned away, however, the work all fell to Williamson, and Munro refused to lift a finger. This was, as Mamen put it, because Munro "doesn't know anything; neither has he any idea of an engineer's work."

There was a new watch regime for the crew, who now worked only from 7:00 A.M. until 6:00 P.M., with their nights free. One man was placed on night watch until 6:00 A.M., the duty changing weekly; in exchange for the night's work, the designated crewman had his days free. There was also a new schedule for meals because rationing was now essential. Breakfast was served at 9:30 A.M., with coffee and hardtack at noon; dinner at 4:30 P.M.; and cocoa, tea or "a mouthful of coffee or rather chicory," according to Mamen, at 9:00 at night. "It is rather long between the meals," he lamented, "but when one has got accustomed to it I believe it will be the best." Templeman thinned the milk and held back the sugar at each feeding, in order to save his stores, and the food continued to be prepared in the usual slovenly way. Dishes were only partially washed, the stove was wiped down with a dirty cloth, and every now and then one of Templeman's cigarette butts found its way into the soup.

The temperature was sinking steadily, dipping down to minus twenty-eight degrees Fahrenheit. The drift had now ceased, and the ice pack was unnervingly motionless. The *Karluk* was still held fast by the ice, at the mercy of the wind and the current. To make matters worse, the days were growing shorter, and soon the men were eating breakfast by lamplight at 9:00 in the morning, and lighting the lamps again by 3:00 P.M. "I suppose the sun will disappear entirely the first days of November," Mamen wrote in his diary, "and when it is gone the long dark winter-night will come quickly, but so much the more welcome [the sun] will be when it returns in January ...."

At Bartlett's request, Hadley and second mate Charles Barker set up shop in the fore-hold, where they built Peary sleds. The captain wanted them ready by February, when they would leave the ship and set out for land, if they had not reached it before then.

In all his years in the Arctic, Hadley had never seen anything like it. He thought it the most ridiculous contraption he had ever come across. Peary had designed the sled himself, based on the experience he'd gleaned in his eight attempts on the North Pole. It measured thirteen feet overall, with each runner measuring three inches wide and one and a half inches thick. The runners were turned up at each end, as was the stern of the sled, making steering easier. Boards of soft wood composed the bed, filled in by pieces of oak, which were fastened by sealskin lashings. The design of the sled made it more flexible than the more conventional Nome model, allowing the driver to turn it around without lifting it. The Peary sled was also more adapted to travel over the rough and uneven Arctic ice.

Mamen was usually supportive of Bartlett, but even he couldn't understand what the captain saw in them. To him, they were cumbersome and strange and he knew they would never work. "I for my part think they are both too heavy and too frail, so I suppose we won't get any satisfaction from them if they are to be used on a sleigh trip. They are only good for being photographed, Mr. Hadley says, and perhaps he is right."

MCKINLAY WAS BEGINNING to gain confidence. In addition to his meteorological work, he had taken up carpentry, something he had never attempted in his life. He constructed a rather crude-looking but functional medicine chest for Dr. Mackay, put up shelves in the library, and built a rough wooden table for the Cabin DeLuxe. He also repaired the gasoline lamp and sewed an entire suit of clothes for himself out of material and blanketing. He couldn't help but feel proud when he surveyed his work.

"There are some people who thought they could only teach school till they came on this trip," Bartlett would shout at him, dropping an enormous bearlike paw onto McKinlay's shoulder. "This is better than teaching school, eh, boy? Just think, you would never have discovered what a fine fellow you are till you came here."

Bartlett was right. It *was* better than teaching school. Before he had signed up to join Stefansson's Arctic expedition, McKinlay could only dream of the type of adventure he was now experiencing. Now here he was in the heart of it, living it. Granted, it wasn't exactly the adventure he had signed up for, but it was an adventure just the same and he was grateful for the experience and excited about what the future might hold.

McKinlay was also grateful to Bartlett, who had been especially generous with McKinlay, Mamen, and Malloch, as if to reward them for not joining the mutinous ranks of Mackay, Murray, and Beuchat. Lately, the captain had been making presents of material and lambskins, as well as knives, pipes, and other odds and ends, to McKinlay and the other two, a poignant gesture that McKinlay knew was Bartlett's way of reaching out. "I sense that he is feeling desperately lonely & conscious that part of the staff indulges in much criticism," McKinlay observed. "At any rate, he is much freer in his relations with Mamen, Malloch & myself; he either knows, or feels, that we refuse to join in the criticism & indeed are prepared to back up whatever he plans."

McKinlay felt for Bartlett and sympathized. He thought that the doctor and his two colleagues were behaving reprehensibly, and he was ashamed to be associated with them in any capacity. He was glad that they left him alone and knew that they did so because his loyalty to Bartlett was clear. He was resolved to stand by the captain and the ship until the end, whatever end that might be.

He just wished there was more he could do for Bartlett than offer his loyalty. He couldn't reach out to that formidable man, and he couldn't make the captain confide in him. Bartlett always kept up a robust, solid front, but lately his face was showing the strain and anxiety he was feeling. McKinlay found himself missing the captain's sharp tongue, hearty smile, and "free & easy, devil-may-care manner."

"I wish to God, McKinlay, I had your even temper," Bartlett told him one day, his usually steady voice uneven.

It was all he said on the matter. But it was all he needed to say. If McKinlay had hosted any doubts about how Bartlett was feeling, those few words painted a clear picture.

THEY HAD LEFT ESQUIMALT four months ago. Daylight was further diminishing and the *Karluk,* still encased in the grip of the ice floe, was drifting steadily northward, sometimes twenty miles a day, sometimes more. By the time she passed Point Barrow, there were only five hours of sunlight each day.

Everyone was feeling the strain. Tempers were short, nerves were worn, and the daily tasks became more difficult to perform. Malloch, normally so cheerful, "the most good-natured chap in the world," according to Mamen, had a tendency to lose control. It came out at odd times—a fierce flash of temper—followed by a return of good spirits.

McKinlay was in the Cabin DeLuxe one afternoon, absorbed in tearing down one of the beds to make more room. He was lost in thought, completely unaware of Malloch, who came into the cabin and stood watching him. McKinlay's back was to the geologist, so it was without warning that Wee Mac was, as Mamen described it, suddenly "encircled by the big bear's arms; to get loose was out of the question and the big bulky fellow went shear berserk on this little innocent man, but when his temper cooled down, he let go his hold and slunk shamefacedly away."

It was a bizarre incident and left McKinlay understandably shaken and Malloch understandably embarrassed. The next day, when the cabin had been rearranged and the extra beds cleared out, the once again sunny Malloch was overjoyed at the change, as if he had thought of it himself. He was contrite, though, over his brutal treatment of McKinlay and crept around sheepishly, removing himself to his bed, embroidering the strips of fabric onto his old trousers. "We may see him early and late with the needle in his hand," wrote Mamen, "singing, a comical figure, naturally good-natured and amiable, but when he gets mad one has to look out for him. It is best to keep at a respectable distance."

While Malloch was becoming prone to violent shows of temper, Dr. Mackay retired to his cabin and began spending most of his days in bed, subsisting on regular doses of strychnine—several a week—to brace himself up. The drug was a tonic, a stimulant, which he had been taking for a while to boost his spirits and his energy, but now he was increasing the dosage. The doses were very large and after he had taken one, he was so weak that he had to stay in bed most of the next day. As days passed, he looked worse— pale and drawn, with dark circles shadowing his eyes and an unusual listlessness about him—until his colleagues worried openly about his well-being. His usual vivacity had disappeared except for fleeting, lightning-quick flashes when he couldn't resist tormenting his favorite target, second engineer Williamson. "For my part," said Mamen, "I believe that he has not long to live, all the strychnine he takes ruins him completely."

Even McKinlay sometimes sank into melancholy. Some days he would sit, book in hand, pipe in mouth, and think about home. His colleagues would catch him, staring into space, and tell him "What's the use?" It was true. There was no use in thinking of his loved ones while he was so far away. Inevitably then, his thoughts would turn to the work that had brought him to the Arctic, and the disturbing fact that, thus far, his choice to leave friends and family was unjustified. They had no leader now, and, even though he tried to stay busy, there was no real work to be done. So what, then, was he doing here?

Mamen confessed his fears only to his journal. He did not confide in anyone, did not burden his friends with his thoughts or worries, did not reveal his own apprehensions. In typical fashion, he tried to remain optimistic. They must take life as it comes. They must be patient. They must trust. Where there is life, there is hope. He believed this above all else, yet he struggled to retain his faith. "Our large ice floe is getting frailer and frailer day after day," he wrote in his journal. "Well, I hope it will be so frail that it will break so we can get out of here. I am now perfectly convinced that we will stay in the ice for a year. Who knows what next year will bring, whether it will be success or death and destruction for all. Yes, when and where this will end is hard to tell. It will probably be a miserable existence for most of us, and the end will be death ... but perhaps it is the greatest benefit that can befall a starved, frozen, and worn-to-death man. No, this is too much. Fresh courage!"

THE FATE OF THE *KARLUK* seemed out of anyone's hands and now they had to wait just as the men of the *Jeannette* had had to wait. As shrewd and experienced as Bartlett was, there was little he could do. De Long himself had also known—perhaps better than anyone—the extreme helplessness of the situation. "No human power can keep the ice still, and no human ingenuity can prevent damage when it begins to grind and break up," De Long wrote. "Held fast in a vise we cannot get away, so we have to trust in God and remain by the ship. If we are thrown out on the ice we must try to get to Siberia, if we can drag ourselves and food over the two hundred and fifty miles intervening; sleds are handy, dogs ready, provisions on deck, knapsacks packed, arms at hand, records encased. What more can we do? When trouble comes we hope to be able to deal with it, and survive it!"

Helpless and unable to do anything for themselves, the staff and crew of the Canadian Arctic Expedition focused their mounting frustration and anger on their absent leader. The men of the *Karluk* gave up hope of seeing him again that year—if ever—and speculated about his whereabouts. Stefansson, they all now realized, had never intended to come back. Perhaps he was at Point Barrow or Herschel Island with the other two expedition ships. Perhaps he was already on his way to wintering in Victoria Land with the Southern Party.

Members of the scientific staff still tried to voice their disgust in private and not in front of the crew. "I suppose there is nobody on board who is sorry for his absence," Mamen wrote in his diary. "I for my part feel sorry for him, if I were in his position under such conditions I believe that I would spend a bullet on myself. He will, I should think, lose his good name and reputation and only be laughed at by the newspapers, yes by each and everybody, poor man, but so it goes when one cannot take care of one's own interests."

Bartlett couldn't give in to criticizing Stefansson, and he didn't have time to waste on lamenting their situation. He left that to the scientists. Although officially in charge of them, he had little control over their avid late-night deliberations regarding the *Jeannette* or Dr. Mackay's plans for mutiny. He focused instead on keeping his crew busy and maintaining his composure.

ON OCTOBER 30, Mamen was lying in his bunk, again studying De Long's diaries, when night watchman Ned Golightly raced into the cabin. Seaman Golightly was usually a quiet boy, calm and reserved, but now he was agitated and breathless. He and the men in the fo'c'sle had heard a loud report at 7:00 P.M. They examined the area around the ship but saw nothing, no sign of where the sound came from. After that, all was quiet. Then, an hour later, Golightly heard the most terrifying noise. It was the ice cracking within ten yards of the ship, surrounding her on all sides, pushing up and raftering, splintering into thin, jagged ribbons, threatening to squeeze *Karluk* like a vise and puncture her vulnerable walls.

Beuchat immediately fell to pieces, scared out of his wits. Mamen assured him that they were safe for the moment and ordered him to get hold of himself. Beuchat calmed somewhat and together he and Mamen raced up and out into the darkness, the bitter, bone-chilling cold, a fierce wind— a blizzard.

It was Sandy who first thought to go after the gear, which was stowed nearby on the ice. Mamen pitched in, and soon all hands were ordered to bring the gear back aboard. The cracks in the ice grew larger as they worked. All about them, the ice was grinding and pressing the ship, as the storm swelled in the darkness. After the supplies were stowed, they went after the dogs, which were reluctant to cross the open water to the ship. The huskies didn't mind ice and cold; they were used to sleeping burrowed in the snow, in the middle of blizzards, if need be. But they hated water. Every time, they refused to cross it. Now as the dark, glassy chasms opened in the ice, the dogs stood their ground and refused to move, or when the men came at them, they ran away, skittering across the ice, away from the open water and the ship.

There wasn't a restful eye in the house that sleepless night. Everyone— scientists, crewmen, Eskimos—suddenly realized quite fully the danger of their situation. It was a reality that Bartlett had been facing from the moment they became trapped in the ice. *Karluk* had survived this time, but would she be so lucky the next? They could no longer push aside the prospect of doom and tragedy. It wasn't a matter of *if* anymore, but *when*.

The ship's engine was still out of commission, and Munro, Williamson, Maurer, and Breddy faced at least another three or four days of repairs, which left the *Karluk* vulnerable and without power should another catastrophe arise. "By that time," Mamen remarked dryly, "we will probably be at the bottom of the sea. If not we ourselves, at least our dear home '*Karluk*' with all our comfort and belongings, and with that the Canadian Arctic Expedition with Mr. Stefansson as Commander would be stranded. But we must hope for the best and be prepared for the worst and we shall see that everything will go well."

ON THE LAST DAY of October, the blizzard raged all day, a furious gale from the northeast that rocked the ship with a violent hand. The ice had fused again late the night before, and the *Karluk* was once more held fast by the pack. The men were bone-weary, aching, and red-eyed from lack of sleep, but everyone was at his post, ready for the worst.

"Oh my, how it blows now," wrote Mamen. "The rigging is swinging to and fro, the masts shake so we feel it now and then, the courage is sinking in most of them, all are prepared for a catastrophe. Well, such is life in the north, it is a gamble, not with money, but with what is more valuable than gold, it is human life one plays with. The strong and hardy ones most often come out of the game with happy results, while the poor and frail individuals may pay with their lives."

They were, as Beuchat observed, the lost and headless expedition.

And so they looked toward November and waited.

NOVEMBER 1913

———— • ————

It is a dreary existence but one must put up with it and be thankful as long as one has a roof over the head.

—BJARNE MAMEN,
ASSISTANT TOPOGRAPHER

By afternoon on the first of November, the gale was so powerful that the men could barely peer outside. Any more than that would have been deadly in the slicing cold and bitter wind. Because all flesh had to be covered or it would freeze instantly, the men tucked themselves safely inside the drafty wooden walls of the ship and stayed there, listening anxiously to the cry of the wind and the crashing of the ice.

When they did look outside they saw a wild and powerful scene. The snow swept and twisted angrily, like the funnels of a thousand small tornadoes. It swirled into clouds and blew with such force that mountainous drifts were forming while some patches of ice appeared flattened—blown perfectly clean and glistening. The ship, still without power, was being carried westward by the current with remarkable speed, at the mercy of the ice floe that held her.

November, it appeared, would bring no relief. Bartlett wore the strain on his weathered, ruddy face, shadows of it appearing around the cracked smile, his keen blue eyes splintered with lines. He was the only one out of the entire ship's company to realize fully the dangers they faced. But he vowed he was never going to let them see his own anxiety.

The men were terrified of losing the *Karluk*, knowing that the swift current would make it near impossible to reach land. If the ship was crushed and lost, their fate would probably be a long and painful death on the ice from exposure or starvation.

Outside, the wind raged sixty miles per hour. A massive snowdrift, blinding and unforgiving, swept over and around the ship. The depth was only thirty-six fathoms now, but the *Karluk* was taking in a good amount of water from a slight forward leak. There was no steam available since the engine had broken down again and was being repaired. The crew and staff—two and two together at a time—used the hand-pump to empty her. It was a long and sobering job, and as they worked they wondered how long the *Karluk* would be able to hold together.

Bartlett ordered a good stock of supplies and provisions to be transferred to the ice nearby. He wanted to lighten the *Karluk*—thus minimizing her chances of being crushed—and give them a solid base of stores, should anything happen to the ship. Working in the teeth of the storm, they began with the sacks of coal and tins of biscuits lined on the poop deck, unloading them onto the ice from 10:00 in the morning until 4:00 in the afternoon.

Afterward, Mamen sat in his cabin, listening with great delight to the tick-ticking of his watch. Many of the men had similar treasures from home. For McKinlay it was the Bible given to him by his local pastor before he left Glasgow; for fireman Fred Maurer a Bible from his mother; and for mess room boy Ernest Chafe his trophies for marksmanship and shooting. For Mamen, it was this watch, which was a gift from his brother Trygve before Mamen had left for Canada. The watch had stopped working months ago, however, and try as he may to get it going again, it had remained silent and unmoving. Suddenly, one afternoon, it began to tick, out of the blue and for no apparent reason. So Mamen sat there now, warm and safe while the storm raged outside, and listened with joy to the sound.

THE DAYS WERE GROWING SHORTER. About noon they caught a glimpse of the sun, which hovered only three degrees above the horizon. It was now dark by 12:30 P.M.

The men were dreading the onset of the long winter night. Day by day, the light slipped away, the sun sank lower on the horizon, and the darkness seeped up and over the icescape, settling oppressively over the ship.

Bartlett kept his men on a strict routine. When there was no work to be done, he invented tasks for them to do. The sense of order was good for them and it was the only way to keep their minds occupied. Mamen, McKinlay, and a few of the others realized what he was doing and appreciated his methods. "Captain Bartlett," wrote Chafe, "kept us to work certain hours every day... just to keep us fit for the hardships we would have to encounter in case we lost the ship, which we expected at any time. As long as we were working, it seemed that we were living for a purpose, and were still a part of the busy world."

A chess league was launched for the officers and scientists to while away the dull evenings, with Bartlett promising a box of fifty choice cigars to the grand prize winner, and a box of twenty-five cigars to the man who took second place. "I for my part have no chances of getting a prize," wrote novice Mamen, "but I promised the others to help them smoke, which I suppose they are not particularly delighted about."

As Bartlett had hoped, the chess tournament quickly became a much-needed distraction. Caught up in the spirit of the game and competition, the men found themselves wholly absorbed in the new nightly activity. It temporarily took their minds away from the loneliness and the great fear—the feeling of being disconnected from the rest of the earth. No radios, no airplanes, no ships could possibly know where they were or reach them if they did know. Because of the rapidly changing drift, even Bartlett and his men had lost all sense of their own whereabouts.

On the morning of November 4, Malloch was shaken awake at 5:30 A.M. by the night watchman, informing him that the stars were out. He pulled himself reluctantly from his bed, dressed hurriedly, and lumbered up to his usual place on the bridge to try for an observation by starlight, as his instruments were still imprecise. But the sky clouded up as soon as he set foot outside. Determined to learn their position, and now wide awake, he stayed out until 9:00 A.M., pacing back and forth, squinting up at the sky and waiting for it to clear, but—with the help of the brilliant star Vega—he was only able to fix the longitude.

Mamen, meanwhile, resorted to climbing up the rickety rope ladder to the crow's nest to take a look around. Each time he made the climb, he prayed he would see land, or at the very least, a way out of their plight. Those minutes seemed to stretch endlessly as he swung up one rung and then another, step by careful step, hoping there would be something wonderful waiting for him at the top. But each day it was, as always, "ice and still more ice as far as the eye could see."

There was a narrow ledge that surrounded the ship for half a mile or so, the result of the shifting ice, which had broken and piled into pressure ridges. These towering ice hills dotted the horizon, but other than that, it was flat and clear and looked like fine going. There was absolute stillness and no sign of life. In fact, as Mamen remarked bleakly, "it looks as if everything were dead ...."

Everyone realized that the ship was unreachable, that even if Stefansson knew where they were, he might have already given them up for dead, and even if he hadn't he would not be able to send help. Yet Stefansson was the only hope.

"Presumably Mr. Stefansson will come in contact with the outer world," Mamen wrote, "and after the weather we have had lately I am sure his supposition is that *Karluk* has gone down and most of us with her. It is this that worries me...."

AFTER DAYS OF grueling work, the transfer of supplies to the ice was, at last, completed. Now when the men looked out on the frosty Arctic landscape, the white blankness surrounding the ship was interrupted by the dark outlines and shapes of boxes stacked and stored on top of the ice. There were 250 sacks of coal, 6 cases of codfish, 5 drums of alcohol, 114 cases of biscuit, 19 barrels of molasses, 2,000 feet of lumber to build winter quarters, 33 cases of gasoline, 3 cases of codsteaks, 4 cases of dried eggs, 5 casks of beef, 9 sleds, 3 coal stoves, and 2 wood stoves.

Kuraluk and Kataktovik went out daily now, diligent and patient, to try to replenish the dwindling meat supply. The Eskimos were respected by the scientists and befriended by some of them. But the crewmen and officers treated them like servants, or worse. Just as the crew's quarters and mess room were separated from the scientists', the Eskimos' quarters were separated from both crew and staff, and they ate and hunted separately. This was fine with them. They wanted nothing to do with the crewmen and were there simply to do their jobs, to fulfill their contracts. Kuraluk and Kataktovik had been hired to hunt and Kiruk to sew, and they went about these tasks quietly and fixedly.

Kuraluk and Kataktovik spent hours in the cold and wind, sometimes sitting by a hole in the ice all day long with no results but a nip on the nose and cramped limbs. They did not complain and they did not give up. On one lucky day, they got ten seals at a lead of water a few miles from the ship.

That made thirty-four seals in the larder now, which they expected would last until the middle or end of January. Beyond that, the men had no idea what they would do. Polar bears were too elusive, and the arctic foxes were sparse. The men were eating seal meat three times a week, and although they were sick of it, they dreaded the day when it ran out.

"It surely will be a dreary winter," Mamen lamented. "There is not a living thing to be seen, neither bear nor fox, and now when the ice has closed up there won't even be seal. Preserved meat and preserved meat day out and day in. Our seal supply will not last longer than Christmas, if that long …."

AT NIGHT, Fred Maurer, Ernest Chafe, gentlemanly seaman Clam, and the rest of the deck crew enjoyed their own gramophone concerts. They spent their evenings in their mess room, much like the staff and officers, playing cards, chess, or checkers, or reading books from the ship's library. During the day, they found themselves with little to do except clean up and chop ice for water. The large tank in the galley was the primary water source right now. It had a small hatch for dropping the ice into; it worked well, but there was a reserve box on deck, just in case of bad weather. Fresh water could be obtained from the old ice floes—the ones that had been around for years. "The effect of the sun upon the ice draws the salt from it," Chafe explained, "thereby rendering it so fresh that the tongue can trace no saltness in it."

Second engineer Williamson removed the copper tank from the Cabin DeLuxe and fixed it up below, running pipes through it from the engine room fire, conveniently located nearby. This way there was hot water for washing, for which McKinlay and Mamen and most everyone else was grateful. It had been at least a month since most of the men had washed their clothes, which were now molding in disreputable and dingy piles on the cabin floor.

Murray's observations showed the ship to be drifting due north, the most northerly and westerly drift thus far. The *Karluk* was still leaking badly, and the staff of the expedition took over the job of pumping her dry. Every day, she had to be pumped free of water, and each day it took longer to do.

Mamen was positive it was from all the bumping in the ice. "I am sure that she has sprung a leak," he wrote, "if so there will be some fun here in the winter, first to labour early and late with pumping to save her, and then it will, I suppose, go with us as with De Long."

NOVEMBER 12 was the last day of the year that they would see the sun. Everyone had risen in the dark, flat morning to eat breakfast, and afterward returned to their bunks to await the slender bit of daylight that remained. It was more of a glimpse than anything else—just a filmy memory of light.

They all mourned the loss of the sun, although a sort of mystical twilight still crept over the sky around noon. But the darkness became more pronounced each day and, in the absence of that bright orb, thanks were given for the moon and the stars.

"People talk about moonshine," wrote Mamen. "Today we have a perfectly splendid full moon, it rose early in the forenoon, it shines so it is a joy to see it, the snow and ice crystals sparkle like diamonds in the light ...."

It was a shimmering, glittering world, and the men often stood outside on the deck or on the ice to admire the exotic beauties of the far north. The Pole star burned almost directly overhead, and sometimes they could forget the dangers they faced when they stood on that drifting world of ice and watched the brilliant light displays of the aurora borealis. "It was difficult to believe that the elements of this beauty were the very stuff from which could spring disaster and tragedy," wrote McKinlay.

He often wrapped himself in his warmest clothes and walked out on the ice at night to enjoy a solitary reverie and to "wonder and admire, remembering that the same moon will in its own time shine on the dear ones at home. What message could it convey to us, if it could? What news of friends and of the world at large? It is at such times that one realises what it means to be this cut off."

———— • ————

WITH THE FALLING TEMPERATURE and no more warmth from the sun, the staff spent the morning huddled in their beds. They were up by noon, though, and the project of the day was to make *Karluk* as warm as possible. Everyone worked together to insulate the main deck with a six-inch layer of snow, and to cover the poop deck, which was above the Cabin DeLuxe, with blocks of snow eighteen inches deep. All doors and windows not used were covered, too. Bartlett would have roofed the entire ship in to make them the most snug and comfortable; but the drift was too unpredictable, and their winter station was not secure enough.

That night, an ominous sound rose above the murmurs of mutiny and the snoring of the sailors—the distinctive rumbling of ice pressure. It was, as McKinlay said, "a noise there is no mistaking."

McKinlay fixed his faulty transit—one of the few magnetic instruments he had on board—and then bundled up in some warm clothes and headed outside for a sighting. Vega was visible to the naked eye. The brightest star in the northern hemisphere, bluish hued and blazing, it was magnificent. McKinlay stayed out to watch it until his right hand became frozen, and the object glass of the transit frosted up, whereupon he went back inside to restore circulation. He rubbed his hand in his hair in an attempt to warm it. His thumb and third finger were skeleton white and badly nipped; but soon the blood began to flow again and he was in agony.

"It is a pain utterly unlike anything I have ever experienced," he wrote that night, his fingers still tender and stiff, "beating toothache all to sticks. I cannot imagine any more exquisite torture than to freeze a man's fingers and toes just so far as they are restorable and then to thaw them out."

Earlier, McKinlay was strolling the deck when, around noon, a glow appeared in the south. He stood there, admiring it, when he noticed, "just tipping the horizon, the upper limb of the sun."

According to the *Nautical Almanac,* the sun was already two days below them, so the only possible explanation for it could have been refraction. But refraction or not, it was light. With great excitement, McKinlay shouted to the others to come look. The men rushed from the saloon, the fo'c'sle, and the engine room to gain one last glimpse of the brilliant star.

They stood there together and bade the sun farewell and thanked it for its warmth. Shoulder to shoulder, crewmen, officers, scientists, Eskimos, and captain, they watched in a deep, awed hush, chilled, their breath escaping in thin, diaphanous clouds. Yet they were strangely warmed. Then, with great sadness, they saw the radiant fireball dip below the earth for the last time, leaving them in the cold darkness.

"Now he is gone!" McKinlay said afterward. "When we will see him again, who can say? For our position is such that we may see him—at the earliest—in two months' time; it may be thrice, it may be—well, one wonders what position we will be in when he does return. But as we watched him go, I had other thoughts. We would miss him, but we would buoy ourselves up with the knowledge that he still shines on our friends at home and with the hope that he will shine for us again."

ON NOVEMBER 15, the ship was buffeted again by screaming gale winds that grabbed hold of her until she trembled from the force of it. It was the most violent storm they had seen, and "it blew and still is blowing so hard that we feel the wind indoors," wrote Mamen, "it penetrates everything, nothing can keep it out, we all shiver and freeze although we are inside ...."

McKinlay was out on the ice when the storm hit, and the ship, only a few yards away, was already invisible in a blanket of drifting snow. Even though there was no sign of open water, Bartlett ordered everyone to remain aboard because of the fury of the blizzard.

The men passed the time as best they could, but they felt their confinement. Mamen, to the delight of his colleagues, spent the day writing out forestry tables, desperate for distraction. *Do you intend to begin a forest station in the Arctic?* they asked him. And he was reminded that he was silly to spend so much time and effort on work that would never be of any use nor ever be seen by the Canadian government. But Mamen was stubborn and did not listen to them. He intended to make his time out here count.

The mess room light burned all day now because of the darkness. The sun was truly gone, and the moon had disappeared, too, into the blackened and clouded depths of the wild gale. Somehow, this made things even more unbearable.

The loss of the sun, the endless waiting, the fear, the quiet, the vacuum of that world—all preyed on the minds of these men. "So long as the sun was with us to measure the night and day, it was not so bad," Chafe wrote, "but when the orb disappeared, a sort of sickening sensation of loneliness came over us."

ONE AFTERNOON, they saw—or thought they saw—smoke in the northwest, a cloud just above the horizon that seemed like the smoke from a steamer funnel. The winds still blew but the snow had cleared. Their hearts leaped at the faintest glimmer of hope that there was another ship nearby. Half an hour later, they saw another spout of smoke, just west of the first one. And later still another stream appeared to the south-southwest, remaining for quite a while in the sky. There was no ship. It was the most curious phenomenon, and something the men were at a loss to explain.

Were they beginning to hallucinate? Their world now filled with eerie sights and sounds, some of them explicable, some less easy to understand. "There is a peculiar weirdness in those silent stretches of the ice pack," wrote Chafe. "No sound is heard except the boom or roar of ice breaking and grinding by its own great weight."

Spirits hit an all-time low. Only the gramophone seemed capable of invoking anything resembling cheer, except to Dr. Mackay, who was quite vocal in his condemnation of it. The doctor had come to view the thing in general—and all of the noise it emitted—as a serious abomination. Even Harry Lander seemed to have lost his charm.

One night—perhaps to placate him, perhaps to quiet him down—Mamen pilfered the handle of the machine and smuggled it to Mackay, who, in an effort to silence the offending beast once and for all, stashed it in his bunk. The staff and officers, as usual, wanted a concert that night. They had come to depend on this evening ritual; it was vitally important to most of them. Williamson tried to wind up the gramophone, but, of course, the doctor had the handle and refused to return it. Not to be outdone, Williamson and McKinlay appealed to the crewmen in their quarters in the fo'c'sle and asked to borrow their gramophone. They set up the borrowed contraption in the saloon and soon were enjoying their favorite music at an even greater volume, as this Victrola played much louder than their own.

It was minutes before Mackay appeared, having done the impossible and dragged himself out of bed. He volunteered the handle, ready to admit defeat—anything to stop the racket. But no such luck. It was with great pleasure that McKinlay and Williamson replaced the handle, wound the machine, and began spinning a record as the crewmen's gramophone continued to blare its own tunes. The result was a thunderous concert of dueling gramophones. Mackay was more annoyed than ever, and completely unamused.

Everyone else was in high spirits over the prank, until the gasoline lamp burned out so that no one could see an inch in front of his own nose. Desperate for light, they lit the dreaded coal oil lamp, which cast a mournful gloom and discharged fumes that caused their heads to ache. One by one, the men retired to their bunks, disheartened and depressed once again. It was amazing the effect that the feeble light of one rotten oil lamp could have. A few stragglers remained, attempting to read or play chess, but at midnight the lamp gave out and plunged them back into darkness.

They depended on artificial lighting, from morning till night, but their supply of coal oil was running dangerously low and Bartlett gave orders for rationing. During the day, lamps were lit only when absolutely necessary. The gasoline lamp in the saloon was still failing, and they were terrified of it dying altogether. Every day, McKinlay took it apart and tried to fix it, but to no avail. It now gave out only a faint light. When it went, it would be like the sun leaving all over again, and the men did not think they were strong enough to deal with this.

Midday brought "a faint, twilight glow in the South," wrote a somber McKinlay, "telling us that there is still a sun shining somewhere in the world, but that is all."

ON NOVEMBER 21, the *Karluk* and the floe that held her began drifting west rapidly, approaching the coast of Siberia. The gale continued to blow through the ship. Mamen, Malloch, McKinlay, and Beuchat felt the gusts of cold air all night as the temperature in the Cabin DeLuxe dipped below freezing. They had no choice but to sleep in their clothes, which was both awkward and uncomfortable. And even with that, it was impossible to get warm. There were two degrees of frost on McKinlay's bunk, and everything that was freezable in the Cabin DeLuxe was frozen and frozen hard. When the men awakened, the room looked like a glittering ice palace. Ice covered everything, and long, jagged icicles shone from the ceiling.

Outside, the rigging shook, the wind shrieked, and the ship trembled from bow to stern. Now the *Karluk* rapidly approached Wrangel Island, following an almost identical path to the *Jeannette,* a fact that did not go unnoticed by the scientific staff and Bartlett.

Some men had already pronounced the *Karluk* dead. Almost all agreed that she would not survive the winter. The scientists held a somber meeting on November 24 to discuss the future. It was more of a wake, actually, complete with mourning over the soon-to-be-departed ship. Still the optimist, McKinlay found himself amused by his colleagues. Everyone was all too aware of the *Karluk's* deficiencies, but there seemed to be no sense in "meeting trouble halfway. Certainly we are in a bad predicament, being as far from Pt. Barrow as from Wrangel Island, while in two months we have drifted 300 miles westward. Should we go much farther West, the chances of breaking free are remote, but then—well, one can never count on the behaviour of the ice, nor can we say where our drift may land us."

As the Eskimos continued to pile snow blocks against the sides of the ship to give added protection against the severe cold, Captain Bartlett rustled up a small alcohol stove, and once they got it going, it turned the frigid Cabin DeLuxe into a dry and warm little home.

By afternoon, the cabin had become so dry and warm that they had to clear the ice off a porthole and open it to let the cool air in. At some point, Malloch announced that he could no longer sleep there, and he was taking himself off to the wheelhouse instead. Because it was full of emergency equipment, he ended up in the chart house, bundled stubbornly in his skins and his sleeping bag. The next morning—and all the mornings afterward—he would sit over his breakfast, pinched and blue with cold, rubbing his eyes and yawning, and refusing to admit that he hadn't slept well. For all of his affability, Malloch was excessively proud and vain and hated to admit defeat, especially after he had made such a fuss. Afterward, he would retire to the saloon, where he could be found catching up on his sleep. He still made his daily observations from the bridge, but most of his days were spent propped up in a chair, his handsome head nodding about as he dozed.

McKinlay, meanwhile, sat down with the saloon lamp, determined to fix it once and for all. He couldn't face another day of the feeble and gloomy light of the oil lamp. He was, at last, successful. Now it burned all night, as bright to him as the sun.

AT MIDNIGHT on November 29, the wind once again hit like a hurricane. The snow blew so fiercely that no one could go outside. The men erupted at each other in frustration and anger. They were edgy, solemn, and quiet, each person in his own way carrying the weight of this frozen world upon his shoulders.

"It is not for themselves they are anxious but for their beloved ones at home," wrote Mamen. "They sleep with open eyes and ears. It is neither sleep nor rest one gets when one has to be on guard against the powers of nature."

BARTLETT LAY IN BED at night, neither sleeping nor resting, and worried about the winter. His patience was thin, his spirits were low, and the uncertainty of their situation was taxing his nerves. It would be better if only he could sleep, but at night he agonized, and through the walls he had to endure the increasing grumblings of Dr. Mackay, Murray, and Beuchat as they gathered in the saloon after hours. While everyone else slept, they continued to plot and plan to leave the ship and head for land.

Bartlett had vowed never to confide in anyone about his worries, but when he and Mamen stood up in the barrel—the wind and the snow whipping their clothes and hair, beating their faces with an icy hand—he suddenly found himself talking about the *Karluk*. It was a relief to speak frankly at last.

Neither captain nor topographer believed that the ship was strong enough to withstand the ice. They both knew that it was inevitable—the *Karluk* would go down, and they would have to save themselves and get out of there somehow.

"Everything that can be done will be done to save her," Bartlett told Mamen firmly, "but whether we shall succeed or not, who knows."

Their talk inevitably turned to Stefansson and his departure from the ship. It was a long discourse and an enlightening one. As always, hovering over them was the specter of the *Jeannette*.

"I have gone to bed lately with a kind of feeling that I shall never wake up again," wrote Mamen, "and when the morning comes and everything is all right, I feel highly surprised to be among the living, it is not exactly a pleasant feeling, but I am now so accustomed to it that it causes me no anxiety. If I must die, let me die like a man and not as a dog. We are all affected... as to whether *Karluk* is so strong that she will stand all the pressing or whether she will follow *Jeannette* and go to the bottom."

In 1880, after a year on the ice, his ship still drifting aimlessly, a weary George Washington De Long had written with a foreboding that the men, Kiruk, and maybe even the two children of the *Karluk* now understood: "There can be no greater wear and tear on a man's mind and patience than this life in the pack. The absolute monotony; the unchanging round of hours; the awakening to the same things and the same conditions that one saw just before losing one's self in sleep; the same faces; the same dogs; the same ice; the same conviction that tomorrow will be exactly the same as to-day, if not more disagreeable; the absolute impotence to do anything, to go anywhere, or to change one's situation an iota. Each day our chances of liberation seem to grow fainter and fainter. Alas, alas! the North Pole and the Northwest Passage are as far from our realization as they were the day the ship left England; and my pleasant hope, to add something to the history of Arctic discovery and exploration, has been as ruthlessly shattered and as thoroughly killed as my greatest enemy could desire. I frequently think that instead of recording the idle words that express our progress from day to day I might better keep these pages unwritten, leaving a blank properly to represent the utter blank of this Arctic expedition."

DECEMBER 1913

———— • ————

We had suffered mishap, and danger had confronted us often; we had been squeezed and jammed, tossed and tumbled about, nipped and pressed, until the ship's sides would have burst if they had not been as strong as the hearts they held within them; we were not yet daunted, but were as ready to dare as ever.
—GEORGE WASHINGTON DE LONG, DECEMBER 31, 1880

O n September 21, the day after leaving the *Karluk*, Stefansson, Wilkins, McConnell, Jenness, and the two Eskimo hunters had reached Thetis Island, just four miles north of the mainland of Alaska. Two days later, a blizzard arrived and the ice, from what they could tell, began drifting swiftly westward. The *Karluk* was, they figured, being swept along with it. Stefansson could only hope that she would eventually free herself and head on to Herschel Island.

In the meantime, he and his group crossed over to the mainland and headed west, and on the morning of October 5, they set out for Cape Halkett. When they stopped at a small Eskimo settlement, Stefansson tried to seek out news of the *Karluk*, but no one knew anything. There was only word of three other vessels—the *Polar Bear,* the *Belvedere,* and the *Elvira*—that were caught in the ice about seventy miles from Herschel Island.

Stefansson decided that he and Wilkins, McConnell, Jenness, Jimmy, and Jerry should make the trek to Point Barrow, camping at Eskimo villages along the way. Afterward, they would all head east to Herschel Island, where they hoped to meet up with the Southern Party.

They had reached Point Barrow on October 12 and, according to McConnell, everyone but Stefansson was anxious to get there, presumably because he was not looking forward to telling the Canadian government that the *Karluk* was missing. They were given a hearty welcome at the Cape Smythe Trading Station and learned that the *Alaska* and the *Mary Sachs* were now docked at Collinson Point, where they were planning to winter.

At Point Barrow, Stefansson was met by Eskimos who told him they had seen a vessel, but that it was too far off to be recognized. Another Eskimo reported seeing a two-masted schooner with no signs of life aboard. Still another Eskimo told Stefansson that he had seen the *Karluk* the week before, and had tried to reach her, but the ice would not permit.

McConnell observed, "It looks as if the *Karluk* is up against it and has drifted past Pt. Barrow, as she must have been five miles out to sea when he saw her and there will be no opportunity for her to get to shore."

Stefansson settled into Point Barrow, sending Jenness and Wilkins on ahead so as to save the cost of boarding them in Cape Smythe. Then he and McConnell got down to the business of writing articles and telegrams and dispatches to newspapers, as well as writing a report to the Canadian government. Stefansson also dictated a form letter addressed to Bartlett to be distributed among Eskimos and "white men" along the coast, in case Bartlett should come ashore.

On the night of October 25, Wilkins saw a light on the northwestern horizon, which gave them hope of finding the *Karluk*. Everyone turned out to see if it was, in fact, a ship, far out in the ice. "A field-glass and finally a telescope was produced—it was the star Arcturus," Jenness wrote in his diary. "There was a fine aurora—a bow stretching from the northwest round to the northeast and almost reaching the zenith."

STEFANSSON WAS ALSO in no hurry to reach Collinson Point, Alaska, where the Southern Party of his Canadian Arctic Expedition was camped. When he finally did arrive on December 15, he found the *Alaska* with a hole in her side and the *Mary Sachs* frozen in the gravel of the beach. No one knew anything of the missing *Karluk*. No one even knew that she was lost or that Stefansson had broken away from the Northern Party.

Stefansson's arrival was something Dr. Anderson and Kenneth Chipman and the other members of the Southern Party had dreaded ever since they had become separated from the *Karluk* back in August. "What we had always expected *might* happen, *had* happened," wrote Chipman. No one was happy to see Stefansson.

The members of the Southern Party were afraid—and rightfully so—that Stefansson would try to take command over them. Anderson and Chipman were especially worried. From the beginning of the Canadian Arctic Expedition enterprise, Anderson had made it clear that he required complete control of the Southern Party without Stefansson's usual interference. Otherwise, he wanted no part of it. He had threatened to quit the expedition in July 1913 and agreed to withdraw his resignation only after he was promised that Stefansson would not challenge his authority. Stefansson reassured him once again that he had no intention of doing so.

Then he promptly began ordering provisions and equipment he felt the Southern Party needed. In addition, Stefansson announced that he intended to take the *Mary Sachs* from them to use as his own vessel, thus replacing the lost *Karluk*. Once again outfitted, he would continue on his way and the Southern Party could hire more men and purchase another ship to replace the *Mary Sachs*.

Stefansson had already sent the story of the *Karluk* to the newspapers, although there were a good many inaccuracies in his version. Stefansson had a habit of changing facts to suit himself, sometimes even changing his own altered facts later, therefore giving several different accounts of the same story. Now he claimed he could get away with these falsities in his reports to the papers because they were just that—reports—so "he could never be held responsible legally."

He broke the story of the *Karluk* to the members of the Southern Party: he said he knew nothing of his ship's whereabouts and had no idea if she was still afloat, or had come aground somewhere, or what condition his men were in.

He blamed the entire catastrophe on Bartlett. Stefansson claimed that he was frightened of the skipper and was unable to stop him from steering the *Karluk* into the ice pack. Yet it was hard to imagine that a man of Stefansson's stature and conviction could really be frightened to the point of intimidation by anyone, even someone as imposing as Bartlett, who had treated his leader with the same polite respect he had shown Peary and, in Stefansson's own words, "always took orders pretty well." Bartlett didn't admire Stefansson as he did Peary. Yet he treated Stefansson with typically polite "yes sirs," and "no sirs," and "anything I can do, sirs."

Stefansson claimed that the captain had scored such a victory in getting Peary to the Pole that he was anxious to repeat that glory with the *Karluk*. The *Roosevelt*, Peary's ship on the triumphant 1909 expedition, had followed leads and gone out into the ice, succeeding beautifully. Stefansson also said that G. J. Desbarats in Ottawa had told Bartlett that he had confidence in him, which Stefansson looked on as interference by the naval service. This official bolstering and encouragement of Bartlett, in Stefansson's eyes, helped to remove from him some of the moral responsibility for the lost *Karluk*.

Stefansson was being criticized sharply by the Canadian Government and by the press for abandoning his ship and her company, and he was quick to defend himself. He had already written his Northern Party off as dead, and as far as he was concerned, the deaths were justified in the name of science and progress. "The newspapers were saying that the entire complement of the *Karluk* had perished, that my plans were unsound, and that the expedition had failed. Editors especially, who presumably had been through high school, were asserting that all the knowledge ever gained in the Arctic was not worth the sacrifice of one young Canadian."

THE MEN OF THE *KARLUK* were disheartened and solemn, grateful only that they had the sanctuary of their ship to protect them. "What a time it would be to be adrift on the ice tonight," observed McKinlay, and they thanked God that they were not.

Bartlett had never known a colder December. The barometer fell steadily throughout the month, temperatures plunging as low as minus thirty-two degrees Fahrenheit. The wind shifted to north-northeast, and the *Karluk* began drifting south, southeast, west, and then north. Everyone, as usual, was on alert. The sky was thick with snow and the wind was unrelenting. The storms seemed to push away the stars and black out the moon, and when these disappeared, dark, heavy clouds took their places.

On December 22, the darkest day of the year, the gale was still strong but the starlight was splendid. The cold and the wind crept into the ship, in frigid, whispering blasts, which numbed the men as they worked and slept.

The *Karluk* drifted strongly to the northwest, and they were now only 140 miles from Wrangel Island's longitude. They had been carried hundreds of miles off course, far to the west of Alaska and Herschel Island, and they were still faithfully following the route of De Long's *Jeannette*.

The ship was leaking alarmingly and it took them at least an hour and a half each day to pump her dry. The men pumped with their own physical power because the steam was still shut off while engine repairs continued.

The *Karluk* vibrated and shuddered continuously from the force of the winds and the movement of the ice. Outside, it was dark as pitch, and the only solace they found was sitting before the dim glow of the saloon stove. They piled as much fuel into the stove as they could.

Enormous snowdrifts mounted around the *Karluk,* covering most of the ship's perimeter. On the lee side, snowdrifts grew higher than deck level, soon towering above the ship, threatening to cave in on top of her at any moment. As the storm roared on, the wind sometimes reached a velocity of eighty miles an hour.

On December 23, the storm was still raging in its sixth day with no sign of relief. Bartlett was extremely anxious, and for once, he wasn't able to disguise it. The men watched him stride the deck agitatedly, pensive and especially withdrawn and were struck with fear to see him this way.

Dr. Mackay, Murray, and Beuchat now began to dwell on the more morbid details of the demise of De Long and his men. The drift of the *Jeannette* was no longer as interesting as the tragic fate of her company. The fate of De Long was, they were certain, to be their own. The doctor and his comrades talked of nothing else, so McKinlay and Mamen began to avoid them altogether.

Maurer, Clam, and the rest of the crewmen were not aware of De Long or the *Jeannette,* but they did know as well as anyone how grave their situation was. They worked every day in the thick of things, and they understood the sea far better than their scientific counterparts. They had no Arctic experience among them, but they could see the dangers.

Maurer wrote, "You would naturally think that a sense of loneliness would come over the crew; but, on the contrary, we were always in good spirits. Each one seemed to realize the situation we were in, but avoided talking about it—except occasionally we would revert to it and wonder how long and far we would drift before we were crushed, and what would be the result."

Meanwhile, the *Karluk* drifted rapidly west. The men could see signs of open water in the distance, and the watchman reported a lead opening up ahead, over a mile away. Low clouds hovered above the horizon indicating land. They could only guess it was Wrangel Island, that barren, wretched place that De Long had written of in his journals.

McKinlay, Mamen, and Malloch found solace in Bartlett's cabin. Each had been keeping busy as best he could and visits to the captain were a welcome reward during those long days.

McKinlay had been teaching English to Kataktovik, who was an eager student, borrowing paper from the magnetician so that he could practice his English and write letters. Mamen, to everyone's surprise, had won the chess tournament, beating the illustrious Dr. Mackay in a brutal tiebreaker, and accepting the promised box of fifty cigars for first place while Sandy took the box of twenty-five for second. Malloch had finally returned to the Cabin DeLuxe after suffering the cold of the chart house for as long as he could. He endured some good-natured ribbing from his friends, but he was too sleepy to care. He could do without pride if it meant being warm again.

The three endured cutting remarks from Dr. Mackay each time they returned from their visits to Bartlett. The drugs, no doubt, had something to do with his bitterness, and the fact that he and the captain were still not on speaking terms.

Bartlett was alone on that ship and he felt it. Despite all of the personality clashes among the scientists and crewmen, they at least had each other. Thus it was that the more perceptive members of the group—McKinlay, Mamen, and, sometimes, Malloch—found themselves in the captain's cabin, passing long hours on those winter days.

Bartlett sat there as they conversed, after the work was done for the day, and told them about his life on land as the toast of high society, a realm he was proud to be invited into, but one where he didn't feel he truly belonged. Indeed, he felt awkward anywhere on land. The captain recommended books to McKinlay so that he could read them and they could discuss them afterward. Bartlett loved to pick up his worn and dog-eared volumes of Shakespeare and Browning and Shelley and Keats—not to mention his favorite of all, the *Rubáiyát*—and read aloud from them. He thumbed the pages with his clumsy, thick-fingered hands, soiled and rough, and looked up at his companion, crinkling his blue eyes with delight.

"Gosh now, that's a mighty fine thing. How do you suppose he knew how to say it that way?" Then Bartlett would shake his head, marveling, and continue to read. For a few moments, it seemed, he was able to forget about the cold and the ice, the helpless ship, the leader who had, it seemed, abandoned them, and the precious lives for which he alone, as captain, was responsible.

THE APPROACH OF CHRISTMAS raised their spirits considerably. Christmas Eve was spent in a flurry of activity and preparation for the celebration. Even the uncaring Templeman bustled around the galley, baking cakes and other delicacies.

There was a beautiful aurora that night. It began in the northwest and stretched across the sky in a broad S-shaped curtain, patterned like a kaleidoscope with patches of brightly changing lights that grew and moved with the blink of an eye. The sky was brilliant, color-swept, and alive.

McKinlay thought the Arctic heavens offered a splendid spectacle. Lunar coronas, lunar halos, the magnificent aurora, and other heavenly phenomena provided a lovely counterpoint to their bleak world. Indeed, McKinlay and the rest of the men felt themselves awaken to life when the moon and stars appeared. The stars were so bright and seemed so close that McKinlay felt he could almost touch them. Refraction caused the moon to look three times its normal size, and as it shone down upon him, its light transformed the nearby ice floes and blocks into "the weirdest possible figures which boggled the imagination," he wrote. It seemed pure magic. When describing the wonders of the Arctic sky in his diary, McKinlay recalled the definition of a phenomenon given by George W. Melville, chief engineer of the *Jeannette,* and recorded in De Long's diary. "'Gin ye see a coo, Jamie, that's no' a phenomenon, & gin ye see a tree, that's no' a phenomenon; but gin ye see a coo climbing up a tree backwards, that's a phenomenon, Jamie, that's a phenomenon.'"

The Arctic sky was, for the men of the *Karluk,* a phenomenon. And the brilliant aurora on Christmas Eve seemed a gift of the highest nature.

That night the staff and crew of the Canadian Arctic Expedition were overcome with the greatest sense of longing they had felt since sailing from Victoria on that now-distant June evening. Mamen crept into his narrow bunk and lost himself in thoughts of Christmases past and the people who meant the most to him on earth. Where were his brothers, he wondered? Were they at home or were they traveling in foreign countries? And what of his parents?

His thoughts kept returning to his fiancée, Ellen. He could imagine tears spilling down her face, as she cried for him. "Yes, poor little one, it is hard to be young and beautiful and to love, without being able to see or to hear from the one one loves. When I think of them, all my beloved ones and the festival, I would rather cry, but I am hardened, the tears will not come. It is on such festive days that longing grips one, one surely does not know how well one is off as long as one is at home, it is only when one gets away that one misses it...."

THEY CELEBRATED a memorable and moving holiday, one of the happiest times they had spent since leaving Esquimalt. McKinlay, Sandy, and Williamson dragged themselves from their bunks at 5:30 A.M. to decorate the saloon. They were bleary-eyed, but excited. December had been a stormy month, but Christmas morning was, miraculously, perfect. The wind had died down to a breeze, the temperature hovered somewhere between minus 13 degrees and minus 22.8 degrees Fahrenheit, cold but bearable now without the wind, and the stars were shining brightly.

McKinlay met the mate and the second engineer in the galley, where they knocked the sleep out of their eyes over a strong cup of tea. Then they went to the saloon where they rolled up their sleeves and did the best they could with the decorations. The brightly colored international code flags were unearthed and draped across the walls, hung from the deck above in festive fashion. For all these months, Hadley had been carrying a good supply of ribbon with him for trading, and now that he wouldn't need it anymore, McKinlay and the others used it to tie up the room with red, white, and blue. They found a large piece of canvas, and on this they splashed Christmas greetings in red and blue paint, hanging it opposite Bartlett's chair at the head of the table so that he would have the best view. So the other fellows would have something to look at as well, they grandly draped the Canadian ensign behind the captain's chair.

When the "lie-a-beds," as McKinlay dubbed them, had finally risen, they were amazed by what he and Sandy and Williamson had done with the saloon. It was a remarkable improvement. The worn and grimy ship, their home for just over six months, had always been dark, dirty, and depressing. The floor creaked and the air was dank and stuffy. But suddenly, all was brightness, cheer, and color, and the change was wonderful. The men felt their spirits lifting, and it actually felt like a holiday.

They had marmalade every other day with breakfast—something each man looked forward to—but for Christmas morning breakfast, they were treated to jam as well as marmalade. Afterward, the three weary decorators each napped for an hour before joining the rest of the ship's company outside on the ice, dressed in their warmest clothes.

McKinlay had spent all of Christmas Eve planning the sports program with Sandy and Williamson. With deliberate care, they laid out the course for the obstacle race and the other races and marked areas for the shot-putting and jumping contests. It was going to be a big event, and for the first time staff and crew were participating together. Until then, everything— chess tournament, nightly gramophone concerts, meals, mess—had been separate, the sailors sticking to their quarters at the front of the ship, the Eskimos to the laboratory, and the staff and officers together at the back.

Fireman Breddy took the first event, the 100-yard sprint. Ten of the men competed, and three or four were injured on the treacherous snow, their mukluks tripping them up and making running difficult. The next two events were the long jump and the standing jump, both won easily by Mamen. As the best athlete on board, he was a fierce and feared competitor. But Bartlett took him aside in the days before Christmas and asked him to participate in only two events so that there would be prizes left for the other men.

When it came time for the sack race, they discovered that all of the sacks they had set aside were frozen, so they had to tie their legs and arms together to simulate what it was like being in one. Sandy came in an easy first, and afterward won the hop, step, and leap event as well.

They retired to the ship for coffee and a smoke because the cold weather froze the tobacco juice in their pipes, making it impossible to smoke outdoors. And then they were back at it in the afternoon, Breddy again winning the first event, this time the 50-yard sprint. Shot-putting was next, and Munro emerged triumphant, in spite of the fact that he had suffered a deep gash in his foot just that morning when he stepped on the jagged edge of a tin buried in the snow. It cut straight through his mukluks and pierced the skin. Dr. Mackay treated the wound, and Munro, now limping, returned to the games, determined not to let his injury interfere with his fun. Mamen also was injured, having twisted his bad knee, but not so badly that he couldn't walk.

There was a comical hurdle race in which all the participants were disqualified. And then Sandy beat both Chafe and chief engineer Munro at the high jump, with a measurement of four feet four inches, not a bad height considering the uncooperative condition of the ice. The highlight for everyone was the obstacle race. McKinlay, Sandy, and Williamson had put great thought and effort into creating a challenging course. One of the obstacles was a snowdrift, which the men had to climb. Half of them slid down the sides repeatedly, unable to get up and over. The bowlines, too, proved treacherous, especially as McKinlay and his teammates had organized them in the most undignified and awkward positions they could contrive. Munro was the unlucky one, getting tangled up, and was left hanging suspended until they helped him down.

At the dredge house, each runner searched for the life belt with his name on it. The results were hilarious. Williamson and Kataktovik ran off with the wrong belts while Breddy found his, but raced off without getting it fastened. Sandy, meanwhile, discovered his belt lacked fastenings altogether, which was made even funnier by the fact that he was the one who had laid the belts out the night before. Chafe, who had fallen to last place throughout the race, was the only one who managed to secure his belt properly, so he ended up taking the prize.

They ended with the tug-of-war, since no sports program would be complete without one. The two teams from aft faced each other first. Bartlett, Hadley, McKinlay, Williamson, and Sandy pulled against Mackay, Beuchat, Malloch, Chafe, and Kataktovik. Bartlett's team won the first and third pulls, which meant they went on to face the team from forward: Maurer, Breddy, Clam, Morris, and Kuraluk. After a ten-minute break for Bartlett's group, they were sufficiently rested to win the first pull. The sailors won the second, though, and then Hadley had to retire because of a frostbitten foot, which meant Munro took his place on the captain's team. With his injury, Munro couldn't match Hadley's wiry strength, and the sailors won again.

It was too dark and too cold then for anything else, so the men retired to the ship to rest and warm their frozen noses, fingers, and toes and to prepare for dinner. McKinlay had typed menu cards for everyone, and these he set at each place at the table. The table itself looked festive, with a small artificial Christmas tree as the centerpiece, and in place of their regular mismatched enameled ware, Templeman had brought out a new set of china. This in itself was a treat because usually there weren't enough dishes for everyone; there were only nine bowls and seven cups, which meant one or two of them ate their soup from sugar basins. Likewise, there were only eight stools and two chairs, so that for all twelve officers and staff to sit down together, someone had to perch on a box or a canister of dynamite.

On Christmas night, however, they didn't seem to notice. As they all took their places, Bartlett produced a bottle of whiskey and filled the glasses, giving only a drop to the teetotalers—himself and Malloch and McKinlay. Before either Malloch or McKinlay could protest even this small amount, Bartlett whispered that they must follow his example.

When asked once why he abstained from drinking, Bartlett had answered, "Because God gave me my body and I propose to take care of it."

"But you drag your body all around and put it out in the cold and get it wet and do a lot of other things that damage it more than liquor would," the inquisitive party pointed out.

"But every time I have a good reason to do so," Bartlett replied.

Now, with just one drop of whiskey in his glass, Bartlett addressed the *Karluk*'s company. "Fellows," said the captain, "I want you to drink one toast. Stand, please."

Everyone rose and held their glasses high, watching Bartlett expectantly. They had not had whiskey since crossing the Arctic Circle on July 27, except for the times Dr. Mackay prescribed it for seasickness, and they knew the significance of this event.

In a solemn voice, the captain continued, "To the loved ones at home."

It was a heartfelt sentiment, and his words were met with silence. The glasses were raised, the whiskey drunk, and the men, too moved to speak, sat down again.

"What thoughts passed through our minds," wrote McKinlay afterward. "For a spell no one moved or spoke; in spirit, we were, each of us, thousands of miles away. How were these loved ones faring? Were they all in good health? Were they prospering? We did not ask ourselves if they were thinking of us, for we knew that their thoughts would linger long on us that day. God grant that any news they may have received of our plight did not cause them any undue anxiety."

After a silent blessing, the men dug into the meal before them. It was as grand and elaborate a feast as they could make from the provisions at hand: mixed pickles, sweet pickles, oyster soup, frozen lobster, bear steaks, ox tongue, potatoes (which had been saved from the start of the voyage for this very occasion), green peas, asparagus with cream sauce, mince pies, plum pudding, mixed nuts, tea, cake, and strawberries.

The men ate until they were stuffed, and afterward, as a special treat, they opened Christmas boxes which had been given to them by the ladies of Victoria, British Columbia, to save for the holiday. One of these contained an assortment of cakes, shortbread, sweets, cigars, cigarettes, and a harmonica for the "baby" of the expedition. It was handed to Mamen, who promptly tried his best to make it hum.

After their feast, the men retired for an hour of rest, rising again at 7:30 P.M. to continue the celebration. But all were exhausted, worn out from the unaccustomed physical exertion. They had no strength left for anything but smoking and listening to the gramophone, which they did until, one by one, they all gave in to sleep.

Mamen felt the pain from his knee injury later that night and discovered his kneecap had been dislocated. Dr. Mackay looked it over and treated it with iodine, but the young athlete suffered for most of the night. Still, nothing—not even this—could dull the excitement and joy of the day's festivities. It had been, as Mamen noted, a happy day in all respects.

THE CRACKING OF THE ICE was like a gunshot, blasting through the silent blackness of their frozen world. They heard the report at 10:00 A.M. on December 26. It was the unmistakable rupturing of the ice. The sound was ominous and everyone rushed above deck to investigate. They had just finished breakfast, most of them lazy and sluggish after the celebration of the day before.

Now as they stood outside, a fresh southeast breeze building around them, they saw the long, spiraling crack in the ice along the entire length of the starboard side of the Karluk. The ice was pressing in so tightly around the sides of the ship—even breaking through the gangway—that the men were afraid she would be crushed that very moment.

They had dreaded this, had prayed against it. With their recent proximity to land, they knew the ship was now especially vulnerable to ice pressure, and Bartlett and his men were terrified that she would end up in the middle of a pressure ridge where she would, no doubt, be crushed once the ice began to move.

Murray and Beuchat swore, in loud and desperate words, that it would be the last of them, and most of the men were deathly frightened. All their plans, all those miles traveled, and here they were. If the ship were crushed, what would become of them? How would they ever get word to the outside world?

Everyone prepared to abandon ship. Pemmican was already laid out on the deck, some of it in the original cumbersome black tins, other portions sewn up in canvas bags. The Primus stoves had been boxed up, and the fuel and the biscuits and the other provisions were waiting on the ice floe that held them. Now the men transferred the tablets of tea into packages that would be easy to carry. Others picked up their sewing with an urgency they had not felt before. They dressed skins for trousers and shirts and prayed that the ship would last, at least until these garments were finished.

The dogs, on short rations now, and given cooked food only every three or four days, were turned loose in the snow so that they could move around and warm themselves. McKinlay and the Eskimos had constructed two shelters for the dogs on the ice, but the dogs showed no interest in either, preferring instead to stay on the open ice during the daytime, doubling up in a circle, nose under tail, remaining still for hours until the snow covered them.

That night, after the skins were sewn, the pemmican laid out on deck, the Primus stoves stored in boxes, and the tea tablets placed in packages, the men tried to sleep, the joy of Christmas now forgotten. The only traces that remained of the holiday were the many aches and pains from the strenuous exercise of the day before.

The next few weeks would be critical. On board the *Karluk,* everything suddenly seemed utterly cold, dark, and grim. Even the stove in the Cabin DeLuxe had gone out after supper that night, leaving the room bitterly chilled.

THE WIND DIED DOWN somewhat on December 27, but it was still blowing strong. The *Karluk* drifted steadily westward, and they were now, the captain calculated, just fifty-three miles from tiny Herald Island, which itself was approximately thirty-eight miles east of larger, albeit equally inhospitable, Wrangel Island. Malloch, taking his daily observations, thought he spotted land in the distance, rising up out of the snow and ice and fog. Sandy climbed to the crow's nest but could see nothing. On deck, the men noticed a long, low cloud, which hovered over the horizon, suggesting the presence of either Herald or Wrangel Island. The men expected to sight either soon.

The sun was still slumbering below the horizon, but little by little the sky lightened every day. As their dark world grew a little brighter, the men were grateful for the reminder that the sun would not be gone forever. December 21 had held special significance for them, because it was the day the sun had reached its southern limit and begun its journey northward. "We should get our first sight of him in about 6 weeks from now," wrote McKinlay. "People at home cannot realise the significance of this astronomical fact."

Prizes were awarded to the winners of the Christmas sporting events, but this did little to take their minds off the ice. It was a constant, fearsome presence. Everywhere they looked, their world was ice. Indeed, the ship was only a dark speck in all that white.

The ice crashed, creaked, and groaned. The men had no rest from the unrelenting noise—the splintering roars and muffled rumblings. "I hope no catastrophe will come before we get the light back," Mamen wrote.

According to the chronometer, they were now fifty miles north of Herald Island, and the *Karluk*, with each day, was still rapidly mimicking the drift of the *Jeannette*. Careful watch was kept in the barrel as they scoured the expansive white vista for land. They strained their eyes and peered through the field glasses; but the horizon was hazy and there was nothing in sight.

Midday on the twenty-ninth, Mamen was working on a pair of skin boots in the captain's cabin, when Bartlett said, "I believe I saw land this morning. I saw the same indications yesterday." There was not just the suggestion of land this time, but actual mountain peaks, which he could see in the distance from the crow's nest.

Meanwhile, up on deck, McKinlay was reading his instruments and studying the icescape. The same low, long cloud hovered in the distance, and the magnetician strained his eyes in that direction until he was positive he could see a rugged peak, rising above the horizon.

"Is that land ahead?" he asked Sandy, who was just climbing down from the barrel.

McKinlay pointed toward the mountain peak and Sandy nodded. He had seen it from the lookout but didn't think it could be seen from the deck. While Sandy took the news to the captain, McKinlay hailed all hands, but by the time they appeared a haze had crept in, obscuring the view. The "bloody scientist" received a lot of ribbing for it, because his shipmates assumed he was pulling a prank, but Sandy confirmed the sighting south-southwest of the ship.

A couple of hours later, the distinctive silhouettes of mountains rose out of the distance, with one peak soaring high above the rest. This, they speculated, was Wrangel Island's highest point, Mount Berry, 2,500 feet above sea level, rising up out of the middle of the island. McKinlay once again summoned the nonbelievers, who gave a rousing cheer at the sight of land. If they could make it to land, they would be safe and they would not have to worry about being stranded on the ice, in the darkness, and in the cold.

They stood there, watching it until the darkness eventually seemed to swallow the island and its glorious peaks. From its appearance, the land seemed too large for Herald Island, which was noted in the *Pilot Book* as being only four miles long. The chronometers suggested it was Herald, but the chronometers had been inaccurate from the beginning of the voyage. The scientists and Bartlett concluded tentatively, therefore, that it must be Wrangel Island instead, especially since the depth agreed with the listed depth northeast of the island. Bartlett placed it at approximately longitude 177 degrees west.

The sighting of land came as a welcome surprise to the ship's company, and it was all the inspiration Dr. Mackay, Murray, and Beuchat needed to put into motion their plans to set out on their own. Immediately, they began preparations to leave the *Karluk,* intent on reaching the island and waiting there for the arrival of a ship and the coming of hunters in summer or fall. Bartlett would not oppose their going, as much as he objected to any breaking up of the party. He recognized their resolve on the matter and was also quite sick of them. It would be, if anything, a relief to see them go. No one, however, looked on their departure with any great confidence or support.

The *Karluk* was drifting straight toward Wrangel Island, the land growing more and more visible, although still faint in the ever-present darkness. However, the closer they drifted toward land, the greater the ice pressure. Indeed the ice was now alive, churning and splintering, leaving long, dark chasms of water, and raftering onto other floes, severing in all directions

around the ship. The men anxiously awaited a strong wind that was threatening to blow in from the northeast. If this happened, the ship would be
in grave danger of being crushed.

They packed all the necessary stores and readied them for transfer to the
nearby ice. Tea was soldered into thin-sheet tin cases, cooking pots were
made by cutting down gasoline tins, and the sewing, as always, continued.

"In one way it looks as if it had been only a few weeks," Mamen reflected, "but when I look back and think it over more closely it seems as if
I had been here for years.... It is really a year since I left my dear home
and fatherland. Yes, who thought then that I would land up in the Arctic,
frozen in ... without a possibility of getting out, drifting with the wind and
currents. I wonder where I will be next year at this time, likely in the ice
or on the bottom of the sea as food for the living things in the depths, or
perhaps back again to civilization."

ON THE LAST DAY of the year, the men were in dangerously low spirits, and as the *Karluk* drifted southeasterly, they tried to distract themselves
with plans for a special New Year's Day football match between Scotland
and All Nations.

But mostly they reflected on their fates and wondered what the year
ahead would bring. "The last day of the year, New Year's Eve," wrote
Mamen in his diary. "Yes, the time goes, 1913 is gone and will never return. New Year's Eve is quiet for us ... but I have chosen this life myself
and will have to be content with it. Well, I am content although it looks
dark many a time, the perils threaten one continuously and one has to be
wide awake and vigilant, but I hope everything will be well and ... that the
new year of 1914 will bring us better luck than the last one did."

For the moment, the *Karluk* was safe. Locked fast in the ice, at the mercy
of the Arctic drift, she had survived these four perilous months. But the
end was clearly upon them.

At 11:30 P.M. on December 31, McKinlay and four of the others turned
on the noisiest of their gramophone records and sang and danced, making
as much commotion as possible in order to wake the ones who were already sleeping. This, on top of the bottle of whiskey given to them by the

captain, roused the early-to-bed out of their comfortable bunks, and a party was begun.

The traditional sixteen bells were struck at midnight, welcoming in 1914. Afterward, McKinlay marched up and down the deck, "raising the devil with the dinner bell." Then they joined together around the saloon table and—six months after setting sail for their great northern adventure—toasted the New Year, with whiskey for the drinkers and lime juice for the teetotalers. It was a toast of hope and ardent wishes for a safe and healthy future.

Munro and Murray were appointed to carry the good wishes and best greetings of the men to Bartlett, along with the rest of the whiskey and a box of candied fruit. They emerged sometime later from his cabin, having shared some cake and whiskey with the captain, much to the envy of their comrades. And then as Bartlett sat locked in his room and agonized over what was to be done, the rest of them rang in the New Year with recitations of poems by Robert Burns, and a heartfelt rendition of "Auld Lang Syne."

Temporarily they could lay their fears aside, flushed with whiskey and cakes and the excitement of the New Year.

JANUARY 1914

———— · ————

We must all do what we can to save our lives.

—BJARNE MAMEN,
ASSISTANT TOPOGRAPHER

Early in the morning of January 2, somewhere in the distance, there was a strumming sound, like a banjo, faint, yet very distinct. It was a thrum-thrum-thrum, at times quite musical, and then there was a loud noise followed by silence.

It was between 3:30 and 4:00 A.M., but McKinlay and Mamen were now wide awake in the Cabin DeLuxe. McKinlay raised himself on one elbow and pressed his ear to the ship's side, listening intently. He couldn't imagine what the sound could be.

Thrum-thrum-thrum. It repeated the same pattern as before, the notes crisp and musical. Then a loud noise. Then silence.

Finally, as the Four-Leaved Clover lay in their bunks and listened, there was a thunderous boom—so strong that the door to the cabin shook.

And then they knew. It was the ice. In the distance, the ice was churning and stirring, splitting into pieces and thrusting up out of the water in great, jagged, diamondlike arcs. The floes of ice vied for position, some of them breaking free, and others violently pushing their neighbors beneath the water. For now the activity seemed to be at a safe distance. The ice immediately surrounding the ship was stationary, but the ice outside this field was in motion, forcing the pack in the direction of Wrangel Island.

McKinlay lay awake until 6:00 that morning, fascinated by the "extreme delicacy of the note which such a fearsome condition of things could produce." Mamen, too, was unable to sleep, and lay in his bunk waiting for the ice to hit the sides of the ship. There were a few light bumps—enough to wake most everyone on board—but that was all. At one point, the mast swayed and creaked so violently that Mamen was certain it would snap in two.

As McKinlay climbed out of bed at 8:30 A.M., the thrumming continued. Up on the deck, he stood in the noon twilight and couldn't see a thing. The sky was too dark and the "crushing and raftering" ice was too far away. "God grant it comes no nearer to us," he prayed.

In the darkness, they weren't able to see the peaks of Wrangel Island, but they assumed, by the depth of the water, that they were about thirty miles from land. It was a comforting thought as the thrumming continued ominously in the endless night.

AT 6:30 A.M. ON JANUARY 3, they were awakened this time to a thump-thumping, which grew into the beating of a kettle drum, and afterward the low throbbing of a bass drum. And then it became a cannonade as the cracking of the ice grew closer and more urgent. Without interruption, the noise grew and seemed to creep ever closer to the ship.

The *Karluk* was drifting southerly at a rapid pace, her speed increasing with the wind. That night, however, Murray's dredge showed that they were again drifting off to the west. As they began to move and as the noise of the crashing ice grew stronger, the anxiety aboard ship intensified. The rumbling of the ice was relentless and often violent. Cracks opened around the ship, more of them all the time, until the horizon resembled a gigantic cobweb of threads and lines. "Cracks and again cracks all around us," wrote Mamen, "they get bigger and more numerous as the time goes by. Well, perhaps one of them will be our grave."

Wrangel Island remained shrouded and invisible so that the men couldn't be sure exactly where it was. Snow fell in the evening, making it frightfully cold and impossible for anyone to see anything at all. The wind was so blistering, the men couldn't keep their eyes open.

They worked in haste, making preparations to leave the ship if necessary. Fred Maurer's twenty-first birthday passed unnoticed as the sailors packed milk into thin canvas covers; Williamson forged cooking tins and packed tea; and Hadley continued work on the third Peary sleigh, even though he still thought it a useless contraption. They fashioned one-gallon tins for kerosene so that it would be easier to carry should they have to leave the ship and set out by sled. They made tea boilers out of gasoline tins and trimmed down the pickaxes to weigh less than three pounds by heating them in the portable forge in the engine room and beating them down. If they were to live on the ice and travel by sled, the less weight they carried, the easier it would be on them down the trail.

Crew and staff worked at their seal and bear skins and clothing, still trying to get their boots and clothes into shape. It was a long process and not an easy one to accomplish in haste. First, the skins had to be scraped with a metal scraper, then heated and cooked until they made a crackling sound when folded. Afterward, the skin side was scraped and washed again to make it soft. It was a thankless and tedious job; the skins were so flimsy and dry that they could barely stand up to the vigorous scraping.

Because rationing was now essential, coffee, tea, and cocoa were watered down until they were unrecognizable, the milk was about 99 percent water, and most of the food was served only half cooked. Sugar and butter were used sparingly and, thanks to Bartlett's orders, seal meat was now being served at every meal in an attempt at preventing scurvy. The men's stomachs were at last adjusting to this unappetizing fare, but they often thought longingly of their Christmas and New Year's feasts.

The constant roaring of the ice did nothing to calm the nerves of Mackay, Beuchat, and Murray. They wandered about the ship, the fear of death on their faces, much to the amusement of their colleagues. While everyone was under great strain and stress, working as hard and fast as possible to prepare for the worst, many of them followed Bartlett's lead and did their best to remain cheerful, if only for the sake of appearances. But Mackay, Beuchat, and Murray no longer cared about appearances. They were scared to death and certain they were all going to die.

First Beuchat went to the captain, asking for a sleeping bag. Murray was right on his heels with the same request. Their tails weren't exactly between their legs, but they were as close to being cowed as anyone had ever seen them. Dr. Mackay had consistently insulted anyone who went to the captain for provisions or supplies, and, since his shipmates were outfitted with furs, he refused to ask for anything himself. Instead, he made cutting remarks to the others and took pride in staying on his own. He hadn't spoken to the captain for weeks, but finally—driven by a chilling, morbid fear—he swallowed his pride and put aside his ill feeling; he, too, went to Bartlett to request a sleeping bag.

Mackay worked diligently making a sled harness and other assorted items he planned to take with him when he left the ship. It was clear to all now that he, Murray, and Beuchat fully intended to make good on their word. They now had everything in order for going ashore and they were ready to leave the ship.

Murray cornered Mamen and warned him to prepare, reminding him that they could all be turned out into the night at any moment and forced to head to Wrangel Island. Mamen regarded Murray with disdain and pity. But he was already prepared. He had organized everything in his knapsack—clothing, affidavits and other valuables, tobacco, and the rest of his cherished personal items—so that the only thing he had to do, when the time came, was to grab his bag and go. But he didn't say this to the venerable oceanographer. Instead, he looked at Murray and said simply, "That time, that sorrow."

Murray stared back at him, his gaze penetrating and questioning, and then muttered something under his breath, which Mamen couldn't make out. But Mamen didn't care. As far as he was concerned, Murray and Dr. Mackay and Beuchat had made their beds, and he had nothing else to say to them. As he remarked later, "It is no use talking sense to crazy people. I am sure of one thing, none of these three will reach land if left to their own resources."

One thing was clear—either the *Karluk* was nearing the crushing ice field, or it was nearing her. In his bones, Mamen predicted trouble. He could feel a storm coming, just as he had predicted it before from his aches and pains. "I suppose this storm may have serious consequences for us if it lasts long," he wrote, "but we have to take it as it comes. It will be worse if we have to take to the ice, I don't know how we are going to manage it, so many together and, besides, such a crowd, for there are many on board who won't stand a week's hard work ...."

Captain Bartlett and Mamen had a long discussion about their situation, and both agreed that everything would be manageable as long as the wind was moderate. Still, they would prepare themselves, hoping for the best, but expecting the worst.

"Look out for next Saturday," Bartlett told his men gravely. "The chances are that we will get a bad one on January 10th." He did not want to alarm them, but he didn't want to mislead them either. He needed them to be ready and prepared for what he knew was coming.

THE STARS SHONE the morning of January 5, and the moon glowed in its last quarter. It was bitterly cold when Mamen went out to check the thermometer: minus twenty-seven degrees Fahrenheit. There was no wind, though, so he didn't feel the chill. It wasn't long before the sky grew overcast, the fog rolled in, the barometer dropped, snow began to fall, and the wind began to blow again; soon they were in the heart of another gale. The snow fell in thick sheets, and then, once on the ground, drifted into great piles. A heavy mist draped the air, clearing only briefly at night, just long enough for Malloch to make his observations.

Late in the night of January 7, the wind shifted and the *Karluk* began drifting rapidly westward. The ice had crashed and creaked all night long, growing ever closer to the ship. But around 2:00 in the morning, the noise suddenly stopped. Everyone waited, listening, expecting it to start up again. But there was nothing. The men breathed a little easier and began to relax for the first time in several days. Perhaps they would be all right after all.

SOON AFTER STEFANSSON'S departure, the captain had moved into his quarters. It was here that McKinlay sometimes spent hours a day engaged in deep conversation with the skipper. Bartlett welcomed visitors, no matter what the purpose of the visit, and seemed to appreciate having someone with whom he could talk. McKinlay and Mamen were, in his words, two souls after his own heart, and in their company he found both intellectual and emotional companionship. The magnetician and the assistant topographer were young, but each possessed a wisdom well beyond his years. Bartlett trusted them both implicitly.

The latest book the captain had given McKinlay to read was *The Inside of the Cup* by Winston Churchill. Bartlett's library was endless and wildly eclectic. One never knew what one was going to find in there, buried beneath the favored classics and stories of sea adventures. One night, among the expected nautical and maritime volumes, McKinlay noticed a slender text called *A Book About Roses* by Reynolds Hole. It was an odd sight, for no one would ever have connected Bartlett with the flower.

McKinlay himself was passionate about roses. They talked about flowers that night and McKinlay was filled with longing for the sight of one of the gardens back home. Bartlett, it seemed, was a prodigious grower of roses when he was back in Newfoundland. He had a deep love for them, and he had a gift for cultivation.

There were no illustrations in *A Book About Roses*, just prose interspersed with poetic lines and stanzas: "He who would have beautiful Roses in his garden must have beautiful Roses in his heart."

Roses in the Arctic. It was, indeed, an odd topic of conversation, considering they were as far from a garden as they could get. But it was a reminder of life and of hope in the midst of all that ice, and it helped remove them—however temporarily—from this dead white world where nothing grew and where they themselves were the only signs of life.

During their talk, McKinlay gazed at the captain and saw him clearly for the first time. He looked tired, neither gruff nor profane, neither scolding nor blustering. No matter how brave and encouraging he seemed in the light of day, at the end of it all he was just a man who craved company and missed his roses.

AFTERWARD, MCKINLAY went up to the deck. There was a full moon that night, making the dark world a little brighter than usual. Knowing he would not be able to sleep for a while, McKinlay decided to go for a walk. The moon lit the ice like a torch, casting shadows over the ice fields and mountains. The frozen world took on a luminous, almost translucent quality. The gale force winds of their recent blizzard had swept clean the great pillars of ice that littered the landscape. Now they glowed like giant emeralds, diamonds, sapphires. The ice statues, sculpted into graceful, breathtaking shapes, shone and glittered. The ice-ground beneath his feet was brilliant and alive, with myriad shades of white, blue, and green.

Rising out of it all sat the *Karluk,* covered in snow and ice crystals, an eerie sight. There was a faint auroral arch in the sky above her and a beau-

tiful corona of vivid reds and blues. That evening the lights were especially brilliant, and McKinlay watched them in awe. At times like this, he
felt nothing could go wrong in the world; there seemed to be no danger,
no doom hovering on the far horizon. There were only reds and blues,
arcs of radiant, graceful light sweeping across the sky.

It was as if McKinlay were the only soul alive, yet, he had the resounding feeling that he was not alone. Something filled him with a wondrous
peace. It was not the first time he had felt that way on this journey. Now
as he stood there savoring the feeling, he was filled with exultation. He
wanted to memorize the moment so that, whatever lay ahead, he would
never forget how he felt at that instant. All too quickly, it passed, but he
was left feeling warmed and at peace. At last, he knew he could sleep.

AT DAYBREAK ON JANUARY 9, disaster seemed inevitable. They
worked in a panic. Ammunition was laid out—one thousand rounds of
Mannlicher, one thousand rounds of 30-30, and one thousand rounds of
.22 shot or shotgun. Tea was divided up in twelve tins of 1200 tablets,
which would hold them for 120 days. Mamen spent the morning doing
what he hated most on earth—washing his clothing. But it had to be done
because his clothes were filthy.

A ferocious wind had blown all night, but by morning only a light
breeze remained. The *Karluk,* at least, was not drifting too rapidly now
because of the proximity to land. "If we only could get about 100 miles
farther north, the drift would be considerably stronger westward," Mamen
wrote. "We must wait and hope for it." If their course would change northwestward, they might reach the mainland of Siberia and be freed.

At 9:30 A.M., Sandy again reported land in sight, although no one else—
no matter how they strained their eyes—could see it. They figured it must
be Wrangel Island, and the thought was a comforting one.

After the wind blew itself out and the weather cleared, Mamen couldn't
resist taking a ski trip. He headed onto the ice alone, happy to be back on
skis once again. Mamen always felt more at home on skis than on his own
two feet. He loved the wind in his face as he glided across the frozen surface, turning this way and that, and jumping when he could. He embraced

any excuse to jump, launching himself off an icy slope or hill and sailing into the air, the earth spinning below him. He was good at it, a champion back home in Norway. Now he stood still and didn't move his legs, using his arms instead to push himself along. He traveled fast and hard across the ice, filled with a sense of freedom and speed as he left the ship behind.

Suddenly, he was aware of the ice cracking and grinding. It creaked terribly beneath his feet and he found himself surrounded by trembling, shivering ice. The sound it made was bone-chilling. It was the same thrum-thrum-thrum, the same beating drum, the same cannonade, but even louder now and more urgent—an entire chorus, uniting in a great, deafening crescendo.

Back on board the ship, Mamen opened his diary and wrote "We may expect disturbances ... any moment now, for it is full moon tomorrow, and according to our own observations as well as those of DeLong, the disturbances always come with the full moon, we have to wait and see what the morrow offers ...."

ON JANUARY 10, between 4:45 and 5:00 A.M., the inhabitants of the *Karluk* awoke to a sound like gunfire. The noise jarred Bartlett, McKinlay, Mamen, and almost everyone else from sleep. Distant, at first, it grew louder. Then it sounded like drums, and then thunder. Suddenly, there was a harsh, grating noise, and the *Karluk* shuddered violently.

It took just seconds for Mamen and McKinlay to leap from their bunks and rush up to the deck. Bartlett and Hadley and a few others were there already, and it was then that Mamen realized he had forgotten to put his clothes on. He slept naked, so there he stood, in the shivering cold, without a stitch of clothing. Bartlett immediately sent him back to get dressed.

In the dark Cabin DeLuxe, Mamen pulled on some clothes, lit the lamp, and awakened Beuchat and Malloch. It was not an easy job to rouse Malloch because he was extremely hard of hearing and probably would have managed to sleep through everything. Mamen shook him awake and they joined everyone else above.

Seaman John Brady had been the night watchman that night, and he had already ventured onto the ice to investigate when Bartlett arrived on the scene. He met the sailor on the ice gangway and Brady gave his report. There was a small crack in the ice at the stern of the ship. Bartlett followed him to the spot and saw that the crack ran in a jagged line in a northwesterly direction for two hundred yards or so.

The wind was now blowing strongly from the north. The ice continued its deafening symphony, until McKinlay covered his ears and thought he would go crazy from the noise alone. Soon the crack in the ice along the starboard side gaped open all around. And then the ship began rising to starboard, shaken and pushed by the ice. Before, the *Karluk's* deck had stood two inches above the ice, but now, as the men watched helplessly, the ship rose six inches above, and then seven, eight, nine, ten, until her deck stood a foot higher than the gangway. By now she was listing badly to port, heeling at twenty degrees, then at twenty-five.

"The ship was now entirely free on the starboard side but still frozen fast in her ice-cradle on the port side," Bartlett wrote; "her head was pointed southwest. On account of the way in which the ice had split the ship was held in a kind of pocket; the wind ... increased to a gale, with blinding snowdrift, and the sheet of ice on the starboard side began to move astern, only a little at a time. The ship felt no pressure, only slight shocks, and her hull was still untouched...."

It was clear to the captain, however, that the *Karluk* would soon be crushed. He immediately ordered his men to remove all the blocks of snow they had placed on her deck and around the outer walls of the cabin. For three hours, they all worked, side by side without speaking. The captain hauled snow just as his men did.

"It was hard to see what was going on around us," wrote Bartlett, "for the sky was overcast and the darkness was the kind which, as the time-honored phrase goes, you could cut with a knife, while the stinging snow-drift ... under the impetus of the screaming gale, added to the uncertainty as to what was about to happen from moment to moment."

The ice was grinding, churning, like an explosion of thunderclouds overhead, and it engulfed them. All at once, the *Karluk* gave an enormous shudder and seemed to settle. The men waited helplessly, not knowing what to expect—rushing water, the flooding of the decks, an abrupt descent into the ocean. Instead, all was silent and still. The sudden hush was as deafening and intimidating as the noise. The ship didn't move. The ice was calm. The night was quiet.

The ice had cracked along the port side and the ship righted itself. The *Karluk,* it seemed, had outlasted the Arctic. But for how long? They had been spared for now, but it was clear their reprieve was temporary. The men retired, on edge, to their cabins, and waited for the worst to come.

"I think we should probably look out for this evening at the turn of the tide," said Bartlett quietly. He then turned and walked away, leaving his men to themselves.

The racket resumed and continued throughout breakfast. Afterward, the ice opened dramatically both at the bow and at the stern. Mamen remarked: "Then it was quite clear to me that our dear old *Karluk* was through with her voyages."

To guard against fire, they extinguished all the stoves and lamps aboard ship, except for the stove in the galley. They also fastened the stoves to the floor to keep them from toppling over with the dramatic listing of the ship. Then the men set to work preparing to leave their home, using hurricane lanterns to find their way around.

Bartlett had made them take every possible precaution to lessen the impact of the loss of the *Karluk.* Their only critical shortage was adequate clothing to withstand an Arctic winter on the ice. They had plenty of untanned skins, but no stock of completed garments. Because of the poor outfitting of the expedition, they weren't even close to being equipped to survive in the frozen world that awaited them outside the ship.

They spent the rest of the day sewing frantically. McKinlay sat on the edge of his bunk, working on a pair of sheepskin socks. Kiruk worked at three times the speed of the rest of them and her older daughter, Helen, helped her. As they sewed, the ice thrummed ominously.

Finally, around 6:45 P.M., there was a horrific blast, right outside McKinlay's bunk on the port side. It sounded like an explosion.

Bartlett raced to the engine room and found Munro already there. As they held up their lanterns, they could see the water pouring in. They struggled with the pump, which had been destroyed by a shard of ice that jutted through the opening, piercing the planking and timbers of the engine room, ripping off the pump fixtures. The port side was crushed amidships, the water crashing in and the holds filling foot by foot. As Bartlett had feared, the ice astern had collapsed, caving and crumbling around the ship with a violent force, and the sheet of crushing ice along the starboard side had smashed against the ship, damaging her beyond repair.

The *Karluk* was beginning to move forward, ahead six yards, and then back again. The stern swung to port and the bow swung to starboard while the ship herself listed to port.

Bartlett gave the orders: "On the poop, clear the pemmican and all emergency stores." The men went to work, heaving their remaining provisions—tents, stoves, skins, paraffin, chocolate—from the deck onto the ice on the starboard side, since the ice on the port side had been crushed to powder.

By this time, the water was rising rapidly in the engine room. Now all they could do was save themselves and whatever provisions they could rescue.

Bartlett then gave the orders they had dreaded hearing and he had dreaded having to give: "All hands abandon ship." He sent Kiruk and her two little girls to the box house that had been built on the ice to start the fire in the stove, and Templeman was ordered to remain in the galley so that the men could have hot food and coffee. The captain then doled out a shot of alcohol to everyone, to help bolster them for the ordeal.

The men were surprisingly calm, even the ones new to sea travel, which was just about all of them. They all moved methodically and swiftly, as if abandoning a ship was something they were used to doing on a daily basis. Because of the unrelenting weather, they could barely see their own noses, much less the emergency stores and equipment they were moving off the ship and onto the ice. Ship, ice, ocean—they couldn't tell what they were stepping on. Too often the loosened ice would up-end and they had to hopscotch to avoid being tossed into the water.

Dr. Mackay was the unlucky one, plunging through the ice, right up to his neck. He didn't seem to realize what had happened or what he was doing because after Sandy pulled him out, he walked about, up and down the ice, with his wet clothes freezing on his body. He had been in a fighting mood all evening, at one point threatening Mamen, who quickly and angrily put him in his place.

But during that most crucial moment of abandoning ship, Mackay was a tornado. The problem, they quickly discovered, was that somehow Mackay had gotten hold of extra alcohol and was completely and utterly drunk.

Bartlett forced the doctor to his cabin afterward, and gave him some more whiskey and offered him some dry clothes. Mackay took the whiskey, but refused the clothes. He was too stubborn and angry, but his shipmates won out, and managed to hold him down and change every stitch of his wet clothing.

For hours, everyone but Mackay, Murray, and Beuchat—who refused to do anything but move their own belongings—transferred boxes of eggs, bacon, butter, and other goods, and finally the precious drums of coal oil. After all the essentials were on the ice, the men returned to the doomed *Karluk* and salvaged all the extra items they had time for, including a camera belonging to Stefansson, which he had left aboard.

By 9:30 P.M., everything they could move was on the ice. To their alarm, however, they couldn't find the little black kitten, who had hidden herself away when the commotion started. They searched the ship throughout, but she was nowhere to be seen. She had been their good luck mascot, their pet, but now there was nothing to be done. As much as they hated to, they would have to leave her behind.

Because a wide lead had opened in the ice on the port side where their camp of supplies had been stored, there was a great deal of delicate maneuvering to be done. They had to heave everything to starboard, then try to bridge with the sled the moat surrounding their stores. The frightened dogs were stranded on the other side of the open water, and one by one the men had to fetch them and throw them across the chasm.

As soon as the lead came together at certain points, the men sledged the stores to the place on the ice where Bartlett had cached the other provisions months ago. As they worked, the men were so focused that they were, as McKinlay noted, "too busy to be conscious of the danger & the discomfort, for in the pitch darkness & the constantly moving ice, every step was fraught with risk."

By 10:45 P.M., eleven feet of water filled the ship's engine room. Scientists and crew continued working, however, helping themselves to hot coffee in the galley when they needed it. This helped warm their frozen hands and bones, and they greatly appreciated it. A gale had blown up from the north by now, and the snow was beginning to blow wildly. The temperature was between minus twenty-six and minus twenty-three degrees Fahrenheit, and the men were soon wet through from snow and perspiration, in a completely miserable state.

Nevertheless, they kept working. Just after midnight, the blue Canadian ensign was hoisted and run down again, and then hoisted once more and left. A ship should go down with her flag flying, said Bartlett.

By 1:00 A.M., the men of the *Karluk* had done all they could do. Although half of the provisions remained on board, Bartlett finally put a stop to their work, with a quiet, "That is enough boys."

The *Karluk* was now listing at thirty-five degrees to port, and the water already covered the engine and the cylinders in the engine room. Thus far, the ice imploding around the ship had kept her from sinking, but now she was visibly settling down at the stern.

Earlier in the day, Kuraluk and Kataktovik had built two houses on the ice, one out of snow, and the other out of snow and boxes, renovating the old dog hospital and installing a stove in one of the shelters. There were fresh boards on the floor and a fire laid ready in the stove. It was to these sanctuaries that the men now turned, weary and frozen. McKinlay, Mamen, Dr. Mackay, Murray, Beuchat, Clam, Golightly, Chafe, and the Eskimos were assigned to the box house, and Munro, Williamson, Breddy, Maurer, Brady, Templeman, Sandy, Barker, Malloch, and Hadley took the snow house, which they would share with the captain. Crew and staff were no longer separated by forward and aft, and would need to learn to live together.

Mackay, Murray, and Beuchat had turned in long ago. As their ex-hausted colleagues wandered into the shelter, the three scientists refused to move or make room, and the rest of the men were left to do the best they could with what was left.

"One cannot speak too strongly of the conduct of Murray, Mackay & Beuchat," wrote McKinlay. "After hauling a sled with nothing but their own personal belongings—they would allow nothing else on it—they re-tired to the house & made no attempt to help us in the work but staked out their claim to about one third of the place." The cramped quarters and the intense cold, along with the barking of the dog Nellie and her new batch of puppies, helped to make sleep "a hopeless job," according to McKinlay.

When Mamen turned in at 4:00 A.M., the *Karluk* was still floating. He had no idea if she would still be there when he opened his eyes again. But she had not given up yet, and after everyone was safely tucked away into the snow houses, Bartlett returned to the ship. Munro and Hadley stayed with him for a while, but then Munro left, and at some point the captain told Hadley to go on and join the others. He wanted to be alone with his ship during her final hours.

The captain went below deck, sat in front of the stove and wound up the Victrola, which he had moved into the galley. One by one, he ran through the collection of records they had on board. He quickly disposed of the jazz and ragtime albums in the pile, tossing them immediately onto the fire without a listen. He never had liked the stuff.

As the boat creaked and groaned around him, he sat listening to music he loved, tossing each record into the fire after the last note was finished. He drank tea and coffee and ate when he was hungry, and he got up now and then to stroll the deck and check the position of the ship. All the while, he listened to the antiphonal sounds of the groaning ship and the encroaching water below, and the classical music (mostly Chopin and Brahms) coming from the mouth of the Victrola.

By 5:00 A.M., water was over the gratings in the engine room, just five or six feet below the main deck. Maurer had gone to bed on the ice that night, bone weary, but wide awake. He prayed the ship would be there when he opened his eyes again, and that he would be able to find the black kitten.

In the box house, McKinlay wrote in his journal and tried, along with Clam and the other sailors, to dry out wet clothing. When the men awoke, the *Karluk* was still afloat but lying much deeper, with the port side of her deck flooded with water.

That morning, the kitten was found aboard ship, finally wandering out from her hiding place. Fred Maurer asked Bartlett for permission to take her off and bring her along with them, and the captain agreed. Everyone loved the little black and white cat Nigeraurak, but fireman Maurer was especially fond of her. When she first came aboard ship, they had kept her in the forecastle. But after a while, she made her way aft and Hadley had taught her tricks. Now she was lifted into loving arms and placed on a bed of skins in a basket in the box house, where she made herself at home.

The first thing McKinlay did when he awoke was to check on Bartlett and the *Karluk*. Bartlett strode up and down the ship for a while as his men watched him. "I am sure that he feels the end of the *Karluk* very keenly …" noted McKinlay. Bartlett went below again and wound the Victrola, listening to more music.

Out on the ice, the men rummaged through the various boxes that lay in wild, unorganized piles in the snow and found some stale bread, cheese, frozen milk, and tins of preserved meat, which they ate cold for breakfast. In the other house, McKinlay discovered, they had found some cigars and were enjoying a much-needed smoke. Bartlett had not allowed any tobacco to be taken off the ship, because it was just one more unnecessary thing to weigh them down, but the cigars had been saved. Having a leisurely smoke seemed an odd thing to do at such a time, but McKinlay joined in, grateful for the pleasant distraction.

Going out later in the afternoon, McKinlay saw that the port side of the *Karluk* was now underwater, and Bartlett was still pacing the main deck on the starboard side. At 2:00 P.M., they took a sounding, which showed the depth at thirty-eight fathoms, and McKinlay took the temperature with a sling thermometer; it read minus seventeen degrees Fahrenheit.

On the gramophone, Mary Garden was singing an aria from *Aida* when the ship began to settle, and soon the lower decks were awash. The *Karluk* groaned, and then fell silent, as if resigned to her fate. Bartlett stood up, placed Chopin's "Funeral March" on the Victrola, wound it one last time, and listened to the first beautiful notes.

As the water splashed its way across the upper deck and began to sweep down through the hatch, the captain raced up top and lowered the flag to half-mast. Then he climbed onto her rail and stood there, moving with the ship as she dipped into a header. He held on to her, clutching the smooth wood, running his hands along it, as if to soothe her. The men had come back, summoned by the thundering of the wood and the ice, and a shout: "She's going." As they stood there watching, no one spoke.

They probably thought he was going down with the ship, their irascible old captain, so stubborn and strange. He had deplored her Arctic seaworthiness when he first saw her, but he did not want to lose her. She was all they had out there, and she had done the best she could. Finally, the rail dipped until the *Karluk* was level with the ice, and Bartlett left his ship.

The bow slipped under and the bowsprit broke then, but she still remained afloat. Then, between 3:15 and 3:30 P.M., they watched her settle slowly by the head, sinking with a grating noise until she was brought up by the bowsprit to meet the ice again. Bartlett stood there on the ice with his crew and watched as she went down by the head. They could still hear the music echoing from the galley.

She sank foot by foot, a slight puff of steam showing that the water had risen over the galley fire. Soon they saw the barrel on the foremast, and then the stern rose. The *Karluk* seemed to straighten with great dignity as the stern sank lower. She disappeared rapidly and gracefully after that, her flag fluttering to the last.

On January 11, 1914, at 4:00 P.M., the *Karluk* went under into thirty-eight fathoms of water. The only remaining signs of her existence were the two umiaks, a whaleboat, and other gear from the deck floating in the water above her grave.

It was the first shipwreck most of them had ever witnessed. It wasn't anything Hadley hadn't seen before, but he was as respectful as the others in those last moments. Mamen and McKinlay, meanwhile, stood together in silence while the tight-lipped sailor Clam revealed nothing. Malloch, his usual affability and good-humored obliviousness faded, was now exceedingly nervous and white. And Chafe, the mess room boy, was overwhelmed by the great loss he felt as the *Karluk* disappeared. "As we watched her settle and sink beneath the sea, a feeling of intense loneliness came over us, but we gave the old ship three hearty cheers as she disappeared. All the water visible was that in which the ship sank."

As Maurer held on to the black cat, he observed quietly, "Our home was gone."

All were sickened and saddened by the sight of the Arctic water closing over the *Karluk*. "She was a good sea-boat, as we had proved," wrote McKinlay, "but that she was quite unsuited for her present purpose was proved by the fact that she failed at the first time of asking. She was gone & we realised that we were at the parting of the ways. Should we win through, we will never forget this day."

As her mast slipped beneath the sea, Bartlett, visibly moved, pushed back his hood and bowed his head. It was always a tragedy when a ship sank, especially one that had been your home for months. And yet he was amazed at how the death of this ship affected him. He had, after all, condemned her from the start. Yet now he could feel the tears welling up as he imagined the *Karluk* in her lonely descent to the ocean floor.

"Good-bye, old girl," he said.

AFTERWARD, THERE WAS ONLY CHAOS. The dogs were wild and fighting, and the men were panicked. Any sense of peace to which they had clung had just drifted to the bottom of the ocean.

Bartlett sifted through the items salvaged from the ship—piles of objects, flung slipshod onto the ice. They had only pulled the essentials from the ship, no personal souvenirs or frivolous items unnecessary to survival or that would take up too much room on the sled.

Still, a few of the men had managed to walk away with one or two treasured possessions. Chafe saved the camera that was given to him by a friend before leaving Victoria, as well as the binoculars he won as first prize for shooting at the long ranges when he was sixteen. "That, and a few medals, were the only things I had saved from the wreck out of forty-seven athletic and sixteen shooting prizes which I had with me on board ...."

Bartlett, too, saved the thing that meant the most to him—his copy of the *Rubáiyát of Omar Khayyám*. Now, in the midst of the madness, he knew where his book was, but he could not find his boots.

"Where in hell are my boots?" Bartlett yelled, but no one paid attention to him. "Where in hell are my boots?" He just kept yelling at the top of his voice. He wanted those boots. It was cold. His feet were damp and half-frozen. His toes ached with the chill.

He didn't know how many times he had yelled that same phrase over and over before he felt a hand on his arm. He shook it off angrily and whirled around in the flying snow. It was Kiruk.

"I fix Captain's boots," she said.

She held them up and he grabbed them out of her hand. Then he noticed that her lips were bleeding.

Bartlett roared, "Somebody hit you?"

"No."

"You fell down?"

"No."

"Well, what in the devil is the matter with your face?"

She didn't even flinch at his yelling.

"I chew Captain's boots."

Then he got it. At the risk of her own life, she had made a dash for his cabin as the ship was going down, just to save his spare boots, something he didn't even think of at the time, too busy playing records and reflecting on the music.

Bartlett knew the boots must have been wet and in bad shape, which is why she had, in the Eskimo way, chewed the thick leather into a pliable state and filled the soles with grass. Between the snow and the freezing temperature and the tough hide of the boots, she had split her lips in twenty places. But she had saved his feet.

Later, the men turned into their houses and sewed and sewed until every bone ached, "preparing for our fight ," said McKinlay, "which has become a tougher proposition than ever." They made hot chocolate, drinking it out of two mugs, which they passed around between them because it was all they had. They were stunned by the ship's demise, still in a state of shock, barely able to digest what had happened in the past thirty-six hours.

One thing was clear to some of them, though. "Mr. Stefansson is to blame for everything," said Mamen. "It is a scandal to bring such a poor ship up in the Arctic, and we could hold both Stefansson and the Canadian government responsible for this; it is terrible to jeopardize so many human lives."

That night, they huddled together in their snow and box houses and slept the sleep of total exhaustion.

It was true, as Mamen wrote, that they "had now only ourselves to rely upon. It is up to everybody to do his utmost so that the outcome may be a happy one, but there are a few here who will be the cause of considerable trouble."

McKinlay still could not sleep more than a few hours. They were lost in the middle of the Arctic Ocean, adrift in the middle of the Arctic night. There was nothing beneath their feet but ice. For the first time in his life, McKinlay knew utter terror, and even though he was surrounded by twenty-four other people who were in the same exact situation, he knew what it was to be completely alone. For once, it struck him how far away from everyone else they were. There was a great, busy, important world spinning below them, far, far away. People were safe and happy and sitting with their families and sleeping in warm beds.

Where was he? What had he agreed to? What would happen to him and the others now? McKinlay had stood there with his colleagues—this strange clan with whom he had little in common, excepting their situation—and stared at the void in the ice where the ship used to be. If the cold had not bitten into his skin, reminding him venomously that he was alive and not dreaming, he might have had to pinch himself.

This could not be happening. It wasn't the sort of thing that happened to William Laird McKinlay, schoolmaster, or to any people he knew. It was the most sobering moment of his life and one he would never forget.

"This has made a man of you," the captain had told him earlier that night, or that morning, he couldn't be sure which anymore. And McKinlay believed he was right. The Arctic was making him a man, and he was doing a man's work. He just prayed to God that he would not fail.

And there, in the great Arctic darkness, he could swear he still heard the strains of Chopin, very faint and whispering, an echo. He could hear the notes, clear, precise, and mournful, a final, distant wail.

Somewhere, thirty-eight fathoms below their feet, perhaps that Victrola was still playing.

By morning, the lead in the ice had frozen over completely. The last trace of the *Karluk* and her descent into the sea was gone. One would never know that she had ever been there at all. One would never know that there had been a lead of water wide enough to pull her down. As far as the eye could see, there was only ice. Ice everywhere. Ice and darkness.

THEY NAMED IT SHIPWRECK CAMP, that particular area of floating ice pack, marked by latitude 73 degrees north and longitude 178 degrees west. They set about making the most of it, willing themselves to forget that it was shifting, fragile ice instead of solid earth, and trying to make the place seem as much like a home as possible. As Maurer remarked, "The ice that held us in its grip and destroyed our ship was now the only means of safety—precarious as it might be."

January 12, their first day living on the ice, was raw and overcast, the temperature hovering steadily at minus twenty-six degrees Fahrenheit. The water's depth was thirty-eight fathoms, and somewhere, in the vast blackness beneath them, lay the *Karluk*.

She had gone down at exactly the point where De Long's *Jeannette* had been frozen in just before she began her westward drift to Henrietta Island, where she was eventually crushed by the opening and closing of the ice— just like the *Karluk*.

By law, Bartlett was still in command of these men, and Kiruk, Helen, and Mugpi, even without a ship. "But I was in command of a shipwrecked party. Had we been on a desert island things might have been brighter. But to be out there on the ever-shifting ice pack, far from land, and faced with the coldest months of the winter night, I could not look ahead without some uneasiness."

McKinlay was awakened at 8:00 A.M. by Seaman Morris yelling "Coffee!" The men stumbled from their makeshift beds and grabbed their mugs, which, by now, were coated with a layer of old cocoa, butter, and tea. They scrambled for food because most of the supplies still had not yet been uncovered, and then all hands were summoned onto the ice. Everyone, except for Dr. Mackay, Murray, and Beuchat, turned out, fatigued and spent from the past two days. Their colleagues, Bartlett included, knew it was hopeless to rouse the trio, so they were allowed to remain in bed all day long.

The rest of the party did their best to sort through the provisions salvaged from the ship. They dug through the furs, skins, and blanketing, piling them all together. They found the pemmican intended for the dogs and put it aside. They found their own pemmican and laid it in another pile. The oil and the oil tins were separated into a stack. The rifles and ammunition were placed in another. So it went, time-consuming and tiring. The men were already exhausted from the exertion of the past two days, a bone-weary fatigue that none of them could shake.

Each of the "living shacks" had a stove at the center. The snow igloo was fifteen feet long and twelve feet wide and had a canvas roof supported by rafters. The box house was twenty-five feet long and eighteen feet wide. The bed platforms were raised and built out from the walls on three sides of the stove. In the box house, Chafe and Clam smuggled out the small stove and replaced it with the former engine room stove, which was much bigger and made their little quarters almost too warm.

Attached to the box house was a room built of boxes and snow, serving as the galley, and another adjoining room for the Eskimos. Then they pitched a tent that would work as a storehouse for their woolen clothing and as much gear as it would hold. Their wool clothes would be useless on the trail because they were neither warm enough nor light enough, but they worked just fine for now and allowed the men to conserve their precious animal skin clothing for later. McKinlay was the only one allowed in the storehouse besides Bartlett, since the skipper had appointed him in charge of the supplies and gear.

By 3:30 P.M. it was too dark to work, so everyone retired to their respective snow houses and continued sewing. They also had their first real meal since leaving the ship—boiled bacon, pea soup, and rice. They ate their soup that night from their tea cups. Templeman had made the broth in the same water he'd boiled the bacon in, and it "tasted as sweet as the finest concoction of the finest of luxury hotels," according to McKinlay. Their cups were dirty, as were their plates, which were encrusted with old remnants of eggs, shells, bacon, grease, and matches, none of which could be rinsed or scraped off as they were frozen to the surface. McKinlay remarked, "We have reached the stage when the dirt on our dishes acts as seasoning; there is no health hazard, since germs cannot exist in our temperatures!" After they devoured the soup, they filled their dirty cups with rice and ate it with their hands. Add hardtack—or biscuits—bacon, and coffee, and they felt like they'd had a feast fit for kings.

Over the next several days, the castaways adjusted to life on the ice. Wrangel Island could now be seen plainly, much to their great relief, approximately thirty to thirty-five miles away to the southwest, although their charts showed they were eighty miles to the north of Wrangel Island and two hundred miles from the coast of Siberia. The sight of land was inexplicably cheering to the members of this lost company. They had been afraid that they had drifted too far east due to the winds, but now there was the island, much clearer than before.

Even with Wrangel Island looming up in the distance, there was no serious plan yet of abandoning Shipwreck Camp and starting for the island. The days were still too dark, and there was too much to be sorted out yet. On January 14, Bartlett spoke with both McKinlay and Mamen about moving the party to the eastern part of Wrangel Island, which should be easier to reach, due to its lower-lying shore. Bartlett was also interested in making the trek to Siberia, although the condition of his men worried him. Many were weak and suffering from frostbite or injury, and he knew this endangered their chances of making such a long journey. Siberia, to his estimation, was approximately 250 miles away over the ice pack, and he doubted whether some of the men would live to finish the journey.

"I sincerely hope that we will stay here until the beginning of February," wrote Mamen. "The days will then be longer and we can drive with our dogs about 12 hours a day. Yes, I hope that with the help of God everything will come out all right but, if not, that we may have a quiet and peaceful death, without too much pain and agony."

During the twilight hours, the men worked to put their camp in order. It was difficult to locate everything, and some items, such as a missing box of ammunition, were never found. Many things were retrieved from the wreckage of the ship—articles from the deck that were thrown to the ice as the *Karluk* sank. McKinlay and Sandy walked through this graveyard of cast-off provisions and tried to take stock—the whaleboat, two kayaks, two umiaks, tins of biscuits, the ice tank, an enormous coal oil tank, a box of Horlick's Malted Milk, a meteorological instrument case.

Mamen and McKinlay labored over the dysfunctional Primus stoves until they were covered with soot and dirt. The small stoves, or lamps, were used for cooking and for warmth, and there were ten altogether, although three were broken beyond repair, which left only seven stoves that could be relied upon.

The days were growing lighter, which brought hope and relief, but they were still, essentially, living in darkness. Bartlett was anxious about many things but his main concern was that everyone get their clothing in order as soon as possible. There was no time now for idling; they must have their clothes ready or they would suffer on the trail. They would be unable to sew once they started for land. Realizing this, everyone worked as fast as he could, even Malloch, who was notorious for spending weeks mending one garment.

As the days passed, the staff, crew, and officers began to think of Kiruk as a mother figure. They had underestimated her worth aboard ship and had never taken the time to get to know her as they should. Now they found a strength and warmth in her that they needed, and from then on she was known as "Auntie."

Auntie was busy making clothes for her family, as well as doing all the cutting for the rest of the company with a piece of circular flat steel with a sharp edge. "She used it with great speed and efficiency, and without any patterns or guides of any kind," Chafe said. "She would cut out socks and other things that would surprise you. I don't think you could find a quarter of an inch difference in any part of twenty pairs...." Fur clothing was heavy enough so that it had to be sewn by hand, but there was other stitching that could be done on the two sewing machines they had saved from the ship. These were used by Auntie and Munro, who was a skilled tailor in his own right.

There were only six sleeping bags for the entire company and not enough skins to make more. Besides this, sleeping bags would be much too heavy to take on the trail. Bartlett ordered that each man make a smaller version—a foot bag, which would cover the feet and reach just up to the knees. For these, he cut up his coonskin coat and divided the pieces among the men.

In addition, they would each need to have four pairs of deerskin or sheepskin stockings and three pairs of deerskin boots. The skins were softened first by scraping them with a piece of iron. This was called breaking the vellum, and sometimes Eskimo women did this by chewing it as Auntie had done.

In the midst of it all, they still found time for games of chess and cards and a concert in the evenings now and then. On rare occasions, they also held dances. With a decided lack of female partners, the men were a strange sight as they twirled each other around the ice. The strangest of all was Bartlett, who once spun his partner so fiercely that they tipped over the stove.

The men, in general, were in surprisingly good humor. If they didn't feel like smiling or looking on the bright side of things, they forced themselves to for the greater good of the company. It was everyone's wish to maintain this sense of optimism, because they knew that, as McKinlay noted, "thus, & only thus, can we win through."

The only exceptions, naturally, were Dr. Mackay, Murray, and Beuchat. Except for getting out of their beds to watch the ship go down, they had been sleeping ever since, waking up only to eat. At night, they kept everyone else awake with their discussions and complaints. "They grumble if the stove goes low," wrote McKinlay; "they grumble about the cold coffee; they grumble & grumble but never venture a helping hand. If trouble comes, theirs will be the responsibility, & God help them for everybody is strained to breaking point with their conduct."

Dr. Mackay frequently unleashed a torrent of verbal ammunition on McKinlay and Mamen, accusing them of being in too tight with the captain. As far as the doctor was concerned, the two young scientists showed great disloyalty by allying themselves with Bartlett instead of their own colleagues. He blamed them for spoiling his chances of getting the captain to take him seriously and listen to his arguments, since McKinlay and Mamen were always there to choose the other side, thus dividing the scientific staff.

Beuchat, in particular, was broken down. He was nervous, edgy, his eyes filled with alarm. Beuchat's already weak heart couldn't stand the strain, and he complained constantly of fever and exhaustion, babbling about the future as if he wouldn't live to see many more days. This kind of behavior made Mamen furious and spurred him to vow: "I have decided to fight for my life as much as I can, one cannot take his fellow-men into consideration, it surely sounds awful to civilized ears, but it is the only right thing here in the Arctic."

THE TEMPERATURE DIPPED to minus thirty-seven degrees Fahrenheit and the castaways drifted southerly on the ice pack. They continued their shipboard routines, as best they could. They ate at the same times, and lights were out at 10:00 P.M. They maintained records of the wind and weather, the soundings, and the temperature. At night, two men took turns at watch, one in each snow house. They were in charge of keeping the fires going, and at 6:00 in the morning, one of them would call Templeman so that he could start breakfast.

The galley provided great and much-needed cheer to everyone, and Templeman, under the circumstances, turned out good meals from the sheet-iron stove. Breakfast brought fried bacon, eggs, hardtack, and coffee, and dinner was bacon, seal stew, and tea.

Bartlett's evenings were spent with the Eskimos in their igloo, so that his men could have a break from him and relax a bit. It was tough to live with your captain under such conditions in such close quarters, and Bartlett knew they would need some time out from under his presence.

While the men were sleeping one night, a dog fight left one dog dead. It was the bobtail Mosse, who just a month earlier had refused to leave the side of his injured brother until he died. Nobody heard the sounds of fighting, and in the morning they discovered the blood-soaked area and Mosse's stiff carcass.

It was a great loss to the men, since there were now only twenty-four dogs remaining, including Hadley's pet Molly, and each one was indispensable if they were to make it to land. "Wouldn't we give a great deal for those twelve dogs taken by Stefansson—the pick of the bunch," McKinlay lamented.

On the evening of January 16, Bartlett invited McKinlay to join him in the Eskimos' igloo to talk about their plans and prospects. The men would ultimately be divided into six teams of four men, and these Bartlett would lead to the Siberian mainland, via Wrangel Island. Bartlett chose McKinlay and Mamen to be in his party on the trail, along with Kataktovik, because, as he said, they were men after his own heart. They would build igloos along the way, instead of using tents, and they would pack as many provisions onto the sleds as the dogs could handle—fifty days' food for the men and thirty-five days' for the dogs, which were being fed every few days now instead of every day. After the dog food ran out, they would be forced to shoot the weaker animals to feed the others. They were fond of the creatures and it wasn't a pleasant thought; but they knew it had to be done to preserve life, both for the stronger dogs and for themselves.

Once setting foot on Siberian soil, they would skirt the shore to North Cape, and then follow the shore to Saint Lawrence Bay, with the option of cutting down through Koliuchin Bay instead. Providing they made it past hostile Eskimo settlements (of which there were rumored to be many), the stronger members of the party would then trek on to find communication so that they could notify the proper authorities while the rest of the party would remain in Saint Lawrence Bay. All told, they would have to travel hundreds of miles.

"Now look here, boy," Bartlett said to McKinlay, laying his hand on the smaller man's shoulders, "we are up against it. The Peary trip is going to look like a picnic alongside this, but we are going to see it through."

"You bet your life," McKinlay replied, trying to sound as convincing as possible, yet wondering all the time if they would.

While they were busy with the preparations, McKinlay and Mamen took the captain aside and told him of an idea of their own. What if he sent a scouting party to Wrangel Island, ahead of everyone else? What if this party could take a load of food and supplies and then remain on the island until the others got there, so that they could explore and learn the lay of the land and report on what kind of game there was, and on ice conditions, before bringing everyone ashore?

The idea had occurred to Bartlett before, and now he thought it over again. When the three of them reconvened, he told them that he had decided to go through with it. It made good, practical sense—the men had been living for so long on the ship, and as a result were not yet hardened to the cold. Nor were they in the best physical shape, and no one except Hadley and the Eskimos had any experience in traveling over the Arctic ice, a rotten journey made even worse by poor light and freezing temperatures. For so many reasons, it made sense to send a few handpicked men before moving the entire party.

Three sleds could be taken, each one led by six dogs and loaded with 400 pounds of provisions. Bartlett wanted to send his ablest men to lead the party, which meant Mamen and McKinlay. But he didn't want them both to be gone at once. He needed one of them to remain with him because they were the only two he trusted.

It fell to Mamen, the stronger and heartier of the two, to lead the scouting party, taking with him Kuraluk and Kataktovik. First mate Sandy Anderson, second mate Barker, Seaman Ned Golightly, and geologist Malloch were designated members of the shore party, who would remain on Wrangel Island and set up camp while Mamen and the Eskimos returned with two empty sleds. McKinlay, meanwhile, would remain in camp to assist the captain, issuing material and looking after various matters.

When Mamen returned, he would, if at all possible, go back to the island with another party while the rest of the group awaited the return of the sun at Shipwreck Camp. When they had enough daylight, they would then join the others, relaying supplies to the island in small teams. This way, they could get enough provisions ashore to last until the birds returned to Wrangel in the spring, and they could also establish a shore camp where the men could rest and dry their foot gear before returning to Shipwreck Camp for more supplies. Bartlett envisioned snow igloos erected along the way, to serve as permanent relay stations.

"We may thus be able to take most of the food & clothing we have here to the island," wrote McKinlay excitedly, "so that we will have something to fall back on, should we need it, when making for the mainland. The announcement of this plan created a great deal of excitement & everyone seemed to welcome it."

Everyone, that is, but Dr. Mackay. The doctor listened with a scowl on his face as Bartlett gave orders in front of the assembled company. It is an easy guess that Mackay would have liked to have been a part of that shore party, so rabid was he to break free from the rest and start for land. This was the worst news he could have. They were finally starting for the island, but not with him. For so long, he had been planning this very journey, and now, at last, the captain was doing what, in Mackay's mind, he should have done months ago. But Mackay was forced to remain behind.

Upon hearing the captain's orders, Mackay completely snapped. He had had enough of the Canadian Arctic Expedition and of Bartlett and his indecisiveness and weak-kneed leadership. He'd had enough of his self-righteous colleagues and the crude and insufferable crewmen. As far as he was concerned, this was the point of no return.

JANUARY 18 BROUGHT WILD, blinding snow, and a fierce gale. Shivering against the cold, Hadley, Mamen, and Sandy loaded the three designated scouting party sleds with biscuits, pemmican, sugar, tents, Primus stoves, alcohol, and various other provisions.

Those who weren't loading the sleds and preparing their equipment set out on the ice with picks and axes to break a trail for the scouting party. The going was fine for the first three miles, until they ran up against an enormous pressure ridge, stretching fifteen to twenty feet in the air. They did their best to clear it, and then returned to camp, feeling satisfied with a day's work. Unfortunately, the snow, the wind, and the drifts took over, and by nighttime all traces of the trail had been destroyed.

With the ferocity of the snowstorm, Bartlett decided that the scouting party would not be able to leave, as planned, the following day. Even if the weather cleared, he would not let his men depart until he could see Wrangel Island distinctly and discern if there was any change in their position or in the condition of the ice pack. If he was not satisfied on all these accounts, the trip would have to be postponed until the weather cooperated.

The sweeping snow and stinging winds were relentless and brutal. It was one thing to suffer through a blizzard inside the walls of a ship, another altogether to be sitting on the ice, unprotected and vulnerable. They were now experiencing an entirely new level of cold, and getting their first taste of living out in the elements. To make matters worse, the ice pack continued to shift and crack, much to the horror of these men who were relying upon its fickle surface as the only thing separating them from the frigid depths of the Arctic Ocean. "All the time, we could hear the booming sound of the immense ice floes grinding against each other," Chafe wrote, "or the sharper crash of an opening lead. Then all would hurry out in the darkness to see whether a lead had opened near our Camp."

They awoke the next day to find the wind blowing from all directions; but they could see the land rising up out of the snow, and its bearing didn't seem to be drastically different. Cheered by this vision, everyone—excluding Dr. Mackay, Murray, and Beuchat—hastily worked at completing the preparations so that the team could start out the next day, as soon as the light allowed.

Finally, the sleds and equipment were ready, with thirty days' provisions for Sandy's land party, and ten days' for Mamen and the Eskimos. The trail was broken again by the same team that had gone out the day before, and now all that was left was for the group leaving to pack their personal clothing.

After supper, Bartlett summoned Mamen and McKinlay to the stove tent, where he outlined his instructions to Mamen. He was to command the party until land was reached, at which point Sandy would take charge of the shore party. He was to land supplies on the island and unload. Then, as long as he deemed it safe, he was to leave Sandy's party to drag the supplies ashore. He should return at once, not stopping to sleep on the island, leaving one sled and bringing back two, along with all the dogs. And last, Mamen was to return to camp if he came to open water and thought there was a risk of losing his supplies.

They spread the charts of the island out before them and estimated that it should take Mamen three days to reach land. By the end of the week, a fire would be lit at Shipwreck Camp to guide Mamen and the Eskimos back in.

McKinlay took night watchman's duties that night so that he could make two copies of the Admiralty Chart of Wrangel Island, one for Mamen and one for Sandy. He worked until 3:00 A.M., a thankless job because he had no way of spreading out the chart but had to work cramped in one position.

There was just one more thing to be dealt with. Malloch was worrying about going. Ever since he received the news that he would be joining the scouting party, he had been anxious and preoccupied. It was too great a risk. His clothes weren't ready yet, but even more than that, he was petrified about going on the trip. His attitude surprised Bartlett and the rest of the staff. Malloch was physically one of the strongest men in the company, and by far the most reckless. He had always been wild and careless when it came to his own health and well-being, and he had a way of laughing everything off when it became too serious. But ever since the ship went down his colleagues had seen a change in him.

Malloch went to the captain not once, but twice, expressing his concern, and even though Bartlett had tried to reassure him, his mind was still uneasy. He asked and then demanded to be replaced. So it was that at 10:00 P.M., on January 19, Seaman John Brady was informed he would be going instead.

IT WAS, AS MCKINLAY described it, a dirty-looking night. The wind had not let up and the snow swept through camp with the venom of a great, white beast. Everyone was to be called at 4:00 that morning, but Bartlett took one look outside and changed his mind. The wind howled and shrieked, and it was savagely raw and cold. The trip was postponed once more.

"It gets on the nerves to wait and wait under these circumstances," Mamen wrote in his diary. "All depends on these trips to the island.... I hope they will be successful, it is my highest desire these days."

Miraculously, by January 21 the breeze had lightened, the snowdrift had mellowed, and the sky had cleared. Bartlett took a good, long look, studying the distant island, the ice pack, the elements, with a weathered, seasoned gaze. And then finally, he gave the word—they were cleared to go.

As Mamen set out to lead his first small expedition of sorts, he reminded himself of all those who were counting on him. It was an enormous responsibility for a twenty-two-year-old, and the first serious challenge of his young life. He thought of his family back home and about Ellen and, most of all, he thought about the journey ahead. If Mamen was good at anything it was bolstering himself up and finding courage in daunting situations. Time and again, he had discovered deep within himself the ability to rise up and fight when all looked bleak. But still, he was riddled with doubt, and overwhelmed by the trust Bartlett was placing in him. "One must take chances and risk something to win," he wrote, "and win we must.... With God's help we will get successfully through with it."

MAMEN WAS LESS THAN HAPPY with their first day's work on the trail. He went to bed that night in their crudely and hastily constructed snow house feeling restless and unsatisfied. He was being hard on himself, unnecessarily. The changeable weather hadn't helped, and neither had the ice conditions. Now he listened to the wind screaming outside and prayed for better luck and an improvement in the weather.

Mamen wanted desperately to prove himself, not only to the captain, but to everyone else as well. He would go out there and lead that party, and it would all be wonderful experience for the expedition he planned to lead someday. He was certain tomorrow would be better. But still ... a weight remained. All were waiting for him to lead them and then return for the others. And now the wind was howling as he had never heard it howl before, and he couldn't see anything in the thick, falling snow.

After breakfast that morning at Shipwreck Camp, they had dug out the snow-covered sleds, and after Bartlett had presented official written instructions to both Mamen and Sandy, the scouting party had departed, Mamen leading the way on skis. Everyone but the captain, Hadley, Murray, Beuchat, Auntie, and the little girls accompanied them for the first four or five miles, making a good, fast start. The dogs were fresh and energetic, but the ice proved rough. The sleds were repeatedly drawn to a standstill by pressure ridges and snowdrifts, and fresh cracks in the ice were troublesome but crossable.

By noon, the extra men turned back to Shipwreck Camp, bidding Mamen's party "au revoir" and "good luck." There was great excitement, everyone full of hope for the future. At last, the moment they had been preparing for had arrived—the men were finally on their way.

Now on their own, Mamen led his party onward, and not long afterward the snow began to blow so that they could not see more than fifty or sixty yards in front of them. It was disastrous because just as suddenly the smooth ice grew rough and uneven, shattering their hopes of a good day's travel.

They headed southwest, relying on the compass at times because the snow was so blinding. Just seven miles from Shipwreck Camp, they came to the first opening in the ice. The ice was thin and the lead wide enough so that they were forced to unload the sleds and drag them across empty so they would be light enough to make it. Then they transferred all of the provisions by hand.

Discouraged, they made camp not too long afterward on a large floe of old ice, building a snow house with a tent for a roof because they were too tired to construct a proper one. Sandy had forgotten to pack the tent poles that Bartlett and McKinlay had set out, they had lost a bottle of alcohol along the way, and the end of one of the rifle butts had somehow broken. Other than that, they were still in good shape. Even though Bartlett had instructed Mamen that the dogs should be fed only once every second day, Mamen went ahead and gave them some pemmican anyway because they were worn out and he wanted them to be fresh for tomorrow.

The wind was so vicious that night that it blew the roof off their snow house three times. Each time, they would chase it down and replace it, finally piling it with Mamen's skis and ski poles, ropes, an Eskimo walking stick, some rifles, a piece of canvas, and a sleigh cover, to give it extra support.

When morning came, Mamen nearly decided to stay in camp and wait for the storm to abate; but gradually the wind began to die down and they set out once more. Huge ridges of ice awaited them on the trail, however—some as high as twenty feet—and these they climbed, pulling the dogs and sleds up and over them. It was an unbearable job and they wore themselves out in the process.

Because of the fog, they hadn't laid eyes on Wrangel Island since leaving Shipwreck Camp, which worried Mamen. Still, he remained hopeful. Surely they would see the mountain peaks again as soon as the weather cleared.

They pressed on until noon on the twenty-second, when they came to an open crack in the ice that stretched far and wide. There was no way of getting across it. The ice surrounding the open water was shaky and thin. They retreated a quarter of a mile and made camp on a large patch of old ice. The total day's progress was seven miles, and they were in worse condition than the day before. Their tent had ripped in two places and most of the party had frozen noses and hands. Earlier in the day, Mamen took a spill into the water up to the middle of his thighs. The water was deadly cold, and he was shivering and blue, dripping wet, his clothes beginning to freeze on his body. But he would not allow the party to stop for him to change clothes; they had to keep going. He paid for his decision with a frozen nose and middle finger, and two frozen feet, the left one particularly bad.

When at last they took shelter in their new snow house, Mamen was sleepless. He lay in his makeshift bed, uneasy and in pain. He was worried about the fact that they were still unable to see Wrangel Island. And he was worried about Kuraluk. The Eskimo was making him a nervous wreck because of his anxiety about leaving his family behind. Kuraluk was very protective of Auntie and his daughters. This was the first time he had been separated from them on this journey, and the first time he had left them alone with those strangers from the ship. Bartlett, he trusted, but the others worried him. He wanted to get back as soon as possible. He would have no rest until he saw his family again.

Mamen also worried about his own frostbitten feet, which gave him so much pain that he could not rest. He got up twice to rub them with snow in an attempt to get the circulation back, not realizing that this was the worst thing he could have done. He should have warmed them against the body heat of one of his comrades instead.

"Oh, what a road we have," Mamen wrote in his diary on that sleepless night. "It is more than difficult and will take longer time than expected."

The following day brought better results, though the high pressure ridges still troubled them and Wrangel Island remained shrouded in fog. The men were in better spirits all around, their outlook improved by eleven miles progress and more accommodating weather. With a little luck, thought Mamen, they would reach Wrangel Island tomorrow.

THEY SET OUT THE NEXT MORNING in snow flurries and a steady, driving wind, which kept up throughout the day. The sky was dark and clouded, and Wrangel Island was still nowhere to be seen. Mamen drove them onward, and they crossed several small openings in the ice, which gave them considerable trouble. The worst came just past noon when they reached a wide, sprawling lead, too wide to cross with the dogs and the loaded sleds.

Mamen and Sandy and the others unharnessed the dogs and threw them across the chasm, dragging the sleds over behind. It was Mamen's bad luck to be caught in the middle of a dog fight, which erupted as he was helping the dogs across to his side of the water. Throwing himself into the middle of the pack in an effort to separate the fighters, he felt a sharp, stabbing pain in his right knee. He buckled, but still managed to push the dogs apart, and then was able to assess the damage. The pain was intense, and he had no idea what he had done. As far as he could tell in his hasty examination, it was either the kneecap or the ligament, but he could not assess the extent of the damage. It was a familiar feeling—the same knee he had injured just weeks ago.

With Mamen virtually crippled, the men were forced to set up camp. Mamen sent Kataktovik out to find a good place, and then the young leader was lashed to Sandy's sled for the drive there. As Mamen was bumped and jostled over the rough ice, his knee shot lightning bolts of pain through his entire body.

They built their snow house, lit the Primus stoves, and ate a quick dinner. Afterward, Sandy and Brady tried to help Mamen with his leg. They pulled it and massaged it, but nothing seemed to help. After just nine miles progress for the day, Mamen was forced into bed, his last thoughts being ones of hope and prayer that his leg might improve during the night and be good enough to walk on in the morning. Otherwise, he would be of no use to his men, only a hindrance, and he would slow them down.

What had he gotten himself into? "I have not yet seen worse luck," he wrote, "I cannot but say that I am much worried both about ourselves and our comrades in the camp. I don't know how to manage everything now. It is worse for the people left behind out on the ice. If the leg is not all right tomorrow, we must do all we can to reach land and then send Anderson and the two Eskimos back, to return now would be folly."

As the temperature dipped to minus forty degrees Fahrenheit, the men endured another sleepless night. They couldn't risk tents or sleeping bags because the ice might shift or break and they had to be unencumbered. Instead, they bedded down on the ice and huddled closely for warmth. Their clothes were wet through from the snow and their own sweat and their exertions over the open leads—the slips, the accidental falls, the dips into the freezing water. It was impossible to dry their clothes, which meant the men were forced to walk up and down periodically throughout the night to keep their blood circulating and maintain feeling in their bodies. They walked even when they couldn't feel their limbs. Sandy seemed to have it the worst. His legs were frozen, and he sat up all night rubbing them vigorously.

They were up at 5:00 A.M. and on their way by 8:30, part of the provisions from Sandy's sled loaded onto Mamen's and Kuraluk's sleds so that Mamen could ride. For the first time since leaving Shipwreck Camp, they spotted Wrangel Island, and they let this spur them on and give them the strength they needed to continue.

There was one other factor that helped them onward: the sun. The great orb had disappeared on November 14 of the previous year, and they could now see it lifting its burning head over the earth. It barely cleared the horizon, but their spirits soared.

They traveled twelve miles that day and were in sight of land. Surely they couldn't have much farther to go. That night's entry in Mamen's diary was proof of his renewed optimism: "We came closer and closer to the island, it is now quite distinct. The mountains rise sombrely [sic], and we can also see the lowland to the west dimly. I hope that we may reach the island tomorrow; it will be a joy both to us and to the others, the sooner we will be back."

Over the next two days, they only traveled an average of nine miles total, however. The uneven ice and loose snow made the going next to impossible. There were increasing numbers of open leads, and Mamen and his team were forced to approach Wrangel Island in zigzag fashion instead of a straight line.

Mamen was still lashed to the sled, unable to straighten his knee or put any weight on it. He felt like the most dreadful burden. If there was anything Mamen hated, it was to be a hindrance. It made him feel weak and angry and frustrated, and yet there was nothing he could do.

There was no rest for the travelers as the nighttime temperature hovered at minus forty degrees Fahrenheit, and they continued to pace the ice, trying to keep warm. All of their clothes were soaking wet, and even the woolen blankets were more like wet dish rags than protective covering. They could not escape the wind and the cold, and "we shiver and freeze more than we have done before," observed Mamen.

They were, at least, coming steadily closer to the island, although Mamen now suspected that the distance from Shipwreck Camp to Wrangel was much greater than he and Bartlett and McKinlay had originally guessed.

January 28 was no better. They were running into more and more open water, and were forced to zigzag more dramatically toward the island. It was maddening to see the land so near, yet not be able to reach it. By noon, they were forced to sit out the rest of the day beside an enormous lead, which they could only hope would freeze over so they could continue. Otherwise, they had no idea how they would get around it.

Making camp was almost impossible because there was no snow to build their igloo. Somehow, after expending a lot of time and energy, they managed a rather crude structure, only to discover that one of their two Primus stoves was no longer working.

They had covered just four miles and their clothes were "wetter and wetter day by day," wrote Mamen. "I don't know how it will go if we don't reach land soon, I don't think the boys can manage it this way much longer and then they have also considerable trouble with me." His leg had not improved at all, but they were so close to the island now—could practically feel the earth beneath their feet—that Mamen insisted they go on.

At the end of the day, they were a discouraged lot and even Mamen was having trouble rallying. He knew Bartlett and the others were already expecting them back at Shipwreck Camp, but he refused to return until they had reached the island. "I have suffered these days more than people might believe," he said, "both from pain in the leg and from the cold, more than I have done in all my life, but my spirits are still high and I look upon the future with bright eyes, however dark it may appear to be."

BACK AT SHIPWRECK CAMP, McKinlay lay in layers of damp clothing on one of the mattresses they'd saved from the ship. He had learned much in the past week from living on the ice. He now knew it was important to remove one's boots before sleeping and to leave them standing because they would freeze during the night. If you left them standing, at least you could fit your feet into them the next day. They tended to get out of shape if you lay them down. Likewise, it was important to remove any clothing that was wet and next to the skin. Most of their clothing was wet by the end of the day, due to snow or ice or water or sweat.

McKinlay's standard outfit now consisted of a singlet, a shirt, overalls, two pairs of underpants, a pair of trousers, mukluks, and reindeer socks. He had also taken to sewing sealskin soles into his socks, with detachable deerskin soles on top of these, at Bartlett's suggestion. The idea was that at the end of the day, he could slip the detachable soles out and let them dry on his chest while he was sleeping. So far, it seemed a brilliant idea.

Each of the two snow houses had a stove in the center of it, and they placed the mattresses surrounding this; but the temperature had dipped to forty degrees below zero, and they soon forgot what it ever was to be warm.

ON JANUARY 25, the sun had appeared over the horizon for the first time in seventy-one days. It was the fourth time Bartlett had seen the sun return in the Arctic, but it was the one which gave him the greatest satisfaction, since so much depended on their having a good amount of daylight. They could also see Wrangel Island for the first time since Mamen had left, situated much farther away than it had been previously. They knew then that they must still be drifting at a greater rate than they had reckoned.

To celebrate the return of the sun, the men had feasted on oysters. Bartlett had found two tins of them in the galley while he was waiting for the ship to go down and had tossed them overboard onto the ice where they broke and scattered. That night, they all went out into the drifting snow and dug for oysters, which Templeman cooked up into a soup.

Afterward, they gathered around the big stove in the box house and enjoyed an impromptu concert, each man reciting something from memory—"Casey at the Bat," or "Lasca"—while Munro offered some of his favorite Robbie Burns's poems. Then they all sang together such popular favorites as "Sweet Afton," "Alexander's Ragtime Band," "Loch Lomond," and "Red Wing."

Auntie sang hymns in her rich, strong voice, and then Helen and Mugpi sang nursery songs. The children helped the men take their minds off their own troubles. It was always easier when there was someone smaller and more vulnerable to worry about, and the children were becoming increasingly important to them. When the little girls sang "Twinkle, Twinkle, Little Star," their mother joined in. It was a memorable moment and, as McKinlay noted, one of the most cheerful times they had had for a long while.

On the twenty-eighth, the day they expected Mamen and the Eskimos to return, Chafe and Clam had reported smooth ice on the trail, stretching across the horizon. There was no open water in sight, which was splendid news. Mess room boy Chafe and seaman Clam, eager to stretch their legs and gain more experience in ice travel, had been out almost every day on the trail and, for the most part, had reported fine ice conditions. The darkness was abating and Mamen now had about eight hours of decent light each day for travel. What, then, was keeping them?

McKinlay knew by the offshore wind that there was a strong probability of Mamen running into open water. There was also a prominent water sky visible to the south, which further backed up the prediction. And as if to prove him right, Chafe and Dr. Mackay returned one day after a hike to report several leads of water, some over a hundred yards wide, a mile or so to the south of them.

Over the next several days, Chafe and Clam went out together regularly, marking the trail every two or three miles with flags. Both young men felt more confident in their abilities now, and it felt good to be useful. They also carried supplies (mostly food and oil) on these short treks, to cache along the trail at spots one, two, three, and four days' travel from camp. Each time, they reported the ice conditions as fine and much improved.

Clam's ear had become badly nipped by the cold, blistering and swelling to twice its normal size. True to his name, he said nothing and did not complain. They were all becoming quickly accustomed to frostbite, although some of them were less careful than others. Malloch was the worst. Now that he had been released from the scouting party, his characteristic affability had returned to a certain degree, and with it his usual thoughtlessness. One day the geologist strode about the camp in a pair of bearskin breeches with his trousers rolled up because his legs were too warm. There were three inches of bare leg showing between the top of his boots and the bottom of his pants. "You are going to freeze your legs, Malloch," Hadley told him, "if you don't wrap them up."

But Malloch laughed it off, saying that was the way Bartlett had said they dressed in Greenland. Hadley just shook his head, once again amazed by the ignorance of all these Arctic greenhorns, and said, "Go to it, old man."

The result was a nasty nip on the leg, which laid Malloch up for several days.

They had postponed setting up the flare to guide Mamen home until the twenty-ninth. That morning, Chafe, Clam, Breddy, and Hadley set out by sled for the first camp made by Mamen's party on the trail. They found it seven miles from Shipwreck Camp and placed a flag there to help lead Mamen home. During the day, a huge bonfire was built out of a whaleboat, thirteen sacks of coal, a couple of cases of engine oil, and ten tins of gasoline. This created an enormous, winding smoke pillar, which billowed into the sky, easily seen at least fifteen miles away. Dusk closed in at 3:00 P.M., at which point they rolled a cask of alcohol down the trail and stood it up on one end before setting it ablaze. They also burned the canoe and three cases of gasoline. The flames were still raging as they lay down to sleep. As Hadley noted, it was a wonder they didn't blow themselves to eternity. "I reminded the Captain of how he had burnt all the hair off his face last winter when he put a package of Eastman's flash papers in the cabin stoves, and I advised him to look out that nothing worse happened."

When Mamen had not arrived by the morning of the thirtieth, Clam, Chafe, and Maurer followed the trail again, this time going as far as the second camp, just four miles beyond the first. They could not understand this slow progress and could not find any sign of open water or anything else that might have slowed Mamen's party down.

One thing was clear, though—they now knew that, for whatever reason, it was too early to expect Mamen's return.

Despite their worry, life continued. The men kept on with their sewing, huddled close over candlelight, since most of their lamps were broken. The dim light was hard on the eyes, as well as depressing. They also mended the holes in their snow houses where the walls had melted away from the heat of the stoves. While the members of the other house took the roof off and rebuilt their walls, the occupants of McKinlay's house were not so eager to go to work. Thanks to Dr. Mackay, Murray, and Beuchat, there was a decided lack of communal spirit, and as a result each man looked after his own corner of the room, propping up the roof and walls as best he could.

The only activity that seemed to interest Mackay and Beuchat was to practice hauling a sled loaded with pemmican cases. These tins of pemmican were about fourteen inches long, five inches wide, and three inches thick. Each tin held six pounds and was marked so that one knew how to take out a pound exactly, which was the standard daily ration for a man in the Arctic, along with tea and a pound of biscuit. The men would open a tin on one side and empty the contents, and then they would open the other side and flatten the tin into a sheet. Bartlett had learned from Peary to mark trails with these flattened pemmican tins. When displayed against an ice ridge, the red or blue sheets of tin were visible for as many as two miles against all of that whiteness. They could be used as an indication of open water or a dangerous fault, or simply to mark the trail. Bartlett had instructed Mamen to mark his own trail this way.

The captain had made it perfectly clear that he had no intention of manhauling anything on the trip to Wrangel Island, yet Mackay and Beuchat were diligently practicing up and down, back and forth. McKinlay watched his comrades warily, trying to ignore the gnawing worry and suspicion in the pit of his stomach.

Bartlett had presented his men with a rough outline of his plans. Following Mamen's return, he would send four sleds with eleven men and all the dogs to the island. When the entire party got to shore, eight of them would remain there (providing there was game enough to sustain them) while the rest of the party crossed the Bering Strait and made for Saint Lawrence Bay to wire for help. If there was no game on the island, they would all go to Siberia.

After months of complaining and plotting and talking about setting out on their own, Dr. Mackay and Murray took Bartlett aside on the morning of January 31 and told him what he had expected to hear long ago—they were leaving. As far as they were concerned, it was much too risky to remain any longer on the ice. They had no desire to wait for Bartlett to lead the team to Wrangel, and then to risk getting left behind on the island while he chose someone else to accompany him on the trek to Siberia. They had to know that after their harsh treatment of him, their chances of being picked to go were almost nonexistent.

Although the news of their departure didn't come as a shock to Bartlett—or to anyone else who had been made to endure their grumbling—it was still hard to believe that the three of them were finally making good on their threats. And it was hard to grasp fully the impact of what they were proposing. It meant, after all, the first complete division of the party. To give it its real name, mutiny.

They presented Bartlett with a list of requested supplies—fifty days' worth—and told him of their plan to reach the island and then, possibly, to continue on to the Siberian coast. Otherwise, they would remain on the island and wait to be picked up by any ships that might arrive there that summer. Beuchat would go with them, which was no surprise, but so would sailor Stanley Morris, which came as a shock to everyone.

There had never been any word about Morris joining them, but he rather sheepishly approached his captain and requested permission to go. Bartlett gave it grudgingly, more willing to let Mackay and the others go than he was to let this decent, sweet-tempered young man leave his own company. While Bartlett was now responsible for the scientists, they were still Stefansson's men. Stefansson had hired them, and they were working for him. But the sailors, stokers, stewards, and officers were Bartlett's, and young Morris was one of the most promising members of the crew.

Morris was also very persuasive and eager, not to mention blindly trusting and completely awed by the Antarctic reputation of Dr. Mackay and Murray. True, they had mastered the rugged Antarctic plateau, but the sea ice of the Arctic was completely different. Continually cracking, splitting, shifting, and moving, the surface of the sea ice was rough and uneven, with magnificent hills and ridges piling up from the pressure. Ever changing, forever in motion, the Arctic pack was unpredictable and could easily turn deadly.

Stanley Morris had wanted to be an explorer since childhood, ever since he was old enough to understand that he was named for the great Henry Morton Stanley, who was sent to find Dr. Livingstone in the wilds of Ujiji, Africa. Now he was in the presence of two bona fide and proven polar heroes, Dr. Mackay and Murray. For some time, he had known something about their plans to leave the ship. He believed in their experience and their authoritative boasting. He also looked up to them as fellow Brits who shared familiar attitudes and methods, while Bartlett was more American in his way of thinking. Morris suddenly saw Dr. Mackay and Murray as men of action while the captain, for some reason, was choosing to wait. Land was visible, after all, and now they were beginning to drift away from it. Better to leave with these brilliant scientists who had proven themselves at the bottom of the world with Shackleton, than to stay here a moment longer on the ice.

Bartlett put up no fight with Mackay over leaving, knowing he would not be able to dissuade him, but he tried to change Morris's mind. The boy would not listen, though. The captain had to resign himself then and told himself that at least Morris could be of use to Mackay and the others because he was so much younger and very handy. Consequently, Morris was granted permission to leave with the scientists.

Bartlett asked that Mackay put his request into writing, stating that they were leaving the main party of their own free will, thus relieving him of all responsibility. After he received their letter, he would issue them fifty days' supplies of provisions and equipment. The captain then passed their request on to McKinlay, because he was in charge of the stores. He also offered Mackay's party their proportional share of dogs, as soon as Mamen returned with them, but Mackay declined the offer. They would haul the sled themselves.

There was one last thing. Mackay told Bartlett that if he and the others decided to remain on Wrangel Island and wait for a ship, they would then "throw themselves on the main party for additional support." A bold statement, considering all they had put everyone through and the now very decisive rift they were forcing upon the party.

Bartlett would have none of it. As soon as he distributed the requested provisions, and as soon as he saw them on their way out of Shipwreck Camp, his responsibility for them was over. That also went for Seaman Morris, who likely had no idea what he was getting into. As hard as it would be for Morris, should Dr. Mackay's party end up on Wrangel Island, their fifty days' supply gone, he would not be able to come to the captain for help. If he chose to leave now, Bartlett's responsibility for Morris was over as well.

It was difficult to tell what kind of impact Mackay's departure would have on the rest of the men. In some ways, it would be a relief to be rid of them, but in other ways, it felt like the beginning of the end. It was true that the *Karluk*'s company as a whole had not always been united in spirit or friendship, but how could anything good come out of such a final and irreparable division?

Somehow it all would have seemed easier to deal with if Mamen would only return. The last day of the month, ten days gone, and still no sign of him.

And then Malloch made a strange and unnerving remark to the captain. His usually sunny face was grave as he told Bartlett that he did not expect to see Mamen again. When asked why, Malloch merely said that if Mamen had managed to reach the shore, he didn't think he was ever coming back.

They brushed it off, but Bartlett, McKinlay, and the rest of the members of Shipwreck Camp were nagged by worry. "We are at a loss to account for this lack of progress," wrote McKinlay, "as the going seemed smooth, & there were no signs of their having been held up by open water. The only explanation we can think of is that they overslept after the exertions of the first day & had only a very short spell of daylight on the second day."

Bartlett put on a positive face for his men and speculated that Mamen and Sandy probably reached land on the thirtieth, and therefore he would not expect Mamen back for a couple of days. Give them until February 2 or 3, and no doubt they would be stumbling, worn and weary, back into camp.

They fanned the flames of the alcohol flare and vowed to keep some sort of fire burning until Mamen and the Eskimos were safely home.

ON JANUARY 29, Mamen, Sandy, and the other members of their party stood rooted in place, not believing their eyes. Mamen had gone over it again and again in his mind, but he still could not figure out what had gone wrong or where they had gotten off track.

They had traveled well that morning, but the afternoon had brought rough new ice, piled into looming ridges and hills, the jagged, slippery surfaces of which must be crossed somehow. They made twelve miles in spite of it all. But then, suddenly, Mamen knew something was wrong. There was the island—but *not* the island. The mountain peaks weren't where they should have been, and the island was much smaller than they had expected. This piece of land, indeed, seemed barely more than a slab of rock jutting out of the ice and water. There were no trees. There was no expanse of land. There was only a sheer, ragged mountain peak.

"I have come to the conclusion," Mamen wrote in his diary on January 29, "that it is not Wrangel Island that we are coming to, but Herald Island. It is a shock to us and to all in the camp...."

It was clearly Herald Island. They were close enough to see that now. Herald Island, without any flat coastal stretch on the southeast side, was comprised of only mountainous ridges and cliffs. It was thirty-eight miles from Wrangel Island and, according to the *Pilot Book,* just four miles long.

From what Mamen knew of the place, Herald Island wasn't fit for any living creature. It was harsh, desolate, and lifeless, and virtually inaccessible. But even a useless, barren scrap of earth seemed better than a block of ice. And in Mamen's condition, and with Golightly's frozen feet, he knew they had little chance of making Wrangel.

It wasn't clear to them what went wrong—whether they had mischarted it to begin with, whether the island they had seen from Shipwreck Camp was actually Herald instead, or whether they somehow got off course in the fog and the snow and the zigzagging across the ice.

Whatever had happened, Mamen and Sandy, Barker, Brady, Golightly, Kuraluk, and Kataktovik were stunned. Unable to go on, they set up camp for the night, but the ice crashed and creaked around them so that no one could sleep. Then, at 10:30 P.M., the ice cracked violently outside their snow house and Sandy, Barker, and the two sailors, frightened out of their minds, raced outside, carrying their belongings, loading them onto the sleds, ready to start away immediately.

Without warning, the ice began to crush. Packs crashed into packs, grating, churning, threatening to smash Mamen and the others flat. The great ice shelves vomited out of the water suddenly, their edges jagged and razor-sharp, crashing on top of nearby floes with resounding explosions. The men could have been crushed at any moment. The dogs barked and howled, terrified. One of the sleds turned over, tumbling half their supplies into the water. The men held on to each other and tried to make their way to a safer plateau, but they were surrounded by the grinding ice and water.

Suddenly, the ice broke up and they were separated from each other, floating on individual shards while the chasms of water widened between them. Even the Eskimos were afraid, shouting to Mamen in Inuit. But somehow they all drifted back together, only to find that now a wide, open field of water lay between them and the island. Mamen didn't know how they'd make it across, short of swimming. There was ice again, closer to land, but it was rougher and looser. The leads of water were wider there. Sometimes there was no ice at all.

The ice quieted suddenly then, and they regained a shaky sense of calm. Sandy and the crewmen set up a tent for Mamen, who rested his lame knee while the other men walked up and down the remainder of the night to ward off the chill. They kept the good stove going and filled themselves with hot tea to keep warm.

They started out again in the morning, south to west, climbing over the immense pressure ridges with their loaded sleds. It was no easy task, but suddenly these ice mountains were springing up everywhere across the horizon; they had no choice but to pick their way up and across them. "It is remarkable that our sleighs stand it," remarked Mamen.

In the afternoon, they ran into thirty feet of open water and were forced to stop after traveling only three and a half miles. Discouraged and exhausted, they once again set up camp as the ice continued to groan and shift around them.

After another sleepless and uneasy night, they awoke on January 31 to see the ice opening up and drifting away from land. The leads of water were growing and they were forced to move camp nearby to a large ice floe, where they felt they would be safer. With the day stretching before them, Mamen tried out his legs for the first time since he had hurt himself. Although he was still suffering and couldn't yet straighten his knee, he made a brave effort to "hop along the best I can, and hope it will get better."

He also came to a decision. It was time to head back to Shipwreck Camp. He would leave Sandy and the boys as close to Herald Island as he could, and then he and the Eskimos would return as planned, taking with them provisions for fifteen days: three boxes of Hudson's Bay pemmican, 200 biscuits, 150 pounds of dog pemmican, tea, sugar, a Primus stove, an ice pick, the two sleds, a gallon of gasoline, and all of the dogs.

Sandy, then, would be left with 6 boxes of Hudson's Bay pemmican, 300 pounds of Underwood pemmican, 100 pounds of dog pemmican, 70 pounds of biscuits, 15 pounds of sugar, 12 boxes of milk, tea, 1 stove, 7 gallons of gasoline, 15 candles, 3½ dozen boxes of matches, and 1 sled.

It is unclear why Mamen chose that moment to leave them. He knew the poor ice conditions; he knew the state of Herald Island. He could have ordered them all back to camp with him, to let Bartlett know of the grave mistake in the identity of the island. He could have stayed to see them through to land, such as it was. But perhaps he knew his knee would only continue to hold them back, and perhaps he felt they could do better without him.

Whatever his reasons, he made the decision. The next day was February 1, and Mamen would be on his way back home with Kuraluk and Kataktovik and all of the dogs, leaving first officer Sandy Anderson, second mate Charles Barker, and sailors John Brady and Ned Golightly to find their own way across the open water to Herald Island.

It would be a perilous journey under the best of circumstances, but none of these young men had been trained in polar survival. And none of them had any experience with Artic ice travel, aside from that of the past ten days.

FEBRUARY 1914

———— • ————

Then to this earthen Bowl did I adjourn
My Lip the secret Well of Life to learn:
And Lip to Lip it murmur'd—"While you live
Drink!—for once dead you never shall return."
— RUBÁIYÁT OF OMAR KHAYYÁM

Before Mamen had left them on the ice, Sandy had asked to go with him back to Shipwreck Camp. There was only open water surrounding the island, and they estimated they were about five miles from land, perhaps less. Sandy had told Hadley before he left that if it came down to leaving him and the others on the ice with no dogs, and open water stretching ahead, he would insist on turning back with Mamen. Sandy was young and inexperienced, but he also had keen instincts. He knew he might just as well sign their death certificates by agreeing to stay.

Something in Sandy's bones told him they would be in for it should they stay out there, just the four of them, trying to make land on their own, so he told Mamen that he thought the party should return to Shipwreck Camp together. But then one of the sailors spoke up—Brady or Golightly—and said, "Give me a rifle and I will walk to Point Barrow." The others were much more confident, and they could afford to be. After all, Sandy was the one in charge now.

He knew the sailor was teasing, but it didn't matter. He hated to be told he was the first to back down or give up. Sandy wasn't like that. He followed orders and he saw things through. He wouldn't have anyone— joking or not—accuse him of being a coward.

So he stayed. But before Mamen left, Sandy gave him a letter to deliver to Bartlett informing him of their plans and the situation. In it, he took responsibility for the choice to go on toward the island, whether or not it was actually his wish. They would proceed to Herald Island as if it were Wrangel and wait there for further instruction—providing, of course, that they could make it across the ice and open fields of water.

The last Mamen saw of them, they were four lone figures, dwarfed by a backdrop of impenetrable ice and open water. They stood small and insignificant against the immense, gray crag of the mountain and the ice that seemed to spread out to all four corners and reach up into the sky.

He couldn't think about this, though, as he and Kuraluk and Kataktovik told Sandy and the others good-bye. Mamen's knee was still troubling him, but at least he could hobble along now and not have to be pulled all the time on the sled. He and the Eskimos made pretty good time on the way back to Shipwreck Camp, passing their tenth camp, their ninth, their eighth, and traveling, in all, fifteen miles.

Later that evening, when they had put up an igloo and were settled in for the night, Mamen picked up his diary and tried to justify his decision to leave Sandy, Barker, Brady, and Golightly. "They will now have to manage by themselves and try to get to the island. I could not wait and help them, as there was considerable open water between the camp and the coast, but the distance is not more than 5 miles at the most so they can manage and get there alone, and there is more use for me as well as for the dogs in the main camp."

There had been a three-mile lead of water between them and the land when Mamen and the Eskimos turned back. Sandy and his team had one sled, two sled-loads of supplies, and no dogs. Golightly's feet were already badly frozen. The ice was young and shifting and it was starting to crush when Mamen left, which meant Sandy and his men would have a hard time of it.

The dogs were starving and sore-footed, but Mamen and the Eskimos drove them on, determined to get home. Kuraluk's spirits had picked up considerably, once they were on their way back, and his enthusiasm to be finished with this journey matched Mamen's. He was going back to Auntie and his girls, to watch over them and make sure they were all right. Openings in the ice caused them trouble, so they made detours now and then, to ford a tricky chasm in the floe, eventually reconnecting with the trail.

On February 3, they unloaded all the unnecessary stores at Camp Two and gave the dogs two biscuits each to help them go on. They started on their way again, a little refreshed, and it wasn't long before they spotted smoke rising up over the horizon. They knew then that they were almost back to Shipwreck Camp.

They soon ran into Chafe and Clam between Camps One and Two. Bartlett had sent them with one Peary sled and four dogs to go out and open the trail for Mamen, taking flags that they would place as warnings at points where leads had broken the ice. They were also to carry provisions to Mamen's third camp and cache them there.

After a quick but joyous exchange with Charlie and Clam, who would continue on to Camp Three with the supplies, Mamen and the Eskimos were on their way again. They soon came up against open water between Camp One and Shipwreck Camp. They dealt with it resolutely, however, going around it as best they could, fueled by the sight of the distant smoke and the knowledge that they were almost home.

MCKINLAY WAS IN the galley, preparing to have a makeshift wash, when he heard Breddy yell, "Here they're; here they're."

Everyone but Dr. Mackay raced to meet them. Kataktovik had led the way, and Mamen came in with the first sled. Kuraluk appeared moments afterward, beaming with happiness at the sight of Auntie. She had been up on an ice rafter in the dark, watching for him, and at the sound of his voice, she ran to him.

Bartlett slapped Mamen on the back and gave him a warm and hearty handshake. "Well done, Norway," he shouted.

They all lined up to shake hands with Mamen, and then they rushed the three weary travelers into the box house, built a huge fire, and stripped off their frozen clothing. They had no spares, of course, so Bartlett and McKinlay peeled the shirts and trousers off their own backs for them.

Templeman cooked eggs, bacon, biscuits, strong coffee, and cocoa, and the three ate gratefully. Mug after mug of hot drink went down them until they felt warmed again. Everyone in camp wanted to know what had happened—had they reached the island, how were the mate and the others, how was the trip, what had taken them so long, and so on. But Bartlett, with a quiet but firm hand, ordered them to wait until the travelers were taken care of and restored to their old selves again.

After dinner, they gathered round and Mamen finally told them about the journey. It was Herald Island, he said, without a doubt, and he had left Sandy's party about three miles from land. Sandy's letter to Bartlett estimated one mile, but the captain feared that they were both underestimating the distance. Regardless, the fact was that no one could decide which island it was. Mamen reckoned Herald Island was approximately eighty-five miles away from Shipwreck Camp, and the captain thought it was probably between sixty and seventy.

The thing that puzzled them the most, though, was that the descriptions Mamen and the Eskimos gave of the island did not agree with the one given by the *Pilot Book*. It was true that Herald Island was in keeping with the positions they had taken with the chronometer, but the land that Mamen had seen looked to be eighteen miles long instead of the four and a half miles cited by the *Pilot Book*. It was too big to be Herald, but the location and contour of the mountains did not match those on Wrangel Island.

Whatever it was, reasoned Mamen, it was land, and that was the most important thing.

WILLIAMSON TREATED MAMEN'S leg that night, rubbing it with alcohol and massaging it so that Mamen could finally straighten it for the first time since his injury. And then bed. "Oh, how nice it felt to get into a bed, soft and warm. I lay awake all night just enjoying existence, sleep was out of the question although I was tired."

The next day was spent in comparative luxury, the travelers doing nothing but eating, resting, smoking, and enjoying the comforts of life. Their shipmates were affable and eager to wait on them, and it was exactly what they required after their journey. Mamen was hungry all day, and his leg was getting better, thanks in large part to Williamson's care.

After a breakfast of codfish, hardtack, and coffee, Bartlett called Mamen and McKinlay into the storage tent to discuss Mamen's report. This island, whatever it was, was neither Wrangel nor Herald, according to Bartlett.

However, as they had nothing else to go on, he was going to proceed on the assumption that it was indeed Herald Island. And he wanted Mamen to go back again, taking Kataktovik and Kuraluk, to try to reach the island and determine its position. Mamen would take a sextant and an artificial horizon with him so that he could do this. Even more than that, Bartlett wanted to find Sandy and make sure that he had landed on the island.

McKinlay would make a copy of the necessary elements of the sun and principal stars to aid in Mamen's latitude observations, and it was decided that Mamen and the Eskimos would leave on Saturday morning, providing his knee was good enough for travel.

Once again, Bartlett had placed a huge responsibility on Mamen's shoulders, but, Mamen reflected, "there is nobody else that he can rely on, and I will do it with pleasure even if it should cost me considerable pain."

DR. MACKAY, MURRAY, Beuchat, and sailor Morris left Shipwreck Camp the morning of February 5. Some of the men had given them letters to mail, in case they should reach land first, and McKinlay and Mamen turned out to see them off and wish them good luck. They would need it, hauling six hundred pounds of provisions themselves.

Murray and Beuchat had given Bartlett the letter he had requested, absolving him of responsibility for their actions. Bartlett told them they could have whatever provisions and equipment they wanted, and that even though they were severing their connection with the rest of the company, he did not want to see them beaten. He would help them, after all, should they need it. He would not turn his back on them as he had originally vowed to do, no matter what their choice now.

Dr. Mackay and his party passed Chafe and Clam later that afternoon. The two crewmen were on their way back to Shipwreck Camp, and Mackay and the others were about a mile from Mamen's first campsite, pulling only half their load. They had quickly discovered that they weren't able to haul everything themselves, which should have been no surprise given the fact that Morris was the only member of the team who had any stamina or physical strength. Beuchat was too weak, Murray too old and out of shape, and Mackay too weakened by drugs and alcohol.

They found it easier to move in two stages, leaving half of the load three or four miles back while they sledged the other half, and then turning back again for the remainder. This slowed their progress considerably, but they were still determined. This setback may have thrown a wrench into their plans, but they were convinced that they would still make land before anyone else.

IT WAS THE AFTERNOON of February 7 and Mamen was miserable. His leg had once again given out, and now he was lashed to the sled, being hauled back to Shipwreck Camp by Munro, of all people, a man he despised. The two had clashed since the *Karluk* sailed from Esquimalt, Mamen thinking the chief engineer lazy and untrustworthy, and Munro believing the young topographer arrogant and impertinent.

Now barely out of camp, not even noon yet, and already Mamen was on his way home. It was demoralizing, especially with so many counting on him, and once again he was unable to complete his mission. Would they soon stop believing in him altogether? When would they decide not to give him another chance to prove his worth?

Mamen had been hopeful starting out that morning. He was up by 4:00 A.M., lashing his belongings to the sled and dressing in his traveling clothes. He was sure they would reach the island this time, since he had had a good rest and his leg was healing.

After breakfast, they harnessed the dogs, and Chafe and Clam set out first, needing a little time to get ahead since they had the oldest and slowest dogs. They were hauling a load on the Peary sled, which they would hand over to Mamen down the trail, along with supplies they had cached days ago. Mamen and the Eskimos would load these onto their three sleds and take them on to the island. Once they landed these provisions, there would be, all told, fifty days' food on the island, leaving fifty-seven days' provisions on the ice.

Mamen's party left camp fifteen minutes after Chafe's, with McKinlay, Maurer, and Munro accompanying them. About a mile and a half out, they caught up with Chafe and a dripping wet Clam, shivering from the cold.

Clam had gone ahead of the dogs while Chafe took the sled handles, the two reported. Someone usually had to run ahead because dogs harnessed to a load often refused to budge unless they had someone in front of them lead-ing the way. So Clam ran ahead. Fifty yards or so, and four miles from Shipwreck Camp, he disappeared from view. When Chafe got to him, the sailor was struggling to pull himself out of the frigid water, with only his arms and head above the ice. Chafe dragged him out and then sent him back to camp, shivering and already frozen. "The temperature was nearly fifty below zero," said Chafe, "so you can imagine how he felt." Chafe then followed him with the sled, and that was when they ran into Mamen and the others.

They advised Clam to run back to camp and made Maurer go with him to watch over him. Munro then set off with Chafe, and they all headed down the trail together, struggling across the young ice, stopped this time by the dog Snooks, which twice plunged through the ice and into the water. They got him out, rolled him in the snow, dusted him off, dried him as best they could, and then set off once more. McKinlay took his leave, think-ing it best to get on his way, since he was the only one going back to camp now, and Bartlett had ordered them not to go any great distance alone.

Mamen now traveled with both Eskimos, Chafe, and Munro. Two miles down the trail, he carelessly banged his injured knee against the sled and once again felt like a helpless cripple. There was nothing to do but go back, because his knee pained him worse than ever; he knew he would not be able to make the trip. He transferred his orders to Chafe, telling him to make the island as quickly as possible and then return right away.

He hated giving this responsibility to Chafe, who was the youngest of them all, and completely unskilled and untested in shouldering responsi-bility. Chafe was competitive and always eager to prove himself, as all of his shooting trophies and awards demonstrated. He and Clam had been training themselves to travel on the ice pack and he had already learned a great deal. But he was still green, and more of a follower than a leader, and besides, it was Mamen's job, not Chafe's. Mamen was the one the cap-tain had entrusted with this mission and the one who should get them there, but he had no choice. And there was no way he was sending Munro.

When they got back to Shipwreck Camp, everyone was surprised to see them, and Munro quickly set out again with the provisions and Clam, now in dry clothing. Again, Williamson worked on Mamen's knee, stretching it and massaging it, making every effort to get it back into the socket, but without success. The kneecap was stubborn and loose and hurt like the devil. Finally, the second engineer managed to slip it back into place and bandaged it with surgeon's plaster to hold it there.

Disheartened and miserable, Mamen holed up in his bed and thought about his chances. He was a burden to everyone now, no matter how much they tried to help and cheer him. He could only pray that his knee would be better by the time Bartlett wanted to leave for the island. He knew Bartlett would want to go before too long, taking the entire company, and Mamen wasn't hopeful that he would be healed enough to join them. If not, he told himself, he would just have to wait there by himself and sit things out until his leg was stronger. Then he would go alone to Wrangel Island and afterward make the journey to Siberia.

He told no one of his plan. Better to wait and travel alone than to hold them back. He could survive easily by himself for a year, with enough fuel and provisions and warm clothing, and in that time he would heal. But then he wondered where he would be in a year—how far he would have drifted, a virtual prisoner of the ever-shifting ice. He could be forced hundreds of miles north and hundreds of miles west, and then he would truly be lost.

But it was better than being a burden. As he wrote in his diary, "I do not wish to be a hindrance and trouble for the others."

ONCE THE DARKNESS set in and the wind howled angrily outside their makeshift igloo, Kuraluk and Kataktovik asked Chafe to pray. Whenever Eskimos found themselves in trouble or in any type of danger, they always prayed, they told him, and sometimes it helped save them. And so they prayed.

Afterward, Chafe told them that if the ice floe were to break up beneath them in the middle of the night, the most important thing was to save themselves and the dogs. Bartlett had always told his men that they should guard the dogs with their lives. "If you lose any of those dogs," he said time and again, "you had better not come back here yourself."

The night seemed endless, and the men awaited the day with enormous anxiety. They awoke to face a trail that was nothing but pressure ridges and open leads of water. Earlier on the second day out, Chafe and the Eskimos had run across a solid wall of ice ridges, growing to thirty feet in height. As they climbed one of them to look for a way through to the other side, a fresh wind swept in and set the ice moving. From their perch, they could see that a lead of water was opening swiftly between their two sleds.

Scrambling down, Chafe and the Eskimos rescued two of the dogs from the water just in time and moved both teams to one side of the lead. But the ice was once more alive beneath them, and new leads opened, splintering in all directions until the three of them—with the dogs and the sleds—were trapped on a floe just twenty-five yards long and ten to fifteen yards wide. Because there was no way to cross, they built an igloo out of loose snow and sled covers and waited out the night.

It was even worse the next day. Slabs of the ice cake had broken off during the night, and now it was two-thirds its original size. They were afraid to move for fear of ending up in the open water, which was everywhere now. They were helpless. The temperature was minus forty-eight degrees Fahrenheit, and they spent another miserable night on the ice floe, huddled together and frightened. It was, as Chafe said, "a night of suffering and waiting—waiting for some good turn that might free us from that awful prison." They prayed the sea would freeze over in the next twelve hours and they would be able to escape.

They had just turned in for the night when there was a deafening crash and the ice split underneath their igloo. Their precious ice floe had collided with another, the impact of which crushed theirs in half. They spent another sleepless night on the now minuscule floe, afraid to move for fear they would lose the only support they had.

When daybreak arrived, they discovered they had been carried within two miles of the island. "Herald Island is only a huge rock four and a half miles in length, and less than a mile in width," observed Chafe, and this was the island they could see at hand. They were sure of it now because just to the west, about forty miles away, was Wrangel, rising up out of the horizon like some grand fortress. Compared to Herald, it looked magnificent.

Chafe turned the field glasses toward land and peered through the lenses, scrutinizing every visible inch of the smaller island. The glasses were strong and allowed him to see even small objects on the earth's surface. He stood there a long time, straining his eyes, running the glasses up and down, back and forth, to this corner and that, but there was no sign of Sandy's party— no sign of life at all.

Chafe took it hard, and he also took it as an omen. "I believe the poor fellows met with the same experience as ourselves, and not being as fortunate as we were to escape, they must have perished in the sea."

Chafe and the Eskimos knew the dangers all too well, having just barely escaped with their own lives from the thrusting, crashing power of the ice. Sandy, Barker, Brady, and Golightly could have been crushed by raftering floes, or lost as the pack suddenly and unpredictably opened, leaving nothing below them but the dark polar sea. They may never have made it to the island. The ice was too forceful, the open water too vast. If one could make it across the fickle ice by some miracle, Herald itself was almost inaccessible, lacking any sort of shoreline, and ringed with imposing cliffs. Perhaps they had gone on to Wrangel Island, as instructed. Or perhaps they were lost. One thing was clear to Chafe now—he and Kuraluk and Kataktovik were not going to make it to either of the islands with these conditions.

Now they tested the young ice that had grown up around their floe, fearing it wasn't strong enough to hold them yet, but deciding to chance it. They couldn't stay stranded forever, so they piled all their provisions on a high ice cake and placed a flag at the center to mark it. Then they grabbed their camping gear and five days' provisions for themselves and for the dogs, loaded the sleds, and headed across the young ice. They separated, traveling twenty yards apart from each other to lighten the weight.

When they reached the main floe, they all breathed sighs of relief. They trudged for five miles before they found their trail again, and by this time it was dark. They made hot tea, fed the dogs, and slept. It was the first full night's sleep they had had in sixty hours.

DAYS LATER, on their way back to Shipwreck Camp, Chafe and the Eskimos found the doctor's party on the icy trail, in bad shape. Mackay and the others had been on the trail for ten days now, and their clothes were frozen as stiff as boards, their boots were worn out and threadbare, and they were clearly on the verge of exhaustion. Mackay did not look well, and he and Murray were man-hauling the sled while seaman Morris stumbled behind them. He had accidentally run the doctor's knife through his left hand while trying to open a tin of pemmican and was obviously in great pain. They said he had blood poisoning, which might be a curable malady back in civilization, but here in the Arctic it could be fatal. The chills and raging fever it brought on meant that Morris was now even more susceptible to the cold and frost. Soon his system would begin to shut down and he would go into septic shock, then die. There was nothing to be done for him.

Mackay and his colleagues were discarding gear along the trail to lighten the sled—mittens, shirts, sleeping bags, notebooks. They had lost half their provisions one night by leaving them on young ice, waking up the next morning to find them soaked with water. They had removed their pemmican from the tins and stored it in bags, and these had gotten wet, turning the pemmican to salt.

Chafe asked Mackay and the others to return to Shipwreck Camp. When that didn't work, he pleaded with them. But Mackay and Murray were as foolishly stubborn as ever. They had made their bed, they told him, and now they were going to lie in it. There was no changing their minds, but Chafe persuaded them at least to accept an ice pick and some seal meat. He offered some of his pemmican, but they refused it. He told them about the conditions surrounding Herald Island and about having spotted Wrangel Island to the west, and hearing this, they changed their course and pointed themselves in the direction of Wrangel. Chafe had no choice. He and the Eskimos dropped back and watched the three weary figures make their slow progress across the Arctic desert, discarding items here and there as they went.

As Chafe and the Eskimos continued back toward camp, they came across Beuchat, a mile or so down the trail. He stood there, utterly lost, a pitiful sight, waiting with the other half of his party's stores. Mackay and the others were coming back for him just as soon as they could, but for now, he waited, unable to walk or move.

Simply to look at Beuchat brought Chafe to tears. His arms hung lifeless at his sides, his hands swollen and bare. He wasn't wearing his gloves anymore because they didn't fit his hands, which were frozen into fists, purplish and swollen, covered in blisters and a thick layer of black skin. Beuchat could not wear his stockings or boots, as his feet were in a similar condition. Instead, his skin boots were only half on his feet, and he was standing on the legs of them, while the soles of the boots were sticking out in front of him on the snow.

He was delirious and in the throes of hypothermia, his breathing slow and irregular, his muscles stiff, his face puffy.

"It's useless for you to try to go any further in the condition you're in," Chafe told him, "so the best thing you can do is to come back with us to Shipwreck Camp."

Beuchat wasn't listening.

"You will be welcomed there," Chafe persisted, "and we will fix you up all right."

He would never live to get there, Beuchat said.

Chafe persevered. He begged and pleaded, but Beuchat was obstinate in his delirium. He had given up all hope of living and expected to die at any time. Mackay, too, had said that he thought Beuchat would be dead by the end of the night.

"Go on," this once elegant Frenchman said at last, "and leave me alone."

Chafe reluctantly decided that there was nothing he could do, and although it was the hardest thing he had ever faced, he must respect Beuchat and let him be.

Before Chafe and the Eskimos left him, Beuchat asked Chafe to give Bartlett a message for him. Please tell the captain that he had absolutely nothing against him. And tell him that it was through no ill feeling whatsoever toward him or anyone else that Beuchat chose to leave the main party.

Chafe promised to deliver the message, and then he, Kuraluk, and Kataktovik shook hands with Beuchat and left him there.

He would die that night, they were sure of it. And Morris, thanks to the blood poisoning, wouldn't last much longer.

THERE WAS ONLY one razor in camp, and McKinlay borrowed it to have a much-needed shave. He washed and then put on a clean suit of underwear, and it was the height of luxury after a month of accumulating dirt and soot and coal oil. He felt quite dapper afterward in pants that shone from the seal blubber and coal oil that coated them. Every seam on the trousers had ripped open and been restitched and patched at least once, but McKinlay was saving his only other pair for the trail.

He was enjoying keeping company with Auntie and the two little girls, who were lonely without Kuraluk. He frequently made malted milk for Mugpi and amused her and her sister by making jumping rabbits and caps out of his handkerchiefs. They would laugh with delight, and it felt good to make them happy.

Now that Mackay was gone, Auntie had begun to look on McKinlay as the official camp doctor. There was little medicine in camp, since the only medical supplies saved from the ship were in a small traveling medical chest that Munro had rescued. For several days now, McKinlay had been treating a deep scratch on Mugpi's chin, just below her lip. Auntie had warned her daughter repeatedly about teasing the cat, but Mugpi couldn't resist. The cat was her playmate and friend, and she loved to chase it about and pull its tail. This time, the cat had gotten its revenge.

On the night before Kuraluk left, Auntie had complained about a pain in her thigh. McKinlay told her to rub it, and she was cured. To further validate his reputation as a miracle doctor, he had given Auntie two cascara tablets for heart pain, and now she was once again feeling fine and thinking him a great "medicine man."

"Thus easily are reputations made!" McKinlay wrote in his diary later that night.

A GREAT DEAL OF OPEN water stopped Clam and Munro from overtaking Chafe and the Eskimos, so they cached their load and returned to camp. Bartlett was trying to give everyone some experience on the trail before they all set out for Wrangel Island. McKinlay, who was in charge of the stores, was the only exception, as he was much more useful to Bartlett in camp and was looked upon by the captain as a confidant and trusted companion.

But for the next trip out, the hapless Malloch joined Munro. They were a pair—between Malloch's blissful carelessness and self-absorption, and Munro's habitual lethargy—and Mamen shook his head as he watched them leave, expecting disaster. Malloch might be a good worker, but he had no clue what he was doing out there; and Munro was one of the most indecisive men he had ever seen.

Their goal was to get to Camp Four, where they would drop off seven cases of dog pemmican and various other stores, including one hundred tea tablets, five pounds of sugar, a half dozen candles, one gallon of alcohol oil, and a stove. Before they left, McKinlay passed out a supply of chocolate to each man from a box he'd found frozen in the ice. They could use it now or save it for the trail; it was up to them.

The temperature was minus forty-five degrees Fahrenheit, and there was a biting wind, which made it seem even colder. It was February 11, one month to the day since the *Karluk* sank, and they were still stalled in the same place.

Soon after Malloch and Munro started on their way, they were held up by a large opening in the ice. They bunked down for the night, and by the next morning, some young ice had formed over the lead. Assuming that it could hold them, they crossed the new ice, tramping over it with their heavy boots, and the dogs, and the sled full of pemmican. Of course the ice wasn't strong enough to hold them. The ice cracked, plunging Munro into the bitter cold water, along with the sled and the dogs. Malloch managed not to get a dunking and soon salvaged Munro, the dogs, the sled, the tent, and their stove, but all seven cases of the pemmican were lost, along with an axe, a pick, and a spade.

They spent a miserable night, cold and wet, with nothing warm to drink because their matches were ruined, and no tent to sleep under because it was frozen stiff as a board and impossible to pitch. It was yet another disastrous and unsuccessful journey, and the routine was becoming disturbingly familiar.

BARTLETT AND MCKINLAY were having a cup of coffee in the galley when Auntie announced that she could hear the sound of dogs barking. They rushed outside, but could see no movement on the horizon. However, every now and then they heard a distinctive bark and an occasional "Mush! Mush!"

They climbed their watchtower, and from there they could see a black spot in the distance. McKinlay grabbed the field glasses and could make out three figures and two sleds. Bartlett and McKinlay met Chafe and the Eskimos as they neared the camp. Chafe told the captain immediately about the condition of Dr. Mackay's party and about what he feared was the loss of Sandy and his men. Bartlett was stunned and didn't speak for several minutes. They walked on in silence, and finally he told Chafe not to say anything to dishearten the other men.

Bartlett tried never to do anything that would discourage the men, even when he knew they were in danger. Instead, he would force himself to laugh, proclaiming, "Why, there is nothing to it," and that he had met with the same thing dozens of times on his trip with Peary toward the Pole.

But he was now gravely worried. Due to the wretched conditions of the ice, it seemed their relaying trips were all for nothing. The most troubling matter, however, was the well-being, and whereabouts, of Sandy's party. He had hoped that they would come back to Shipwreck Camp with Chafe and then they could all make the final march to Wrangel Island together. But Chafe and the Eskimos were back without the first mate.

Even if Sandy and his party had experience with ice travel, Bartlett knew that Herald Island, with its precipitous sides and rocky face, was unreachable. He hoped they would venture on to Wrangel Island instead. In his mind, he urged them there. In either case, it was best that the rest of them leave for land immediately. He decided it then and there. They would take the trail toward Herald Island, in order to pick up the stores cached at Camp Four and to look for Sandy and his men, and then they would go on to Wrangel.

WILLIAMSON HAD BEEN WORKING on Mamen's leg, and now Mamen was finally starting to feel better, although the knee was still swollen and sore. There was hope, thought Mamen. Maybe I will make it after all. Everyone had been taking such good care of him, including Bartlett, who wouldn't even let him take the night watch, and instead took it himself. "You must keep quiet," the skipper told him, "and get well in your leg before you think of anything like that."

They could see Wrangel Island clearly now, west of Herald. It seemed to be much closer than they had expected. Indeed, they now appeared to be drifting closer and closer to the island, although this may have only been some sort of optical illusion caused by the light.

Chafe was back now, along with Kuraluk and Kataktovik. Mamen thought about Sandy and his mates and wondered where they were. He told himself that they had probably gone on over to Wrangel Island, and would be there waiting for him, Bartlett, McKinlay, and the rest of them when they got there. Dr. Mackay's party seemed more hopeless. He pitied them out there, struggling over the ice. "They have a hard time, I should think," he wrote. "I suppose that Beuchat has left this world, poor fellow. He did not know what he did when he left the camp."

Bartlett was emphatic that they all leave soon. Mamen's knee was well enough now so that he had given up the idea of staying in camp alone. He would be able to go with them. And the truth was, he didn't want to be left by himself. He was a brave young man, but he didn't savor the thought of being left behind.

They would divide into four teams, with two teams starting out first, and the other two following within a day. Munro would lead the first two teams—Hadley, Williamson, Breddy, and Maurer on one, and Munro, Malloch, Chafe, and Clam on the other—and Chafe was put in charge of the dogs. Bartlett, of course, was leader of the other two teams. For his own foursome, he chose the pick of the litter—Mamen, McKinlay, and Kataktovik while Kuraluk and his family would travel with Templeman.

There would only be five dogs per sled, since two were too injured to pull and would probably be shot early on for dog food. They had already had to kill Nellie's puppies because they would only be a hindrance on the trail, as young and weak as they were, and to take them along as passengers was impossible. This way, too, they would save Nellie's strength so that she could work. The dog power was too limited for Bartlett's tastes; there were too many injuries, and they were always at one another's throats. So he ordered each man to make a man harness, in case it should come down to having to haul the sleds themselves.

Bartlett made no bones about it. They would be in for one of the hardest struggles men could ever come up against, certainly the hardest struggle any of them had ever faced. The work ahead was tough, tougher than they could imagine, he told them, but if they used care and caution, all would be well in the end.

Malloch was especially careless, and Bartlett lit into him about his habits. The geologist had never dried out his shirt and foot bag from his unfortunate relay trip with Munro, and now they were still wet and already stowed away for the upcoming journey. He would never make it on the trail like that, and Bartlett warned him that he would end up like Beuchat if he wasn't more careful.

All worked to ready themselves, until they were dripping with perspiration. Everyone sewed warm clothing and loaded up the sleds for the upcoming journey. McKinlay was busy issuing stores to Munro, since his teams would set out first. Each sled would bear a load of nine hundred pounds, Munro's carrying five cases of man pemmican, two cases of biscuits, eighty-four tins of milk, and two gallons of oil. Hadley's would carry identical stores, but with six cases of pemmican instead of five.

Munro would lead both of his teams directly to Wrangel Island while Bartlett's teams would head first for Herald to look for Sandy and the others. After they either found them or ascertained that they were not to be found on the island, they would continue on to Wrangel.

At 5:30 A.M. on February 19, all hands were called and everyone hurried about making final preparations. There was much swearing as the men tried to locate last-minute additions to the load—mittens, socks, bags. Tempers were short and the men were anxious, particularly the ones starting out that day. One or two of the crew complained that the weather was bad, trying to postpone the inevitable. They wanted to stay in Shipwreck Camp, where they felt relatively safe and where everything was familiar. Now that the ship was gone, it was home, and they were loathe to leave it.

The weather, however, was fine and clear, a brisk easterly breeze stirring the air. It was a fresh wind, but it would be at their backs, steering them away from their home on the ice, and propelling them, at long last, toward land.

WHENEVER THERE WAS any movement on the ice that sounded even the faintest bit like footsteps, one of the men would shout, "There is a bear outside, Charlie!" And they would all break up into laughter.

Chafe had made the mistake of telling them about the time he and Clam were camped out on the ice and heard what they thought was a bear running outside their tent. Each time Chafe would race out into the night with his gun, there was no bear to be found. It was only later that they learned that ice, grinding at a distance, sent vibrations over miles through the ice floes, which made a thumping sound that closely resembled a person walking, or a bear running at a slow trot.

Chafe knew he should never have told them, but now he brushed it off because the laughter was good for them. It was important they keep their spirits up.

Their faces were frozen and the drifting snow and strong winds made traveling unpleasant. Under Munro's leadership—so different from Bartlett's commanding and confidence-instilling influence—the two teams followed the trail marked by the various sledging parties.

They learned quickly about life on the ice, something none of them but Hadley had experienced before. The surface of the ice was fissured and uneven, interrupted everywhere by large ridges and hummocks, which had formed by lateral pressure. Sometimes they could get around these, and sometimes they had to climb them with pickaxes, forging the way step by careful step. Then they had to wrest the sleds over, being careful not to topple the provisions, and then wrangle the dogs across. It took hours sometimes, and it was the most tedious work imaginable. Everyone was discouraged and frustrated, and there were always one or two who wanted to turn back.

They had ten decent hours of daylight now during which to travel; this helped immensely, especially since the trail was broken up and hard to maneuver, a result of the constant shifting of the ice. There was no earth beneath their feet; the ice was the closest thing they had, and it was disconcerting—and at times, terrifying—to feel the quaking and trembling underneath them. Sometimes the ice made a break of three or four miles in the middle of the trail, and then they had to figure out a way around and across, and then once again try to locate the trail. It could take a day as the men headed east and west until someone found the trail, following it for three hundred yards or so to make sure it was passable. Other times, the trail would disappear altogether, ending abruptly because of ice movement, and they knew to look for it two or three miles to one side or the other. They usually found it to the left, "for the farther away from Wrangel Island the ice was," noted Hadley, "the faster it was drifting to the west."

They ate two meals a day, usually pemmican and biscuits, and they did their cooking over a Primus stove, also using it to melt ice for water so they could make their tea. At the end of each day, they built snow houses that were four feet high by seven feet long, and as wide as the number of people sleeping in them. The houses were just large enough for everyone to lie down close together, which was fine because they had nothing other than body heat to warm themselves.

The first thing that had to be done in building a snow igloo was to find a level field of ice that was heavy and strong. Snow knives were used to cut the blocks of snow. The knife had a steel blade, a foot and a half long, two inches wide, and about a sixteenth of an inch thick. The handles were usually six inches long, but Bartlett had his men lengthen the handles of their knives by lashing hatchet handles to them. Sometimes they also used handsaws to cut the snow blocks, which they carved into different sizes. The bottom of the snow house was made up of large blocks, as much as two feet thick, and the blocks in the upper part of the house were smaller, tapering at the roof.

Inside, they built a bed platform of snow, and they lay skins on top of this. They slept in their clothes, sometimes without any other covering, just so they could be ready at a moment's notice to leap up and run, should the ice give way. Other times they used blankets. Each man also had his foot bag, which, after he removed his skin boots, he would draw over his legs, just up to the knees.

They were always aware of the cold; it was simply an element of their lives now, a constant force. But they never caught pneumonia or influenza or even a head cold because these things did not exist in the Arctic, beyond, as Bartlett said, "the limit of habitation of civilized man."

When it came time to leave Shipwreck Camp, no one wanted to abandon the cat, even though she was, technically, another mouth to feed. Bartlett said Munro's party could take her along, so Maurer and Hadley stitched a deerskin bag to carry her in, and that is how she rode on the trail to Wrangel Island. Sometimes, she traveled in state on the sled, and other times Maurer wore the bag round his neck, and she snuggled safe and warm against him for the journey.

At night, they brought her into the igloo and let her out of her bag and everyone would give her something to eat, one by one, down the line. She lived mostly on pemmican scraps, which she seemed to enjoy. Then, quite contented, she would crawl into one of their foot bags and curl up on top of their feet. Here, she would sleep through the night, until they began again in the morning, when she was once again put into her deerskin bag and tied round Maurer's neck.

In a typical day, they would build the houses, feed the dogs, brush every bit of snow from their clothes, and then crawl inside the igloo through a small door, which was just big enough for them to squeeze through on their hands and knees. They covered this hole with a blanket, packing snow around it to keep out the wind and the cold.

And then they would make tea. Bartlett had written an ode to tea once: "Tea! Thou soft, thou sober, safe and venerable liquid…. I owe the happiest moments of my life, let me fall prostrate." His literary effort was perhaps a bit overzealous, but it was nonetheless a fair summation of how vital a resource tea was to men on the Arctic ice. Its value was inestimable, and after a long day on the trail, in the frigid winter climate, there was nothing that warmed the men better or faster.

They were always keenly conscious of the ice, and the constant danger they faced. Nights were the most harrowing, when they lay in their snow houses, listening to the ominous creaking and grating of the ice. There were no bear jokes then as they rushed out of the igloos now and again, searching for the source of each ear-splitting boom or crash they had heard. They paced up and down in darkness, searching the ice around their camp, on the lookout for dangerous leads. One night, the ice snapped right across the floor of one of the snow houses. Tumbling out into the darkness, the men found they were surrounded by open lanes of water. They walked about gingerly for the rest of the night, trying to keep warm, careful to keep a foothold on the capricious ice.

On February 25, Munro's two parties broke camp and not long afterward were halted by the most enormous pressure ridge they had ever seen.

They estimated it was at least fifty to seventy-five feet in height, and possibly more. The great monster sprawled eastward and westward, seemingly endless in all directions.

They absolutely did not think they would get across it. They split up into different parties, setting out in all different directions to find a way through or around the great ridge. They spent the entire day clambering about the ice, scaling the massive frozen mountain, following its eastward or westward progress for as long as they could. But when they reunited, no one had found a way through.

Discouraged, anxious, and utterly daunted, they returned to the previous night's camp, crawled into their snow houses, and talked things over. They decided to travel east until they came to the end of the pressure ridge—surely, it had an end—or until they found some way across it.

AT SHIPWRECK CAMP, they sewed until they couldn't stand it anymore and enjoyed themselves now that the rest of the company was gone. Truth be told, it was wonderful to be on their own. Of those who remained at camp—Bartlett, McKinlay, Mamen, Kataktovik, and the Eskimo family—only Templeman wasn't particularly easy to get along with, but at least he earned his keep by cooking for them.

Blistering winds forced them to stay indoors. McKinlay dreaded the actual pitching and breaking of camp because the snowdrift had buried everything, including the supply tent, which now lay beneath eight feet of snow. The men didn't go outside if they could help it, but each time they were forced to—as when they needed to feed the dogs in the other igloo—they had to dig their way out of the box house. This meant that they had to delay their departure, not only because the weather was unrelenting, but because the whole object of their staying in camp while Munro's teams went on was to make an inventory of everything they were leaving behind.

The temperature dipped to minus fifty degrees Fahrenheit now, and the windstorm raged. As they huddled in their snow house, McKinlay and the others were worried about Munro's first-division parties. The blustering wind and drifting snow would certainly cause them trouble, and they wouldn't have been surprised to see their comrades return to camp.

At last, on February 23, the snowdrift moderated and the wind died down. The temperature warmed to minus forty degrees Fahrenheit, and they hastened to finish preparations so they could leave camp the next day. They would take three sleds instead of two, Bartlett decided, with Bartlett driving one, and Kuraluk and Kataktovik driving the others. Each would be loaded with pemmican, biscuits, milk, tea, and oil.

Kuraluk and his family led the way with Templeman, with Auntie carrying the toddler Mugpi on her back. Eight-year-old Helen would walk the entire way on foot, sometimes helping her father with the sled. An hour later, Bartlett set out with Mamen, McKinlay, and Kataktovik. They took one last survey of camp, making sure they hadn't forgotten anything, and then Bartlett wrote out a memorandum. "Canadian Arctic Expedition, Shipwreck Camp, Feb. 24th, 1914," it read. "Left Camp 10 a.m. Wrangell [sic] Island bearing SSW... We go with 3 sledges, 12 dogs and supplies for sixty days."

They all signed their names to the document, and then Bartlett placed it in a copper tank and buried it in the snow. It was a way of leaving their mark, and proof that they had been there in this drifting camp, which refused to be claimed for very long. They also left the British ensign flying over the ice.

The camp had been their home for over a month now, giving them refuge—such as it was—after the loss of the Karluk, and they would all feel a certain degree of attachment to the place, long after they'd left it. With the Karluk gone, Shipwreck Camp was the only home they had in the Arctic, and it made that vast, cold world seem less daunting. It had given them familiarity and, as minute as it was, a sense of place. But they had to leave it. As soon as the spring thaw arrived and the ice began to break apart, their temporary home would cease to exist.

THEIR SLEDS WERE heavily loaded and the dogs were almost useless, even though Bartlett had given them all they could eat before they left camp to strengthen them for the trek to the island. Bartlett finally had McKinlay harness up and help pull his sled while he guided and drove the dogs. It was a miserable job—not even time to catch one's breath—but McKinlay was determined to endure.

Mamen's dislocated knee made him too fragile to do much of anything right now, except limp alongside Kataktovik's sledge, doing the best he could to keep up. The knee bothered him constantly and popped out of place again at least once on the trail. He was suffering silently, but everyone knew the pain he was in. He bristled at what he viewed as his own weakness, and there was nothing any of them could do to bring him out of it. Bartlett kept reminding him how indispensable he had already been to them, and what invaluable work he had already accomplished, but it did not help his spirits.

Captain Bartlett was eager to reconnect with the rest of the party, and in a hurry to reach land. Too much had happened already, with the loss of Dr. Mackay's party, and the uncertainty about the fate of Sandy, Barker, Brady, and Golightly. The captain wanted to get his people on any kind of land, and then move on to Siberia as quickly as possible.

Because of his hurry, Bartlett had made the mistake of not building a snow igloo that first night on the trail, and they suffered for it in the tent, which dripped steadily, all night long. It was the coldest night of McKinlay's life. As he lay there, huddled closely between the captain and Mamen, he remembered some advice he had gotten before leaving Scotland: "Wriggle your fingers and toes and wrinkle your face. Give your ears an occasional rub." So he did.

It wasn't long before he heard the captain's sleepy voice. "If you can't lie still, boy, get out."

McKinlay immediately lay still, but it was so cold, he couldn't sleep. Instead, he stared up into the darkness, feeling the cold penetrating skin, muscle, and bones. Unable to stand it anymore, he slipped out of the tent and tramped around in the snow, trying to get the blood back into his limbs.

It was still dark the next day when they broke camp and continued on their way. Sometime in the afternoon, the captain let McKinlay take a turn driving the sled while he walked ahead with his pickaxe, carving the trail. McKinlay had never driven a sled before, but he had watched Bartlett do it and felt fairly sure of himself. He was doing fine until the bow of the Peary sledge struck the edge of an ice hummock and the whole outfit turned over, including the dogs, who ended up in a horrible, snarling tangle. The blood rushed to McKinlay's face as he stood there, cursing them. He went on, each oath worse than the last, until he felt his head might explode with rage. He had never been so angry. He let those dogs have it and, of course, they paid no attention to him. They stood in a crazy, mixed-up pile howling at each other. McKinlay roared at them and the dogs roared back.

Suddenly he looked away and noticed the captain, rolling on the ice, helpless with laughter.

"Oh boy," Bartlett said, "I thought I knew all the swear words, but you have sure taught me some new ones."

McKinlay had to laugh, too, in spite of himself. In his previous life as a schoolmaster, he'd never even uttered a mild "damn," much less the barrage of foul language he'd just unleashed.

Kuraluk had been traveling so far ahead of them that they hadn't even caught a sign of him yet. Now they ran into his party near Camp Five. Just two hundred yards away was the second cache left by Chafe, which had originally contained fifteen gallons of coal oil. Now there were only six, and the others were nowhere to be found, no doubt buried by the snow or swept away by the ice. The loss of oil was such a serious one that Bartlett sent McKinlay and Kataktovik back to Shipwreck Camp the next morning to bring back as much oil as possible. They were also asked to fetch some skins, tea, candles, seal meat, ammunition, leaves from the *Pilot Book,* and chocolate.

For supper that night, Bartlett, Mamen, Templeman, the Eskimos, and McKinlay polished off three mugs of tea each and some pemmican. The Hudson's Bay brand was too fatty, and the Underwood pemmican too sweet, they had decided. Neither tasted good, especially to a novice like McKinlay, but he was glad to have it anyway.

The ice crashed and growled all night long, and cracks opened everywhere, one twenty feet wide, another just behind the igloo where Bartlett, Mamen, McKinlay, and Kataktovik were resting. As the ice churned and crushed, the snow house shook violently, finally forcing the men out onto the ice. There they found, as McKinlay described it, a "world in torment."

With lightning speed, they rescued their supplies and moved them to a safer floe of ice some distance away. "The ice was breaking up into small cakes," McKinlay wrote, "if one did not take care to step on just the right spot on a cake, it would sway & tilt & one had to jump for it. And the darkness made matters worse."

In the midst of it all, Kuraluk's igloo cracked from corner to corner with a great roar, and there was now a lead of water where he and Auntie and the little girls had been sleeping. They nearly lost Mugpi to the water and the ice, but she was rescued and they escaped just in time. For the rest of the night, Bartlett, Kuraluk, Mamen, McKinlay, Kataktovik, and Templeman paced up and down while Auntie and the girls moved into the captain's igloo and tried to sleep.

The racket in the ice continued all day, until the men expected the ice to open up beneath them or to split their igloo in two. Fortunately, neither happened, and finally the ice quieted. McKinlay and Kataktovik then set out on the trip to Shipwreck Camp, making good time in spite of the breaking ice and open water, bringing back fifteen gallons of coal oil, as well as the other items Bartlett had requested.

They started out early the next morning, heavily loaded, both men and dogs harnessed up and pulling the sleds.

A few hours later, Bartlett and his men were surprised to see Munro's two teams traveling toward them. "No way of going through," they told the captain when they reached him, and then Munro described the monstrous pressure ridge. They were going back to Shipwreck Camp, he said. There was no way of getting to the island.

Mamen was characteristically disgusted: "Certainly a fine party .... some fine specimens, indeed." McKinlay and Bartlett were equally unhappy with the chief engineer's decision to turn back.

Bartlett asked the men what they planned to do when they got back to camp, and it was obvious they hadn't thought it through. He was furious and made it clear in the strongest of terms that they were going forward, not back, and the pressure ridge be damned.

The captain then took the lead, followed by Mamen, McKinlay, Kuraluk, and Kataktovik, and they picked their way through three hundred yards of rough ice. Then they made camp on a small floe of smooth ice, the only smooth patch in the midst of miles of the roughest ice they had ever seen. Bartlett ventured ahead, clambering up any peak he could to study the conditions of the trail that lay before them.

All he could see were the immense ridges; the vibrating, tumbling, voracious ice; the sprawling leads of water. The icescape was alive and uneven. They were lucky to have made it this far. But what of Sandy's party? And what of Mackay's? There would be no hope for them if they were caught in this chaos.

And there it was—the imposing ice ridge, or rather a series of immense ridges run together, stretching east and west toward land for miles and miles, like a great, sprawling mountain range, blending into the horizon without end.

Bartlett had never seen anything like it. Neither had Hadley, in all of his twenty-five years' experience living in the Arctic.

There was no end to it. No way of going through. No way of going around.

That decided it. They would have to build a road across.

MARCH 1914

———— • ————

It really does begin to look as if we have all the seeds of disaster for the future.

—WILLIAM MCKINLAY, MAGNETICIAN

Vilhjalmur Stefansson told the *New York Times* that he was certain the missing *Karluk* was fine, as were her men. He could not imagine that they had come to any harm and he conjectured that, most likely, the ship was probably still wandering across the Arctic Ocean, held fast by ice.

In reality, no one knew where the men of the *Karluk* were, or what had happened to them. The Canadian government had nothing to say to the families of the missing men it had hired to staff and crew this expedition. They did not want to raise false hopes, nor did they want to dash any expectations. The *Karluk* might just as well be found as not found, her men alive rather than dead. The official stance was that they had every confidence that the *Karluk* would withstand the elements and her passengers would survive.

Thus, Bartlett's mother, McKinlay's parents and siblings, Mamen's brothers and fiancée, Murray's wife, and all of the relatives of the other men could do nothing but pray and hope for the best and wait for word of their loved ones.

There had been sightings over the past few months—the masts of distant ships, a "white man's" tracks crossing the sea ice, heading toward land. Not much to go on, but there was hope.

Stefansson, however, did not see any reason to act. He was at Collinson Point with the Southern Party, busy outfitting himself to head once more into the Arctic. When he heard news of the sightings, he gave Dr.

Anderson instructions "that no 'relief expedition' be sent out on the ground that the search for a ship placed like the *Karluk* has only infinitesimal chances of success and a vessel so sent out would be likely to be no better situated herself...."

No search party would be sent then. There was, Stefansson said, nothing they could do for her.

THE MEN SURVEYED the road ahead and felt their hearts sinking. It was going to take them a week to break a trail through the ice barrier if it could be managed at all. Bartlett and the Eskimos led the way, marking out the road while everyone else followed with picks, axes, and shovels, cutting their way through the huge walls and boulders of ice. In some parts the ice was pressed into great, soaring ridges eighty feet high, with sheer, vertical faces that would have to be scaled and made passable for men, dogs, and sleds loaded with provisions. "The front of it appeared to us like a great prison wall," said Chafe. "It was as smooth and perpendicular as if built by a stonemason." Some still preferred taking their chances at Shipwreck Camp. Better to live on the fickle ice, they felt, than to have to face this devil.

But Bartlett was determined. The captain sent periodic relay parties back to various camps where stores were cached, to pick up extra supplies, and luckily the weather, although horrendously cold, was calm enough to work in.

If they could just make it over the other side of the massive ridges, they would be safe from shifting ice. These hills stood as the division between the drifting land-fast ice and the floating sea ice. The hills had been formed by the drifting variety, driven by onshore winds blowing against the grounded ice.

It was the slowest, most grueling work imaginable, toiling to make a narrow path, three or four feet wide at most, through three and a half miles of ice mountains. After chipping away at the pass, they then had to make it as smooth as possible so they could drag their sleds over it.

"To look at the ice, one would think it impossible ever to get through it," McKinlay wrote in his diary. "In some parts there are ridges of 60 or 70 ft. in height, some even higher, with a sheer vertical face on one side as smooth as if they had been built by human hands. And we must get over & through & we must camp here until we have made that possible, which will take some days."

The chasms between the ice ridges were as wide as the ridges were tall. All able men climbed up one steep side of the mountain, where they posed precariously, cutting chunks of ice from the top, which they then rolled down into the chasm below until it grew to half the height of the ridge itself. This was harrowing work, and Bartlett was having to train the men as they went.

Afterward, the men "would grade a road down to it, go across and grade up the side of the next ridge; then fill up the next chasm in the same way, and so on till the whole thing was finished," wrote Chafe.

Then they had to maneuver the sledges over the tops of the ridges, which meant fastening a rope to the nose of each sled and hauling it up the incline. Once at the top, they untied the rope, fastened it to the rear of the sled, and lowered it down the other side. Sometimes, they held the sled at the top and ran a rope from it to another sled below. Then as the first one slid down the incline, it would pull the second sled up. At the bottom, they simply moved to the next ridge and repeated the same process all over again until they eventually crossed the entire range.

Bartlett sent Kuraluk and Kataktovik ahead through the rafters to scout out the ice conditions. They reported that the ridges ahead resembled a small mountain range. As Bartlett said, "Building a road across them was like making the Overland Trail through the Rockies."

MALLOCH HAD SOMEHOW gotten his feet frozen again—two toes and the heel of each foot this time. Malloch, being Malloch, didn't tell anyone about it and just laughed it off and tried to ignore it in the hopes that it would go away. The result was that he had gotten himself into a real mess. The heel of the right foot was now a mass of raw flesh, and Mamen clipped off the skin and bandaged it. Malloch was increasingly careless with himself and his clothing, and no matter how many hard lessons he was taught, he never seemed to remember or pay them any mind.

Maurer, too, had a frozen heel, and he and Malloch stayed inside, worthless invalids. Frozen feet were a serious handicap in the Arctic, not only to the victims, but to the progress of the entire party. Mamen couldn't help being annoyed by Malloch's lack of concern for himself. His thought-lessness was starting to affect everyone now, making him unable to work and do his share. But Mamen took care of Maurer and Malloch as best he could. With Dr. Mackay gone, everyone took a turn at doctoring, particularly Mamen, McKinlay, and second engineer Williamson, who seemed to have a special knack for it and didn't appear to be bothered by the more squeamish aspects of the job.

Bartlett ordered Mamen to stay in camp to rest his leg while everyone else toiled over breaking the trail. According to Mamen, the captain told him, "You will have use for it before you and I get through." Mamen's job was to rest. Impatient, he tried to remind himself that this was just as vital to the expedition as carving the trail or moving provisions across the ridges. Bartlett needed Mamen's leg to strengthen and heal so that Mamen could go with him to Siberia. He hadn't told the topographer this in so many words, but Mamen knew it just the same.

Little by little, as the pass across the ridges was being carved out, Bartlett and his men moved camp to the other side. The distance over the ridge was three and three-quarter miles, which seemed much longer given the tremendous trouble they had getting the stuff across. Bartlett himself made three round trips over the bad ice, and fireman Breddy was on his fourth of the day. He was a typically indolent young man, always eager to hand responsibility over to someone else, but now he worked with unchar-acteristic energy and enthusiasm.

Mamen had gone over with the second load and there he had stayed. Kataktovik built an igloo, so Mamen had shelter, and nothing to do but watch the men toil and struggle.

While everyone else worked on cutting the trail, McKinlay, Hadley, and Chafe were sent back to Shipwreck Camp to bring back more supplies. After much trouble in the morning picking up the trail to camp, they ar-rived there later that same afternoon. They loaded eight hundred pounds of provisions onto the sleds the next day, so that when they were finished, the only items remaining in camp were cases of pemmican and various smaller items.

On the return trip, they perspired so much from the exertion that Chafe peeled off all the clothing on his upper body except for a sweater. Finally, they decided to cache part of the load at Camp One so they could make better time. At this rate, it would take them about six days to reach the main party, and they needed to move faster than that. Bartlett would need the dogs, and the manpower.

The next day they lost the trail and searched for an hour before finding it again. When they did, the trail was smashed up and too rough to drive the sleds over, so they had to cut a new one. Hadley was an imposing, irritable figure. He was also, next to Bartlett, the one who knew the most about cutting trails and maneuvering over ice, so McKinlay and Chafe followed his lead.

McKinlay was chopping his way through the towering, raftered ice, when the barking of the dogs made him turn around. He saw Chafe heading for the ice hummock, carrying his axe. Then he saw an impressive young polar bear—ten feet from head to toe—standing behind him. Before McKinlay could say anything, Chafe called out to Hadley, who hastily cut his rifle off the sled. The old man pulled the trigger but the grease on the cartridge was frozen. Their hearts raced as the bear lunged after the dogs. In an instant, Hadley tossed out the useless cartridge, loaded another, and fired a shot, which sank the bear to his knees. A second shot finished him off.

They were busy fixing up one of the igloos at Camp Five when a second bear appeared, much larger than the first and with a beautiful coat. The bear also went after the dogs, three of which had broken free from their harness, and now ran around the bear in circles, barking and snapping at him. The bear sat on his haunches and swung at them with his paws, nearly destroying one of them with a scrape to the back. Hadley, on tiptoe, crept over to the sled and again took down his rifle. At first, he tried to scare the bear off so that he wouldn't have to kill him. But the bear was already terrified of the dogs and paid no attention to Hadley. Finally, to protect the dogs, the old man took aim and fired, wounding the bear, which ran twenty yards before Hadley's second shot killed him instantly.

Later, as McKinlay was retrieving ice to make water for the tea, he heard the dogs barking as before. Standing beside the dead bear was another of the giant creatures. He was still and silent, eyeing the dogs warily as they raced around him. And then came Hadley again—boom—with another shot. The bear ran, dropping about a hundred yards away, but as McKinlay, Hadley, and Chafe started for him, he rose again and loped off, disappearing from view.

The next morning, Hadley found the injured bear three hundred yards or so away from camp. He was gasping for breath, and the old man shot him to put an end to his pain. Hadley cut open the bear to let the gas escape, and then they fed the dogs from the carcass and cut off a leg to take on the trail with them.

When they reached the ice mountains, they paused to take in the scenery. There was no smooth ice to be seen anywhere in that great, vast field before them. The enormous ice boulders, large as buildings, were piled on top of each other, scattered like mammoth rocks on a giant's playground. A parallel series of ridges mirrored these, their icy heads looming above and beyond. They were all you could see for miles and miles. It was through these that the trail had been forged, because there was no way around them.

Bartlett and his men had divided the loads and dragged them across as carefully as they could. The sleds were heavy and awkward, and it was slow going over the ice. To make matters worse, there were deep chasms in the ice at some points. They had to be especially vigilant: one wrong step and a man could plunge to his death. So they moved stealthily, cautiously, dragging the sleds over the ridges, all hands hanging on to them as they slid—as carefully as possible, so as not to get out of control—down the sheer incline on the other side.

At last, the ridge was completely subdued, six days after it was begun. Six days' labor over three miles. They had not yet reached the land-fast ice, but they were over the worst part. Bartlett was anticipating more pressure ridges before they reached land, but for now, the men were relieved. It was calmer on this side of the mountains. There was no wind, only a light breeze; just forty more miles or so, and they would reach the island.

Once they were on the other side of the ridges, the men could see more clearly how the mountains must have formed. Blizzards had pushed the moving ice against and across the stationary ice, which threw the ice into, as Bartlett put it, "fantastic, mountainous formations that are as weird as that astounding picture of Chaos before the Creation that used to ornament the first volume of Ridpath's 'History of the World.'"

They were thankful to be on the other side of them, and the men—particularly the polar novices—could not believe they had won their way through. "It was with a sense of intense relief," wrote Chafe, "that we looked back at this monster wall, and then gazed over the vast, almost level, stretch of ice before us."

They moved in the teams Bartlett had designated when leaving Shipwreck Camp, which meant McKinlay worked with Mamen, Kataktovik, and the captain as they moved forward over the ice, on the last leg of the journey to land.

Land. They could scarcely believe they were so close. Just a couple more days' march, Bartlett said.

McKinlay and Mamen had set out before sunrise with a load for the next camping place, seven miles closer to Wrangel Island. They were working in relays again, carrying forward supplies, which they cached at the next camp, and then returning and bringing the rest. Some of the men remained in the new camp to build the snow houses for that night while the rest of the men went back for the remaining stores. It was a system that seemed to work well.

They still had to cut their way through the ice in spots, but now there was smooth ice in patches, which helped their progress.

Then, as Bartlett had predicted, they came upon another pressure ridge. They knew the drill by now, and everyone set to work—just as they had before—to build yet another road across the Arctic.

FOR SOME REASON that Mamen couldn't figure out, the skipper had turned selfish. He and Kataktovik kept to themselves now, always walking ahead together to break the trail, and in Mamen's opinion, Bartlett couldn't do a thing alone without Kataktovik as his nursemaid.

There had been a large portion of bear meat, their share from the one Hadley had killed, which Bartlett had proposed they wait to eat. While the other teams were enjoying theirs, they waited. Bartlett said he was too tired to cook it and they should save it for later.

Afterward, when Mamen and McKinlay asked for their share of the meat, they were told it was already gone.

"I don't give a damn now till we get the things in to the island," Mamen reported Bartlett as saying, "and then to hell with them, with everybody, I know damn well to look out for myself. I am not going to starve."

McKinlay sensed there were other reasons for Bartlett's strange behavior. Still, it was baffling. Bartlett was usually so generous and fair, and now he seemed to think more of himself. On March 7, the captain got two stoves going just to dry out his own clothes. "I have also been disappointed," McKinlay wrote, "to find that Captain is not sticking to the scale of allowances he himself has laid down; he & Kataktovik today took with them 2 lb. pemmican over the ration."

In their tent, a tin of Underwood pemmican was lasting them only one day instead of the prescribed one and a half days. He could only blame it on Bartlett, since he and Kataktovik were still taking two pounds of the stuff with them when they went out breaking the trail.

Bartlett told McKinlay "'it don't matter' to him, as he is not going to stint himself before he reaches the island. The reason is obvious, of course, he will start off fresh supplied from the island & we will have what is left."

What McKinlay and Mamen could not know was that the captain was thinking ahead of the long journey to Siberia. He knew now that most of his men were too weak to make the journey. He had already been toying with the idea that he himself would make the two-hundred-mile trek to Siberia, and the five hundred miles beyond that of rugged Siberian wilderness. Mamen expected to go, but Bartlett knew Mamen would never make it, thanks to his lame knee.

Better to let his men think the worst of him than to explain that their own survival depended upon his physical condition. He had to strengthen himself for the long, arduous journey that lay ahead. If he was not strong enough, he would never make it to Siberia himself. They, on the other hand, would be waiting for him on an island, which, by all reports, teemed with enough game to get them through. Bartlett and Kataktovik would be crossing mostly ice and wilderness, and there was no telling what chances they would have at obtaining fresh meat. He couldn't very well tell his men they were going to die if he didn't have extra pemmican, so he took the extra rations and let them wonder.

THEY AWOKE ON THE MORNING of March 12, determined to reach land at any cost, even if it meant traveling in the dark.

Bartlett's party was up by 3:00 A.M., and on their way before 6:00. The other teams followed later. At 1:05 P.M., Bartlett, Kataktovik, McKinlay, and Mamen were still in the lead. Kuraluk and his family were not far behind.

Kataktovik was up ahead, breaking the trail, when they heard a shout. He was kicking the snow with his foot. "Nuna!" he was yelling. "Nuna!"

Land.

McKinlay and Mamen gave a cheer for the solid earth—the first they had set foot on since leaving Port Clarence, Alaska, in July 1913.

Wrangel Island was a rocky, barren wilderness, covered in ice and snow. Fifty miles wide and a couple hundred miles long, it lay four hundred fifty miles northwest of Alaska and two hundred miles from the Siberian coast. It was rough country, harsh and unfriendly, almost entirely mountainous, its peaks rising some twenty-five hundred feet. There was little vegetation or wildlife, aside from polar bears and offshore seals. It was, as Chafe said, "the most desolate looking place I have ever seen, or ever wish to see again."

But it was land.

Bartlett and his men stood on the northeast side of the island, where three sandy spits jutted out from land into the water, or, more accurately, ice. They had reached Icy Spit, which was the middle one. The shore was littered with dead trees, their gnarled roots piercing the air. There were mountains and valleys near the coast, and higher peaks rising from the middle of the island. Everything was buried in snow and, except for the mountains, it was impossible to tell the difference between land and ice. There was driftwood everywhere, which was a wonderful sight, because they would need it for fuel before their stay there was over. There was no trace of game yet, but they were hopeful. And what's more, they were safe.

While they waited for their comrades, they began building an igloo for the night, their spirits soaring. The only dark cloud was that there was no sign yet of either Sandy's party or Dr. Mackay's. They had not really expected to see Mackay and Murray, Beuchat and Morris, but they had hoped—and prayed—to see Sandy and his team waiting for them.

They now began to fear the worst. If Sandy was not on Wrangel Island, where was he? Had they even made it to Herald Island? Were they waiting there now? Or were they lost in the ice?

It was too horrible a thought.

They quickly built fires out of wet driftwood so there would be smoke, which would be visible from far away. If Sandy were to see it, or Mackay, it would guide them.

Two miles offshore with the rest of the men, Maurer could see Bartlett's team across the ice, elevated in the distance, and he knew the captain must have reached land. They saw the mountains beyond—not ice mountains this time, but real mountains of rock. And then they could see glorious smoke rising from an unseen fire.

Maurer and the others quickened their pace. Some of the men had thought they would never set foot on firm ground again. They couldn't believe it when they actually did. Dropping on hands and knees, they dug through the snow. Tears welled up when they saw the earth. They picked up the pebbles and rocks and held them, rocks pressed to faces, lips. They had never appreciated the ground beneath their feet until they had lost it and found it again.

They knew it was a temporary shelter. They knew one or all of them would have to make the two-hundred-mile journey over the dangerous sea ice to the Siberian mainland. They knew that even after reaching Siberia there were still hundreds of miles to traverse before reaching civilization where they could send word for rescue. But at that moment, they only wanted to celebrate.

"What a sense of security we enjoyed for the first time in months," wrote Maurer. "We were almost wild with delight. We were on land! No more open leads—no more midnight alarms."

They left their provisions in the open that night, out on the sandspit, and then turned in to their snow houses and slept, for the first time since the *Karluk* was crushed, peacefully and with easy minds.

"No braver man, nor one more loyal to duty than Captain Bartlett, can be found in the world," wrote Maurer afterward. "He shared all the dangers and hardships, and worked as no man ever before worked, for the safety of the men. He kept them in good spirits, and would face any danger for them. I can truly say that if it had not been for Captain Bartlett, not one of us would ever have reached Wrangell [*sic*] Island."

In the week that followed, Bartlett pondered over what to do. The rest of the men busied themselves searching for game, gathering driftwood, returning for provisions cached along the trail, and setting up camp.

There was a story Bartlett knew about a student who was asked to name five Arctic animals. To which the student replied, "Three polar bears and two seal." Even if bears and seals were all they should find on Wrangel Island, they would survive. Bartlett prayed there would be enough of them.

Kuraluk suspected they would not find much game in the vicinity of Icy Spit because there did not seem to be much open water there, and there were no seal holes within twenty-five miles of land. After some exploration, he reported seeing bear tracks, but he determined that there were no reindeer or caribou on the island, probably because the animals would not be able to survive in an area where it would be so difficult for them to get food. He also took a long walk along the western part of the shore, to Berry Spit, looking for Sandy and Dr. Mackay. He returned to camp, having seen no sign of either.

For a long while, the captain had made it clear to his men that there were only two choices—either he would go ahead to Siberia alone or they would all make the trip. At first, Bartlett had been of the mind that they should all go, but some of the men were now too weak or injured, in particular Malloch, Maurer, and Mamen, who would only slow the journey down. The last thing they needed was to pull Mamen with his bum knee, or Malloch with his frostbitten feet, or to wait while some of the slower members of the party hemmed and hawed and asked to turn back to land.

They were on land and comparatively safe, but to wait for a ship would be foolhardy. The whaling industry had declined so drastically in the area that the captain did not expect any ships to come out this far. And although they were off the treacherous ice, there were still hazards to be aware of. They no longer had to worry about being crushed by ice, but now they might freeze or die of starvation if help didn't come before too long.

Bartlett decided that he would have to go for help. He would make his way across Long Strait from Wrangel, and then to the coast of Siberia.

And he would take Kataktovik as his sole traveling companion. The Eskimo was young, but he had some experience of ice travel—certainly as much as anyone else Bartlett had to choose from—and he was used to surviving in the cold and ice. He understood life in the Arctic and he had proven himself to be dependable.

Bartlett knew they would need to travel light and they would need to travel fast. The later in the season, the worse the ice conditions would grow as the ice began breaking up and the leads of open water multiplied.

They had been out of touch with the world for months now. Bartlett needed to get word to the Canadian government as soon as possible.

They had food enough on the island to last the group eighty days, which would get them through most of June. And hopefully by then the birds would be back on the island, and seals would be easier to find offshore.

On March 14, he told the rest of the company his plan. Mamen, as expected, took it the hardest. He had counted on going with Bartlett and made no attempt to hide his disappointment. Bartlett had made up his mind. He knew what was best for the party, which meant Mamen and his injured knee remained on Wrangel Island.

He would take seven dogs and leave the rest. He wanted Mamen, Chafe, and Clam to go back to Shipwreck Camp for the remaining supplies and was leaving Mamen in charge of that short expedition. Small consolation, but a big responsibility nonetheless. Mamen's orders were to bring as many sled loads as possible across the pressure ridges, caching them on the shore side of the mountain range, where the stores should be safe from shifting ice, and easier to bring to land.

Bartlett addressed his men with confidence, which soothed their worried minds and imbued them with hope. But the truth was that the skipper knew as much about Siberia as he knew about Mars. He had the reports of the *American Coast Pilot Book*, but those were several years old, and other than these, he had nothing to go on. He would just hope for the best and figure it out when—and if—he got there.

BY THE MORNING OF THE FIFTEENTH, a blizzard raged outside their igloo. They were forced to lie inside all day, except when Kataktovik had to cut his way out to fix the roof, which was falling in, and to fetch more supplies. The house was buried under several feet of snow, so it took the men hours to make a path out.

And then Mamen put his knee out again, just moving around in the confined space of the snow house. He would not be going with the captain to Siberia. And now, he would not be going to Shipwreck Camp. Chafe had fallen sick with something mysterious, as had Williamson and Templeman, and now Munro and Breddy would go with Clam instead.

The next day, the Shipwreck Camp team was supposed to start out, but the weather stopped them. Mamen once again twisted his knee, knocking the troublesome cap out of its socket, and his comrades spent hours pulling and massaging it back into place.

Because Bartlett was leaving, Munro would be left in charge. Until Sandy returned—if Sandy returned—John Munro, as chief engineer, was next in line and must be left in command of the party, even though Bartlett was worried about this, and rightfully so. Munro's character was questionable. A fundamentally decent man, he was no leader. He had a tendency toward shiftlessness and underhandedness and wasn't always forthright in his dealings with the other men, and there was tremendous bad feeling between Munro and two of the scientists, Mamen and Malloch. They had been at daggers drawn with the engineer for some time, and the captain knew this could cause problems. Munro and Williamson were also at odds, which was worrisome. Williamson was coarse, headstrong, and unpredictable, and he and Munro had never been able to get along. Still, Bartlett had no choice.

The men would be free to settle where they wanted to on the island, but always remaining under Munro's charge. Bartlett divided the group into four parties and instructed each party to make a different camp, so that they would be able to hunt in separate areas and, he hoped, secure more game. He also felt smaller parties would be more manageable and that the men would be more apt to get along. With this in mind, he put some thought into the assignment of party divisions.

The remaining scientists—Mamen, McKinlay, and Malloch—would be separated from the crewmen, except for Templeman, who was to be the fourth member of their group. The Eskimo family would be on their own with Hadley, who, for all his bigoted remarks, felt more comfortable with them than with anyone else. And the crewmen were divided into two separate teams: Munro, Breddy, and Clam; and Williamson, Maurer, and Chafe. This way, the discordant Munro and Williamson could be kept apart. So, too, could Fred Maurer and the usually rash, unruly Breddy, whose caustic tongue had helped make them adversaries months before, when they had worked together in the *Karluk's* engine room.

McKinlay, as provision master, was given the task of allotting supplies to the men while Bartlett was away. Bartlett asked each man to write a short letter home, which he promised to deliver. They brought out pencil and paper and everyone wrote a letter, so that by the time Bartlett left, his pockets were bulging.

On New Year's Day, he had asked his men to avoid anything that would lead them to quarrel with one another. Now he made the men promise again that they wouldn't argue amongst themselves while he was gone. He knew that the Arctic conditions could bring out the worst in men—even in the best of individuals—and he also knew the dangers of this. It was his greatest fear in leaving them. They were a motley crew, with several volatile and unstable personalities in the mix, and he feared that the peace he had managed to maintain would be shattered. So keep up your courage, he told them, live peacefully, and do the best you can.

They promised him they would, and there was little else he could do.

THE THOUGHT OF BEING without their leader was difficult to digest. McKinlay had long ago stopped thinking of Stefansson in that role. He was no leader, as far as McKinlay was concerned. Stefansson was no one with whom he even wanted to be associated. But Bartlett was their leader, without a doubt. They would have died without him.

The captain would take one sled, seven dogs, and rations for sixty days. On Wednesday, March 18, the sled was loaded. Bartlett, Kataktovik, and McKinlay hitched up the dogs while Mamen, from his bed, made a cup of tea for the travelers.

Then Bartlett bid good-bye to everyone and asked McKinlay to accompany him for a while. He had left instructions for Munro, and now he had some for McKinlay. Keep the peace, he asked him, and help Munro. Bartlett had wanted to leave McKinlay in charge instead, but because

McKinlay had no official position on the ship, he couldn't. It was all right with McKinlay, who didn't want the responsibility. He wouldn't have it, he told the captain, for all the tea in China.

"Canny Scot," Bartlett said smiling.

Again he asked McKinlay to assist Munro in any way he could, and to do whatever he could to keep peace among the men. This last was the most important, as otherwise it spelled disaster.

Then they said good-bye and McKinlay watched Captain Bartlett and Kataktovik embark at last on their long and lonely journey. So much rested on their shoulders—the lives of twelve men, one woman, and two little girls. If McKinlay and the rest of them were ever to leave Wrangel Island, Bartlett and Kataktovik were their only hope.

WITH BARTLETT'S DEPARTURE, a sense of great loneliness swept over the camp. They missed the captain and his encouraging words. For his sake and theirs, they tried not to think of what would happen, should something horrible befall him and keep him from reaching land.

The weather didn't help their sinking spirits. The joy of being on land had worn thin, quickly replaced by weariness and illness, and irritation at the relentless raging wind and sweeping drifts. They went outside only for supplies and ice, otherwise remaining in their snow houses for the duration of the day, although, as McKinlay remarked, "it is neither comfortable nor cheerful."

To make matters worse, everyone was complaining of sickness, and the large igloo had been turned into a kind of hospital. Chafe and Williamson were sick but improving while Maurer had fallen seriously ill. Malloch and Templeman were weak and scarcely able to move, and Hadley was suffering from rheumatism. The sick men were afflicted with a mysterious malady, marked by a peculiar swelling in their limbs. No one could figure out what it was.

Munro, Breddy, and Clam had left for Shipwreck Camp to fetch the remaining supplies the day before Bartlett set off. At last they returned, unable to reach camp thanks to the blizzard, the strong drift, and the rough conditions at the ice ridges. Besides, now Breddy was complaining of cold, and Clam was as sick and swollen as his colleagues on Wrangel. As the new invalids moved into the hospital igloo with the rest of them, McKinlay worried about this recent turn of events. The sickness was strange and no one could put a name to it. Each of the victims suffered from great swelling to the face and body, and overwhelming feelings of weakness, which made even the smallest movement difficult.

It was all so discouraging. They had counted on the extra stores from Shipwreck Camp, but with Munro unable to make it there, and with the addition of two more sick men to the company, McKinlay didn't know how they would survive.

There were only 104 pounds left of the dog pemmican, which would only last another week. The animals were placed on short rations, and soon, because they were starving, they began tearing about the camp, eating everything from mukluks to sled lashings, and anything else the men forgot to put away. They also ran off now and then with tins of pemmican, which they tore open and devoured.

On March 20, one of the dogs was racing across the top of the snow hospital when the roof caved in on top of the sick men. Unable to move, they were in danger of being smothered by the great wall of snow now covering them. McKinlay and the others frantically dug through the snow to reach the men, whom they pulled out from the ruins one by one, transferring them to Kuraluk's igloo while the healthy few worked at repairing the roof of the hospital. It was then they discovered that Chafe had frozen all of the toes on one foot four days ago, but hadn't said a word about it to anyone.

They were in even worse shape than McKinlay had suspected.

THE FIRST NIGHT ON THE TRAIL, Kataktovik and Bartlett finished building their igloo and crawled inside, weary and cold, looking forward to a cup of tea. Then they noticed the hole in the boiler. The thought of a hot drink had kept them going during their long first day, but now it seemed they would have to go without.

Then Bartlett remembered something. One Saturday morning when he was a boy, he had been berry picking with his folks. They had taken along a large iron boiler in which to cook their dinner, but when they tried to use it, it leaked. Sure enough, there was a crack in it, and there went dinner. But Grandmother Bartlett pulled out a couple of pounds of hard Newfoundland biscuit, the kind that you could chip a tooth on, and soaked it. Then she took a handful of the soaked biscuit and plastered it inside the boiler, right over the crack. And it worked perfectly.

Now he chewed up a small piece of hardtack. He took the piece of biscuit from his mouth and fixed it over the bottom of the boiler. Perfect. It didn't surprise him a bit. Aside from the berry-picking time, he had once built a dam out of sixty-five pounds of biscuits and used the makeshift plaster to plug up a leak in the bow of his ship. The stuff was handy.

It was a hundred and nine miles from the southernmost point of Wrangel Island to the northern coast of Siberia. But Bartlett and Kataktovik were traveling an extra hundred miles around the shore of the island, heading east and south so that they could pass by Herald Island to look for Sandy and Dr. Mackay's missing parties. He refused to give them up for dead.

Bartlett and Kataktovik were only half a mile from Icy Spit when they were assaulted by the withering northwest wind, which gathered itself up until it was blowing with great ferocity. They couldn't see more than a dozen yards ahead of them, but the snow was hard beneath their feet, which made that part of it good going. They followed the shore to Bruch Spit and stopped in the evening near Skeleton Island, where they built their igloo for the first night.

As they followed the shore the next morning, they strained for any sign of the lost parties. So far, nothing, and conditions along the shore were discouraging. High cliffs plummeted down to the water's edge, obliterating any sign of a beach. They passed Hooper Cairn, built by a group from the United States revenue cutter *Corwin* in 1881. They did not see any game, except for one raven and a lemming.

The wind nearly knocked them off their feet at times, especially when they passed under the high cliffs, where the wind would sweep in after them as if trying to carry them away. A cloud of snow seemed to shroud the island permanently, which explained why Wrangel was always so hard to spot from Shipwreck Camp. The snow, mixed with pieces of shale from the cliffs and bits of sand, sliced at their cheeks, the only exposed part of their bodies.

On the twentieth, two days after leaving Icy Spit, they crossed the spit on the south side of Rodger's Harbour, which was on the southeastern shore of the island. Then they followed the beach, searching for encampments or signs of life. They had hoped that maybe, just maybe, Sandy and his party, or Dr. Mackay and his men had landed here. But again, there were no signs that anyone had been there before them.

Bartlett had planned to head from Rodger's Harbour across Long Strait, and then to Cape North on the Siberian coast, but he suddenly realized that they would have to take another route. The ice off the coast of the harbor had been pressed into great ridges, and valleys of snow swelled in between. Better to stick to the shoreline instead. To build a road through the ice rafters and chasms of snow would be too dangerous and would waste time they didn't have to spend.

Another decision had to be made then—whether to travel on the island or on the shore ice until the point where they had to head out across the sea ice. The surface of the land was rocky and rough, and the ice onshore was so jumbled and uneven that they needed a pickaxe just to get across. They were discouraged and weary, having journeyed for two days, and were still on the island, no nearer to Siberia than they were when they left Icy Spit, or so it felt.

They tried again the next day to conquer the pressure ridges and valleys of snow. Surely, they could find a way through it. But they had to give up. They would just have to find another way.

As they followed the shoreline westward, the conditions began to improve, so much in fact that they made it past Selfridge Bay and all the way to Blossom Point, at the southwest corner of the island.

They were finally on their way, but they had seen no sign of the missing parties. Bartlett prayed that Sandy and Dr. Mackay would find their way to the others, and then he set his sights fully and finally toward Siberia. It would be a long haul across the ice, and he knew, by what he had seen already, what kind of conditions they were in for. The air ahead of them was heavy with condensation, which meant open water. Not a good sign.

And at the edge of the stationary ice, just five miles from land, they ran into a towering ice ridge. It took them two hours to cut a road through.

They slept in their snow goggles, just to get used to them. The goggles were vital out there in the high winds and the snow. A man could go blind without them. Bartlett's left eye was already giving him trouble.

Immediately after leaving Blossom Point, the captain and Kataktovik lost sight of the island. The sky was too overcast, the air too thick, and the snow, once again, covered it in a great shrouded blanket of white.

THE CAPTAIN HAD ONLY been gone a few days when the dissension began. All the team spirit they had developed on the trail was quickly deteriorating and, without Bartlett to keep them at peace, the different personalities began to clash.

Templeman had an unbridled tongue and an almost pathological capacity for lying, not to mention his excessive drug habit, which had been significantly curbed since they had been shipwrecked. Then there was Hadley, with his pungent way of speaking, and his gruff demeanor. McKinlay liked him in spite of it all; he was a good man to have on your side, but McKinlay tried to stay out of his way and to bother him as little as possible. And there was Munro, who seemed completely overwhelmed by his appointed charge.

They began to quarrel, and the thing they quarreled most often and most violently over was food. The first bone of contention was the division of the biscuits. In all, they had five cases, each of which contained five hundred biscuits. Munro and McKinlay consulted and decided to distribute one case and an additional 214 biscuits to each party of four, and one case plus thirty-six biscuits to each party of three. This arrangement actually gave each man in the three-person party one-sixth of a biscuit more than the rest of them, but Williamson and Breddy, who were in one of the three-person parties, couldn't seem to understand this. Instead, they demanded the biscuits be divided evenly among each group, regardless of the size of the party.

There was much complaining, too, about the wasteful way in which the Eskimos were using their provisions. They burned the stove all day and smoked fresh tea instead of being frugal, seeming to think they would fall back on the other parties when their supplies had run out. The men blamed Hadley, who shared their igloo and who should have known better.

They had begun to ration their food now, due to Munro's failure to reach Shipwreck Camp. In McKinlay's tent, McKinlay, Mamen, Malloch, and Templeman cut themselves down to five biscuits per day with one pound of pemmican. They were hopeful, though, because Templeman had taken a short walk earlier and found a feather on the ground. They couldn't tell what type of bird it belonged to, but it was a good sign.

Through it all, McKinlay acted as counsel to Munro, who sought his advice about everything. McKinlay was also called in frequently to smooth over hard feelings or difficulties. He was pleased to be of help, and happy to know that he had some influence with the other members of the party. It made him feel useful, and pleased that he was not letting the captain down.

Per Bartlett's instructions, Munro and McKinlay were planning a search trip to Herald Island to look for Sandy and the rest of his party, leaving in two days, no matter what the weather. Mamen, meanwhile, had asked Munro for permission to go to Rodger's Harbour, seventy miles or so across the island on the southern coast. He would take Kuraluk and they would find the most suitable camping places along the way. Once everyone reconvened at Icy Spit, another attempt would be made at reaching Shipwreck Camp. None of the trips would last more than a week due to the shortage of dog feed.

As the weather mercifully began to improve over the next few days, so did the health of some of the sick men. Williamson and Breddy were soon able to move around a bit. The healthier members of the party even managed, after a great deal of swearing and urging, to get Templeman and Malloch outside into the good weather, to dry out their skin clothing in the warm sunshine. The sky was clear, and for the first time, they could feel the warmth of the sun on their upturned faces. A pronounced wind still chased through now and then, awakening the drifts again, but it remained the best day they had seen in a long time.

THERE HAD BEEN A CHANGE in plans, and now Malloch and Templeman were going with Mamen and Kuraluk to Rodger's Harbour.

They would set up a camp there, and afterward Mamen and Kuraluk would return with the dogs for the journey to Shipwreck Camp. The captain had instructed them, after all, to settle in different camps about the island, and Mamen argued that now was as good a time as any to do so. Mostly, though, he was sick to death of Munro and anxious to get away from him. McKinlay would join them as soon as he returned from Herald Island.

On the morning of March 23, the men loaded up the sleds, and the two parties set out—Mamen, Malloch, Templeman, and Kuraluk for Rodger's Harbour, and Munro and McKinlay for Herald Island.

THE ICE BETWEEN WRANGEL ISLAND and Siberia was always shifting and breaking up beneath their feet. Great leads of water surrounded them on all sides, and each step required thought and caution. It was the most treacherous kind of Arctic travel, and Bartlett and Kataktovik quickly developed a routine to get through it.

The dogs and sled were left beside an open lane of water while Kataktovik headed in one direction and Bartlett took the other, searching for a point where they could cross. When they found one, the person who discovered it would fire a revolver or climb up to the nearest ice ridge and signal, providing the drifting snow and heavy fog allowed him to be seen. The ice didn't always cooperate, God knows, and more often than not the best they could do was to find a place where the ice almost formed a bridge across the water. Then they would hurl the dogs over to the other side and drag the sled quickly as they jumped for it. When this wasn't an option, they searched for a floating ice floe, which they could use as a sort of boat to transport them to the other side.

It was lane after lane of open water and uncooperative ice, and it slowed down their journey immensely. So many times, the sled plunged through the young ice, soaking various provisions, including their sleeping gear. Whenever this happened, the dogs would huddle, terrified, in a pack, which was too much weight for the fragile ice beneath them. Bartlett was taxed, calling on all the experience he had ever gleaned as a Newfoundland sealer and an Arctic explorer.

At night, they spent three quarters of an hour building their igloo and stayed up to mend their clothes, which were ripped every day on the ragged, jutting ice.

At last the weather began to clear. And then, even better, they shot a seal in a lead of open water and Kataktovik retrieved him with a special device the Eskimos used for just such a thing. It was a large wooden ball, with hooks projecting from it, and a handle about ten inches long. Attached to this was a white cotton fishing line, fifty fathoms long, to which Kataktovik sometimes added lumps of ice to add weight and increase momentum. Then he would spin the contraption around by the handle and send it sailing out beyond the body of the seal. Drawing the line in, he would hook the seal and pull it to the edge of the ice floe. Lying down on his stomach, he then edged himself out over the thin ice to the water's edge and hooked the seal. Bartlett stood back several feet, attached to Kataktovik by a rope, and as soon as he had the seal, the skipper would haul them both back onto the solid ice.

The good weather came and went, and the light conditions suddenly worsened. Nights were restless and often sleepless, because the ice was constantly in motion; they were afraid of it splitting beneath them as they slept. To save time, they would forgo making snow roofs for their igloos and would use instead a small tent, which they weighed down with pemmican tins, snowshoes, snow blocks, and a rifle. One night, however, the wind blew so hard that it tore off the canvas roof and they were temporarily buried in snow.

They had numerous problems with the dogs. They chewed through their harnesses and devoured anything in their path—clothing, sled lashings, provisions. Sometimes Bartlett had to tie their mouths to keep them from chewing themselves free.

The dogs were fond of running off when they were unleashed; once the entire team got away from the sledge and started running over the trail, the harness dragging behind, in the direction of the island. Afraid that he and Kataktovik would be stranded without the dogs, Bartlett grabbed a pemmican tin and headed stealthily toward them, pretending to open it. The dogs watched him warily and then, drawn by the pemmican, crept back to him. Bartlett quickly took hold of the harness and they behaved for the next several hours.

One night, Kataktovik gave a great shout as Bartlett was brushing the snow off their sleeping robes. There, at arm's length, was the largest polar bear Bartlett had ever seen. At least thirteen feet from head to toe, the bear fell at the second shot of Bartlett's rifle. He was an old bear, from what they could tell, a stunning creature. The skipper cut off a hind-quarter, which was all they could carry, and they had a generous helping of the raw meat because there was no time to cook it. The dogs had not even noticed the bear, a sign of how exhausted they were, and now they fed the animals all they could eat.

The next morning, they discovered a wide lead that had opened during the night just near their camp. Splitting up as usual, Bartlett heading in one direction, and Kataktovik in the other, they searched to no avail for a crossing point. They met again at the sledge and decided to cross there. A thin layer of young ice filled the lead, too weak to hold a man, but workable, Bartlett thought. He remembered something he had learned among the Newfoundland sealers and figured it just might work here.

Kataktovik was lighter than the captain, so he laid tent poles across the lead—just as Bartlett had seen the sealers do—and crawled over the young ice, a rope fastened around his middle so that Bartlett could pull him up and back if the ice broke.

He reached the other side safely, and then they drew the sledge across with only a few of the provisions. Kataktovik unloaded these on the other side and sent back the empty sled, which Bartlett loaded with a few more items. They did this over and over again until all their stores rested on the other side of the ice. The dogs got across on their own, except for one that had to be tied and pulled across, given his penchant for running away. Then Bartlett lay face down on the empty sled and held on for dear life as Kataktovik threw the rope over his shoulder and ran as fast as he could, pulling Bartlett clear, just as the ice buckled.

Afterward, they began the long, laborious job of digging their provisions out of the steadily drifting snow and loading them back onto the sledge. "It was a slow job," Bartlett wrote. "Everything was white; boxes, bags, sleeping-robes, all the objects of our search, in fact, were blended into the one dead tone, so that the effect on the eye was as if one were walking in the dark instead of what passed technically for daylight. The drifts all looked level but the first thing we would know we would stumble into a gulch of raftered ice, heaped full of soft snow, or a crack in the ice, covered by a similar deceptive mass."

All in all, though, it had been the best day's work they had done since leaving Wrangel Island. And that night, they were able for the first time to build their igloo on a solid and reliable floe of old ice. They had their first good night's sleep, free—at least for the moment—of worry.

BY EARLY AFTERNOON, McKinlay and Munro came within view of Herald Island, about fifteen miles due west of the northwest point of the island. There was no way they could get through. The ice here looked like the bad ice they had encountered on the journey from Shipwreck Camp to Wrangel Island. It had taken the entire party a week to build a road through that, and now, standing on top of a pinnacle of ice twenty-five feet high, they could see that this bad ice stretched clear to Herald Island. It was like some sort of tortuous obstacle course and it took their breath away. A trail would have to be cut to make the ice passable, and they knew, standing there, that it would be impossible for two of them to do it.

McKinlay and Munro trained their binoculars on the island, scanning it for any signs of a camp or of human life. The glasses were powerful, and they could see the island clearly. But there was no Sandy, no Barker, no Brady, no Golightly. There was no Dr. Mackay or Murray or Beuchat or Morris. As far as they could see, there was no life at all. No means of living either. Herald Island was, indeed, little more than rock, and it was impossible to reach. They suspected then that their search was fruitless. Sandy was not there; they could see that.

With heavy hearts, they turned back, retracing their steps, and made camp. They fed the dogs the rest of the pemmican before turning in, determined to return to Wrangel Island tomorrow.

On the way back, one of the dogs collapsed, and McKinlay and Munro had to put him on the sled. They were pitiful creatures now, barely resembling the fine animals they were when Scotty Allen had sold them to Stefansson. They were skin and bones, weak, and voraciously hungry.

Back at Wrangel Island, McKinlay and Munro were told that Mamen and Kuraluk had quarreled on the journey to Rodger's Harbour, and because of it, Kuraluk had returned. No one knew exactly what had happened, and the Eskimo wasn't talking; so they were left to wonder what went wrong. On his way home, though, Kuraluk had shot a female bear and two cubs, which was the first good news they had had since reaching land.

Mamen returned the next day, reporting that he had only gotten as far as Skeleton Island because Malloch was quite ill again and unable to go any further. He had left him there for the moment with Templeman and would return to them after the trip to Shipwreck Camp. He also said that the trouble with Kuraluk was over the building of an igloo, and that he had ordered the Eskimo to return to Icy Spit.

Kuraluk and Munro set out the next day to retrieve the bear meat. It was a hard trip, heading into a gale blowing from the east; they walked against the wind, their eyes creased into slits, nearly shut from the blast of cold. Everyone else was too sick to go, including McKinlay, who was now planning to move into the big igloo with the rest of the invalids.

When Munro and Kuraluk returned, they cooked up a grand feed of bear meat and bear broth in the battered pots Munro and Williamson had made from kerosene tins. It was, to everyone, a welcome relief from the pemmican, which they had been eating every day with little variation.

On the last day of the month, Munro, Chafe, and Clam spent the day preparing to leave for Shipwreck Camp. Munro had decided it was time to make another attempt, now that Chafe and Clam were feeling better. They would take two sleds, the remaining twelve dogs, and their portion of the bear meat. Mamen, meanwhile, was preparing to return to Skeleton Island. He didn't want to leave McKinlay, but Munro insisted he go back to look after Malloch and Templeman. So Mamen was to leave tomorrow, and McKinlay would have to suffer it out in the big igloo with the other sick men.

He could not think when his feet had felt warm. For as long as he could remember, they had been frigidly, fearfully cold, and they were now swollen to twice their normal size, and he was in great pain. When he began feeling unwell, he had prayed that it wasn't the mystery illness that plagued everyone else. But soon McKinlay, too, was unable to rise from his bed. It felt like influenza, with every limb aching, and his body horribly weak. He tried raising himself on one elbow, but was forced to lie back down. It was too much for him.

Now, with Mamen and Malloch moving to Rodger's Harbour, McKinlay was, at the moment, the only "bloody scientist" remaining in camp. He would join them just as soon as he was well again.

THE OPEN LEADS OF WATER were more numerous now. Bartlett and Kataktovik hopscotched across them, unharnessing the dogs and pulling animals and sled across from floe to floe. They stepped lightly, afraid of upsetting everything into the water that now surrounded them.

They had now been out on the sea ice for nine days. That night, there was a clear and beautiful sunset, and the sky was clean and cloudless. Bartlett squinted toward the southwest, trying to make up his mind about something. His eyes were in such pain right now, from the days of travel over the blinding white of the ice, that he didn't trust them. He picked up the field glasses and turned them toward a shadow on the horizon.

Still unsure, he called Kataktovik and pointed. "That land?"

Kataktovik said that it might be. He took the glasses from Bartlett and climbed to the top of a nearby ridge to have a look. He came back down in a moment and handed Bartlett the binoculars. It might be an island like Wrangel, the Eskimo said, but it was nothing bigger and therefore useless. He was already discouraged and this seemed to darken his spirits even more.

"We see no land," he told the captain, "we no get to land; my mother, my father, tell me long time ago Eskimo get out on ice and drive away from Point Barrow never come back."

Bartlett assured him that they would come back, that he had been out on the ice for long distances with Eskimos and they had all returned safely in the end. But Kataktovik was not comforted.

The captain climbed up to the top of the ridge and took another look through the glasses. Kataktovik's eyes were better than his, but he was determined to figure out what this was. In his bones, he was certain that it was land.

In the igloo that night as they made their tea, Kataktovik asked to see the chart they were following. When Bartlett showed him the course they had taken and the place they were headed, the young man's spirits brightened. It still was not Siberia, in his opinion, but probably an island not written on the chart.

Bartlett tried to encourage him. "If you 'fraid," he said, "you no reach land." But Kataktovik remained unconvinced and slept fitfully that night.

The next morning at sunrise, every object seemed more clearly defined, and when Bartlett looked through the field glasses again with rested eyes, he saw the land distinctly.

Kataktovik had already been up on the ice ridge and said excitedly, "Me see him, me him nuna."

"What you think of him?" Bartlett asked. "You think him all right?"

"Might be, might be, perhaps," the Eskimo replied.

Yet Kataktovik still doubted that it was Siberia. Before they had left, both at Shipwreck Camp and on Wrangel Island, Bartlett had gone over the charts with Kataktovik, explaining how to read them and showing him where they were headed. He taught him about Siberia, as much as he himself knew, and how far away it was and how far they would have to travel to reach it, comparing the length of the journey to trips Kataktovik was familiar with, such as Point Barrow to Cape Lisburne, and so on.

But now Kataktovik said it was not Siberia. It couldn't be because his people had told him Siberia was a low land, and the land they were seeing was not. The captain explained that the shore, or tundra, was indeed low in places, but that the hinterland was easier to see right now because it was higher. The Eskimo was still skeptical and, it turned out, fearful. He had heard that Alaskan Eskimo were not well liked in Siberia, and that the Siberian Eskimo would kill them if they came ashore. He was terrified, convinced he was going to die if they set foot on that land. Finally, Bartlett thought, he understood the root of the problem. The captain did his best to reassure the young hunter, but nothing seemed to work.

They set out toward the island or Siberia or whatever it was, Kataktovik wary and depressed, and Bartlett cheerful. The captain knew now that they would be on land in just a few days and estimated it was about forty miles away. With their pickaxes, they crossed the usual open leads of water, skittish young ice, and pressure ridges, and then stopped to make their tea and have some bear meat. The meat was convenient when they were traveling, because they could cut off small pieces now and then on the trail, thawing it by rolling it in their shirts and letting their body heat warm it until it was soft enough to chew.

As they had crossed the ice ridges and raftered ice, with the deep snow valleys buried in between, Bartlett took a hard tumble and hurt his side. His eyes were still giving him a lot of pain and he was in bad shape. But as he lay in the igloo that night, battered and worn, he was in the best of spirits. They were almost to land. Just another few days and they would be there. And then it was down the coast of Siberia, to bring word of the *Karluk* and her men to people who could help them.

APRIL 1914

———— • ————

It's Hell all right.

—JOHN MUNRO, CHIEF ENGINEER

The ice split them down the middle, leaving Chafe alone on his side of the open water, with five of the dogs and all of the food. He could barely see Munro and Clam on the other side of the lead. Munro was shouting, but Chafe couldn't make out the words. The weather was awful—blinding snow and winds—and Chafe's eyes were bad to begin with. All three of the men were nearly snowblind because their goggles had frosted so badly that they'd had to take them off, and their eyes were so weak that they could only keep them open for ten or fifteen minutes at a time. Their eyes were red and swollen and tears ran down their cheeks. They took turns, fifteen minutes each, cutting the trail and leading the dogs while the other two rested their eyes. When it was his turn, Chafe took hold of the handles on the sled and shut his eyes to ease the pain, letting the dogs lead him.

The trail had been especially difficult and easily lost. They were surrounded by vast fields of open water. It was as if the entire Arctic Ocean had opened beneath their feet.

On the night of April 7, they had decided that they had done their best to reach Shipwreck Camp, but that it was impossible. The way was too rough, too dangerous. Their food was getting low, as was their oil, so it was clearly time to turn back to Wrangel Island.

The next day, they were met by open water. Over one lead in particular, Munro and Chafe got into an argument about which way to go. Since Chafe was breaking the trail at that point, he got his way, and they followed his direction. Chafe went first, testing the ice with his pickaxe, and

Munro followed with one sled, with Clam and the other sled bringing up the rear. They were cautious, careful, but suddenly, they heard a shout. Clam had plunged into the water with the sled and dogs on top of him, pushing him under. Down he went into the frigid black depths, again and again. Up for a gasp of air, and then under, the weight of the sled, the supplies, and the dogs pushing him beneath the water's surface.

Chafe and Munro thought they had lost him. Quickly, they grabbed a bamboo pole from the other sled and held it out to him, but just as he managed to get hold of it, the ice gave way under Chafe and Munro, sending them into the water as well. Struggling against the cold, knowing they would not last long in these temperatures, they somehow pulled themselves up onto the ice and once again held the bamboo pole out to Clam. He grabbed it again and they pulled him to the edge of the ice and heaved him out of the water. They were all soaked through by this time, but at least Clam was safe. Freezing, but safe.

They rescued the dogs and the sled next, brushing the dogs off with dry snow to help warm them and prevent them from freezing. The rifle was gone off the sledge, as well as Chafe's binoculars and his treasured camera, both of which meant the world to him. The binoculars, especially, had sentimental value, being the first prize Chafe had won shooting at the long ranges when he was sixteen. He had saved them from the *Karluk,* but still the Arctic Ocean had claimed them.

While Chafe continued to carve the trail, Munro fell to work taking care of the sled and the dogs, whose traces were tangled. Clam stood, dripping wet and miserable, trying desperately to get warm. He had spent about three minutes in the water, long enough to have done some damage, and now he was shivering and shaking, his teeth chattering so badly that he couldn't speak. Chafe gave Clam his mittens, since Clam's had been lost in the water, and changed to a woolen pair. They did the best they could with Clam and prayed he could hold up and somehow get warm when they started moving again.

The open water seemed to have doubled since the accident, and now the ice was crushing and drifting swiftly. A hundred yards later, they were faced with another lead, at least four feet wide. Chafe jumped across, bringing Munro's dog and sled with him. Then he went on ahead while

Munro doubled back to help Clam with his sled. By the time he and Clam reached the lead, it was ten feet wide and growing.

"Work round the water," Chafe yelled to them. And then he told them he would meet them on the other side.

"You can't," shouted Munro, straining to be heard over the howling Arctic wind. "You're adrift from the other side as well."

And he was. He drifted away from them rapidly until they were separated by three hundred yards.

Munro yelled to Chafe to cross the lead where they stood, but the words fell dead against the strong wind. Chafe couldn't hear a word or see well enough to find a way out. Munro headed across the young, fragile ice to reach him, but Clam urged him not to, shouting to be heard. As Munro turned toward Clam, the engineer broke through the ice and landed in the water. He scrambled out and they assessed the situation.

Clam and Munro were on one side of the steadily growing lead with the sled and six dogs while Chafe was on the other side with the food, the gear, and five dogs. They waited an hour, praying the ice would close again, but Chafe drifted farther and farther away. He could not see or hear them anymore and soon he was alone in the ice, the snow, and the howling wind.

The weather was thick all around him. He was completely isolated except for the dogs, stranded on a floe of ice. He could do nothing but wait. He built an igloo, which looked more like a coffin, between fifteen inches and two feet high, but long enough for him to lie down in. Throwing the sled cover on top for a roof, he crawled into the snow shelter feet first, with his head to the door. With little room to move, he lit the Primus stove and boiled a cup of water. Because Munro and Clam had the tea, he put a bit of pemmican in the water to make a kind of soup. It tasted awful, but it was hot and it helped warm him.

He was utterly frozen, and as he lay there he willed himself to stay awake. His clothes were frozen solid now, and he was terrified of falling asleep for fear he would freeze to death. Instead, he lay there, shivering, teeth chattering, thinking about Munro and Clam. Mostly Clam, who had been in the water so long. Chafe knew Clam would most certainly freeze to death if he stayed out there, and he prayed they would head back to Wrangel Island. *Please don't wait for me,* he urged them silently. *Please go on.*

He fell asleep after an hour or so and was awakened two hours later by the ice rising beneath him. He crawled outside and saw that the wind had changed, bringing the ice together now. The floes were joining with such pressure and force that the floe he was sleeping on had buckled. He gathered his things quickly and broke camp, setting out to look for his comrades.

He searched for their trail, but when he didn't find it, he looked for the old Shipwreck Camp trail instead. The dogs were weak and useless so he unhitched them from the sled and led them over the pressure ridge, where he fed them. The one named Bronco ran off, and Chafe was unable to catch him. He returned to the sled and camped for the night, exhausted and discouraged.

Should he leave the sled and try to reach Wrangel without it? This was the next decision to be made. If he left the sled behind, he would have an easier time of it over the fifteen miles of rough ice that waited between him and the ridge, and from there he could make the island in two days. But if the ice opened up again and he was left adrift or if he was lost in a blizzard, then he would need the camping gear, which was on the sled. Without shelter or equipment, he would certainly perish.

In the end, he took the sled because it was the safest way to travel and because they would be able to use the provisions on the island, should he make it back. With his ice pick, he set to work cutting the trail, chipping away for every two or three hundred yards, and then going back for the dogs and the sled. He pressed onward, traveling three miles for every one he advanced. It seemed endless.

He worked for eighteen hours the next day, but only made seven miles. His oil was gone, which meant he couldn't make tea or soup, so he lay in his igloo that night and sucked on ice and snow. One of his feet was disturbingly numb and he knew it was badly frozen. His right hand was also frozen and growing quite sore.

When he awoke the next day, he discovered one of the dogs, Blindie, lying dead in the snow. The dogs had been working constantly for three months now, with only a pound of pemmican per day or every other day. The last several days they had had nothing.

Now with only three dogs left, he unharnessed the rest and tried to move the sled over the ice ridges, through which they had only recently cut a trail on their original journey from Shipwreck Camp. It took him more than an hour to haul the sled over the first grade, which slanted at a sheer and precarious angle, twelve feet skyward. He unloaded the sled, tying a rope to the nose of it and pulling it up from the top of the ridge. But when the sled wouldn't budge, down Chafe went again, pickaxe in hand, to chip away at the incline. Over and over, he did this, until he finally managed to pull the sled up the face. At each incline, he repeated this process until finally he crossed the ice mountains at 10:00 P.M., just an hour after darkness had fallen.

He opened his eyes the next morning to a savage blizzard, which had blown up from the southwest. With a frozen hand and foot, and dogs that now refused to head into the blinding snow, Chafe decided the only thing he could do was leave the sled and head for Wrangel Island. Carrying his blanket, pickaxe, and snow knife strapped to his back, he chained Hadley's dog Molly to his wrist and let her lead him. The other two dogs ran ahead, untethered, following the trail.

Chafe was on the verge of collapse, feeling his knees buckling and his strength giving way. He was so weak now that he could barely walk. Molly pulled him along behind her, and he prayed she knew where she was going. The direction seemed all wrong to him, but he could only trust and be led. They traveled all day like this until it grew dark and he could no longer see. Still Molly kept on.

All he wanted to do was lie down. The first cake of ice that was big enough to shelter him from the blizzard would do. His right foot throbbed and he could barely walk on it. He could no longer feel his heel or one of his toes. His pants were ripped at the seam and one of the legs was filled with snow. His right hand was useless. But Molly kept on, tugging him along, refusing to stop. She was the smallest of all the dogs and by far the best trail hunter, as she had proven when she disappeared from the ship in October and found her own way back. She was Hadley's own pet and had gone along for the ride, just like Hadley, not expecting to be put to work.

And now she worked, pushing on through the bitter cold and the blowing snow toward land. Chafe had no choice but to hold on and follow. To stop for the night in his condition would be fatal. He knew this, and yet he yearned for rest as he bumped along behind Molly, his sore eyes closed against the storm, his blanket clutched against his chest.

THURSDAY NIGHT, APRIL 9, Munro and Clam returned to the island without Chafe. The two of them appeared in the door of Williamson's house, which was the designated hospital. They were a pitiful sight. The men at Icy Spit quickly set about warming them up, feeding them, and making them tea. They were soaked and frozen and both had swollen hands. Munro's foot was badly nipped by the cold, and the soles of Clam's boots were worn bare. His feet were in horrendous condition. They all sat there, drinking tea, and taking turns rubbing his feet and holding them against the warm flesh of their stomachs to restore circulation. While they warmed Clam, he and Munro told the others what had happened.

They could neither see nor hear Chafe after they became separated, and then he just floated off without a sound. Chafe had taken over breaking the trail because Munro's eyes were so bad from snow blindness. And that was when it had happened. It had seemed useless for Munro and Clam to try to take the sled back through the ridges of ice in their poor condition. Both were soaking wet from falling into the water, and Clam was half frozen. They'd left the sled and marked it with a pole and, letting the dogs loose, they headed to the ridges on foot.

That night, they had walked up and down to try to warm themselves, because Chafe had their Primus stove on his sled. He also had the food, so they ate ice and snow to keep their strength up—such as it was. After that, they'd headed south, searching for the pressure ridges. They thought they were lost when suddenly the weather cleared and they found themselves inside the ice mountains. Driven by the thought of food and shelter and dry clothing, they pushed on toward Wrangel Island.

They were hopeful that Chafe would make it back. At least he had the food, the gear, and dogs; if he could just make it across the treacherous ice, they felt his chances were good.

After a day of rest, Munro set out alone to look for him. McKinlay, still bedridden, was too weak to go with him, and no one else seemed eager to go except Clam, who was too badly frozen to move. Munro asked Kuraluk to make him a sled out of skis, and then set out with five days' rations. Unable to find the trail, he returned to camp the next day.

At the main camp, McKinlay and the others remained desperately ill. McKinlay, for one, was living on his milk ration, which, thankfully, he had saved. Everyone else had used theirs up on the trail, and now they were suffering for it. The only thing they had to eat now was pemmican, and the thought of it turned McKinlay's stomach. It was a bitter concoction to face, especially day after day. But then Maurer cooked some bear meat, and for the first time in a long time, they actually enjoyed a meal.

Little by little, McKinlay was able to get up and out of the igloo, trying to help out with the cooking or take a walk. He was not able to go far just yet, but it felt wonderful to be out in the fresh air.

On April 13, a blizzard swept through, blowing the snow into huge drifts. The wind was fierce and chilling, and they all feared for Chafe, lost somewhere on the rough and unpredictable ice pack. Had he followed the same course as Sandy's party and Dr. Mackay's?

Later that night, McKinlay moved into the Eskimos' igloo with Munro and Hadley, and they had just sat down to tea, when they heard a sound at the door. It was Chafe, almost unrecognizable because he was so worn down and battered.

"Is that you, Charlie?" Munro asked, not believing his eyes. They had begun to lose hope, and they were thrilled at the sight of him. "Come in, come in." They ushered him into the igloo and began to fuss over him.

Munro lighted a candle and got the Primus stove working. While the water boiled, Munro and McKinlay took off Chafe's skin boots and socks and trousers. The socks and boots were frozen together in a block of solid ice, and his pants were packed with snow. His hand and foot were covered in blisters, which Munro lanced with a needle and then bandaged. They gave him dry clothes and filled him with hot tea as he told them his story.

It was Hadley's little dog, Molly, who had saved Chafe's life. Chafe was convinced he could not have gotten to Wrangel without her, and he said that after she led him thirty miles over the snow and ice and deposited him at Icy Spit, he fell to his knees and hugged her and thanked her for saving him. Then set her free and watched her run ahead, following at his own slow pace. Molly had brought him home.

The blizzard blew all night and the next morning. McKinlay dug his way out through five feet of snow piled over the door. Other than that, no one ventured outside, and the sick men in the hospital igloo were nearly asphyxiated from the lack of fresh air. Chafe lay in his bed, eyes swollen shut from snow blindness. It would be days before he could open them again.

When the weather cleared, they all turned outside and had a good feed of bear meat. McKinlay took short walks up and down the Spit, trying to regain his strength, and played nursemaid to the invalids, even though he himself was still quite weak. Munro, Chafe, and Clam, meanwhile, tried to doctor their frozen limbs. As usual, Hadley and Kuraluk went hunting in the morning, but also as usual, came up empty-handed. They did spy the first birds of the season, two snow buntings. Day after day, it was the same. They went out in search of game, and always came back with nothing. The men did not know how much longer they could stand the all-pemmican diet, but for now, at least, they had no choice.

IT WAS CLAM'S left big toe that was giving him problems. It had gone gangrenous and would have to be amputated. They had no doctor, now that Mackay was gone, and they had no surgical instruments or anesthesia. The only equipment they had was a skinning knife and a pair of tin shears used to make cooking pots out of empty gasoline cans. The only medicine they had was a small supply of morphine, which they would save to treat him after the operation. Williamson volunteered for the role of surgeon.

They held Clam down, a man on either side to grip his arms, and one to hold his head turned away so that he couldn't watch. The shears were sharp, but not meant for cutting bone, and McKinlay could tell Williamson was struggling with them. He leaned into them more and finally had to kneel against the shears to cut his way through. It was a gruesome sight and McKinlay had to turn away himself to keep from getting sick.

But Clam didn't flinch. Through it all, his lips remained tightly closed and his eyes open. Except for a slight twitching of his facial muscles, he didn't move, nor did he speak. McKinlay had never seen anyone live up to a nickname so well. Indeed, it was the greatest act of bravery and strength he had ever witnessed.

After the operation, some gangrenous area still remained, but Williamson thought it best to wait until Clam had a chance to do some healing before he removed it completely. He felt the sailor had endured enough for the time being, even though Clam, obviously in pain, was his usual stoic and pleasant self, quiet and uncomplaining.

THE WEATHER ONCE AGAIN WORSENED, the wind raging more than ever, the snow blowing heavily. The men were forced back inside, with only pemmican and tea for nourishment. Once in a rare while, they cooked some of the bear meat, which gave them great relief from the pemmican, until finally all that remained were the bones and the fat.

Chafe had been unable to eat at all lately and was still suffering the effects of his ordeal. Both he and Munro underwent Williamson's surgery, Munro having the dead matter cut from his heel, and Chafe having the dead area removed from his toe and heel with a pocket knife. The lingering pain killed Chafe's appetite and he ate only two pounds of pemmican in ten days. As soon as his foot began to improve, though, his appetite came back and his strength returned, until finally he was able to crawl outside of the igloo and sit by the fire.

Williamson decided Clam was now strong enough to have the rest of his toe removed, and once again, he was an exemplary patient. McKinlay didn't know how he endured it, although the toe was clearly causing him immense discomfort. Williamson put silver nitrate on it to form a scab and then he prescribed morphine, which Hadley administered, to dull the pain.

They were a party of cripples, Munro observed, and it was true. Those who weren't frostbitten or maimed were still bedridden and swollen from the mystery illness. McKinlay, recovering from the sickness, was also suffering from frostbite, his nose and hand inflamed and beginning to peel.

McKinlay had become increasingly important to Munro, who relied on his advice. As soon as he was physically able, however, McKinlay planned to join Mamen and the rest of his group at Rodger's Harbour. He was still too weak to travel, but he longed to be with them. "I wonder when I will be able to join my own party," he wrote wistfully, "I hope it will be soon."

For now, though, Munro made it clear that he was thankful for McKinlay's presence. "I don't know how we would get along without him," wrote the chief engineer. He would do whatever he could to detain McKinlay for as long as possible.

Hunger became a hard fact of daily life. They still had no game, except for a couple of bears shot by Hadley and Kuraluk at the beginning of the month. They counted on their tea supply, relied upon it, because it helped wash down the pemmican, even without sugar or milk. For breakfast, they drank a pot of tea with a bite of pemmican each. "Everyone here swears they will do bodily injury to anyone who denies that tea is the finest thing in the world," said McKinlay. "But as I write, I dream of a breakfast of porridge, ham & eggs, tea with sugar & cream, toast & rolls, butter & marmalade."

Every day when the weather allowed, they built a log fire out of driftwood and gathered around it, talking almost entirely of food—of the good meals they would eat when they got back to civilization, foods they missed, foods they loved. They created elaborate imaginary multiple-course dinners and sumptuous fictitious feasts. It somehow helped satisfy the cravings they had for something other than pemmican and kept their minds off their growling stomachs.

"Another month gone is the general greeting today. Let us hope the weather improves quickly now," McKinlay wrote on the last day of the month, "& we will be happy, even though hungry."

ON APRIL 27, Hadley and Kuraluk set out on a hunting trip to the ice ridges, where they hoped to find more game. There was no sign of anything where they were—no seals; no birds, except for the two buntings they had spotted; no fox; and no bears since the first of the month. Their only hope right now was to find another hunting ground. They took three of the dogs with them and struggled across the ice to the range of pressure ridges, wading through snow up to their stomachs.

Once they reached the ridges, they were enshrouded by a thick black fog, "the worst going I Ever saw," said Hadley. Still, they managed to get four seals down by the water. At last. There were bears, too, but the dogs chased them away before the hunters could grab their guns and leave the tent. They followed the great, lumbering beasts for a while, but had to give up because the bears were too far ahead and traveling too fast.

Then both the old man and the Eskimo came down with snow blindness and were forced to lie confined in the tent, helpless to move. Aside from the seals and the escaped bears, there was nothing out there. But if the group were to survive until help arrived—if help arrived—the two knew they would have to cover the area and then cover it again until they found something to eat.

THINGS HAD NOT GONE WELL for Mamen's party as they headed for Skeleton Island. And now Malloch worried him. He was so careless, as he had always been careless with himself, not using sense or logic. He was sick all the time, just as they all were, but he did nothing to help himself. Instead, Mamen had to do everything, the looking after, the feeding, the cleaning up. When Malloch "made water" on himself one night because he could not get up to go outside, Mamen had to clean him. When he wandered off without socks or boots on the snow and ice, it was Mamen who had to look after his frozen feet.

And now the toe would have to be amputated. It was not a challenge Mamen welcomed, but there was no one else. Templeman was sick as well, and there was only Mamen. They leaned on him and expected him to save them. He was tired of it already. They fought like cats and dogs, Templeman's sharp and insulting tongue clashing with Malloch's violent temper. Mamen did not enjoy being in the middle of it. Yet there was no shaking it. Somehow, he alone had been saddled with the responsibility for them. It was not supposed to be this way. "I could swear at and curse Captain Bartlett who has foisted [Malloch] and [Templeman] on to me ... yes I could curse all three of them, for that matter, for they are of no help and of no use, only in the way."

The trip to Skeleton Island had worn Mamen down. He was too tired, too weak, and he was having trouble with his sled. He had started for Skeleton Island manhauling a Peary sleigh, but it was too heavy and the distance too far for him to pull it. So he improvised, something he did skillfully. He took a pair of skis and rope, and some pieces of wood, and made a small sleigh, just large enough to transport his knapsack and footbag, three skins, one bear ham, and the rest of the provisions he was taking with him.

Skeleton Island was just a few square yards in size, lying a hundred yards or less off the east coast of Wrangel Island, halfway between Icy Spit and Rodger's Harbour. Eight miles from Skeleton Island, he parked his sled and unloaded his footbag, one skin, a snow shovel, and a rifle and, carrying these, marched toward camp. When he reached Hooper Cairn, he could see two small dots in the distance and a pillar of smoke. He quickened his pace, and when he was near camp, Templeman came to meet him.

They had had a terrible time of it while he was away. Templeman said they had been near death and had not expected to live to see Mamen again. When he reached camp, he could see the damage. Their igloo was in horrible shape, and their provisions and tools were covered in snow. Malloch was still frightfully ill, and now Mamen felt his own eyes swelling shut, a sure sign of snow blindness. He had some eye medicine in his knapsack, and after Templeman brought him a cup of water, Mamen bathed his eyes. As he lay there in darkness, he agonized over "being in poor shape myself, too," and worried about how it would all end. One thing was certain: he had no time to be sick right now, with Templeman and Malloch unable to care for themselves.

Over the next three days, Mamen was confined to bed, unable to open his eyes. Templeman brought him water three times a day for an eye bath, but it didn't seem to help. In the midst of it all, on April 5, Mamen spent his twenty-third birthday. It was, as he observed, the worst one he ever had.

When his eyes improved, he was able to be of use again. Templeman and Malloch badly needed him, and Mamen hoped he could get them back into shape soon. Templeman's toes were frozen and Malloch's knee was giving him trouble. They were weak as newborn puppies, but Mamen was in rotten shape himself. His eyes, although better, still couldn't stand the light for long, so he was forced to stay inside with the others.

On the tenth, Mamen and Templeman headed the eight miles out of camp to fetch Mamen's abandoned sled. At Hooper Cairn, Mamen sent the cook back to camp with orders to get all the skins out and start on a new igloo. It was the least Templeman and Malloch could do, he thought, while he was manhauling the sled all by himself.

He used snow goggles, but his eyes were in misery. He had to stop and polish the glasses every other minute, or dry them off, and it slowed his progress considerably. Finally, he retrieved the sled, and when he at last made it back to Skeleton Island, he found Templeman and Malloch deep asleep in the old igloo. The skins were nowhere to be seen and there was no sign of a new snow house. He woke them up and gave them both hell. The weather was too cold, they said, and they just couldn't bring themselves to go out in it.

Mamen remained spitting mad. "Yes, I see now what I will have to put up with," he wrote vehemently. "Yes they are both some fine specimens." Mamen made a cup of tea and then started on the igloo himself, building it without any help from Templeman or Malloch, who simply lay watching him. He finished all four walls before turning in for the night, and the next day he built the roof. Then he beat and brushed the skins and transferred everything to the new igloo. He lit the Primus stove and then they settled down to some tea and biscuit and pemmican, not enough food, by any means, but enough to quiet their hunger. Mamen was cook now, just as he was everything else, and for a treat he served up some bear steak from the meat he'd brought with him.

His knee had popped out of the joint again, a worrisome thing, but something he was getting used to by now. He worked at it for half an hour and finally got it back in place.

That was the day Malloch had urinated in his pants because his hands were so frozen that he couldn't use them and the pull string on his trousers was twisted into a knot. Too proud to call for help from the others, he simply lay there and the accident happened. He was barely recognizable now, and as exasperated as Mamen had been with him lately, he pitied the poor fellow.

———— • ————

ON APRIL 13, Mamen heard a sound outside the igloo and clambered out in his stocking feet to find himself face to face with a small arctic fox. Grabbing Malloch's rifle, he shot the fox before it could get away and nabbed their first catch on Skeleton Island.

The wind was blowing stronger now and they found themselves in a full-force blizzard. They stayed in the snow house, bringing a load of ice inside to give them several days' supply of water for tea and soup. But the snow and wind also found their way inside the shelter, until soon the snow was piling up around their beds. "Happily it wasn't so very much," said Mamen, "and it confined itself nicely to my corner of the igloo." He rose from his snow-covered bed and filled up the cracks in the walls and ceiling of the igloo and then brushed off all of the skins and coverings.

The health of Malloch and Templeman wavered all the time, but they were at least beginning to get the color back in their cheeks. Malloch, in a moment of lucidity, was suddenly overcome with gratitude toward Mamen. He had been such a burden, he realized now, and he didn't know how to thank his friend. He could only say simply, "I have you to thank for my life."

Mamen alternated between pity, sympathy, and disgust at Malloch's situation and behavior. Even with moments of improvement, Malloch seemed to be getting worse every day. He was too weak to move, or else he just didn't want to move, and he slept day and night. Mamen suspected him of laziness, and as he repaired Malloch's skin anorak, which was in wretched shape, he found himself lost in thought over it all. "Malloch is certainly a peculiar fellow; I begin to get sick and tired of him; he needs a nurse-maid wherever he goes ... he certainly is the most careless fellow I have seen, both with himself and his clothes...."

To make it worse, Malloch was eating more than his share of the pemmican. He also ate as much as he could of the fox meat while downing soup and biscuits and tea. Neither Malloch nor Templeman made any noise about trying to supplement their precious food supply, and indeed Malloch in particular seemed to believe that as long as they had something to eat, there was no reason to go in search of other food. "We will soon be ruined the way he carries on," Mamen complained. "He must reef his sails if he wants to be with us."

It was a month now since Bartlett and Kataktovik had left for Siberia. This weighed heavily on Mamen's mind. Bartlett's decision not to take him along still stung and the burden of his two companions weighed him down until he feared for his own health and well-being. He prayed Bartlett would win through "so that we can get out of this situation as quickly as possible, for if I have to stay here longer than to the fall, I am sure I will go to pieces, for Malloch and [Templeman] are of little help."

Their oil was gone and now, Mamen felt, it was time to move down the coast to Rodger's Harbour where he hoped to find more game. His leg had given out yet again, but he felt determined to make the trip. Bartlett's instructions to them, after all, had been to move about the island in different camps. They would have better chance for game that way, and besides, someone from the company needed to be at Rodger's Harbour when help arrived. Even though they didn't expect the rescue ship before July, Mamen wanted to be there waiting for it. There was no use staying where they were, and Skeleton Island seemed to fit its name all too well. There was no sign of life or of game for miles.

Before setting out, Mamen penned a note, which he left for McKinlay. He couldn't understand where the magnetician was, as he was supposed to have joined them some time ago. "It is a month now since we left Icy Spit," he confided in his journal. "I wonder if another month will pass before we see McKinlay, or what is the matter with him or the others up there. Has Munro not come back, or is illness raging?"

They left Skeleton Island on the morning of April 24, manhauling two sleds loaded with provisions and equipment. Mamen pulled the heavier one, which carried 225 pounds, while between them Malloch and Templeman pulled the 60-pound sled. They switched at Cape Hawaii, which was half way to Rodger's Harbour, but soon had to stop as Templeman and Malloch were too weak to manage the heavier load even with their combined strength.

Mamen removed some of the provisions from the lighter sled and added them to the heavy one. Then he let Malloch take the light load, while he and Templeman hauled the other. Overheated and overexerted, Mamen peeled his skin shirt off his body for the first time since leaving Shipwreck Camp. He never got any peace. Even now, while he was straining under the larger load, he was playing referee to the other two, who were at each other's throats the entire way to Rodger's Harbour.

They stopped overnight and stayed inside their igloo for twenty-six hours, sleeping and resting. The trip so far had worn them out, and although they longed to keep going, they needed the rest. They had enough food for only two meals each—one pound of pemmican and five biscuits a day. It wasn't very much, especially with their recent physical exertions.

On the road to Rodger's Harbour, in the midst of the snow and ice, they caught beautiful glimpses of spring. Mamen found an arctic willow in bloom, and they heard the unmistakable song of a bird, although they couldn't see him. It was a sign of returning life and "with the spring comes new life for man and beast," wrote Mamen.

Everything seemed more promising when they arrived at Rodger's Harbour on April 27. They found no sign of shelter or game at the harbor, but there was driftwood in abundance, which was encouraging. They could at least build themselves a little cabin to use until the ship arrived.

They put up their tent and settled in. Mamen had planned to send Malloch and Templeman back to Skeleton Island to retrieve the rest of their stores, but Malloch was in immense pain. His feet were far gone with frostbite, and his toes stank of rotten flesh. One of them, in particular, was badly frozen, and Mamen feared he would have to amputate it if it did not show signs of improvement. Yet Malloch still walked about the tent and about camp without his mukluks on. It was the most maddening thing imaginable.

Soon it was clear that the toe had to come off, and Mamen would have to do the cutting. He promised Malloch he would do what he could for him, but without responsibility for anything that might happen afterward—infection or disease. Malloch agreed, and the operation was underway. Mamen cleaned his instruments—a small pair of scissors and a lancet—with boiling water and some antiseptic. Then as Malloch gritted his teeth, Mamen did the job, wrapping the foot afterward in gauze. It had gone as well as it could have, under the circumstances, and Malloch bore up impressively.

They would wait a few days to make the trip to Skeleton Island for supplies, Mamen decided. Malloch needed looking after now, and when it was time to go, Mamen would go in his place. While Malloch remained in the tent and tried to recover from his operation, Mamen and Templeman walked as far as they could along the shore, in search of life. They saw nothing, not even tracks, and the singing bird was now silent. They were too weak to go far, and when Mamen returned to camp, he picked up his diary and wrote, "I don't know what ails me nowadays, I feel infinitely weak, my body has swollen, my legs are worst, they are about twice as thick as ordinarily. I can hardly walk, I move like an old man."

Over the next few days, he began to feel worse and had no choice but to lie inside the tent and rest. Malloch, for once, was feeling better, but Mamen lay in bed, weak and exhausted, listening to the wind that blew through camp and rattled the walls of their tent. He was worried the tent would cave in or fly away at any given moment, but he was helpless to do anything. Luckily, it withstood the gale, and Mamen was able to rest, nourishing himself with a drop of tea, but nothing more. He couldn't stomach the thought of pemmican right now.

It was mysterious, this illness. He had no idea how it had gotten him or what it was. He did not recognize the symptoms. He only knew that he was terribly weak and tired all the time. Malloch was improving daily, but still he relied upon Mamen. He and Templeman both looked to Mamen to lead them now, even as he lay in his bunk, unable to rise or eat.

"I don't know how this will end," he wrote in his diary on the last day of April. "The prospects are certainly not bright."

BARTLETT KNEW LITTLE about the northeast coast of Siberia except for the history. Captain James Cook had made the first examination in 1778, followed by Admiral Ferdinand von Wrangel in 1820. In 1878, Baron Nordenskjöld sailed along the coast in his ship *Vega*, before becoming frozen in at Pitlekaj. In 1881, Lieutenant Hooper of the USS *Corwin* further examined the coast, and it was his descriptions and findings that had made their way into the *American Coast Pilot Book,* better known as the seaman's Bible.

Bartlett had looked at Nordenskjöld's book, *Voyage of the Vega,* aboard the *Karluk,* even though it was written in German and he didn't speak the language. But he studied the pictures, which gave him an idea of what they would be facing once they reached land. There were woods, apparently, which stretched down to the shore at points, and if the pictures could be relied upon, reindeer lived there.

What the *Pilot Book* didn't tell him, though, and what he especially wanted to know, was what the Siberian natives were like and what condition they were in, meaning what food they ate and if they were overrun with tuberculosis, as was the case with other "primitive races" that had come into contact with civilization. It had been thirty years since the last reported data on the region, and so much could have changed since then.

Kataktovik grew more terrified of reaching land. It was the Eskimo, he said. "Eskimo see me, they kill me," he told the captain. "My father my mother told me long time ago Eskimo from Point Barrow go to Siberia, never come back, Siberian Eskimo kill him."

They had been through numerous narrow escapes—cracking ice, shifting ice, crushing ice, ice in motion everywhere. The ice now moaned and thundered and ground its fearsome teeth. The dogs were nervous and uneasy at the noise and almost useless now.

On April 4, Bartlett had left the dogs and sled in camp and then set out with Kataktovik. With pickaxes, they made their trail through the hazardous ice. The captain scaled a tall rafter and scanned the horizon. Up ahead, he could see the field of rough ice and then, lying beyond this, an open lead. On the other side of the lead, lay the ice foot, the Arctic term for the ice "which is permanently attached to the land and extends out into the sea."

He hoped they could reach land by nightfall. As Kataktovik continued cutting the trail, Bartlett went back for the dogs and sled, and they forged their way over the moving ice until they reached the open water. They dragged the dogs across and then jumped across themselves, the lead opening wider all the time. To make matters worse, there was a blizzard blowing, stirring up the snow around them.

But now, at last, they were on land ice. It would be easier from here on out, with only rafters and deep snow to worry about. The snow was so deep that they were forced to don their snowshoes, which they had not yet worn on the trip because the ice conditions were too rough. Bartlett was grateful now to have them because, as he said, "snowshoes are indispensable in Arctic travel and I should as willingly do without food as without snowshoes."

Kataktovik had been in better spirits for the past few days, and now he said that he smelled wood smoke coming from the land. They were not close enough yet for Bartlett to detect the scent himself, but he trusted the Eskimo's keen senses.

Finally, early on the evening of April 4, after two hundred miles traveled and seventeen days' march, they set foot on land. The first thing they saw was the trail of a sled.

"Ardegar," Kataktovik said, which meant "that's good." "Eskimo come here."

Bartlett asked him if, at last, he thought it was Siberia. Kataktovik said yes, he believed so.

"Where we go?" the captain asked him, and Kataktovik pointed east.

That night, they built their igloo, made some tea, and turned into their bunks, thankful to have made it across the treacherous ice pack. Then they slept like the dead. As Bartlett commented, in typically understated fashion, "It seemed pretty good to sleep on land again."

The snowstorm was still raging the next morning, and they could see little of their new surroundings. Later, Bartlett discovered they had landed near Cape Jakan, which lay about sixty miles west of Cape North. The land was swept clean of snow, which made traveling easy across the Siberian tundra. They followed the sled tracks, and after the horrific conditions of the ice, they now felt the worst was over. The dogs were all but useless now, and Bartlett and Kataktovik were feeling worn themselves; but they were encouraged because they had, miraculously, reached Siberia.

Suddenly, Kataktovik, who was walking ahead while Bartlett drove the dogs, stopped in his tracks. He turned back, meeting up with the captain and pointing to distant black objects on the horizon.

"Eskimo igloo," he said. His expression was difficult to read.

"Ardegar," said Bartlett heartily and urged him onward.

They pressed on, until suddenly the skipper found himself in the lead. Kataktovik was a good, strong walker, but now he fell back near the dogs, and then behind them. Kataktovik was certain that the Siberian Eskimo would kill him, no matter what the captain said.

The captain told him it was hogwash and repeated all he had already told him about the hospitality of these people. They were safe now, he said, and these Eskimos would give them a place to dry and mend their clothes. Perhaps they could get some new dogs to help them on their way, or convince one of the Eskimos to go with them on their journey, which would make it easier for them.

Kataktovik would have none of it.

"Maybe," Bartlett said, in one last effort to appease him, "we get tobacco."

The younger man was still skeptical, but at this prospect, he agreed to go on.

The objects on the horizon were soon revealed to be people, who were running about, back and forth, excited at the approach of these strangers. Kataktovik fell back again behind the dogs, and Bartlett told him, "You drive the dogs now and I will go ahead." He saw the relief in the Eskimo's face as he strode forward.

When Bartlett was within yards of the Siberian Eskimos, he stuck out his hand and said in English, "How do you do?" The Eskimos shook his hand excitedly, talking rapidly in a language he didn't comprehend. They greeted Kataktovik the same way, and neither he nor Bartlett could understand a word they were saying. The language of the Siberian Eskimos was vastly different from that of the Alaskan Eskimos, and none of the Siberian Eskimos seemed to speak any English. Although the captain tried to explain who they were and to tell them what had happened and where they had come from, they clearly didn't know what he was talking about.

They were hospitable, though, and quickly unhitched the dogs and fed them, then transferred the sled to a section of their house, where they stored it away from the bad weather. A stooped old woman led Bartlett by the arm, pushing him into her house. His head knocked against the low ceiling and he took a seat in the spacious room. The house itself was built of driftwood and covered with a dome-shaped roof of saplings. Over the entire structure were stretched walrus skins, held in place by ropes and fastened to the ground by heavy stones.

The Chukches, as the Siberian Eskimos were called, did not use snow igloos. Instead, they built these arangas, as they termed them. Inside, this particular living space measured about ten feet by seven and was separated from an outer room by a curtain. In the outer room they kept sleds and equipment, and this was where Bartlett's sled was being stored now.

The old woman fussed about Bartlett, brushing the snow from his clothes with a tool called a snow beater, which was shaped like a sickle. She gave him a deerskin to sit on and hung his boots, stockings, parka, and fur jacket up to dry. As Bartlett pulled on a pair of deerskin stockings she had given him, he looked over at Kataktovik to see how he was faring.

The young man appeared stunned but relieved. He was being fussed over as well, and soon both of the weary travelers were sitting in front of a dish of frozen reindeer meat, "eating sociably with twelve or fourteen strangers to whom, it might be said, we had not been formally introduced."

The Chukches lighted and heated the aranga with a lamp fueled by walrus or seal oil. They also used this for cooking. In all, there were three lamps in this house, which meant the temperature rose to about a hundred degrees.

There were three families, all neighbors, gathered tonight in the aranga to eat and drink with the strangers. They brewed strong Russian tea, which they were terribly fond of drinking. The old woman dusted off her best cups, unwrapping the exquisite china from dirty cloths, and then spat into each cup to clean it.

Bartlett decided to hell with being polite and asked Kataktovik to fetch his own mug from the sled. There was no way he was drinking from those cups, and when Kataktovik brought him his mug, which was much larger than the cups she was offering, the woman looked hurt. He couldn't tell, though, if it was from her disappointment because he was not using her finest china, or her alarm that, given the size of his mug, he obviously planned to drink more tea than anyone else.

After the reindeer meat, their hosts served some walrus meat, which smelled rancid. Bartlett did his best with it, but had to push his plate away. The taste was overpowering and he didn't trust the meat, which was obviously quite old; but Kataktovik loved it.

As far as Bartlett could tell, they thought the captain was a trader; but Kataktovik escaped them and they didn't seem to believe that he was an Eskimo. When he spoke to them in his native language, they held up their hands, touching their faces to say they did not understand him. Then they would speak to him, at which he would throw up his hands helplessly, saying, "Me no savvy."

Using his charts, Bartlett showed their hosts where they had come from and, by drawing pictures, managed to tell them about the *Karluk* and what had happened to her. From what he could learn, he and Kataktovik could expect to run into various settlements of Chukches along the coast. He also learned that there were two kinds of people native to the northeastern Siberian shore, coast Eskimos and deer men. The former made their living by hunting, and many of them traveled between the different settlements in skin boats. The latter were an even hardier people. Tuberculosis had indeed become a fixture in the lives of many of them. When they became too ill or old, they apparently were left to die, their bodies given over to the animals to eat.

All night long, Bartlett listened to the incessant coughing of his hosts and hostesses. The air was stifling, thick with the smoke from their Russian tobacco, and the lamps burning all night long. Bartlett slept fitfully and, finally, unable to stand it any longer, he sat up, barely able to breathe. The lamps had burned themselves out and he tried to light a match, but with no luck. He tore open the curtain and breathed deep breaths of the cold, clean air. His hosts regarded him with some surprise and polite disapproval, but didn't say a word.

The next day, on the anniversary of Peary's supposed discovery of the North Pole, Bartlett and Kataktovik set out toward Cape North, one of the bigger rustic settlements in that vast wilderness.

With luck, Bartlett thought, he and Kataktovik would now reach civilization and wire word to the authorities about the men on Wrangel Island. He thought of them all the time and agonized about how they were. "I wondered how the storms which had so delayed our progress across Long Strait had affected Munro's chances of retrieving the supplies cached along the ice from Shipwreck Camp and getting safely back to the main party, and how the men would find life on the island as the weeks went by …."

IT WAS MINUS SIXTY DEGREES Fahrenheit on the trail, and Bartlett could not remember ever feeling this cold. His hands were frozen, and it was the first time in his life that he was not able to block out the chill or the frost.

Siberia meant "Sleeping Land." It was wild country and the coldest region in the northern hemisphere, with temperatures falling to minus ninety degrees Fahrenheit in deepest winter. Only in the heart of Antarctica did temperatures ever dip lower than they did in northeastern Siberia. It was Bartlett's first experience in this place, and he had never known such bitter, destructive cold or such harsh weather, even near the North Pole.

They were caught in a blizzard on their way to East Cape, the wind blowing with hurricane force, the snow sweeping across the land with enough power to knock a man down. It was frightening, but beautiful. Even as it produced mayhem, the Arctic could create great scenes of beauty. Ice crystals often seemed to float in the air, sometimes forming glowing halos around the sun and the moon. And on quiet nights, there was a rustling in the air that the Eskimos called the "whisper of the stars."

Along the way, Bartlett and Kataktovik ate the usual pemmican and some deer meat given to them by Chukches at Cape North. They had long ago used up their supply of ship's biscuits, most of it ruined by the salt water they had run into on the ice from Wrangel Island. Now Bartlett's arms pained him, and Kataktovik was suffering from sore hands and feet. The sled was growing lighter every day as their food supply diminished, but the dogs still pulled badly. They were worn down and, as Bartlett observed, practically dead on their feet. One of them, Whitey, finally lay down and refused to go on, so they picked him up and put him on the sled. Whenever they stopped at an aranga, Bartlett bartered with the people there and tried to persuade them to sell him a dog or two, but no one seemed willing, or else they had no dogs to spare.

They stayed one night with a man who had seven good dogs, and the man said he would let Bartlett borrow one of them, as long as the captain promised to send it back to him when he reached East Cape. At the next aranga, Bartlett traded his forty-five-caliber Colt revolver for a small but strong dog, which he named Colt.

That night on the trail, he decided not to take any chances and brought both of the new dogs into the igloo. He left their harnesses on and then tied their traces together, Bartlett and Kataktovik both lying on top of the traces to keep the dogs from running off.

The temperature outside was at least fifty below, and sometime in the night, Bartlett woke from a sound sleep, shivering with cold. Opening his eyes, he saw the hole in the side of the igloo where the dogs had broken through. They were both long gone. At daylight, Bartlett sent Kataktovik back to the last aranga where they had gotten Colt to see if he had fled home. Hours later, the Eskimo returned with the dog, but there was no sign of the other one.

That night, Bartlett tied Colt's mouth to keep him from chewing his harness and again brought him into the igloo. Once again, Bartlett and Kataktovik fell into a deep sleep, and once again, the skipper awoke in the middle of the night to a blast of cold. Colt had chewed himself free once more and escaped. This time, Bartlett gave up. The dog was too far away by now, and it was better just to go on their way and not waste any more time on the matter.

Down to four dogs again, they made slow and halting progress. Whitey was recovered enough to limp behind the sled, but he could do little more than that, and the others were broken. That night, after Bartlett and Kataktovik had made their camp, some men arrived with Colt. His owner had sent him back with them to give to Bartlett. The captain was astounded by the integrity of this man. It was, as he said, "one of the many instances of fine humanity which I met with among these Chukches. All honor and gratitude to them!"

THEY REACHED CAPE WANKAREM on April 15. The land was low and rough, and Bartlett and Kataktovik stopped the night at the nicest aranga they had seen so far. It was clean and comfortable, and the people were wonderful. They had heard of these strangers who were journeying along the coast. Men had brought word of them the day before. They seemed honored to have them as guests in their house, and the man proudly brought out copies of old magazines—*National Geographic, Literary Digest, The Illustrated London News*—which he handed to Bartlett.

The captain politely declined, because his eyes were feeling the strain of the hours on the ice and snow, the glare of the sun against all that white, and the stinging snowdrift, which always seemed to follow them. His eyes needed a rest, and he could hardly make out objects or images right now.

THEY PASSED CAPE ONMAN in a blinding snowstorm that made it hard to find their way. Even so, they could see that the place was a ghost town. Empty arangas were the only sign of life left, and they found out later that everyone had moved to Koliuchin Island. They followed the trail, which took them away from land and out onto the ice, until they came to Koliuchin Island.

There was a vast difference in this landscape and Cape Onman. Here, there were signs of prosperity, and a dozen or so arangas littered the area. A young man approached them from one of these, saying, "Me speak 'em plenty English. Me know Nome. Me know trader well. Me spend long time East Cape. You come in aranga. Me speak 'em plenty. You get plenty eat here."

The people of Koliuchin had also already heard about Bartlett and Kataktovik and knew they were trying to reach East Cape. After a dinner of frozen deer meat, cooked seal meat, flapjacks, and tea, the young man who had greeted them said, "I bring you East Cape; how much?" He said he had a good sled and plenty of dogs and could get them there in five days.

Bartlett had forty-five dollars loaned to him by Hadley before he left Wrangel Island.

"How much you pay me?" the man repeated.

"Forty dollars," said Bartlett. He didn't want to part with the money, but it would be worth it to get to East Cape so quickly.

"All right," the boy said. "You show me money."

"No."

"Maybe you have no money."

"I have the money."

This seemed to take care of things for now. Kataktovik was suffering from severe pains in his legs, so they delayed the trip a day so that he could rest. They would leave their sled and possessions at Koliuchin Island, and travel on the young man's sled. When they reached Koliuchin Bay, they were told they would find an American trader named Olsen, about whom Bartlett had heard many tales along the coast.

They left on April 19. Bartlett harnessed their four dogs to the young man's sled. He wanted to take their own sled as well, but the Chukches would get more use out of it, and it would only slow them down now.

Now Bartlett, Kataktovik, and their driver headed back the way they had come, past Cape Onman, and from there followed the shore toward Mr. Olsen's house. Two hours before reaching him, their guide halted the sled and announced that he was not going to East Cape after all.

Bartlett gave the boy five dollars for taking them to Koliuchin Bay, and then their guide turned his sled back toward home and was gone. The captain and Kataktovik were left without a sled and no way of reaching. Olsen, who lived several miles away. That night, however, Bartlett managed to barter with another Chukche who promised to take them to Olsen's place in exchange for a snow knife, two steel drills, and a pickaxe.

In the morning, they harnessed their dogs to his sled, and by noon they reached Olsen, a thirty-eight-year-old trader who knew about the *Karluk*'s expedition, and who offered to hire them a guide. From Olsen's, they headed for Cape Serdze, traveling through Pitlekaj. After Pitlekaj, they arrived at an aranga near Idlidlija Island, where Olsen's guide turned back. They paid him off first with a spade and tobacco, and Bartlett realized he had now given away almost all of his tradable items.

They reached Cape Serdze the following afternoon, with the help of two Chukches and their sleds. It was, at last, beautiful weather. The temperature, while still well below freezing, felt more bearable, and the sun's rays warmed them as they traveled. Once again, Bartlett's eyes suffered from the glare of the sunlight upon the snow. It was bright as a mirror, and he was forced to pull a cap over his forehead, and a hood over this to shield his eyes from the light.

At Cape Serdze, they met Siberia's most famous hunter, a man called Corrigan. He was the most prosperous Eskimo Bartlett had met, and with the assistance of a Norwegian neighbor of Corrigan's, the captain was able to convince Corrigan to take them to East Cape. It was ninety miles distance, but they covered it swiftly. They headed out over the sea ice just off the shore and traversed numerous steep inclines, sliding along at rapid speeds. It was a hair-raising and thrilling experience to travel with Corrigan. He maneuvered the sled as deftly as Bartlett steered a ship. His sixteen dogs were first-rate and one of Corrigan's buddies came along for the ride, bringing his own sled, upon which Kataktovik rode.

They passed great jutting cliffs that stood over a hundred feet high. They made fifty miles the first day, the traveling made easier by the nearly twenty-four hours of sunlight and the improving weather. When the temperature rose the next day to freezing point, it felt almost balmy. Traveling was rougher the second day, however, and they were forced to stay close to the cliffs. This wasn't the safest path; the warming sun was melting the ice and now and then boulders would come crashing down from above them, thundering across their paths.

Corrigan knew very little English, which frustrated him immensely because he wanted to tell Bartlett stories of his exploits. He was a hero, the "daredevil of northern Siberia," and he was proud of his conquests.

He had heard all about Bartlett's adventures from the Norwegian, and he grew more and more animated as he related stories about his own narrow escapes and great hunts. Bartlett could pick up a word here and there, but the more excited Corrigan grew, the less the captain could understand him. Soon he was just nodding at everything the hunter said until Corrigan realized Bartlett had no idea what he was saying. Grabbing his head in despair, the great hunter moved onward in frustration, driving the sled fast and hard over the ice.

On April 24 at 6:00 P.M., Bartlett, Kataktovik, Corrigan, and his friend reached Emma Town, a few miles southwest of East Cape. "The second stage of our journey from Wrangel Island was over," wrote Bartlett. "We had been thirty-seven days on the march and … had actually travelled about seven hundred miles, all but the last part of the way on foot. There now remained the question of transportation to Alaska, and the sooner I was able to arrange for that the better."

AT EMMA TOWN, Bartlett gave his letter of introduction to Mr. Caraieff, the brother of a man he had met at Cape North. Then Caraieff and Bartlett discussed ways to get to Alaska. Because of the season, it was too late to travel by sled and too early to travel by boat. It would be at least June before any ships could reach East Cape. Bartlett could get an Eskimo to take him in a whaleboat to the Diomede Islands, Caraieff said. From there he could take another whaleboat to Cape Prince of Wales. He would have to wait until May to do this, though, and even then the ice conditions would be unpredictable.

Bartlett was most concerned about sending a wire to the government in Ottawa to alert them of the *Karluk* tragedy and of the castaways on Wrangel Island. He knew time was critical, and that every day that passed would be harder on the men he'd left behind. The closest place with a wireless station was Anadyr, at the tip of the northeastern Siberian coast, just off the Bering Sea. This, he knew, was where he would go.

Caraieff helped him make the arrangements. Some local Eskimos would take Bartlett to Indian Point, and from there he would find other Eskimos to take him to Anadyr. Kataktovik would remain at East Cape. He wanted to go to Point Hope, Alaska, he said, even though he had joined the expedition at Point Barrow. Bartlett planned to give him provisions enough to last him until he could get a ship across to Alaska.

And so the plans were set into motion. They would start in the next few days.

Bartlett went to bed feeling satisfied at last. He was on his way for help. He would be there soon and the wireless message would be sent to the authorities; then they would do everything possible to rescue his men as soon as they could. It had been a long, difficult journey, but soon help would be on the way.

The next morning, Bartlett awoke to find his legs and feet rapidly swelling. He was in tremendous pain and could barely move, and he couldn't imagine why. The only thing he could attribute it to was the harsh pounding his legs and feet had received, day in and day out, from the long and tiresome trek across ice and water and cliffs and snow. Whatever it was, though, he had become an invalid overnight.

Three days after Bartlett had arrived at Caraieff's, a distinguished Russian dignitary from Emma Harbor came to visit. His name was Baron Kleist, and he was the supervisor of Northeastern Siberia. The captain was thankful to run into Kleist. He had been hoping to track him down while he was there. Kleist was leaving May 10 for Emma Harbor and asked Bartlett to go with him. This might be faster, they decided, than traveling to the wireless station at Anadyr.

But for now, all trips, and the telegram to Ottawa, would have to wait. Bartlett was utterly helpless. He was no longer in pain, but the swelling in his limbs was so severe that it drained him of every drop of energy. He had lost forty pounds and, aside from the swelling, was dangerously thin. Kataktovik was pale and gaunt as well, and suffering from sharp pains in his legs.

They had won through. They had traveled over seven hundred miles of perilous ice and savage Arctic wilderness. But the journey had beaten them, and now they were too weak to move, too ill to continue. They were completely unable to take those final steps to bring help to the cast-aways back on Wrangel Island.

MAY 1914

———— • ————

I will lift up mine eyes unto the hills, from whence cometh my help. My help cometh from the Lord, which made heaven and earth.... The Lord shall preserve thy going out and thy coming in from this time forth, and even for evermore.

—PSALM 121

DIARY OF BJARNE MAMEN
RODGER'S HARBOUR
FRIDAY, MAY 1.

May has begun with bad weather, I wonder how it will end.

Our biscuits are gone now—it lasted April out—but luckily it won't be so very long now before we can change our diet. The birds will soon be here, and fowl and eggs will taste magnificently after this long and hard diet—pemmican diet.

I feel stronger today, I hope to improve steadily now, so that I may get back my strength and buoyancy.

TRY AS HE MIGHT, McKinlay could not keep the peace. Now Kuraluk was afraid of Hadley, and Hadley was mad at Kuraluk; Munro and some of the others were furious with Hadley; and then Munro had it out with Williamson, who, in turn, seemed to be getting on everyone's nerves and enjoying stirring up trouble. He and Breddy were constantly quarreling and got into a violent argument one day, although McKinlay had no idea what provoked it.

"Tempers seem to be wearing short," he worried in his journal; "what will happen if things ever get really bad, I cannot imagine, for there have been some little signs that some dispositions will not stand much strain."

McKinlay was torn. He longed to join Mamen and Malloch down at Rodger's Harbour. He was feeling stronger now and more able, but not strong or able enough to make the trip. And Munro now relied so heavily upon McKinlay's counsel and opinion that McKinlay would have felt bad leaving him, especially with the tension in camp.

Their oil was running out now, so they could only cook and make their tea over driftwood fires. They traveled two miles from camp to find wood because they had already used up everything in the immediate area. Unfortunately, the weather wasn't always cooperative for fire building, and when it was windy or snowing (as it always seemed to be), they had to forgo the fire and eat their pemmican cold and dry "and dream of better," McKinlay wrote wistfully.

By chance, they had discovered something that made the pemmican more palatable. Williamson was heating a tin of the stuff one day, trying to open it, and without meaning to, overheated one side. The result was a bit of fried pemmican, the taste enhanced 100 percent. From then on, they would fry it in seal oil. They also found they could cook blubber and make it palatable, although no one but the Eskimos could stand to eat it alone.

They enjoyed three or more mugs full of tea for supper. "What a godsend is tea to us these days—the only warm dish we have," McKinlay wrote. "The two hours I had to stand shivering while making it were well worth it."

McKinlay was suffering badly from the cold. Even though the temperature increased, it was still well below freezing. He was used to the biting winds and low temperatures of Scotland, but Wrangel Island was a different place altogether. His parka was riddled with holes, and he cursed Stefansson for purchasing such cheap secondhand furs. He tried patching the garment, but it was beyond repair. Whatever he did, he couldn't seem to keep warm, but he did not complain to his colleagues. There was no one here in whom he could confide, and it wouldn't help matters anyway. Besides, as he said, "we have sufficient of the loud-voiced variety in camp these days...."

The crippled men were progressing nicely, except for Chafe, who refused to eat or take proper care of his heel, which had turned a frightening shade of black. Williamson would have to perform another operation to remove the dead flesh even though the second engineer himself was ailing, showing the same signs as the rest of them—swelling accompanied by great weakness. McKinlay wondered where it would all end. He was suspicious of the pemmican and wondered if it had anything to do with how they were feeling, but there was no way to be sure. And even if it was the pemmican, there was little else to eat.

Auntie did have a way of surprising them with food she had stored and hidden away. She was much better at rationing than the men were, and every now and then she would present a bit of meat from, as it seemed, thin air, and they would have a brief reprieve from the pemmican.

Several flocks of eider ducks flew over the camp, but the men could do nothing because Hadley and Kuraluk had all the guns with them at the ridge. By May 7, McKinlay and the others were beginning to worry about the long absence of the two hunters. Auntie anxiously waited for her husband's return. She was frightened while he was away, especially of bears, so Williamson had moved into the Eskimos' tent to help settle her nerves.

Kuraluk appeared in camp at midnight that same night, dragging a small seal. There were three more at the ridge with Hadley, he said, and the next day the men ate their share of the animal, frying the liver in a pemmican tin as a special treat. It was, thought McKinlay, the tastiest bit of food they had eaten for as long as he could remember.

But then the trouble started. Williamson, who had remained in the tent with the Eskimo family, began reporting things that he claimed Kuraluk had told him. He said that Hadley had tried to persuade Kuraluk to take his family out to the Ridge to live so that they would have fewer mouths to feed. He said that Hadley didn't want any of the rest of them to eat. He wanted to have all the meat for himself so that he alone would survive. Williamson also reported that Hadley had not been hunting at the ridge, instead lying in the igloo all day or taking walks on the ice.

The tempers of the crewmen were already volatile from hunger, and now everyone but McKinlay and Munro cursed Hadley and boasted about what they would do to him, the next time they saw him. The matter of food was not to be treated lightly, and they would teach him a lesson once and for all for wanting to deny the rest of them their share. Trouble had already been brewing, and McKinlay felt a great sense of unease as he listened to the threats against Hadley, who wasn't even there to defend himself.

Munro had a long talk with Kuraluk, who claimed to be afraid of Hadley, although he said nothing regarding the rumors Williamson had been spreading about the old man. Kuraluk did say he thought Hadley was in charge and that he needed to do whatever the old man told him to do. The Eskimo had wrenched his back, which put him in a great deal of pain, but he was planning to head back to the ridge the next day in spite of it, because he was afraid not to follow Hadley's orders.

Nonsense, Munro told him; he should rest his back first and recuperate. Then, when he was well enough to go to the ridge, some of the other men would go with him. They were all eager to get their hands on Hadley even though most of them until now had been content to lie about camp, their greatest exertion being talking of food and complaining about their situation.

The wind blew strong and hard, sweeping over the landscape until the snow was blown away and dark patches of earth remained. It was the season of the midnight sun, and they now went to bed in sunlight at 11:00 P.M.

Kuraluk set out for the ridge on May 11, with Munro, Breddy, Maurer, and McKinlay following the next day. They took with them a mug and some pemmican and followed Kuraluk's trail. The snow was deep with a firm, thin crust, which sustained them briefly with each step before they sank into it up to the thighs. McKinlay went along to keep the peace, dreading the moment of confrontation. "I hope some of the tempers cool somewhat before then," he wrote, "or there may be trouble."

About 10:00, as the men left the snow and crossed onto the level ice field, they spotted a black object on the horizon. From where they stood, it looked like a sled, but they soon decided it was only a piece of ice. After another mile or so, however, they saw that it was indeed a sled. As they approached it, they soon saw a dejected-looking figure, muttering over and over again, "Me no good lose."

Kuraluk was snow-blind and had lost the trail. The men asked him what he wanted to do, but it was hard to understand him. Finally, they all turned back to camp, guiding Kuraluk, who could barely see. McKinlay also felt the onset of snow blindness, his eyes painful and gritty, as if they were full of sand. The light was strong that day and it was impossible to wear goggles because they frosted up so quickly.

The next day, Hadley arrived in camp. No one was happy to see him and the crewmen demanded that Munro come to some sort of understanding with the old man. "Munro's job is not an enviable one," McKinlay observed. "To provoke ill-feeling would probably make our final state worse than at present."

Something had to be done. If Munro didn't take care of it, the rest of the men would—and not so diplomatically. The following morning, the engineer took Hadley aside and had a private talk with him. McKinlay and the others had no idea what they said to each other; but at the end of it all, they seemed to be on remarkably good terms, and Hadley, it appeared, was forgiven. Some of the more vocal members of the group were not pleased about the private discussion and demanded that they have a "round-the-fire" talk to straighten things out. Williamson, in particular, was unhappy that he wasn't privy to their conversation, and upon Munro's return from the meeting, complained bitterly about it.

Afterward, Hadley avoided the second engineer completely. He would never forget that Williamson's antipathy nearly cost him his life. Munro had been heading out there to the ridge to have Hadley killed. He had ordered Breddy to do the deed for him so that he wouldn't have to do any of it himself. If they hadn't come across the snow-blind Kuraluk, Breddy would have done it. And it was all thanks to Williamson's lies.

Some time ago, Hadley had thought Williamson a decent man and had even loaned him his rifle as a sign of his belief in him. That, however, was before he discovered that Williamson was a "contemptable rotter." He had stolen from Hadley's knapsack and he had made threats. In Hadley's mind, the second engineer had been out to get him ever since the ship went down.

"I would not Live another winter on this Island another winter with this push for the Dominion of Canada if the ship fails to show up," Hadley wrote with obvious disgust. "[T]he general plan is to push on for Siberia because it will be Impossible to make a living here any way and Everybody is free to come or stay but if they come They must keep up or get Left."

Munro and Williamson had never gotten along well. But now Munro's dislike for the man had turned into a deep-seated hatred and anger. Williamson had started the trouble and now, Munro could see, he was not to be trusted. The story about Hadley had been a fabrication, from Williamson's lips to their ears. Most of the men had been so quick to believe it that Munro had never asked Kuraluk to back up the story. Munro realized he would have to be careful what he believed from now on.

It was always something with Williamson—he was never happy and always complaining. Williamson still had the rifle Hadley had lent him, but was doing nothing with it. In fact, now that they were on the island, Williamson had done nothing at all—except for performing the operations on their feet. Other than that, he never lifted a finger, never walked when he could ride, never did more than his share, and sometimes did less than that. And now he was trying to stir up trouble.

"It's hard to have to listen to all his hard words," Munro wrote in his diary, "but I have made up my mind not to quarrel with him so must pass it off, but as there is a God above who spares both of [us] to get out of this, it will do him no good. I'LL get my own back. I have come to the conclusion as many others in the party that its that class of Englishman who has got the English despised the world over. When out of this I pray to God I may never see him again."

> *DIARY OF BJARNE MAMEN*
> *RODGER'S HARBOUR*
> *THURSDAY, MAY 14.*
>
> *I for my part was out for four hours today, but I don't know whether it did me any good or not. I swelled up frightfully after it, my whole body, yes, how this will end is hard to tell....*

HADLEY HAD FIRST OBSERVED the glorious midnight sun around May 6, and the men planned to sit up and watch it on the night of May 14. Mugpi turned four years old that day, so there was more than one reason for celebration. They built an enormous fire and sat there shivering and waiting, but at last had to turn in around 11:00 P.M. because of the cold.

The night of May 15, a heavy fog crept in, obscuring the sun and making the temperature drop rapidly. By the next day, snow was falling in thick, white clouds, and the men spent a miserable day in camp. Bad luck seemed to plague them, whether on land or on ice, and they were, as Munro observed, "fed up with everything" by that point, the weather only making things worse.

A nasty case of snow blindness kept McKinlay from making a trip to Skeleton Island to fetch some medication for Chafe and Clam's feet. It was there in McKinlay's knapsack, along with his compass and other belongings, which Mamen was leaving for him. Breddy was sent in McKinlay's place, although that was worrisome because the fireman was notoriously lazy and couldn't be trusted to finish a thing once he had started it.

Clam's toe was healing well, but Chafe desperately needed the medicine. His foot had gone black and was worse than ever, which meant he was forced to undergo another operation, this time to remove the dead matter from his heel. They were all in rotten shape. Maurer was suffering from snow blindness, as was Kuraluk, who was still hoping to return to the ridge as soon as he was better. Munro would go with him so that they could bring back the remaining seal meat.

Everyone was sick of the pemmican and barely able to hold it down. It made them sick to eat it. They had sixteen days' full rations of pemmican left now, so they figured they would be fine until the middle of June. But they knew they had to get some fresh meat soon or they would be in dire straits. On May 23, things looked up when Hadley and the Eskimo saw the first seal on the ice near camp. Kuraluk shot but missed, his snow blindness hampering his vision.

The weather had been miserable all month, and it stayed that way. The snow blew continuously, and Munro had to postpone his trip to the ridge until further notice. Kuraluk now announced he did not want to go back to the ridge, and Munro knew he could not force him, even though they were all reliant upon Kuraluk, who was their most skilled hunter. Munro knew he had to handle him delicately, being careful not to offend him for fear he would give up the hunt altogether. So he said nothing about Kuraluk's decision to stay in camp, confiding instead to his diary, "It's Hell to be in a position like this."

Then, to everyone's surprise, Kuraluk left Icy Spit the morning of the twenty-fourth with a loaded sled. He didn't say a word to anyone before leaving, just headed off alone, tight-lipped and stoic.

In the midst of it all, Breddy returned from Skeleton Island with a note to McKinlay from Mamen. He and Malloch and Templeman had been sick and suffering and now they had moved down to Rodger's Harbour. It was a long way across the island to the harbor—about seventy miles—but no one else at Icy Spit was willing to make the trip. So McKinlay would go alone. Munro would have to keep his own counsel because Mamen, it was clear, needed McKinlay's help more.

ON PEARY'S 1909 NORTH POLE expedition, while the admiral and Bartlett and the rest of the company were camped at Cape Sheridan, Dr. J. W. Goodsell and Professor Donald B. MacMillan had opened a case of books and afterward had come down with violent colds. The books were brand new and had never been read or owned by anyone. But they had, apparently, been packed by a man infected with a cold.

Bartlett thought of this as he sat in the relative comfort of civilization and suffered through an excruciating case of tonsillitis. Because of the extreme cold and remoteness of the region, germs didn't breed in the Arctic as they did in more normal climates. All those weeks trudging through the Arctic freeze, snow, blizzards, without so much as a sniffle, and now he was laid up in East Cape, his throat ulcerated and searingly painful. He coated it with peroxide and alum, which eventually seemed to help, and finally he began to recover.

On May 10, he was still weary and ill, his legs and feet mysteriously swollen. His host, Baron Kleist, was eager to leave for Emma Harbor, aware that, this late in the season, a thaw might come at any moment, breaking up the ice and thus complicating their sled journey. Bartlett could only walk with difficulty, but he decided it was time to depart. It would be best not to wait for a complete recovery, since there was no telling how long it would take for him to be fully well again.

Kataktovik saw them on their way. Bartlett gave him the rifle they had carried with them from Wrangel Island on their journey across the ice and wilderness, and then he shook hands with him and thanked him for all he had done. Bartlett was indebted to Kataktovik, and he told him so, thanking him for showing faith in their mission and having faith in Bartlett himself. He had been the bravest and most reliable companion the captain could have wished for and Bartlett was loath to say good-bye.

The distance from East Cape to Emma Harbor was about the same as the distance from New York to Boston. With dog drivers and sleds, Bartlett and Baron Kleist set out shrouded in fog in the late afternoon of May 10. Both the captain and Kleist were worried about how they would feed the dogs; the season was so advanced that the meat supply of the Eskimos was beginning to thin. Bartlett left his own dogs at East Cape.

They traveled through heavy snow and thick fog, rain, and wind, frequently finding their way strictly by compass because they were unable to see ahead of the dogs. They often drove on through the night, stopping at different arangas for nourishment and rest.

Bartlett had searched for an oilskin coat at East Cape because his fur clothing was soaked through from his trek across the Siberian wilderness. There were none that fit him, though, and now he worried about the effect these wet clothes would have on his already poor health. He rode on the sled most of the time, to save his strength, and this gave him a chance to appreciate the views of this wild and unfamiliar country. But now and then he walked alongside to keep warm. His legs were still weak and swollen, and before long, he would climb back onto the sled.

They were headed for a reindeer settlement on the north side of Saint Lawrence Bay. On their way there, they lost all sense of direction, and as the dog drivers stopped to discuss the matter, the dogs suddenly took off, tearing across the ice with the sled flying along behind them and a surprised Bartlett hanging on for life. The path was scattered with boulders and blocks of ice, and Bartlett expected to be thrown or crushed at any moment. Somehow, though, they reached the bottom of the hill and the dogs stopped, having momentarily lost the scent they were chasing—the scent of reindeer.

But there, miraculously, was the trail they were searching for, bringing them right into Saint Lawrence Bay. Here, Bartlett saw his first Siberian reindeer. Because spring was arriving, the animals had just moved to the coast from parts inland, where they had wintered.

Bartlett and his group were averaging five miles an hour on the journey, and the captain admired the skill and speed of their dog drivers. He didn't speak their language, but they were colorful and memorable characters, especially a man called "Little," who was a strapping four feet tall. Little promised Bartlett that he would take him in his motor boat to Alaska, if the captain wasn't able to find a ship at Emma Harbor. Bartlett was touched by the offer and promised Little he would take him up on it if it came down to that. Little knew a few words of English and was quite proud of his vocabulary. "Me make baron speak 'em plenty English," he boasted many a time.

They crossed the ice of Saint Lawrence Bay and followed its shores east. From there, they traveled over land for several miles before setting out on the ice again, this time in the mouth of Mechigme Bay. They stayed along the coast, heading west, and then drove across the opening of the bay until they reached the southern shore. After this, they traveled the coast for twenty miles and then once again took a land route to Neegchan.

The air was heavy and damp with fog, and Bartlett was often wet to the skin. At the various arangas, he was often able to give his clothes a cursory drying, and was thankful for this because his throat was still vulnerable and not yet healed. He feared a relapse. Once you became sick or injured in the Arctic, it was twice as hard to heal as it would have been in the rest of the world. Resistance was down, and without adequate shelter from the cold the body's immune system wasn't able to do its job, which meant a relatively simple thing—tonsillitis or a cut on the finger—could soon prove fatal.

They were, at last, entering the final stretch of their journey. Here and there, they stopped for tea at one of the many arangas they happened upon, and in one of them an Eskimo told them he had heard of a whaler at Indian Point with a master named Pedersen. From the description, Bartlett decided it was the same man whom Stefansson had originally hired to skipper the *Karluk*. Bartlett knew Captain Pedersen personally, and the fact that he was in the area was good news. Perhaps Bartlett could persuade the captain to take him to Alaska.

————— • —————

MAMEN HAD SKIED in the mountains, taken leaps off of cliffs, trekked through snow, scaled rocks, jumped over precipices and ravines. He fell down, he got injured, he got back up again, he kept going. He was invincible. He could do anything and nothing could touch him.

Because his father was the leading funeral director in Christiania, Norway, Mamen had grown up with death, but it never changed his feelings of immortality or his firm belief in his own strength. Life just kept going, and he knew it always would.

But now he had to face the thought that he was weak, that Malloch was ill, that Templeman was helpless, and that the entire expedition might not make it off Wrangel Island alive. The worry never left him. Yet despite his own weakness, he roused himself every day to take care of his two comrades, both of whom had come to depend almost entirely upon him.

Malloch was still careless with his feet. Just as they were beginning to improve he would get them frozen again. He was in a kind of delirium now. He seemed helpless and unable to look after himself, but remained blissfully ignorant of the harm he was doing to his body. Mamen would find him outside in his stocking feet, wandering through the snow, a smile on his face.

When Mamen was too weak to tend to him, Templeman took over, washing out bandages for the patient under Mamen's supervision. But mostly it was Mamen, who went without food, giving his rations to Malloch and tending to his feet when he was negligent, which was all the time. He was, as Mamen said, "the worst man I have seen in all my life ... he will never do what other people do, it is no use telling him anything...."

It made Mamen all the more determined to see Malloch and Templeman better and to beat this mystery illness himself. Though still weak, he was improving steadily and soon hoped to have his usual good health back. Their biscuits were gone, the pemmican inedible, but they looked forward to the birds that would soon be there and the eggs they could already taste in their vivid imaginations.

The weather could not have been worse. Hurricane-like gales blew snow and threatened to rip their fragile tent apart. Unable to build a fire and with little oil for the Primus stove, the men often had to content themselves with dry meals—plain pemmican, with no tea to wash it down. They had enough pemmican to last them through the rest of the month but it was now their only food source and, as Mamen observed, "Half a pound of pemmican twice a day is certainly not much, but we have to be glad as long as we can get that. It will soon be better times for us, as soon as the birds come from the south and the ice breaks up the sun will shine for us day and night."

As the gale raged on for days, the men were confined to the tent, making tea sparingly on the Primus stove out of water from melted snow. There was only enough for a mouthful for each one of them, and the flavor was unsavory; but they were grateful for a hot drink.

When the weather cleared at last, leaving sunshine, Mamen left the tent to go walking. He headed down the sandbank, but his strength soon gave out and he was forced to turn back.

On May 5, as the wind began to blow about the tent and another blizzard swept through the camp, Mamen lay inside and remembered the people he had left behind when he'd set out on his quest for adventure a year ago.

If only he didn't feel responsible for Malloch and Templeman. He felt such a mix of pity and disgust for them, forever fluctuating between anger and sympathy. Malloch's left foot got so frozen that Mamen held it against his own stomach for three hours just to get life into it. He was sick of taking care of this man. "I for my part will have nothing whatever to do with him now," he wrote. "He will have to take care of himself. I have ruined myself completely for him."

The night before, Mamen had dislocated his knee yet again, but he had no time to think of himself. It was always Malloch now, and although he was not about to turn his back on his comrade, no matter what his private threats, he did ask the geologist for a written statement noting that Mamen had done all he could to help him, and that Malloch alone was to blame for the condition in which he found himself. But the worst part of it was that Mamen was overexerting himself on his colleagues' behalf. They were too weak to make the trek to rejoin the main party, but Mamen sorely needed the help. "I feel weaker and weaker for every day that goes," he wrote on May 6. "I don't know how this will end, if only McKinlay could come down here and help me a little. This hard work with Malloch and Bob has been too much for me."

Mamen had taken over most of the culinary duties since the three of them had been together, but Templeman helped when he could, making Mamen hot water for tea or giving him a nip of whiskey to brace himself up. It was little comfort, though, and Mamen felt hopelessly and wretchedly alone. Malloch had been a good friend, but now he wasn't himself. No one would have recognized this shell of a man, rambling and defeated, helpless as a child. The strapping, cocky fellow he had been only weeks before had vanished. Mamen knew that Malloch might lose his right foot and possibly the left one from frostbite, and now he worried that Malloch was losing his mind as well. "It is getting darker and darker for us instead of brighter," Mamen wrote. "Malloch has truly been of much trouble to me from the beginning, I have worn myself out for him.... I suppose he is kind of insane. He became a little sad when I told him tonight in what condition his feet were, but right afterwards he was merry and content, They are not any worse than my fingers were, he said.... I sincerely hope that I may have strength to keep him alive until we are taken from here. It is my only wish...."

Malloch had not had many moments of mental clarity lately, but whenever he did, he realized that if it were not for Mamen, he would be dead. He was grateful then and, although such moments were fleeting, Mamen at least knew that Malloch was aware of all he was doing for him.

Mamen prayed for the weather to clear and for his strength to grow so that he could make the trip to Skeleton Island for the supplies they had left behind. But by May 10, Mamen's body was so swollen from head to toe that he had a great deal of trouble moving around. The strange thing was that he was not in pain—he just found it difficult to move or walk. There was no rest to be had, though, and on the eleventh he operated on Malloch's finger, cutting off the nail and the dead skin. He hoped he would not have to remove the finger itself, especially since it appeared that one of Malloch's toes would have to be amputated before long. To make matters worse, they were nearly out of bandages.

Mamen fixed breakfast on the morning of the eleventh, and afterward had to lie down because he was feeling extremely weak. The next day, he could do nothing but lie in the tent, unable to eat or move. He wasn't able to keep the pemmican down, and now he was in a great deal of pain. Malloch and Templeman prepared breakfast as best they could and Malloch washed and bandaged his own foot, doing such a bad job of it that Templeman had to redo it.

Templeman was weak and Malloch helpless, but they were still fighting like cats and dogs, shouting insults and threats at each other until Mamen thought he would lose his mind. To make it all worse, Malloch urinated on himself again so the stench in the tent was unbearable for days afterward. His feet were worse because he refused to take care of them, and he was always running outside in his stockings. Templeman was doing the best he could to look after him; but his reserves of strength weren't as strong or as deep as Mamen's and he was quickly wearing out.

Where there is life, there is hope. Mamen had clung to that axiom, but suddenly, he did not know if there was hope. He could not walk or move; there was no one to care for him or explain to him what was happening to his body or to tell him how to get better. For the first time, he truly could not imagine how it all would end.

He wrote letters to his parents and to his fiancée to tell them he loved them, and to thank them for all they had done for him in this life. In case Mamen did not survive, he made Templeman promise to deliver the letters for him once the ship came and they returned home. Death, Mamen wrote his mother, would be a welcome release. He could only hope for the chance to do better work in the world beyond.

They were able to move outside the tent on May 14. On May 15, Mamen took a three-mile walk, bringing back armfuls of wood to camp. He felt stronger afterward, but his body began to swell again so that he knew he had overdone it. Still, he craved the exercise and physical activity. Malloch, on the other hand, was a firm believer in lying in the tent all day without moving. He said he just couldn't see the sense in wasting what little energy he had.

Mamen's strength continued to return, although his body was still swelling frightfully. Somehow he managed to cook breakfast and tend to Malloch's feet, which had been sadly neglected ever since Mamen became so ill. But Malloch, as always, didn't seem to care about anything anymore, least of all himself, and Mamen did not know what else he could do for him.

On the morning of May 17, the sky cleared, the snow drifted about camp, and Malloch lost consciousness. Alarmed, Mamen and Templeman did all they could to rouse him, but nothing worked; he remained still and silent, his breathing falling evenly and steadily, as if he were sleeping.

They spent an anxious day, not knowing what to do for him, and afraid of the worst. Finally, at 5:30 that evening, he "stretched his legs and drew his last breath ...." George Stewart Malloch, renowned Canadian geologist, was dead at thirty-three. Nearly a year ago, those in charge of the expedition had been afraid that the young topographer hired to assist him would be a hindrance and a burden to this talented, dynamic man. Now that young topographer felt an overwhelming sense of grief, having done all he could to save his friend's life.

All he could do was thank God that Malloch's death had been a quiet one and that he was no longer in pain. For all of Malloch's recent foolishness, Mamen would miss him and would mourn him.

"Yes, this 17th of May has indeed been the worst I have had so far," Mamen wrote in his journal. "It will in all events be a day that I shall remember as long as I live."

They were too weak to move Malloch's body from the tent, and even if they had been strong enough to do so, they could not, in good conscience, leave him outside in the snow and the wind and the cold. So Malloch lay there as he had died, and as they slept beside him they tried not to notice the stench of death or his stiff, lifeless features, his eyes forever closed, his hands forever still. Mamen was haunted by him. The memory of his staring eyes as they clouded over in death was constantly before him.

"I don't know how this will end," wrote Mamen. "Is it death for all of us? No, with God's help we will get out of it, I am still weak, but as long as there is life there is hope. There is something that still keeps me alive, all my beloved ones, and with God's help I hope to be at home, hale and hearty, and spend Christmas with them. It is two months today since Captain Bartlett left Icy Spit. I hope to see him again in two months now, at the latest."

THERE WEREN'T ANY DOGS to spare so McKinlay knew he would have to walk the entire way to Rodger's Harbour—a good seventy miles. His eyes were still not completely healed. He didn't have a gun, which he knew he should have, especially since Breddy had spotted bears at the Skeleton Island camp. And Bartlett had always warned the men against traveling anywhere alone. But McKinlay felt he had no choice. It had been so long since they'd heard anything from Mamen, except for his rather urgent note, and besides, Mamen had in his possession some antiseptic, which they could use for the sick men.

McKinlay left camp at ten o'clock in the morning on May 17, accompanied by Munro. The chief engineer had a lot on his mind and he needed someone to talk to. He walked with McKinlay for several miles, worrying about the state of relations back at camp and how best to handle the increasing tension between the men. Then he turned back.

The snow, deep and difficult to walk in, was falling heavily and drifting badly. McKinlay sank with each step up to his thighs or his waist, and he could only see about twenty yards ahead. He had to lie down and rest over and over again, in order to keep on going.

On May 18, at three o'clock in the morning, McKinlay reached Skeleton Island and collapsed. He didn't care anymore about bears or the wind chill or frostbite. All he wanted was sleep. The roof of the igloo had fallen, but he found some old skins Mamen had left behind and brushed the snow from them and lay down, right there in the open. He awoke at noon, buried in snow.

He had a difficult time of it the last thirty or so miles to Rodger's Harbour. His right leg was cramping and his left leg was bleeding from the constant chafing it endured on the journey. At times, he had to lie down in the drifts, always on the lookout for bears. But he kept on and finally he saw it, there in the distance: Rodger's Harbour. The black mark on the beach a little over a mile away was Mamen's camp.

Mamen and Templeman greeted him with gratitude and joy. Malloch had died the day before, they said, and he still lay in the tent. There was already a horrible smell emitting from the body, and during the night, McKinlay was violently ill. Mamen and Templeman were still too weak to move the body and McKinlay too exhausted from his long hike. But he did what he could for Mamen, especially, who appeared to be on the verge of collapse. McKinlay summoned up every consoling word he could think of to try to make Mamen forget the hell he had been through since they had last seen each other.

The next morning, McKinlay and Mamen rolled Malloch's body into the tent cover and placed it out of harm's way. They placed logs around him to keep the wind away until they could give him a proper burial. It was all they had the strength to do. The three of them stood over him and bowed their heads and, at Mamen's request, McKinlay said a few words of prayer.

Afterward, they went back inside the tent and lay down. They agreed that their best hope was to go back to Skeleton Island and then to Icy Spit. Mamen had left the main party to get away from Munro and the crewmen, which McKinlay couldn't blame him for—after all, "the 'scientist' was not a 'persona grata' with many members of the party, which did not tend to make life agreeable...." But now going back seemed the only sensible thing to do. They must have food and fresh meat and be looked after.

They were set to leave on May 20, but Templeman was not feeling well, so they postponed the trip until the next morning. Mamen was alarmingly swollen but anxious to leave. Both he and McKinlay prayed he would have the strength to make it to Skeleton Island.

Then a blizzard came from nowhere, bringing with it winds and snow, which hammered the men relentlessly. Everything was so white, heavy, and thick that it was impossible to tell the land from the sky. McKinlay tried repeatedly to go outside in search of the game they badly needed, but the gale was too fierce. The three men stayed in the tent. Neither Templeman nor McKinlay was in great shape, but Mamen was terribly weak. The Underwood pemmican grew increasingly unappetizing and Mamen couldn't hold it down anymore; so McKinlay gave him warm milk from the rest of his own milk ration. It was the first food Mamen had had in four days.

"It is a most curious illness," McKinlay observed, "I cannot understand it; it seems to get worse after he eats. The only meat they have had besides one bear ham, is a fox.... What is the cause of this strange sickness? Can it be the pemmican?"

McKinlay stumbled out briefly to check on Malloch's body and added logs and stones to cover him so that any animals that happened by would leave him alone. If the ground had not been frozen, they could have given the dead man a proper burial, but there were no tools to dig with anyway.

There was nothing to do but wait out the storm and hope that Templeman and Mamen would grow strong enough to travel. McKinlay was exhausted but could not sleep. Instead, he lay awake, thinking of poor Malloch, and worrying about Mamen and Templeman. He fretted about getting them to Skeleton Island and then to Icy Spit. He worried that Mamen would not be able to make the journey. He prayed for strength, for himself, for Templeman, and especially for Mamen.

Finally, on May 23, the weather cleared and the men were free to set out. Templeman and McKinlay packed up a few necessary supplies and checked on Malloch's body one last time. Then there was only one problem—Mamen couldn't walk. They helped him to his feet and he collapsed. After that, they couldn't raise him, and even if they could have, they knew they wouldn't be able to carry him all the way back to Icy Spit.

They hadn't had any fresh meat since McKinlay had arrived, and Mamen still was not able to eat the Underwood pemmican. At a loss, McKinlay suddenly remembered that he had left some of the Hudson's Bay pemmican back at Skeleton Island and thought if he could get this to Mamen it might give him strength and make him better. It was more digestible than the Underwood brand he had been eating, and McKinlay thought the variety, at least, might sustain Mamen until he could find some game for him.

He left Templeman to look after Mamen, and at 3:00 P.M. on May 23, McKinlay set out alone for Skeleton Island. He took only tea, matches, and a tin of condensed milk. He was planning to make the trip as quickly as possible because he knew that every minute was precious, and crucial to Mamen's survival. He would bring back the Hudson's Bay pemmican and the biscuit scraps that he had seen in camp. And soon they would have Mamen well again.

EARLY ON THE MORNING of May 16, Bartlett and his companions passed Chechokium and crossed the divide to Emma Harbor. The fog and mist were still thick around them, parting now and then to reveal the mountain peaks on the peninsula that lay between Emma Harbor and Providence Bay. Bartlett thought the peaks "stern and forbidding." To reach the harbor, they had to climb up the great divide, a ragged cliff that acted as a fierce and protective barrier, its sides steep and unyielding. It took all that was left of their strength to make the climb, and when they reached the top, Bartlett "could look down to Emma Harbor and see open water out into Providence Bay. The land was white with snow and the ice nearer shore was unbroken, so that the open water beyond seemed as black as coal-tar, shining against the white."

They tumbled down the other side of the divide, nearly breaking their necks as the dogs ran free and the sled slid out of control, teetering from side to side in a maniacal zigzag, so fast and hard that it "almost took a man's breath away."

They reached the Baron's home in Emma Harbor at 7:00 A.M. on May 16. It had taken them six days to make Emma Harbor from East Cape and, as Bartlett noted somberly, "two months had gone by since I had parted from the men on Icy Spit, Wrangel Island. If all went well I should be back for them in two months more and I hoped they were holding out all right and would be in good shape when I reached them again."

The Baron's personal physician, Dr. Golovkoff, tended to Bartlett after he arrived. He still had some swelling in his legs and feet, although he was feeling much stronger now, and his throat, though mending, was still giving him pain. Golovkoff was attentive and highly skilled, and Bartlett was soon feeling, if not like a new man, at least a much-improved one.

He was anxious to reach Alaska, and he began to send word out that he was looking for Captain Pedersen. Pedersen's *Elvira,* it turned out, had been crushed, sinking off the northern coast of Alaska during the fall of 1913, at the same time *Karluk* was enduring the stormy season and being carried offshore. After his ship sank, Pedersen had hiked overland to Fairbanks and traveled on to San Francisco, where he took over the whaler *Herman*. Bartlett met a trader named Thompson at Emma Harbor, who told him Pedersen had passed through on his new ship. Through Thompson, Bartlett sent a letter to Pedersen and told him his situation and where he could be reached. In the letter, he also broached the possibility of hitching a ride on the *Herman* to the American shore.

Bartlett sent out several other letters to Pedersen, sending them by different Chukches who, he hoped, would be able to reach the captain. On May 19, one of the Eskimos arrived on the Baron's doorstep and reported that he had searched for Pedersen in John Holland Bay, but that by the time he got there, the *Herman* had already sailed for Cape Bering. Bartlett sent word there to try to catch Pedersen, but there was no need. Pedersen had already heard of Bartlett's quest to find him and on May 21, the *Herman* steamed into Emma Harbor.

AFTER HE HAD WALKED several miles, the winds started up again and McKinlay reached into his overshirt for his goggles. The pocket was empty. He stopped walking. Frantically, he searched all of his pockets. The goggles weren't there. This was very dangerous, and he knew it. To travel in the Arctic without eye protection was slow suicide. The reflection of the sun on the ice and snow was blinding, and the murderous wind flung sand and dirt into your eyes, often swelling them shut. One of the deadliest problems an Arctic traveler could face was snow blindness, especially while traveling alone and unarmed. If his eyes closed up, he would be helpless.

In his mind, McKinlay retraced his steps. He had already been traveling for a couple of hours and he could have lost his glasses anywhere along the way. They could be buried in snow by now. Or he could have left them back at Rodger's Harbour.

Against his better judgment, McKinlay decided to keep going, but before too long he wished he'd gone back for them. His eyes were starting to bother him and he was afraid. He knew that snow blindness, once you had it, could come back more easily, and he had already suffered one unforgettable bout. He was struck with an image of himself, stranded in the snow, blind and helpless, while Mamen and Templeman wasted away back at Rodger's Harbour, waiting for him to bring help. Mamen was depending on him. Mamen needed the pemmican to survive.

McKinlay's eyes were useless now. They were painful, and fast swelling shut. For the first time since the ship sank, he panicked. This was worse than losing the ship because this time someone was depending solely on him. The image of Mamen was vivid in his brain. McKinlay saw him lying in the tent, swollen, unable to walk or eat or move, growing weaker and weaker.

It filled him with fear. He felt utterly helpless and ill and disgusted with himself for being so careless with his goggles. It was a stupid mistake. But he made himself go on.

He knew it would be impossible at this point to find his way back to Rodger's Harbour, so he headed north, as best as he could tell, hoping to reach Icy Spit so that he could send Munro and the others to bring food to Mamen. He lost all sense of time and direction. He did not stop to rest or sleep. He was exhausted, but he pushed on. He walked and when he couldn't walk, he crawled. The ground was rough and treacherous, covered with knifelike rocks of different sizes and shapes. He tore his clothing and gloves on the sharp rocks and pebbles beneath his hands and knees. They ripped holes in the soles of his boots and scraped his feet until they were raw and bleeding. He was wet through from the snow and the water and the ice, and his skin was freezing. One eye was swollen completely shut, and he could barely see through the other. He was forced to travel by touch, giving his "good" eye a rest.

Through it all, he heard the words inscribed to him by his local Clydebank minister in the Bible given to him before he set sail from Glasgow the previous year. They had meant little to him then as he was embarking upon his great northern adventure. *I will lift mine eyes unto the hills, from whence cometh my help....* Now the words gave him strength and pushed him onward. *The Lord shall preserve thy going out and thy coming in from this time forth, and even for evermore.*

And so, by some miracle, at 4:30 in the morning on May 25, two days after McKinlay had left Mamen and Templeman, he reached Icy Spit. The seventy-mile journey had taken him thirty-eight hours, without stopping to sleep or rest. He woke Munro before collapsing, telling him, as best he could, what had happened.

Afterward, wet and miserable, he passed out and slept until the next day. When he awoke, his only thought was of Mamen.

> *DIARY OF BJARNE MAMEN*
> *RODGER'S HARBOUR*
> *THURSDAY, MAY 21.*

> *The barometer is falling; it now stands at 29.4. In the tent all day, cannot eat now, feel infinitely weak.*

THEY LEFT EMMA HARBOR immediately, Bartlett only taking time to thank Baron Kleist for his kind hospitality before boarding the *Herman* for the 240-mile trip across the Bering Sea. Pedersen was a godsend. Not only was he delaying his trading voyage to make the unexpected journey to Alaska, but his crew—including second mate John F. Allen, the original first mate on the *Karluk* before being dismissed by Bartlett—was working entirely on shares and would have their paychecks delayed by the detour.

On May 24, they reached the edge of the ice pack off Nome but could get no closer than twelve miles offshore. There was no harbor in Nome, just open beach, which made it dangerous for ships to travel in and out. When the ice field was as heavy as this, it simply meant a ship was immobilized until the pack broke up—if the pack broke up, for it often stayed firmly intact, stubborn, and impassive.

They waited for three days, gazing longingly at the shore, which seemed, especially after all the time passed and distance traveled, so maddeningly close. Yet it was impossible to reach. Bartlett thought he would lose his mind, with nothing to do but read magazines and stare at the shoreline while somewhere his men were struggling to hold on.

On May 27, Pedersen had had enough and changed course for Saint Michael, southeast and down the coast. They steamed across Norton Sound and arrived at Saint Michael on the twenty-eighth. Here, too, the harbor was frozen solid, but they took down one of the smaller boats and rowed to the edge of the ice, making the rest of their way on foot. Earlier, Bartlett had shed the polar furs he had been wearing for all those months and changed into some American civilian clothing given to him by Pedersen.

At 8:00 that evening, Bartlett once again set foot on American soil, for the first time in nearly a year. It was the greatest feeling of relief. Pedersen went with him to the town's wireless station, but the windows were dark and the office was closed for the night, so they went in search of a hotel. Along the way, they met Hugh J. Lee, a well-known United States marshal to whom Bartlett had been introduced in Nome the previous summer.

Lee was surprised to see Bartlett now, and the captain quickly related his story. Lee took over then, ushering Bartlett over to the town's winter hotel. The two men stayed up all night, talking about the *Karluk* and her captain's journey to get help for her survivors.

The first thing the next morning, Bartlett was at the wireless office, a military station of the Signal Corps of the United States Army. With a careful hand, Bartlett wrote out his message to the Canadian government, but the sergeant in charge refused to send it. Bartlett had little money left at this point, but due to regulations the sergeant would not send the telegram without full payment.

Bartlett had walked nearly seven hundred miles over the past two months and he was worn out, ill, fed up, and exhausted. He had come so far—farther than this man could ever imagine—and he had gone through hell to get here. Suddenly, he felt that slow-boiling temper of his beginning to rise, and all the familiar rumblings that indicated an eruption.

And then, just in time, Hugh J. Lee walked in, explained things to the sergeant, and that was that. The wire was sent to the naval service in Ottawa, Canada, relaying the story of the *Karluk* and Bartlett's recent journey and the men now waiting on Wrangel Island.

Then Bartlett turned all his attention to finding a ship to rescue the men. The rest of the month was spent in a flurry, trying to locate available ships to make the voyage up north once navigation opened in midsummer. Until then, no one would be able to get through the Arctic ice pack.

The government heads in Ottawa had believed the *Karluk* and all her company to be lost, and now they sent word to Bartlett expressing their great relief at the news of survivors. In communication with them, Bartlett showed optimism that both Sandy's party and Dr. Mackay's party would be found. He expected the missing men to have joined everyone on Wrangel Island by now. Whether Bartlett truly believed this or whether it was wishful thinking is hard to tell.

In any case, Ottawa was thrilled. How should they proceed, they asked the captain, and requested his advice on ice conditions and arrangements for rescue. He wrote back with ideas, suggesting they contact the Russian government, since their ice breakers were strong and powerful. He also suggested a United States revenue cutter named the *Bear*, which was currently cruising in the Bering Sea. Thirty years earlier, the *Bear* had been one of the ships that rescued the survivors of the lost Adolphus Greely expedition. Now, perhaps, she could rescue the survivors of the *Karluk*.

DIARY OF BJARNE MAMEN
RODGER'S HARBOUR
FRIDAY, MAY 22.

In the tent the whole day, I have now had nothing to eat for four days ....

As soon as this weather abates, we will make an attempt to reach Skeleton Island, I for my part cannot stand staying in here.

MUNRO LEFT FOR RODGER'S HARBOUR on the afternoon of May 26, taking Maurer with him. McKinlay was still miserable with snow blindness and would be out of commission for some time. Munro had wanted to leave immediately after McKinlay returned, but the weather made it impossible.

The purpose of the trip was twofold. First, and most important, they were going to look after Mamen. And second, they would scout out the conditions at Rodger's Harbour, with the idea that, if conditions looked favorable, they might move the entire company down there.

They arrived at Skeleton Island at 10:00 A.M. on May 27 and spent the day digging out the igloo, the pemmican, and the rest of the gear that was buried beneath a hill of snow. They had a difficult time of it, with nothing but a piece of tin for a shovel, but eventually they uncovered what they needed. There were birds in the cliffs and they longed for a shotgun, but again they were ill prepared and had to move on empty-handed, dreaming of the feast they could have had.

As they approached Rodger's Harbour, Munro was impressed with what he saw there. Driftwood seemed to lie about in abundance, and abandoned birds' nests were scattered everywhere. In the distance, they could hear the geese and the ducks, which seemed to have made their feeding ground nearby, and Munro wished to God the entire company was already down there. The conditions were so much more promising than they were at Icy Spit.

Finally they reached the camp at Rodger's Harbour. Dropping their gear, they called out for Mamen and Templeman and took in the surroundings. The tent would have to be moved to new ground, that was clear, and it was already in an awful state, battered and beaten by the wind. Munro made a note to himself to take care of it in the morning. And then Templeman rushed out of the tent, appearing frightened at the sound of their voices. He seemed lost and anxious and broke down, hysterical. He wept like a child, so relieved to see them.

It had been two days, he told them—and it was hard to understand him—two days alone in this place. Two days frightened and two days praying that someone would come.

Mamen had worried himself a great deal over McKinlay's absence. When the magnetician didn't return, Mamen was clearly frightened, but he didn't make a fuss and he didn't complain about feeling sick. Instead, he made plans. They would build a hut for winter. He would gather fossils for his Spitzbergen collection back home. He would ski to the Siberian coast as soon as his knee was healed. He talked about seeing his mother and his girl.

Because Mamen could not stomach the pemmican, Templeman fed him condensed milk mixed with whiskey, even though Mamen found it "by imot"—revolting.

At midnight on May 26 he slept, and at 4:00 A.M. he called Templeman and asked him to light a fire for the tea. Templeman did so and then turned in again. Half an hour later, he called Mamen, but the topographer was sleeping heavily and could not be roused.

He had waited as long as he could, held on to life until the last. *Where there is life, there is hope.* Mamen maintained that hope even in the final moments of his life. But at 5:00 in the morning on May 26, death came swiftly.

It was hard to believe that Mamen was gone. He had been so young and full of bravery and fight. His diary gives a haunting glimpse of a young man who foresaw his fate, but who, until the end, clung to life. He had great belief in honor and the triumph of strength over weakness. He was twenty-three years old and had many plans—to be married when he returned home, to lead grand expeditions of his own one day, to be a good person, to do good work.

Now he was gone. But perhaps, as Mamen had hoped, he would have the chance to do even better work in the world beyond.

JUNE 1914

———— • ————

A letter from Mrs. Murray arrived yesterday with a clipping from a Liverpool paper—a copy of a letter from Mr. Stefansson.... He says again that the men are in no danger he thinks.... I think about them a great deal—all the things they said to me, and I wonder, wonder what has become of them.

—MRS. RUDOLPH MARTIN ANDERSON

In the aftermath of the assassination of King George I of Greece in 1913, violence had spread throughout Greece, Serbia, Bulgaria, and Albania until, on June 30, 1913, the Second Balkan War had broken out. In the United States, Woodrow Wilson would enter the second year of his presidency in 1914 as conflict in Europe escalated ominously, and there were rumors of impending world war.

In the midst of it all, international press attention was riveted on the fate of the twenty-five missing people who had sailed from Victoria, British Columbia, on June 17, 1913, and vanished into the Arctic. They had been given up for dead by their former leader, by the Canadian government, and by everyone else. But now the world was transfixed by the story of the *Karluk* disaster and the surviving castaways on Wrangel Island.

The boys at the wireless station in Saint Michael, Alaska, gave Bartlett their back files to read so that he could catch up on current events. He had been away from the world for nearly a year and, as he always did when away for a long period of time, he found much had changed and progressed. It was good to get back to civilization, to become once more a citizen of this familiar world. It was an adjustment, but one he was used to making.

Under the care of Dr. Fernbaugh, the government surgeon, he was recovering nicely from the mysterious swelling in his legs and feet, as well as from his tonsillitis. Soon he would be completely revived and then he would be able to do the work before him. He was anxious to get on his way to Wrangel Island, even though it was still too early in the season for traveling. July would be the best month to make a trip to Wrangel, since the ice should be at its weakest by then, but Bartlett was spending all his time now trying to find a ship to take him north.

He had suggested three possible rescue ships to the Canadian government—the Russian ships *Taimyr* and *Vaigatch,* and the United States revenue cutter *Bear.* The Russian ships were noted icebreakers with good records of service. The *Taimyr* had forged through the icy Arctic waters in 1913, and its master, Captain Vilkitski, discovered Nicholas II Land, now known as Severnaya Zemlya, an archipelago located between the Laptev and Kara Seas. Both ships were similar to the steel vessels Bartlett had used in the Newfoundland seal-fisheries, and both were fitted with powerful engines.

The *Bear* had actually been built in the 1870s for those same Newfoundland seal fisheries. She was three-masted, her keel molded in greenheart, reputedly the world's hardest wood, from the West Indies. When Adolphus Greely and his men became lost in the Arctic, the United States government sent the *Bear* to rescue them in 1883.

Bartlett felt that if any ship could maneuver its way through the impenetrable ice surrounding Wrangel Island, it was the *Bear.* Bartlett had never met the *Bear*'s current master, Captain Cochran, but from what he knew of his reputation, Cochran wasn't afraid to put his ship into the ice.

Bartlett knew the *Bear* was presently headed to Nome from San Francisco. She would be the first ship from the "outside," as they called it, to come to Nome that year. But the ice in Nome's harbor, as Bartlett and Captain Pedersen had discovered upon trying to land there in the *Herman,* was especially thick and forbidding, so the *Bear* was forced to land at Saint Michael instead.

Bartlett went aboard and met with Captain Cochran. Together with the *Bear*'s officers, they discussed the castaways on Wrangel Island and what was to be done. Cochran and his men were eager to make the trip, but now they had to await the official government go-ahead from Washington, D.C.

Bartlett was hearing disturbing rumors about the thick, inaccessible ice that surrounded the coast. People were saying ice conditions were the worst in history. The news was deeply troubling and the waiting excruciating. He sent out word to captains of any ships leaving for northern waters, asking them to try for Wrangel Island if they were in the area. If he was not able to reach his men yet, perhaps someone else could. It didn't matter who brought them home, just as long as McKinlay and Mamen and Hadley and the Eskimos and all of the others were found.

While Bartlett and Cochran awaited word, they sailed on the *Bear* for the Siberian coast. As she was on her way across, Cochran received the official orders over the wireless. He was to leave for Wrangel Island, as soon as conditions permitted, and rescue the lost men of the *Karluk* expedition. Captain Bartlett was to go with him. They still had to wait for the season to open and, most likely, would not be able to leave until July. But Bartlett believed he had found his rescue ship and that it was just a matter of time before he was on his way to free his men.

McKINLAY WAS FEELING stronger every day. His feet were still sore from the rough journey, but as long as he moved around he felt better. He thought that exercise had much to do with his relative good health. The crewmen were ill, but they didn't get up at all; they just lay there in their beds and refused to move about.

He was still living in the big igloo with the crewmen Williamson, Breddy, Chafe, and Clam, and playing nurse. Clam was the latest victim, his legs badly swollen. It was a miserable job tending to the invalids, especially with a demanding patient like Williamson, who always needed something and always complained, testing McKinlay's great reserves of patience.

The weather was growing warmer now, which meant the igloos began to melt, becoming so wet and unlivable that the men finally swept the snow from the nearby spit and pitched tents there. They spread dry sticks on the ground to lie on, and it was a big improvement over the damp and cold of the snow houses.

They were down to their final case of pemmican, which would last about twelve more days. After that, as Hadley said, they would be "up against it & have to Depend on our own Efforts as Hunters to live...."

Unfortunately, Hadley and Kuraluk were having no luck on their daily hunts, and the men were subsisting on the nauseating pemmican, which, by now, they could barely swallow. Their precious tea, too, had become repulsive, boiling black from the worn tins it was cooked in.

Kuraluk suggested that they move to Skeleton Island, where they would have better prospects—more wood and more game. He and his family, along with Hadley and McKinlay, left on June 4 on a scouting trip. They traveled between the sandspit and the island, Kuraluk breaking the trail. Hadley drove the sled while Auntie and her little girls walked along the spit. McKinlay tagged behind, unable to keep up even with Mugpi. He was still weak and walking was still difficult for him, but he was determined to keep on.

After traveling ten or eleven miles, they stopped for the night at Bruch Spit. They pitched a tent and ate a meal of blubber soup and pemmican, then fed the dogs with deer hair soaked in blubber soup.

McKinlay and the others were worried about Munro and Maurer, who should have returned by now with Mamen and Templeman. McKinlay wondered what could be keeping them. He had not been asleep long when Munro and Maurer awakened him. They were alone. No Mamen, no Templeman.

They brought the worst possible news. Mamen was dead and Templeman was out of his mind. They had left the cook there because he wasn't strong enough to make the trip to Icy Spit.

The news was unfathomable. Mamen had died waiting for McKinlay to return with the pemmican, not knowing where McKinlay was or why he did not come back as promised. The men took the news of Mamen's death hard. Their spirits, already low, dropped drastically, and they felt more hopeless than ever.

The way he had died was deeply disturbing. This wretched mystery illness was plaguing all of them, leaving them so weak and crippled at times that they could not even stand erect, but had to crawl about on their hands and knees. McKinlay had long suspected the pemmican. Hadley was beginning to suspect it as well. "Underwood Pemmican again," he said. "That makes 2 in that party … the cook is the only one that's Left There & he is nearly crazy."

Tragedy aside, however, Rodger's Harbour was, Munro and Maurer said, an oasis. The beach abounded with driftwood; the cliffs teemed with birds. Munro had confiscated Malloch's Mauser pistol and he and Maurer had apparently had a feast of ducks along the way back to camp. There were seals as well. They had only come back to fetch whatever supplies they needed for the new camp, and to let the others know that Munro was going back to Rodger's Harbour to live.

If there had only existed some sense—even a hint—of camaraderie, their ordeal would seem more tolerable. But they had been strangers when the expedition began, and they were still strangers. There was no common bond. Nothing—not even the tragic predicament in which they found themselves—could bring the men together. With Bartlett as leader, they had gotten along better. Munro was in charge, but he wasn't well liked among the group; and he wasn't the leader the captain was.

In Bartlett's absence, the worst in each man had begun to surface. Character traits that had before seemed more like quirks and minor flaws were amplified in the Arctic wasteland. Admiral Peary had once observed, "A season in the Arctic is a great test of character. One may know a man better after six months with him beyond the Arctic circle than after a lifetime of acquaintance in cities. There is a something—I know not what to call it—in those frozen spaces, that brings a man face to face with himself and with his companions; if he is a man, the man comes out; and, if he is a cur, the cur shows as quickly."

Templeman, in addition to being a drug addict, was a pathological liar. Breddy made a lot of noise about everything and couldn't be counted on. Williamson was a troublemaker and untrustworthy. Chafe was impressionable. McKinlay had previously thought him to be a decent young man, but now that he was living with Williamson and Breddy, Chafe showed all the signs of having fallen in with the wrong crowd. He picked up their foul language and let them influence him. Of the crew, only Clam was dependably diligent and thoughtful.

Hadley was harder to figure out. He made no bones about his disgust for the "dirty Indians," as he insultingly called Kuraluk and his family. Yet McKinlay knew he'd had an Eskimo wife, that he'd loved her, and that he had come to the Arctic to escape her memory.

McKinlay did not want to stay any longer at their present camp. He did not want to see how those traits would continue to manifest themselves in these men he cared nothing about, and who, he knew, cared nothing about him. It had been different when Mamen and Malloch were alive. Their scientific interests gave them something to talk about, a common ground. He and Mamen had been especially good friends, but now he found himself completely alone. Munro was the closest thing he had to an ally.

McKinlay couldn't stand it anymore, and if they accused him of abandoning ship, then so be it. Mamen had left weeks ago because he didn't want to be around the rest of them, and McKinlay intended to do the same. So he asked the engineer if he could go with them to Rodger's Harbour. It was his due, after all. McKinlay was supposed to have moved there in the first place with Mamen, Malloch, and Templeman.

Munro told McKinlay that he wanted him to stay with the main party. The chief engineer was firm. He wanted everyone to move from Icy Spit to Cape Waring. There was a bay there with driftwood on the beach and thousands of crowbills nesting on the cliffs. They would be fine until the ship came. Munro, meanwhile, would return to Rodger's Harbour. Someone needed to be there to await the rescue ship, as per Captain Bartlett's orders. But he needed McKinlay to stay with the main party and tend to the sick men while Hadley and Kuraluk hunted. What's more, he wanted McKinlay to take the sled back to Icy Spit and transfer the sick to Cape Waring. Afterward, once all the men were safely deposited in the new camp, Munro told McKinlay to return to Skeleton Island and bring back any useful gear he could carry.

It was only the beginning of June, which meant they could not expect a ship before July. While McKinlay would not accuse Munro of only looking out for himself and abandoning the rest of his men, he suspected it, and so did Hadley. Munro had not wanted the responsibility of these men in the first place. He was anxious about their poor health, but he was also anxious to be free of them. "I think," Hadley observed, "that its because of his belly that he is going he will have a rifle and only himself and cook to keep."

——— • ———

AS MUNRO HAD INSTRUCTED, McKinlay, Hadley, and the Eskimos reached Cape Waring early on the evening of June 5 to set up camp. By now all of the Eskimos, especially Kuraluk and Mugpi, were suffering from snow blindness.

In spite of his weakened eyes, Kuraluk went off to hunt seals and crow-bills with Hadley. They returned hours later with a small seal, sixteen gulls, and a goose Kuraluk had shot from a flock flying overhead. It was a life-saving abundance of food. Auntie cooked part of the seal for supper, and they gave thanks, silently, each in his own private way. "Behold, there is corn in Egypt," mused McKinlay; "get you down thither, and buy for us from thence; that we may live, and not die."

After dinner, Hadley called McKinlay aside. He was pointing to a strange form of ground plant, which seemed to cover the area. McKinlay bent down to give it a look. He had never seen anything like it before. Hadley peeled off a bit of bark. The best he could figure it was some kind of stunted form of Arctic willow. Hadley sniffed the bark, then tasted it with the very tip of his tongue. After a moment, he smiled.

Hadley had a stack of books, which he had somehow managed to save from the *Karluk* before she slipped beneath the water. Now he and McKinlay ripped a few pages out of one of these and rolled cigarettes, using the bark and leaves from the mysterious plant as tobacco. Then they enjoyed the first smoke they'd had in months. They sat there, on the ground outside the tent, not talking, just smoking. For the first time, McKinlay felt a strange kinship to this irascible old man. They had nothing in common, outside of their situation. They had little to say to one another. But at that moment, it didn't matter.

Afterward, as McKinlay got ready to make his first trek back to Icy Spit to fetch the others and the rest of their supplies, Hadley and Kuraluk approached him and extended an unexpected invitation. Would McKinlay move into their tent when he returned? McKinlay was taken aback by their kindness, but immensely grateful. "I take it they see how difficult it is for me, living with some of the others," he said, "Hadley gave a hint to that effect."

The invitation meant a great deal to McKinlay. With Munro and Maurer gone to Rodger's Harbour, Hadley knew McKinlay was alone, and that the "bloody scientist" would never be welcome in the other tent, filled with crewmen, even though he played nursemaid to them and had been taking care of them for weeks.

McKinlay thanked Hadley and Kuraluk and told them he must first consult Munro before accepting their offer. The engineer, after all, was still in charge, and McKinlay felt it was a matter of necessary courtesy to ask Munro's permission. But he hoped to God he would say yes.

MCKINLAY ARRIVED AT ICY SPIT at one o'clock in the morning. There was still endless daylight, so they could travel—and often did—at any time of the day or night. When he reached camp, the men rushed to greet him, not because they were glad to see him, but because they were anxious for any meat he might have brought them. Auntie had given him six gulls—one for each of them—and these he handed over now.

Munro and Maurer were still there, with all of their gear and supplies sorted. Munro was restless and anxious to be off, and Maurer, it now seemed, was going with him. Somehow he had convinced Munro to let him join the party at Rodger's Harbour. McKinlay was incensed but said nothing.

He was irritable and weary from his journey and asked to take a rest, but Munro wanted to leave immediately. Before he could get too distracted with preparations and orders, McKinlay asked him for permission to move in with Hadley and the Eskimos. To his great relief, Munro said yes.

They set out after a breakfast of gulls. McKinlay's plan was that he would drive the sled with the gear halfway to Cape Waring and then come back for Clam and Williamson, who were too swollen to walk. Breddy and Chafe, although still weak, would walk it at their own pace and stop when they got to the gear and have everything ready when McKinlay arrived with the invalids. They would put up the tent and have a meal waiting for McKinlay and the others and then help the scientist unload.

Munro seemed to approve of the plan wholeheartedly, and he and Maurer set out on their own toward Cape Waring. McKinlay had not slept since he had reached Icy Spit, but soon he was on his way with the gear, guiding, and often helping, the three dogs pull the sled. Eight miles later, he unloaded the supplies and turned around. By mid-afternoon, he was back at Icy Spit, and after a cup of black tea, he loaded Clam and Williamson onto the sled. Half an hour later, he was off.

The journey was arduous, and it seemed longer than eight miles. It was a heavy load for the dogs and also for McKinlay, who again had to help the dogs pull. Williamson complained the entire way.

When at last they reached the halfway mark, there was no sign of a tent or a fire, no smells of food. For a moment, McKinlay was alarmed, fearing that Breddy and Chafe had somehow wandered off-course and were lying injured somewhere off the path. But a closer look revealed that the two crewmen lay in the middle of the ground, sound asleep.

Now McKinlay was furious as well as exhausted. He unhitched the dogs and fed them, then made himself a cup of tea. At midnight, he at last lay down to sleep, "in no very amiable frame of mind. But 'Least said—' will be the soundest policy, it seems to me."

MUNRO WOKE MCKINLAY at 8:00 the next morning, having finished breaking down the old camp. After breakfast, they headed to the new camp at Cape Waring. Maurer, Chafe, and Breddy were going to walk it, and Munro and McKinlay were going to load the sled with the tent, some of the more necessary gear, and Clam. McKinlay would return later for Williamson and the rest of the gear.

They hadn't gone a mile before Munro and McKinlay broke into an argument. McKinlay's anger at and resentment of Munro had been building for some time. Now they argued over which route to take to Cape Waring. Munro wanted to travel over the land, McKinlay over the ice. Munro insisted on going his way, and McKinlay gave in, allowing for the fact that Munro had made the trip three times to his one. Hours later, they were lost in the fog, and McKinlay had to figure out the right direction and lead them—over the ice—to Cape Waring.

It was the last straw. McKinlay felt Munro was pushing him away, that he was alienating McKinlay in his selfish decision to go to Rodger's Harbour. He felt Munro was neglecting his responsibilities as leader by abandoning the men. It was too reminiscent of Stefansson. True, the chief "seems to be in trouble all around," McKinlay observed, "which may account for his desire to be at Rodger's Harbour; I certainly cannot blame him as some do not seem to be happy unless they have a grumble." Munro was on the outs with Kuraluk, Hadley, Williamson, and Breddy, but Captain Bartlett had left him in charge of them.

Suddenly McKinlay spied a small streak of color under the ice and snow. Munro was still talking as McKinlay knelt down. The earth bled through the ice in spots, and in these spots were patches of the prettiest, hardiest little wildflower he had ever seen. He couldn't begin to identify it, but it was beautiful—deep, pungent purple, brilliant in its contrast to the white landscape. For so long, everywhere and everything had been white, as far as the eye could see. He could barely remember the world before the ice. But now, suddenly, there was color—rich, vibrant color. McKinlay knelt on the hard, cold ground brushing the snow away from a cluster of flowers. Even under the snow, the blooms were alive and growing.

Suddenly, his anger was forgotten. And he felt full of hope. This delicate little flower had survived—was continuing to survive—in this vast wasteland, here in this remote, unfriendly strip of earth at the very top of the world. Perhaps he himself would survive after all.

THEY REACHED CAPE WARING to find that Kuraluk and Hadley had shot a seal and several crowbills. They celebrated with a dinner of underdone seal meat—the way Eskimos preferred to eat it—and then McKinlay rested for half an hour. Breddy, Chafe, and Maurer appeared an hour later, tired from their walk, and happy to have reached camp. As they turned in for the night, McKinlay set off to retrieve Williamson.

It was 9:30 P.M. He was exhausted and so were the dogs, and they made slow progress. Even though the sled was empty and lighter than the loads the dogs were used to, they were too tired to pull McKinlay, so he walked; he didn't reach Williamson until two o'clock in the morning.

They were on their way by 4:00 A.M., Williamson riding on the sled. McKinlay felt somewhat invigorated after his brief rest, and they moved along at a decent pace, even though he had to do a bit of maneuvering over the pools of water that were forming on top of the ice. Newer ice melted on top of the old ice, and sometimes—as they quickly found out—the old ice was very thin beneath the water. One or two times, as they rushed across these pools, the sled broke through and was saved from sinking only by their speed. It was harrowing, and McKinlay was suddenly wide awake. Williamson, he could tell, was frightened, and so were the dogs.

There was no stopping, even though McKinlay longed to turn back. They were skimming along with fair success when the unthinkable happened: as they were crossing a particularly precarious pool of water, the dogs suddenly drew up short in the middle of it, stopping right then and there, and their entire outfit broke through the ice. As McKinlay and the dogs scrambled to safety, soaked and shaken but unharmed, the sled and Williamson slid further into the water at a frightening angle. Williamson let out a yell and McKinlay leaped to his feet and pulled the sled back onto the ice. It took all his strength, and as he was balancing the load on more solid ice, the dogs broke their traces and bolted for camp. He tried to catch them, but they disappeared over the horizon.

Now they were in a spot. They were still ten miles from camp, and McKinlay knew there was no way he could haul Williamson there by himself. For an hour, he followed the dogs. But each time he crept toward them, off they would go again, until he knew it was hopeless. Eventually, he rejoined Williamson, who sat, helpless and frightened, in a pathetic heap on the sled.

Williamson said he would try to walk. McKinlay freed himself from the harness and helped the second engineer, as gingerly as he could, off the sled. Immediately Williamson's knees weakened, and McKinlay caught him as he buckled. He was shaky but determined, and he supported himself on the handles of the sled while McKinlay dragged it. After fifty yards, however, Williamson was unable to go on.

Although the sun was still high in the sky, the bitter wind had picked up again. McKinlay suggested pitching the tent over Williamson while he went after the dogs, but Williamson wanted to remain on the sled. McKinlay then spread thick layers of skins beneath Williamson, who lay on top of these wrapped in two blankets, a traveling rug, and the tent cover. McKinlay made sure his face was covered to protect it from frostbite.

As McKinlay walked the ten miles to camp, the snow began to fall heavily while the ever-present sun softened what already lay on the ground. He sank in snow to his knees and then to his thighs. Because his eyes had begun to trouble him and he was seeing double, he had to rest now and then, afraid his suffering vision had gotten him off his path. His eyes had swollen nearly shut by the time he reached camp hours later. Learning that Kuraluk and the dogs, which had all returned unscathed, had already gone back to get Williamson, McKinlay stumbled into his new quarters with Hadley and the Eskimo and collapsed into sleep.

McKINLAY'S SNOW BLINDNESS was so bad that his eyes remained swollen closed. He could see nothing. He wanted only to rest, to give his eyes a chance to heal, but Munro and Maurer were leaving for their new camp at Rodger's Harbour and wanted McKinlay to accompany them long enough to bring back the dogs and sled. On his way back, he could stop at Skeleton Island for more gear and the Mauser pistol, Munro told McKinlay, who was lying there, blind, in the worst pain he had ever experienced.

McKinlay was obviously incapacitated and in pain, yet there Munro stood, over his bed, reciting their plans for departure. Finally, Munro gave up and decided to take fireman Breddy instead, but Breddy always hated working, preferring instead to do what he wanted when he wanted; so he avoided Munro until his departure. In the end, Munro and Maurer left for Rodger's Harbour alone. It was what they had wanted anyway—to be alone, away from the rest of the men.

Once again, the men of the *Karluk* had been abandoned by their leader.

McKINLAY LAY IN THE TENT for days, his eyes bound up. Hadley tended to him, bathing his eyes with zinc sulphate, which gave only momentary relief, and injecting them with cocaine from their meager medicine chest. Nothing seemed to help, though, and McKinlay remained in a miserable state. He had to be fed and led about camp like a blind person. All of them were suffering. Clam's condition was much more grave, but as usual, he said little about the pain. Williamson, although not as ill, complained enough for the both of them.

Captain Robert Bartlett, the ice master whose leadership and courage rallied the crew of the *Karluk* when disaster struck.

The scientific staff of the Canadian Arctic Expedition of 1913, taken in Nome shortly before the *Karluk* sailed. Front row, left to right: Dr. Alister Forbes Mackay, Captain Robert Bartlett, Vilhjalmur Stefansson, Dr. Rudolph Martin Anderson, James Murray, Fritz Johansen. Back row, left to right: Bjarne Mamen, Burt McConnell, Kenneth Chipman, George Wilkins, George Malloch, Henri Beuchat, J.J. O'Neill, Diamond Jenness, John Raffles Cox, William McKinlay.

3

HMCS *Karluk* in Victoria Harbour in June 1913. The ill-equipped, run-down ship attracted huge crowds to speed her departure.

4

Diamond Jenness and William McKinlay aboard the *Karluk* in June 1913. Jenness, an anthropologist, and McKinlay, a magnetician, were known as the twins because of their short stature.

George Malloch, geologist, on board the *Karluk* in June 1913. His comical, easy-going nature provided welcome comfort to his shipmates.

5

lexander "Sandy" Anderson, promoted
first mate when his predecessor was
ismissed before the expedition set sail.
is youth and relative inexperience were
lly compensated for by his enthusiasm
d dedication to duty.

Bjarne Mamen, at twenty-two the
youngest member of the scientific staff,
begged to join the expedition and was
accepted despite his lack of experience.

illiam McKinlay relaxing
n the deck of the *Karluk*.
Scottish schoolmaster,
cKinlay had long dreamed
f being an explorer but
ntil now his only experience
f the Arctic was from the
ooks he had read.

9

Kuraluk and Kiruk (who became known as "Auntie") with their two children, Hele then aged eight, and Mugpi, aged three. They were hired to hunt and to sew winter clothes for the members of the expedition

Chief Engineer John Munro who, though lazy and ineffectual, was left in command on Wrangel Island by Captain Bartlett.

George Breddy, the *Karluk*'s stoker, and one of the more volatile crew members. His instability and deviousness would lead to one of the most traumatic incidents of the entire expedition.

The *Karluk* forcing a path through the ice pack in August 1913, as an early winter set in.

With the *Karluk* trapped in the ice, the scientists and crew began to unload supplies onto the ice pack.

Bjarne Mamen in the regulation polar
explorer's kit. The clothes on board were
thin hand-me-downs, purchased cheaply,
and not issued to everyone.

Vilhjalmur Stefansson, a renowned
explorer who believed that anyone
could survive in the place he called
the "friendly Arctic."

"Goodbye, Stefansson. We did not then know that those of us who were left on your
luckless ship were not to see you again." From the notes of Fred Maurer, September
1913.

The last photograph of the *Karluk* before she went down. The ice blocks surrounding the hull were cut from the ice pack in an effort to insulate the ship from the bitter cold of the Arctic winter.

Shipwreck Camp.

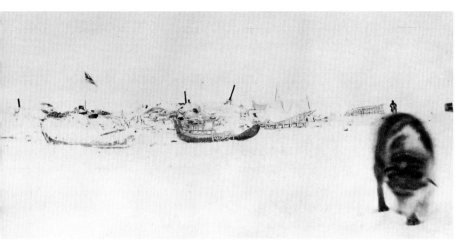

19

"To look at the ice, one would think it impossible ever to get through it. In some parts there are ridges of 60 or 70 ft. in height, some even higher, with a sheer vertical face on one side as smooth as if they had been built by human hands. And we must get over & through & we must camp here until we have made that passable." William McKinlay, March 1914.

"Wrangel Island is eighty-five miles long, and varies from twenty-eight to thirty-five miles in width, and is practically all mountainous. It lies one hundred miles off the coast of Siberia and is the most desolate-looking place I have ever seen, or ever wish to see again." Ernest Chafe, March 1914.

Kataktovik on Wrangel Island
shortly before he and Captain Bartlett
set out on their extraordinary 700-mile
journey across the ice to Siberia to
get help. Apart from Helen and Mugpi,
Kataktovik was, at nineteen, the
youngest member of the expedition.

Auntie with Helen and Mugpi on Wrangel Island, skinning a seal. The Eskimos were
the hunters and were responsible for finding at least 80 percent of the game on the
island.

Nigeraurak, the ship's cat and good luck mascot. Little Mugpi used to tease the kitten and was rewarded with a deep scratch, which left a distinct scar.

Mugpi, now four years old, with one of the ship's dogs.

25

From left to right, Ernest Chafe, John Hadley, Robert Williamson, Kuraluk, Mugpi, and Helen butchering a walrus. Chafe is holding the animal's flippers.

The meat rack. After butchering game, the meat would be left to dry in the sun to preserve it for winter supplies.

John Hadley, a trapper who had joined the *Karluk* to escape his grief following the death of his Eskimo wife. He is shown here with his faithful dog, Molly.

28

William McKinlay, Robert Williamson, George Breddy, Ernest Chafe, and "Clam" Williams. A rare photograph of scientists and crew together. The divisions between them, already noticeable onboard ship, became even more marked on the island. The camp would ultimately split in two, with McKinlay joining the Eskimos' tent.

29

William McKinlay, exhausted and suffering from snow blindness, lying outside his tent at Cape Waring.

The camp at Cape Waring. The divisions in the camp are all too clearly visible, with the crewmen's tent on the left and the Eskimos' tent—shared with McKinlay and Hadley—on the right.

"Clam" Williams with one of the ship's dogs on Wrangel Island. The only member of the crew on the island to behave honorably.

John Munro and Robert Templeman, the *Karluk*'s cook, at Rodger's Harbour, 60 to 70 miles south east of Cape Waring. They had established a camp there to await the rescue ship for which the *Karluk*'s survivors were so desperately hoping.

The Canadian flag flying at half mast over the grave of George Malloch and Bjarne Mame at Rodger's Harbour.

The longed-for ship, the *King and Winge*, which forged through the ice to reach the survivors on Wrangel Island in September 1914.

Mugpi, Helen, and Kuraluk on their way back to Alaska.

The survivors of the Canadian Arctic Expedition, from left to right: John Munro (at the back), Robert Templeman, Robert Williamson, John Hadley, Captain Robert Bartlett, Auntie, Mugpi, Helen, William McKinlay, Kuraluk (seated in front), Ernest Chafe, "Clam" Williams, and Fred Maurer.

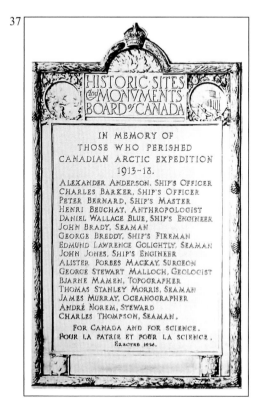

37

The plaque commemorating those who died. In a curious twist of fate, this plaque is itself now missing, having been lost when the National Archives of Canada moved buildings in the 1960s.

Fortunately, there were now plenty of birds at the new camp, and Hadley and Kuraluk were having tremendous luck with the gaming. Chafe began hunting on a nightly basis, and rarely came home empty-handed. The catch was always divided equally between the two tents, in the ratio of five (Hadley's tent) to four (Williamson's tent), with Helen and Mugpi counting as one adult. At first, the dividing of game seemed to go smoothly, all hands being present during the sharing out so that everyone could make sure he was getting his proper ration.

The members of Williamson's tent, however, were rotten at rationing the food among themselves. They ate through their stores quickly, in one or two sittings instead of saving the meat for later, and nothing Hadley or McKinlay said could make them realize the importance of being frugal.

On the evening of June 12, McKinlay, Hadley, and the Eskimos were awakened by groaning from the other tent, followed by panicked shouts from Williamson. He couldn't breathe, he was shouting over and over. Someone from the crew tent ran to fetch Hadley, and McKinlay and the others spilled outside and saw Williamson sitting on a log, "the fear of death" on his face. It was his heart, he gasped. He was done for.

After a careful examination, Hadley concluded that it was no such thing and that, instead, Williamson was suffering from nothing more than a case of acute indigestion. Hadley questioned Chafe, Breddy, and Clam and discovered that each of them, including Williamson, had eaten two crowbills and then divided two small gulls among them. Hadley lectured them about being more careful with their stores of food and then, since he was in charge of the medicine chest, gave Williamson some tonic before they all turned in.

The lesson failed to make an impact, because the next night the men in Williamson's tent finished all of their birds at supper. What they did was their business, of course, but it soon became clear that Hadley, McKinlay, and the Eskimos would suffer from it. Hadley and Kuraluk were away on a hunt one day, and McKinlay was in the tent mending his clothing when he heard steps outside and peered through a small hole in the tent. There were Chafe and Breddy, helping themselves to some of his tent's soup—Hadley's soup, McKinlay's soup, the Eskimos' soup. "They went about it so freely," he wrote, "that I was sure that they thought no one else was in camp. Breddy then handled the birds in our store tin, apparently counting them, and later, when I checked on them, they were at least one short." He could not believe men would steal food from other hungry men, much less from a woman and two little girls.

There was more trouble on June 13. Chafe and Breddy had gone hunting and sometime afterward Breddy returned, reporting to his tentmates that there wasn't a crowbill to be seen. He had only gotten one gull, he said. At 7:00 A.M., Chafe returned and McKinlay overheard him report having gotten four gulls, although they later told Hadley and McKinlay that they had gotten only two.

Another time, Chafe shot eight crowbills, giving four to Hadley's tent and keeping the other four for Williamson's tent, even though these were not the proportionate shares they had agreed upon. And afterward Hadley had seen Chafe cooking three birds for himself and Clam, which left Breddy and Williamson unaccounted for. Did Chafe really get eight birds as reported? Was he cooking three of their four for himself and Clam, thereby cheating Breddy and Williamson? Or had he actually gotten more birds than reported, in which case were they really cheating Hadley's tent?

Hadley and McKinlay were growing increasingly concerned. The men in the other tent, with the lone exception of Clam, were loose cannons. They didn't trust them. If the crewmen were, in fact, stealing from them and cheating them out of birds, it was something to be gravely worried about.

"Hadley declares they are not dealing squarely," McKinlay wrote. "We may be unduly suspicious; but things have not always gone so smoothly as they might have done, if everybody were to hang together a bit more."

McKinlay's eyes had gradually improved, and on the evening of June 13 he set out for Skeleton Island to retrieve his knapsack and the ammunition for the Mauser pistol. Before he left, he asked Williamson for the Mauser so that he could have a chance at game on the way, but Williamson refused. Munro had given strict orders that the pistol shouldn't leave Williamson's tent, he said. This seemed odd, given Munro's intense dislike of the second engineer, but there was nothing McKinlay could do to change his mind.

Munro, it appeared, had already removed most of the gear and provisions that had been at Skeleton Island, so McKinlay loaded what was left onto his sled and turned immediately back toward Cape Waring. He had retrieved 270 Mauser cartridges, one empty biscuit tin, one empty coal oil tin, and seven tins of pemmican, as well as his own knapsack. When he got back to camp, however, he found several items missing from his bag, including his compass, a cap, one sack of boot packing, several pairs of socks, a notebook, and a tin of pemmican. Munro must have taken the things on his way back to Rodger's Harbour, Breddy said. There seemed to be thievery everywhere now.

ON JUNE 16, Kuraluk took his family and headed for the cliffs. He would only be gone for a day, but he feared that was too long to leave his family alone in camp. Hadley would be joining them there later, which would have left only McKinlay to look after Kuraluk's wife and children, and the other men never seemed to listen to McKinlay like they did to Hadley. They were a bit afraid of Hadley, but the scientist didn't scare them.

So Kuraluk took Auntie, Helen, and Mugpi with him to the cliffs to hunt for eggs and birds. The men in the other tent had guns and used fierce words and made threats. He was not going to leave his family alone in that camp.

Kuraluk was depressed and he didn't expect to live. Every day, he asked his younger daughter, "Are we going to live?" and "Will we live through this?"

Each time Mugpi replied, "Yes, we will live."

Perhaps he should not have let Mugpi know his fear. He was the father after all, and she was just four years old. But she comforted him. They were so much alike, both comical and funny, more light-hearted than Auntie or Helen. Maybe this is why he reached out to her now when he should have been protecting her. Or maybe it was because he was in a desperate situation—one he had never before experienced or dreamed of experiencing—and because he was afraid.

"Are you sure we will live?" he asked.

"We are living now, aren't we?" said Mugpi.

CLAM FOAMED AT THE MOUTH, blood streaming from between his lips. His eyes rolled about, unable to focus, and he couldn't breathe. He had been ill for so long, sicker than any of them, and had borne every-thing so well—not only the amputation, but a terrible bout of the mystery illness. For some reason, he had been hit the hardest, although he never complained or asked for help or cursed his luck.

They expected him to die at any time. For an entire week, they kept him propped up in a sitting position because when he lay down he would begin to choke again, and his eyes rolled back into his head so that only the whites showed. One night, they almost lost him. McKinlay was called into Williamson's tent, and somehow they managed to bring Clam back around.

After that, he began to improve; but the progress was slow and it seemed doubtful he would ever return to his robust, handsome self. Would he follow the fates of Mamen and Malloch?

Williamson, as Clam's surgeon, had prescribed dosages of morphine to ease the pain from the amputation of his toe and to help Clam sleep. Hadley was in charge of the stock of medicines and refused to take responsibility for giving Clam another dose until the patient himself requested it. In Clam's weakened condition he might die from another dosage, especially a substantial one, and Hadley wasn't about to take that risk. Clam would have to ask for it himself. This was doubtful, since Clam was stubborn about asking for help, but two or three days after his last dose, he broke down and asked Hadley for half a grain. When it had no effect, Hadley made him write a note, which absolved the old man of any responsibility for any bad effects suffered as a result of the drug, and only then did Clam get more morphine. That, Hadley said, would be the last of it. He was wary about handing out the stuff, knowing how powerful it could be. He did not want Clam to become addicted to it, and he also had to preserve their supply.

THE ESKIMOS RETURNED from the cliffs on the evening of June 16, bringing forty-three crowbills. Later that same day, someone from Williamson's tent stole a bird from Hadley's stores, which left the old man's tent one short for two meals. There was no doubt about it now. In addition to cheating and lying, the other tent was stealing from them. And

McKinlay and Hadley were sure they would catch the thief in the act if he kept it up.

They had been lucky in June. Hadley, Kuraluk, and Chafe had managed to kill a few seals and scores of birds—crowbill ducks for the most part, called "atbah" by the Eskimos—which afforded them two good meals a day. It was certainly more fresh meat than they had been used to for some time.

Kuraluk frequently climbed to the top of a nearby hill to look out over the land and ice, scouting for seals across the horizon. They were not having much luck with seals lately because a good many of them had been frightened away by the shooting around the cliffs. The seals, too, were losing their blubber in this summer season, which meant that they sank in the water immediately after they were killed, making it impossible to retrieve them. They must be shot in the brain, the men discovered, as opposed to the heart. Unless they were shot through the brain, they managed to get away, slipping into their holes and disappearing from sight.

While this worried them, there was a matter of greater concern. The ammunition would not last forever, and they had used up an alarming amount of it already on the birds. Now Kuraluk set about making a bow and arrows so that he would have another method of shooting crowbills.

Hadley, McKinlay, and Kuraluk had decided that they would also need to hunt eggs to supplement their diets. The only problem with this was that it was dangerous work. They named the place where they shot the birds Crowbill Point. It was a fantastic series of five separate cliffs that reached into the sea for a hundred yards or so. The birds nested high in these jagged, rocky cliffs, which meant a man would have to be lowered over the top of the peaks and down the face to reach the nests. McKinlay, being the smallest and lightest, was the only choice. They made a bo'sun's chair to be used in the lowering, and constructed an especially long ladder for climbing the peaks.

Auntie did her own share of hunting now and then, going out with the bow and arrows, sometimes taking the little girls with her. Helen caught a pirate gull one day by attaching a piece of blubber to a feather quill. She tied a piece of string to the quill; when the gull swallowed the blubber, the quill stuck in his stomach and he was held fast by the string. Even the indolent Breddy made an attempt to hunt, although on his way to the cliffs he lay down on the beach to sleep, and "then came back complaining of stomach-ache. We have come to the conclusion," said McKinlay, "that he is another shirker ...."

Munro and Maurer arrived at Cape Waring at 1:00 A.M. on June 18 to retrieve more ammunition. No one was happy to see them. Everyone looked on them—especially Munro—as deserters, and they were treated to a chilly welcome.

Munro and Maurer brought with them eight or ten crowbills, which they cooked up immediately and ate in front of everyone, not offering to share. Afterward, Maurer turned into Williamson's tent to sleep, but Munro refused to sleep beside Kuraluk in the other tent; so he stretched out on the ground nearby.

McKinlay was still curious about the disposition of the Mauser. When he questioned Munro about it, the chief engineer denied leaving orders that the pistol was only to be used by Williamson's tent. True, he had loaned it to Chafe with ammunition, but that didn't mean it was not to be used by the others as well.

McKinlay also confronted Munro about the missing items from his knapsack. Munro said he had left McKinlay's bag untouched and knew nothing about the items. Only one other man had been in the camp at Skeleton Island—Breddy—leaving McKinlay to wonder which of them was the thief and the liar.

The men were beginning to quarrel like selfish children over every scrap of food and ammunition. This was not child's play, however. It was a life-or-death struggle to survive. When Munro demanded fifty rounds of ammunition from Hadley, the old man gave it to him under protest. This would give Munro, all told, 170 rounds of ammunition for three men, and Hadley and Kuraluk would be left with 146 rounds for ten people. Munro and Maurer slept all day, and when they woke they begged birds from Hadley's supply.

Munro couldn't believe what a mess this camp was. The crewmen had been stealing from the Eskimos, and now the Eskimos were afraid of them and wouldn't go near them anymore. Williamson and the rest were also, apparently, cheating on birds and lying about how much game they were getting, keeping it all for themselves, no doubt, and then eating it right away. Everyone was ill and swollen and often crawling around on hands and knees when they couldn't stand erect from the illness. But the crewmen ate like horses in their tent, as many as four birds a day, which, if you asked Munro, was "fairly good for people who are dying. God knows how everything is going to end."

Munro had seemed in no hurry to check on the sick men in the crew tent until Breddy appeared, demanding in the strongest of language that he call a meeting of the entire party. Grievances needed to be aired and this was the time to do it. Tension had built for too long and it was finally at a head now that Munro was back, and showing little interest in the condition of his charges.

Everyone—even the invalids—attended the meeting, and the pent-up feelings of the past several months erupted. Williamson, Breddy, and now Chafe didn't like the Eskimos, despised Hadley, and considered McKinlay only a "bloody scientist." The Eskimos were afraid of the crewmen, and McKinlay and Hadley knew the other tent was stealing from them. And everyone was furious with Munro and felt they had been abandoned by him.

Like a rapid-fire gunfight, accusations and recriminations shot back and forth. The language was loud and obscene as Williamson and Breddy demanded that the party stay together for the sake of looking after the sick men and hunting game. Either that or Maurer should stay with them and McKinlay should go back to Rodger's Harbour with Munro. They would rather have one of their own looking after them.

Maurer said that he had absolutely no desire to stay with his former party, and then the "orgy of charges and countercharges" truly began. When Breddy again demanded that Maurer stay with them and McKinlay go to Rodger's Harbour, Munro proclaimed that McKinlay had absolutely no wish to be at Rodger's Harbour. He said that McKinlay wanted to stay at Cape Waring.

It was an outright lie. "This, Munro well knew, was untrue, as I had all along gone out of my way to do all in my power to help him in his plans; & it was his own wish that I should remain to look after the sick," wrote McKinlay. Munro knew full well that McKinlay had pleaded to let him move to Rodger's Harbour. More than anything, McKinlay wanted to be away from this place and these people. He was sick of playing nursemaid.

McKinlay had put up with a good deal for the sake of peace, testing the limits of his physical and mental strength as well as his patience, but now he snapped. He would not stand for lies. He gave Munro a much-deserved piece of his mind.

To soothe the party as best he could, Munro announced that he and Maurer would return to Rodger's Harbour for Templeman, and then, as soon as the water cleared off the ice, McKinlay would head there with the dogs and the sled to get them. Thus, the three of them could rejoin the main party at Cape Waring. This seemed to satisfy even the loudest of the men—Breddy and Williamson—who, although still bristling, seemed to think it a fair plan. Munro, Maurer, and Templeman were returning. That was all they had wanted in the first place.

When the meeting was over, McKinlay turned in, exhausted and irritated, only to be called outside by Munro. The engineer steered him out of earshot of the others and told him to disregard everything he had said about fetching them from Rodger's Harbour. Do not seriously attempt to reach us, he said. Instead, McKinlay should set out and only go part of the way, then return and report to the others that the trail was impossible. That way, Munro and Maurer could remain as they wanted to at Rodger's Harbour with Templeman, and no one would be the wiser.

Any remaining respect McKinlay had for Munro vanished in that moment. McKinlay was not going to lie for Munro, nor would he help him deceive the rest of the men. When the time came, McKinlay said, he would make the journey to Rodger's Harbour and he would do everything in his power to get there and bring them back. Furthermore, he told Munro that he was "informing Hadley of his suggestion, but would not mention it to any of the others, in order to avoid causing what, I was certain, would be unavoidable trouble."

Williamson, Breddy, and the rest of the men, he knew, needed no further reason for despising Munro, and if possible, McKinlay wanted to avoid what was likely to be a violent showdown.

McKinlay reported Munro's suggestion to Hadley, who shared the scientist's outrage. "I believe he leaves to night for Rogers Harbour again," said the old man, "so I suppose that we shall not see him again before the ship comes ... and it Looks to me if They Both wanted to shirk the responsibility of Looking after the sick people."

He recorded the incident in his diary, and McKinlay did the same, and true to his word, they never mentioned it to the others. But after that, McKinlay lost all desire to go to Rodger's Harbour. For the first time, he was glad he had been left behind.

They were an even sorrier bunch after Munro departed. Between them, Munro and Maurer had consumed enough food to last both Hadley's tent and Williamson's tent for a day and a half. Everything had come to a head, all of the tension, anger, and resentment that had been building for months, but the confrontation with Munro had done little to quell this or improve the situation. If anything, it had made things worse, because now feelings were bruised, tempers were raw, and no one was in a civil mood.

Munro had only been gone four days when Williamson took McKinlay aside and suggested that it might not be a good idea, after all, to get Munro and the others back from Rodger's Harbour. While both Williamson and Breddy had been adamant about Munro returning, Williamson was now afraid of having three more mouths to feed. Right now they were experiencing trouble enough feeding themselves.

The sharing of the food was the point of contention. Hadley asked the men in Williamson's tent each time if they were satisfied with the division of the game. Lately, even when they had been agreeable and claimed to be satisfied, they would return to their tents and eat their entire allowance and then begin to complain loudly that Hadley and the others were cheating them out of their rightful share.

Meanwhile, in Hadley's tent, Auntie worked magic with the portions. She was in charge of the food and she made it last. Hadley, McKinlay, Kuraluk, and Auntie were still hungry, but they were nourished and she could make their meager rations go a long way. Always, they made sure that neither the little girls nor the kitten went hungry. All three were well fed and fussed over, and the men were more likely to give up shares of their own meals than to let the children or the cat suffer.

All that fuss over a cat might have seemed unlikely, but they were devoted to her. She helped sustain them on long, dark days. She gave them something to think about other than themselves, just as having Helen and Mugpi to worry over helped to take the focus off their own suffering. As long as the cat was alive, they felt they would survive. She was, after all, their good luck charm.

One evening, Hadley came back with ten gulls, which Auntie divided evenly between the two camps. An hour or so later, Breddy returned from hunting claiming there wasn't a crowbill to be seen, and McKinlay saw Chafe come back not long afterward with four gulls. Chafe slipped into his own tent without seeing the scientist and emerged with four more.

On June 24, Williamson's tent ran out of food. They had eaten all of their shares greedily and carelessly, and now they had nothing left. Hadley had warned them countless times about the importance of rationing themselves, but they never listened. Now they claimed they were being swindled by Hadley, McKinlay, and the Eskimos out of their rightful share of the catch. They grumbled all day and threatened to keep everything they shot for themselves. To prove their word, Breddy and Chafe returned from hunting with two good-sized eggs and five birds and made no move to share these with the other tent. Instead, they cooked the entire lot and had their own private feast.

The crew had lived separately aboard the *Karluk*, and now they insisted on living separately here. The camp was bitterly divided and there was nothing McKinlay could do about it. He agonized. He had, after all, promised the captain to keep the peace. Even though he and Munro were on the outs, he had done the best he could. But he hadn't accounted for hunger and greed. He had not foreseen the stealing and the betrayal and the paranoia that seemed to plague all of them when it came to their precious supplies and food. There was no rational thought. There was only fear and hunger and survival—and now every man for himself.

———— • ————

MUNRO WAS NEVER SO THANKFUL as he was upon reaching Rodger's Harbour. He and Maurer were exhausted from the trek and worn out from the conflagration up at Cape Waring. Munro was relieved to be safely back at this camp, miles away from the rest of the party. Now that they were back, they could concentrate on getting game, surveying the area more closely, and settling themselves into their new home.

He was glad, once and for all, to be done with the others. He was sick to death of the whole miserable lot of them, especially Williamson and Breddy, who never seemed to do anything but complain. He hoped he would have some peace and quiet. As far as he was concerned, he and Maurer and Templeman would just wait it out at Rodger's Harbour. There was no reason to go back to Cape Waring, or to see the others until the rescue ship arrived.

The weather was raw and cold and a heavy mist lingered in the air. Munro, Maurer, and Templeman stayed near camp until the fog lifted enough for the engineer and Maurer to go in search of seal down by the river. They also set out a net for catching birds. Whenever they went hunting, Templeman remained at camp, too weak to join them. Lately, he was suffering from indigestion because he'd eaten too much pemmican and—like the rest of them—had not had enough fresh meat.

On June 24, they found one duck in their net, and then Munro went out that afternoon and saw two seals. He crept toward one of them, careful not to make a sound, but that seal escaped. Munro then headed for the other one, lying down on the ice about seventy-five yards away from it. He studied the creature and tried to get up his nerve to fire his gun. For five minutes, he lay there on his stomach, trying to convince himself to shoot. His heart was beating so loudly that he was sure the seal would hear it. The creature was stretched gloriously in the sun, unaware of Munro, whose hands were shaking as he aimed the rifle. For minutes, Munro aimed his gun at the seal until he realized that his hands were too shaky to hit his target.

"It was a terrible predicament," he said. "Our very lives were at stake, and here I was with an acute attack of something akin to 'buck fever,' although much more serious than that well-known affliction."

He tried to get himself together, to clear his mind and gather his courage before the seal disappeared. He aimed again but, as he noted, he was so nervous that "in that state I could not have hit a barn, so I had to wait."

In an effort to cheer himself on, he clenched his teeth and called the seal all sorts of names. "I'll get you!" he threatened over and over again. And then the thought came to him. "If you miss him you will starve...."

He aimed and fired. He had done it. His first seal.

Maurer loaded it on the sled and that night they had a grand "stew up," which they had promised themselves upon getting their first seal. There was so much food that Templeman was unable to finish his meal.

The next day, with new confidence, Munro and Maurer headed out on the ice again. There were numerous seals in the distance and they were sure to get at least one. But they couldn't get near enough to the animals to get off a decent shot, so they had to return to camp empty-handed. The next day they tried again, but they still couldn't get close enough. On the twenty-seventh, they returned to the hunting ground, but a heavy fog quickly sent them back to camp, where they were forced to amuse themselves for the rest of the day with various odd jobs. They repaired their gear, mended their sled, and found a flag pole—or a piece of wood that would make a perfect flag pole—and set it aside for later. As soon as they had the strength and as soon as the frozen ground allowed, they would plant the pole and raise the British flag they had saved from the *Karluk*. They also created a storage space for their meat—a hole in the ground, lined with skins and blubber. They threw the seals in and then packed ice on top of them. Even with this, the seal meat rotted, but they ate every scrap of it, except for the hides and the blubber. Afterward, when there was nothing else, they were forced to eat those, too.

The mist lingered, but on the twenty-ninth it cleared enough for Munro and Maurer to go sealing. This time, they managed to kill two seals, and that evening they dined on fried liver. They were feeling more hopeful now, their moods much improved by all the food. Indeed, they felt like kings, and Templeman kept busy cooking all the time. As Munro said, "We are living high."

———— • ————

IT WAS BETWEEN 6:45 and 7:15 on the morning of June 25 when they heard the gunshot. Hadley had awakened McKinlay at 6:30 a.m. when he left the tent, but the magnetician soon drifted off again. When he awoke the second time, he stuck his head out of the tent to look for Hadley, figuring he was out shooting at the ducks. Instead the old man was lying in bed.

A few seconds later, they heard a shout. It was Williamson. "Clam! Call Hadley! Breddy has shot himself!"

McKinlay was out of the tent in a flash. Hadley and the Eskimo were on his heels. They ran to the other tent, tore open the door, and burst inside.

"What is the matter here?" Hadley demanded.

Williamson was sitting up in his bed. Now, he pointed at Breddy and said simply, "Breddy has shot himself."

Clam and Williamson both said they were asleep when it happened. The shot woke them up. Chafe was out hunting. He had gone the night before.

Breddy lay in his bed, rolled partially on his left side, his right arm stretched alongside his body, his left flung across his breast, his hands open, his eyes closed. Hadley turned Breddy over and they could see the damage. The bullet had entered the right eye, exiting on the left side of his head, just two inches or so above the ear. His right eye was "powder-burned and blackened" where the bullet had entered. It must have made a perfect pass through his brain. He would have died instantly.

Williamson handed Hadley the gun—a Colt revolver—which he picked up from Breddy's left side. Hadley snapped, "Have you another gun in here?"

"Yes."

"Give it to me and I will look after it. You don't need guns in here, anyway. You ... are scarcely able to move."

The weapon that killed Breddy was a '41 .345 caliber Colt DA revolver, owned by Hadley and loaned to Breddy. Clam and Williamson handed over their other gun, a .401 Winchester rifle, which had also belonged to Hadley, loaned to Williamson at Shipwreck Camp, back in the old days when Hadley had thought Williamson was a decent guy.

Williamson and Clam also gave Hadley all that remained of their ammunition, just twenty-four revolver cartridges and three of the original 83 to 100 rounds of rifle ammunition, "and there has been nothing to show for it," observed McKinlay.

The men carried Breddy's body outside and, in the presence of everyone, Williamson went through Breddy's personal effects. The dead man had kept everything on his person, apparently not having trusted his tent mates any more than he trusted Hadley and the others. All of the missing articles from McKinlay's knapsack were there, including his compass, which was hidden in a sock.

Chafe had gotten in the habit of going out every night to hunt. He usually left around 8:00 or 8:30 P.M., returning the next morning, and Breddy usually went with him to help carry the birds. The snow on the ice was melting daily and deep pools of water were forming. Chafe had to wade through these every night, up to his knees or his waist, until his legs became numb from the cold. Each morning, he couldn't wait to get back to camp so that he could take off his wet clothes and warm himself.

His foot was still so painful from the operation that it was hard for him to walk. For this reason, it would sometimes take Chafe twelve hours to make the trip to the cliffs and back again, even though they were only two to five miles from camp. "Of course," he said, "a lot of the time was wasted, for every time a shot is fired the birds leave the cliffs and fly away to sea; then I would have to wait till they returned and settled, before firing another shot." The crowbills went out to sea every third or fourth day to feed, staying away twenty-four hours or more. Whenever these went away, Chafe tried to shoot seagulls, which nested on top of the cliffs.

Chafe had landed a goldmine on his hunting trip of June 24, killing twenty-three birds, an exceptional night's work. Because the birds were too heavy and because Breddy wasn't there to help him this time, he dragged them along behind him over the ice as he headed back to camp on the morning of the twenty-fifth.

Half a mile from the camp at Cape Waring, Chafe spotted McKinlay coming to meet him.

"Charlie, there has been more trouble in camp," McKinlay said by way of greeting.

"What is the matter now, Mac?"

McKinlay told him about Breddy. Chafe felt all his strength leave him. He could not believe what he was hearing. McKinlay took the birds from him and they returned to camp, where Chafe saw his friend's body lying in the open, covered with a blanket, and stretched out beside a log.

According to Chafe, Breddy had come to him the night before, as Chafe prepared to go hunting. "Breddy … said he was not going with me, but was going to get up early in the morning and clean his revolver, and was going to go out to one of the seal holes to try and get a seal. The poor fellow must have done as he intended—got up early, and was in the act of cleaning his revolver when it accidentally went off and shot him."

The birds Chafe had killed were divided between the two tents, twelve going to Hadley's larder and nine to Williamson's. This time no one grumbled at having to share, and Williamson confessed to McKinlay that Chafe had admitted he and Breddy had been cheating on birds. "Wednesday last, they really obtained 6 eggs and 5 birds instead of 2 eggs and 4 birds, as they had reported, and also… Breddy stole the bird noted on June 16."

Kuraluk and McKinlay worked all day at digging a grave. They chose a small hill beyond the camp, but the ground was still frozen. They used an axe to break up the earth and a piece of board for a shovel.

That night, they had a quiet supper and later, about 8:00 P.M., after the invalids and Chafe had turned in, Hadley, Kuraluk, and McKinlay carried Breddy up the hill on an improvised stretcher made of poles and canvas. They lowered him into the grave, but it wasn't deep enough. His body was still so swollen from the mystery illness that they had to take him out and lay him on the ground. Covering Breddy's body with the canvas, they agreed to finish the work tomorrow and started back down the hill.

There was something odd about the body, which had nagged at Hadley since he had first seen it on the floor of the tent. Something strange about the way Breddy's shooting hand was positioned.

MCKINLAY COULDN'T IMAGINE why Breddy would have killed himself. Breddy had been a cocky, self-assured young man in good health, especially compared to some of the others. He had always done exactly what he wanted to, including stealing food from his fellowmen, and he had never allowed himself to be burdened with work he didn't feel like doing. Perhaps Chafe was right, and maybe he had been cleaning his gun when it accidentally went off.

Williamson and Chafe were doing all they could now to ingratiate themselves to Hadley and the rest. Indeed they seemed quite chastened and frightened by what had occurred, worried about losing favor with their estranged comrades. They even seemed a little scared of Hadley, McKinlay, and the Eskimos. To the best of McKinlay's knowledge, Clam had not participated in the lying, the stealing, and the cheating, and as far as he could tell, Clam had little in common with his tent mates, aside from being a crewman. He was instead stoic and silent, and when he did talk, he was soft-spoken and polite and seemed to have little reason to need to ingratiate himself as Williamson and Chafe were doing.

Williamson, in particular, was eager to make peace with Hadley, McKinlay, and the Eskimos. The night before, he had been all too happy to volunteer the fact that Chafe and Breddy had been cheating at birds— so generous of him to turn them in while not implicating himself when he had been, most likely, participating in their scheme. If not, he had al- most surely reaped the benefits. Also, he was suddenly now making a habit of giving little presents to the children, scraps of pemmican and useless trinkets, in the hopes of bribing Auntie into giving his tent some seal meat.

McKinlay spent the day after the shooting deepening Breddy's grave while Hadley sat by a seal hole for hours, with no luck. There were no seals any- where on the ice. That night, they had a quiet supper and for the first time since they'd reached the island, both tents ate together. Williamson, Chafe, and Clam not only shared their store of food with McKinlay, Hadley, and the Eskimos, but they ate with much more restraint than usual.

McKinlay was tempted to tell them about Adolphus Greely and the way he had sentenced a man to death for stealing seal thongs, which was all he and his men had to eat when they were stranded in the Arctic for a win- ter of 250 days and only forty days' rations. "The temptation recurred, but I resisted it," he said. "They would have failed entirely to appreciate my grim sense of humour. What a sorry bunch we were!"

After supper, McKinlay, Hadley, and Kuraluk walked back up the hill to the grave and deepened it further. They lifted Breddy's swollen body from the ground and at last laid him to rest, to be covered later with wood, skins, and moss.

Keep the peace, the captain had told McKinlay. But Bartlett could not have foreseen a tragedy like this.

Of the rules they were used to—the laws that had governed them back home—none of them applied in this strange world. It had truly become every man for himself.

If the tension subsided between the two tents, at least for the time being, it was now building violently between Hadley and Kuraluk. It was hard to tell what the problem was except that Hadley was his usual surly self, and Kuraluk was intimidated by him. Hadley, too, had been in a fury lately over having to cook breakfast because Auntie, who usually performed the task, now refused or slept in.

Unfortunately, he and the Eskimo were the two best hunters, and the ones everyone else relied upon for nearly all of their food. Kuraluk, especially, was skilled and indefatigable. The only thing was, they had to keep him happy. The moment he felt unwanted, unneeded, or depressed, he would refuse to hunt. He was as stubborn as Hadley; in fact they were very much alike.

The days passed as usual, with Kuraluk and Hadley hunting each morning, and Chafe hunting each night. The weather turned warmer so that McKinlay's tent had to sleep with the flap entirely open to let in fresh air.

Hadley and McKinlay lengthened the egging ladder, which was now about thirty-five feet tall. As soon as it was ready, they took it to the cliffs and McKinlay climbed to the top, fetching twenty-one eggs. As Chafe observed, the eggs were in a well-advanced state of development, "and would not have been considered marketable under the Pure Food laws of any country. But there were no Pure Food laws on Wrangel Island, so we ate anything that would sustain life." Ever since moving to Cape Waring, they had been lucky with birds and seals. Even McKinlay had been out hunting now and then, enjoying feeling useful and active.

They kept themselves to small portions and two meals a day. McKinlay did not know what would happen to them if the seals went away entirely, as they appeared to be doing, or if the birds left or if the eggs disappeared. They had not seen polar bears or arctic foxes in a long time. Auntie soon announced that the pemmican was finished, so anything they ate from now on, they would have to catch themselves.

The strain was unbearable. Throughout their ordeal thus far, McKinlay had managed to maintain his faith and a strong sense of hope, but often—especially lately—he felt burdened with a wretchedness that he probably would not have felt had he not been so completely alone. He rarely spoke to the men from the other tent anymore, except when they were arguing with Hadley over food. Williamson, Chafe, and because he lived with them, Clam, were greater strangers to McKinlay now than they had been at the beginning of the journey. With Bartlett gone, and Munro having abandoned everyone for Rodger's Harbour, they were without an official leader, and McKinlay had no influence over them. They would not listen to him, and they had nothing to do with Hadley or the Eskimos or McKinlay.

There was something else disturbing McKinlay. It was a horrible thought, and one he tried to push from his mind. But it lingered and refused to go away. It was about Breddy. He and Hadley had examined the body after death and made some unsettling observations.

"One point I noted in addition to those already noted," McKinlay confided to his diary. "His right hand was not in such a formation as would hold a revolver, the four fingers being bent slightly at the first joint & the thumb quite straight & hard against the first finger."

McKinlay was not sure what it meant. He had no experience with dead bodies. He was not a doctor or a detective. But he knew enough to know that something was amiss, and that thought alone was enough to keep him up at night.

"Our suspicions have been raised," he wrote, "by Williamson's strange conduct & by other circumstances, that Breddy did not die by his own hand—either suicidal or accidental."

ON THE EVENING OF JUNE 28, McKinlay and Hadley trudged up the hill to cover Breddy's grave with another load of wood. This time, they took Chafe with them. Hadley and McKinlay had already discussed the matter, and now they wanted Chafe to see what they already knew themselves. They wanted another pair of eyes to witness this and another brain to help process what it might mean.

The day before, Hadley had asked Chafe to grill Williamson about Breddy's death. Specifically, he wanted to know where the weapon was found afterward—where the gun lay that Breddy was killed with. Was it in his hand or on the floor? And if it was on the floor, then what position was it found in? Williamson said he couldn't remember where the revolver was, whether it was on the ground or in Breddy's hand. Yet when Hadley had demanded the weapon, Williamson had handed it to him, picking it up from Breddy's left side.

Uncovering Breddy's body now, they showed Chafe "that Breddy's Eyes were closed," wrote Hadley, "and that he was shot through the Eye Lid and that his hands were Laying not Like a man that Held a gun and shot himself …."

There was only one answer and one reason for this, and now Hadley believed without a doubt that the thing he had suspected was true. That evening Hadley wrote in his diary, "I think its nothing but *Murder*".

JULY 1914

———————— • ————————

Now that time is wearing on, our anxiety increases. When will our relief come? Will we be relieved this summer, or must we winter? God forbid! Our chances are thin.

—WILLIAM MCKINLAY, MAGNETICIAN

Williamson had murdered Breddy. Hadley was convinced of it. The positioning of the dead man's hand, his closed eyes, and Williamson's strange behavior were all damning clues. Breddy didn't look like a man who had shot himself, accidentally or otherwise. He didn't look like a man who had put up a fight or who had even been awake at the time. He looked like someone who had been taken by surprise, who was probably asleep in his bed when the barrel of the gun was pointed at his right temple and the trigger was pulled.

Hadley and McKinlay had examined the body carefully several times, but what now? How did you live with a murderer, especially in such close quarters? Where they were living, there were no courts of law, no trying of evidence, no judge and jury, no punishment for the guilty. Williamson knew Hadley suspected him, and he must have sensed McKinlay's guarded skepticism as well. With a kind of desperate earnestness, he continued giving little presents to Helen and Mugpi and was as nice as possible to Hadley and McKinlay. But he was still up to his tricks. On days when Hadley and McKinlay weren't in camp and Kuraluk had gone off hunting, Williamson tried to bribe Auntie into giving his tent food.

Hadley took it all as proof. He and Williamson had been at odds for many months, it was true, and once crossed, Hadley had a hard time forgiving any man. But this wasn't just Hadley being vengeful or Hadley being unforgiving. This was Hadley being convinced that Williamson was a murderer.

Chafe had been hunting at the cliffs, so there was no reason to suspect him. Clam, who was in the tent at the time, was so deathly ill that it seemed impossible he could even hold a gun, much less commit a murder. Besides, Clam didn't seem capable of such a brutal act.

That left Williamson, who had been doing nothing but causing trouble since they landed on the island, deliberately stirring things up by spreading lies about Hadley and Kuraluk, so that everyone in camp was furious with Hadley; and then Munro almost killed him. What's more, Williamson and Breddy had fought violently just weeks before, although no one ever found out what they were fighting over. Afterward, they had both argued vehemently in favor of convincing Munro to return to the main party; then, just a day or so before Breddy's death, Williamson had changed his mind. *We would be better off with fewer mouths to feed,* he had told McKinlay. *Don't bring Munro back.*

And then, the day before Breddy died, Williamson's tent had run out of food. They had cheated Hadley and the others out of birds, and they had even stolen meat from their larder, but still they had nothing left to eat. Had Williamson killed Breddy to save a mouth to feed?

No one would ever know what happened on the morning of June 25 or what, if anything, might have passed between Breddy and Williamson before Breddy died. The only thing they knew, and would probably ever know, was that Breddy was dead and the wound did not appear to be self-inflicted.

ON JULY 2, Kuraluk took his family egg hunting at the cliffs. They stayed out there for two days but wanted to stay longer. It was good to be away from the other men at camp.

Mugpi was a sunny child. Kuraluk had made her some miniature sleds out of ivory to have as toys. She played with them for hours, her laughter sparkling and bright. But Helen was solemn and she felt the hardship of their situation as keenly as Kuraluk and Auntie. She helped her father with the hunting and her mother with the cooking and now and then would chase the cat with Mugpi, but mostly she worked. Auntie was tough and strong and could have survived on her own out there, without anyone's help. But the family was thankful to be together.

If Kuraluk could have stayed at the cliffs with Auntie, Helen, and Mugpi, he would have. So much rested on their shoulders—the expectation that they would find food for the party and prepare the food and keep everyone fed and warm. Kuraluk did not want to go back to camp. But if he didn't, the men would come after him and make him return. Still it was good to take a break and go to a place where they could breathe and relax and sleep without worrying, even if it was only for two nights.

ON JULY 1, Chafe had gone hunting as usual and brought back two crowbills and one small gull. Williamson, Chafe, and Clam had not offered to share with Hadley, McKinlay, and the Eskimos this time, and instead ate the entire catch themselves.

The strain of living under this tension was wearing on McKinlay. Relations were disturbingly tenuous between the two tents, and McKinlay found himself worrying a great deal about what might happen next. He was still in shock from Breddy's death and was trying to adjust to the thought of living with someone who might be a murderer, not knowing, always wondering, afraid to turn his back on Williamson and not fully trusting Chafe and Clam.

Bartlett had said he could size up a man in an instant. "One good look and I can tell what a man is like," he liked to boast. "A couple of questions and I know his character. I can tell whether a man can be counted on or not in a pinch. I can almost say how he will behave when he dies."

Would Bartlett have been able to predict this? As much trouble as Williamson had caused during the past few months, as unpleasant as he could be, would anyone have ever picked him to be a killer? And under different circumstances, in a different world, would those violent tendencies have ever come out? McKinlay's faith in essential human goodness was being sorely tested. He hated even entertaining the possibility in his mind. He wished he could forget and move on and not think about it anymore.

Lately, he seemed to be suffering the effects of their all-meat diet, with excruciating stomach pains, but at least, thank God, they had not gone hungry yet. At times, he was so weak and sore that he would have to lie in the tent all day, unable to move. He was not the only one. Everyone seemed to be suffering from a stiffening of the joints, their limbs so dead that, as Chafe said, they "could pinch them hard and not feel it." Chafe's legs were so stiff that he was unable to leap across the cracks in the ice, even the smaller ones of three or four feet in width. Consequently, he began to take a sled with him when he went hunting. When he came to a lead, he would use the sled to form a bridge and walk across it to the other side.

Kuraluk was not interested in hunting lately, preferring instead to sleep late and stay around camp. He seemed despondent, but Hadley said it was typical of an Eskimo with a well-stocked or semi-stocked larder to become a lazy hunter. Kuraluk, in turn, said they were in no danger of starving as long as they had some blubber on hand. So Hadley went out by himself day after day and tried, with no luck, for seals or birds. One day he counted fifty-four seals on the ice, but they were lying on a smooth, flat area, which meant there was no way to reach them without being seen.

Kuraluk did begin work on building a kayak, at Hadley's urging. Now that the ice was beginning to break up and the leads were beginning to open, the men knew they would have better luck at hunting seals from the water. And as there was much open water along the beach now, it was almost impossible for the men to go out onto the ice anyway.

Kuraluk worked on the kayak daily, constructing a paddle out of a log to go with it. His only tools were an "adze," made from a hatchet, and a knife, but with typical resourcefulness he somehow was managing to create a magnificent frame of driftwood, the pieces lashed together with sealskin. Soon it began to take shape as a small skin boat, pointed at each end like a canoe. Unlike a canoe, however, the kayak could only hold one person in the small, round hole that would be carved into the wooden frame and covered in seal skins.

Hadley was unable to kill any game lately, although he miraculously caught two seals during the first week in July, which left everyone feeling hopeful and much relieved.

Chafe, as usual, went out on his nightly hunts, but when he was lucky enough to find game, he rarely offered to share it with anyone other than the men in his own tent. Hadley's seals, meanwhile, were still divided equally.

Before the new meat was shared out, Williamson appeared at Hadley's tent, asking how Hadley and the others made their meat last for so long. Williamson, Chafe, and Clam had already run through their share of the last three seals, divided out in June, and now they had no more food. Williamson begged for meat from Hadley and, grudgingly, the old man gave Williamson a large portion from their larder. Hadley wasn't going to let them starve to death, no matter how much he felt they deserved to.

Breakfast in Hadley's tent—when there was food to be eaten—was usually between 7:00 and 8:00 A.M. Then they had meat and tea and fed the dogs soup. Between noon and 2:00 P.M., on the rare days when they had enough for three meals, they ate lunch, usually tea and cold meat left over from breakfast. Supper was eaten after 6:00 in the evening, again tea and meat, the latter eaten from a pan with cooked blubber. Hadley, McKinlay, and the Eskimo family sat in a circle and ate out of the pan, combining the meat with the chunks of blubber to fill out the meal. "I am sure I eat ten times as much fat as ever I did at home," said McKinlay. And then, before bed, they had a snack of blood soup.

By July 5, Williamson's tent had devoured their entire share of the new seals, and somehow he persuaded Auntie to give him the intestines from one of the seals so that they would have something to eat. In Hadley's tent, meanwhile, they used what they called "salad oil," which McKinlay described as being "made by cutting blubber into small pieces & putting it into a 'poke,' which is a sealskin cut in such a way that the skin is complete except for a hole at the neck & another at the tail." The poke was left out in the sun until the blubber became a sour tasting oil, which the Eskimos could then use in the wintertime. Their poke had rotted and torn and, as a result, the oil wasn't fully ready; but Auntie served it up anyway and showed the men how to dip their meat into the oil before eating it. It was, said McKinlay, an "acquired taste."

In early July, the temperature hovered just below the freezing point, and rain began, beating down upon their tents in a torrential downpour. It lasted for days, and there was nothing for the men to do except lie inside, sleeping, sewing, and eating. Only Kuraluk ventured outside to work on his kayak. He was sporadic about working lately and sometimes picked up the kayak and sometimes just laid it aside. The men were anxious for him to finish it, but there was no way to hurry him.

Part of the trouble was that Williamson had installed a stove in his tent, which he had constructed out of a coal oil tin, and which the Eskimos loved. The entire family had started spending their evenings with the crewmen, gathered around the warmth of the stove, and enticed by the strong tea Williamson offered them at midnight. Kuraluk had never tasted anything like it, and he and Auntie found themselves awake all night and sleeping well into the next afternoon. One morning, Auntie was so exhausted that she fell asleep in the middle of fixing breakfast. Kuraluk, too, was tired and did not have as much energy now to work on the kayak.

It was maddening for McKinlay and Hadley, who suddenly found themselves alone and alienated from the rest of the camp. Were they being purposely excluded? McKinlay couldn't be sure, but even if they weren't, the midnight tea parties were taking their toll.

When the rain stopped, a thick fog crept in and the men moved camp to the north end of the beach. The rain had done a good deal of damage to the ice, which they were happy about, and in the distance, they could see that the great and powerful series of ice mountains, which had caused such grief to them on their trek to Wrangel Island, had now begun to crumble as the ice broke up. Open leads slithered everywhere across the horizon, wider and wider as the ice traveled south rapidly. "Eight days of this weather & one seal! The silver lining to our black cloud is that most of the winds we have been having are S. and SE.—the most favourable for any rescue," wrote McKinlay.

And then the rain set in again, cold, misting, and blowing and making it impossible to hunt. They lived on blubber for thirteen days while they waited for the weather to improve and for Kuraluk to finish the kayak. McKinlay and Hadley went out every night to pick and eat scurvy grass. The land surrounding them was barren, with only a scattering of flowers, grass, moss, and other plants. But there was scurvy grass in abundance, a seashore plant which grew flat against the ground and featured clusters of small white flowers and plump oval pods resembling green beads. More than anything, it was a good source of Vitamin C, which was almost impossible to get from anything else they were eating.

Chafe managed to kill a few birds, which he shared with Hadley's tent; during the odd break in the weather, Hadley went out sealing. There was one seal, far out on the ice, tantalizing but unreachable. Every day, Hadley watched it wistfully, and every day he returned to camp empty-handed. The ice and water conditions would make sealing nearly impossible now until the kayak was finished. They gave up for the time being. They also gave up on getting any more eggs. Chafe had been for a walk on the top of the cliffs and reported that the slope down to the edge was too steep and too dangerous to lower anyone down to fetch them. McKinlay often wished he could go hunting, but the two rifles were better off in the hands of Hadley and Kuraluk. Williamson's tent still wouldn't give up the Mauser, which Chafe used on his hunting trips.

Their supper table, as McKinlay observed, would have "created shocked surprise on a civilized table." Now they were surviving on old blubber and oil; thin soups made of seal blood; and, now and then, a rotten seal flipper, several weeks old, hair and all, which only the Eskimos seemed to enjoy. Before the meat supply had been completely exhausted, they had eaten anything that was even remotely edible—tails, neck pieces, wings, and various other "sundry parts," as McKinlay described it. They now had to make use of every single part of the animals they caught. The blubber—that thick layer of fat, which lay between the hide and the flesh of the seal, and which the Eskimos used for cooking and lighting—made McKinlay's stomach turn, but it was all they had now. Kuraluk and Auntie were amused by his efforts to swallow the stuff. "It helps to fill a hollow if nothing else," said McKinlay.

THEY AWOKE ON JULY 13 to find the entire ice pack on the move, heading south, blown by a temperate north wind. Wherever the ice met the land, it piled into thick, towering ridges, and numerous leads formed as the ice split apart and dissolved into the depths. McKinlay and Hadley had begun a routine of walking up a nearby hill to view the ice conditions, and now they headed back to camp, only to find the ice had vanished from the north end of the beach and a gigantic lead sprawled out toward the sea from the mouth of the Cape Waring bay. It was a good sign. "A few southerly gales will bring our ship," McKinlay wrote hopefully, "God send it soon."

Chafe's birthday, July 14, came and went. He had gotten a sea gull, which he said he enjoyed more than any birthday dinner he'd ever had. Hadley also managed to kill a few birds, but he could only retrieve half of them; the others fell into the water or were carried away by the pressure ice. Luck turned against them in all areas, it seemed. Even when they managed to kill a bird or seal, they could seldom retrieve it.

On July 17, Kuraluk finished the kayak frame at last and brought it inside the tent out of the rain to cover with skins. The next day, he took it out on its maiden voyage. At first, it seemed that the kayak would solve their problems, since it took Kuraluk within range of three walrus. He was frightened of the walrus, aware of the damage they could cause both to him and to the kayak. They were typically gentle creatures that turned fierce when attacked, but he went after them anyway. He shot at them, but they managed to get away.

Now there was no more meat in camp, and the next morning Williamson awoke McKinlay, Hadley, and the Eskimos to beg for blubber. He and his tent mates had run out of food again and had nothing left to eat. He was so pathetic and pitiful that Kuraluk reluctantly gave him some.

They rose in the afternoon now because there was no breakfast to eat. McKinlay was constantly suffering from acute indigestion from the blubber they had been living on and his legs were so sore he could barely walk. "Rain, fog and mist are all we have been having this month," he wrote wearily, "and conditions inside the tent are such that we will be having sickness around." Yet they were surprisingly philosophical about their lack of food and their now constant hunger. They viewed the days ahead—sure to be hungry ones—with understandable fear, but there was something else, too—determination. Things could be worse and probably would be before it was all over, but the temperature was gradually warming now and the rain was breaking up the ice, which would make way for the rescue ship.

On July 19, all they had left was tea. In desperation, Hadley gathered the last of the ammunition, loaded his revolver, and set out to find some birds.

"Let us pray that something will turn up," wrote McKinlay, "before things become too bad...."

BOTH THE *Bear* and the walrus-hunter *Kit* had reported heavy ice up north. The *Bear* was just back from Siberian waters, and *Kit* had returned from a recent trip up the Bering Strait. The ice was interminable, they said, and impenetrable. The *New York Times* reported these were the worst ice conditions in the history of the Arctic.

The *Times* was closely following the story of Bartlett and his quest to reach Wrangel Island. Newspapers around the world reported on his every move, and ships from Russia to Scandinavia to America were sent in search of the castaways. As ship after ship was forced to turn back due to the relentless ice, the fervor to reach them grew. All the while, the leader who had abandoned them maintained a noticeable silence. Stefansson was far away from the public and press now, deep in the heart of the Canadian Arctic.

In Nome, Bartlett had been anxious to be on his way. He had been sitting idle for over a month, waiting for word to come from the government, and for a way to open so that he could embark on the rescue mission. He had left his men on Wrangel Island in mid-March, and it was now July. At this rate, and with the ice conditions, he knew the earliest he could hope to reach them would be August 10.

On July 13, the *Bear* left Nome with Bartlett on board. He shared the captain's cabin with Cochran and spent much of the time in the chart room, where Lieutenant Dempwolf, the navigating officer, taught him a great deal about Alaskan and Siberian waters.

As well as being a mail boat, the *Bear* had numerous other duties. Missionaries and schoolteachers who needed to transfer to different points up and down the Alaskan coast often hitched rides, and the *Bear* also brought aid to the needy in different ports, providing essential supplies, provisions, and care. In addition, according to Bartlett, she acted "as a kind of travelling law-court."

The downside of this, for Bartlett at least, was that the *Bear* had many stops to make on her journey north before she made for Wrangel Island. The reindeer Station on Saint Lawrence Island was the first stop, followed by various other stations on the island, where the ship dropped supplies for the local schools. Saint Lawrence Bay on the Siberian coast followed, and then Lütke Island. At Emma Town, they picked up Lord William Percy, the distinguished son of the Duke of Northumberland and a well-known ornithologist. Also at Emma Town, Bartlett saw his old friend Caraieff, who had accompanied him and Baron Kleist to Emma Harbor. At last, the captain was able to settle his debts, paying off the money he owed to everyone who had helped him.

Afterward, the *Bear* headed up the coast to East Cape, and then to nearby Ugelen, and from there she steamed across to Teller, Alaska, where they visited many different settlements.

The delays were frustrating, and Bartlett wished the *Bear* could have made a more direct path to Wrangel Island. But he was lucky to find the *Bear,* and she had her own business to take care of first. He knew, too, that they could only benefit from waiting for the ice conditions to improve. Perhaps there would be a helpful break or shift in the ice pack before they entered the Chukchi Sea, that frigid body of northern water that surrounded Wrangel Island. At least he was on his way. He had to remind himself of this whenever he became impatient or anxious.

"It was a great relief to me to be really doing something at last, after so many weeks of inaction," Bartlett wrote. "My thoughts were constantly on the castaways and I wondered how things had been going with them since the middle of March."

BURT MCCONNELL was an ambitious young man, so ambitious, in fact, that most who knew him would say *overly* ambitious was a more accurate description. For months, Stefansson's personal secretary had grated on the nerves of the men in the Southern Party, who found him exceedingly pushy and overbearing, and Stefansson, at last, had given him his notice. This was right before Stefansson hired more men, purchased another ship, and vanished into the Arctic. McConnell, meanwhile, would be returning home to Los Angeles as soon as his year with the Canadian Arctic Expedition was up.

On June 1, the day on which his commission with Stefansson expired, McConnell had written a letter to the Honorable Robert L. Borden, prime minister of Canada, regarding a proposed expedition to rescue the *Karluk* and her men. Word had not yet reached the Southern Party, still headquartered at Collinson Point, Alaska, of the *Karluk*'s destruction or of the men stranded on Wrangel Island. All they knew was that the ship was lost and drifting somewhere to the northwest.

McConnell was now free, as he suggested, to lead a rescue mission to the Arctic to retrieve his lost comrades. The idea that Stefansson's twenty-five-year-old former secretary should be entrusted with such a grand charge—particularly when he had no real Arctic experience—was a preposterous one, but he had thought out every step, every necessity that a journey such as this would need. His letter ran for pages, with detailed plans for how the mission should proceed and why he, Burt McConnell, was just the one to lead it.

It was, as McConnell himself realized, "SOME letter for a kid like me to write." A noble and grand plan, yes, but typical of McConnell's notorious ambition. He had hoped to continue with Stefansson on the Canadian Arctic Expedition, even though they hadn't always seen eye to eye. He liked the notoriety of the position and had expected to be promoted. But Stefansson had sent him home due to his ineptitude and impertinence, and now he felt dejected. He did not want to return to Los Angeles to resume yet another ordinary secretarial job, nor did he want his polar career to end.

McConnell had posted his letter to Borden in June, and in July he followed up with a shorter one, which reiterated his desire to head north in search of his former shipmates. "At the time I wrote to you my sole reason for wishing to lead a relief expedition into the Arctic was for the benefit of the twenty-five people aboard the KARLUK at the time she disappeared," his letter stated. "Now, however, a month later, another reason has presented itself, viz., Mr. Stefansson and his two men ... have not returned from their Ice Trip and are already six weeks overdue."

His mission now was even grander than he had originally dreamed. If he was going to save the men of the *Karluk*, he figured, he might as well save Stefansson, too. He was hungry for the glory it would bring him. What McConnell didn't know was that Stefansson was neither in need of his help nor in need of saving. On the contrary, he was doing what he had wanted to do from the start of this expedition—heading as far north as possible in search of undiscovered land.

As JULY OPENED, Maurer, Munro, and Templeman had been riding high from June. The last weeks of June, ever since they moved to Rodger's Harbour, had been good for them. They had gotten much game and eaten well and it seemed as if their prospects in the new location were good.

Before leaving Cape Waring, Maurer had entrusted Helen with his kitten. The cat really belonged to everyone, but he felt quite possessive of her; she had bonded with him in a way she hadn't with the others. Still, he thought it best to leave her at the main camp instead of taking her on the long trip to Rodger's Harbour, so he left her with Helen, who promised to look after her.

On Wednesday, July 1, they had raised the Canadian flag in honor of Dominion Day. They finished the flagpole that morning, although in the end they had to choose another pole, since the first one was too heavy for the three of them to lift in their weakened condition, even when they worked together. The months of meager diet had broken their strength.

As the Canadian ensign was raised for the first time on Wrangel Island, Maurer felt happy. "It was a great celebration of Dominion Day," he wrote. "The entire population of Rodger's Harbor was there and what is more I knew the names of everyone of them." Their meat safe held three and a half seals so far. There was just too much now for them to eat at once, and it was a lucky thing, because they only had two tins of pemmican left. Templeman was still lazy and getting on Munro's nerves. But for the most part, they were in fine spirits. Sometimes Maurer would go hunting with Munro, and sometimes he would stay in camp to deepen the meat safe or to prepare the seals.

July had begun beautifully, the sun shining, the air warm and calm. But by July 5, the sky had opened and it had begun to rain, so that there was nothing for the men to do but stay in camp and cook. They took advantage of every opportunity to stay out in the open and breathe the fresh air because the tent was small and cramped, with "little room for anything but sleeping," according to Maurer.

On July 16, a strong easterly wind had sprung up during the night and continued throughout the following day. The rain had lightened into a miserable, dank mist, and there was nothing to do but sit about camp and wait for the storm to break. Maurer had been working for the past two days digging a grave for Malloch and Mamen. It was sobering work, and as he stood in the rain, the water dripping down his face in cold, shiny rivulets, his hands stiff and sore from digging, he reflected on his own life as well as the lives of the two scientists. He was feeble, having lost a good deal of weight. He could have dug that hole in a day back home, in good health, well nourished. But the ground was still partially frozen and he was terribly weak. It was discouraging to feel the limits of his strength.

Since May, the bodies of Mamen and Malloch had lain under their canvas covers, anchored by stones and wood. Maurer and Munro had waited this long to bury them because they had expected a ship in early July and wanted to take the bodies home so that Mamen could return to Norway, and Malloch to Canada, as they had dreamed of doing.

But no ship had come, and they had no idea when one would arrive. It did not seem fair to leave the dead men out in the rain and the elements any longer. They would have to rest where they had died, on desolate Wrangel Island.

AUNTIE LAY AWAKE at night, listening to the cries. They were haunting, unearthly sounds, which chilled her bones and caused the hair on her skin to bristle. It had been going on for days, and she was the only one who could hear them.

They came from a mythical creature—a sea serpent of sorts, monstrous and vile. Its tusks were enormous, great grappling hooks that could crush a ship with one blow. Its teeth were long and jagged, sharpened to great, luminous points. The description alone, McKinlay remarked, "was enough to inspire terror." Hadley said it was a being that existed only in the mind of the Eskimos.

But it was real to Auntie, and the cries were growing louder every day. Her blood ran cold, and all she could do was listen to the calls of that distant, menacing creature and wait to see what destruction it caused.

Every soul in the camp was discouraged and disheartened. They could feel their bodies weakening and slowly wasting away. They sat with their shoulders slumped, their heads hanging down in defeat, not saying a word to each other. There was nothing to say now when everything looked so bleak.

On July 20, the men collected all the bird wings they could find lying about on the ground, plucking the feathers from them and tossing them into a pot of water to make a sort of soup. The wings were really nothing more than bones, but at least it was something, and more than they had had to eat in days.

The wings had been boiling for an hour when Hadley raised his binoculars in the direction of a distant object, creeping toward them down the beach. Everyone else was gathered outside around the fire, anxiously awaiting their soup, which, they hoped, "would give us new life and strengthen us," said Chafe.

Hadley interrupted the silence with a shout, "Hey, boys! The native's got a walrus."

In an instant, they were all on their feet, passing the field glasses around so that each man could see it was true. Then they removed the pot from the fire, tossed the bird wings onto the ground, and put fresh water on to boil in preparation for the walrus that Kuraluk was bringing them.

An hour later, he reached camp. The walrus weighed at least six hundred pounds, and it had taken five bullets to kill him. It took all hands to cut up the animal, since its hide was nearly an inch thick and, according to Chafe, "is so hard that every two or three inches you cut, takes the edge off your knife, and you have to sharpen it several times before the job is completed."

For most, it was their first taste of walrus. Chafe pronounced the flesh similar to seal, the blubber, when boiled, much like cornstarch pudding. It reminded McKinlay of beef, "both lean and fat; and the soup made from it was not to be compared with anything I had ever tasted, it was delicious. As our Scotch saying has it, 'Hunger's guid kitchen.'"

Despite the strangeness of taste, the men were immensely grateful to have meat in their empty stomachs. Their spirits had lifted considerably from the catch and the fact that they now had meat in the larder. "Thus does our mental state depend on our stomach!" observed McKinlay happily.

Momentarily, things seemed to be looking up. Auntie sewed a piece of calico onto the end of Hadley's tent and they lengthened the ridgepole that held it so that the tent was roomier and now large enough to hold a stove. This they installed the next day, and all were grateful to have the warmth. But on July 23, a dense fog billowed in from the east, making it miserable for the men, whose old, rotting clothing could no longer withstand the low temperatures. They had been wearing the same clothes now for the past six months and they were in a pitiful state—filthy, torn, pocked with holes, stained with blood, and soaked with oil. The stove did little to combat the chill.

A brisk northwest wind swept in on the heels of the fog, bringing the broken ice back together and closing up all of the open water outside the bay. The men were understandably defeated. "No more unfavourable conditions could exist for us," McKinlay observed, "while the wind means delay in our relief." With the ice pack reformed and solid once more, no ship would be able to reach them now until the end of August.

After breakfast, Kuraluk and his family walked over to the headlands to get a good view of the east coast. When they returned, they reported nothing but solid ice across the horizon, as far as the eye could see. On July 24, it began to snow, the fog was thicker than ever, and the wind blew until McKinlay and his fellow castaways were chilled to the bone. To make matters worse, Hadley's tent was feeding on walrus hide now, which they boiled vigorously until it resembled jelly. A little of that meal, thought McKinlay with disgust, went a long way.

Over the next few days, the wind changed to the east and, as a result, the ice began crushing in the bay. The men were despondent. Their rescue was at the mercy of the weather. Should the winds decide to change again, they would be doomed. As it was, the thick ice of the pack was barely moving, the bay still congested. This relentless fog and snow and wind grated on their nerves and depressed them, as did the waiting. Camp was shrouded in a thick, gray mist that covered them like a great, suffocating blanket so that they couldn't see more than a hundred yards in front of them. What little glimpse of Arctic summer they had had was now gone, and winter seemed to be returning.

In spite of the weather, Kuraluk and Hadley went hunting, the Eskimo in his kayak, and the old man on foot. Hadley shot a seal, a walrus, and an uguruk—or bearded seal—but was unable to reach any of them. Kuraluk stayed out overnight in the kayak, and just when they had begun to worry, he returned with an uguruk. The animal had sunk after he shot him, but Kuraluk had managed to fish him out with his nixie, a handy tool he had created to hook a dead or wounded creature and pull him up on the ice. The nixie was not strong enough to retrieve this powerful five-hundred-pound creature, but Kuraluk had gotten it in the end. Hadley, of course, claimed it was the very uguruk he had wounded just a day or so before. He couldn't stand to see Kuraluk become the only provider in camp, and it had been days since he had brought back anything himself.

The uguruk intestines provided a new dish, the kind McKinlay and the others had been more than willing to leave to the Eskimos until now. It seemed too revolting, too nauseating, but now that they were so famished, they tried it. The inner lining of the uguruk was washed and dried, the lining often used as material for everything from windows to raincoats. The outer skin was cut up with the blubber and served as quite a delicacy. It suggested raw clams, thought McKinlay, and although not a tasty dish, he had to thank God for the nourishment.

The next day, Kuraluk crawled out onto the ice and shot another uguruk as it lay near its hole. Hadley and McKinlay helped him haul it back to camp, trudging through the rotten ice, and towing the uguruk through the water. They were forced to walk most of the way in the water themselves, "often on ice perforated all over with small holes and very often above the knees so that the water poured in over the tops of our boots," wrote McKinlay afterward.

This uguruk was similar in size to the first one, and the Eskimos compared the sizes by studying the hollows in the claws of the flippers of each animal. It had taken Kuraluk, Hadley, and McKinlay two hours to haul the uguruk into camp, and when Auntie had cut it open they discovered its stomach was full of worms, but otherwise empty. Not an encouraging sight for the men. If the uguruk was starving, what then were their own chances for survival?

Toward the end of July, the wind shifted once more and the ice, loosened by the eastern blow, once again grew impenetrable. Young ice formed over the open leads every night and was at times so thick and strong that it would pierce a hole in the kayak. Fortunately, this was easily fixed by a patching of boiled seal oil, which the Eskimos used as a pitch substitute.

On July 29, Hadley thought he saw the smoke of a ship in the distance. There was great excitement as everyone took turns peering toward the horizon through the field glasses, but there was no ship. There was nothing. Only ice. McKinlay wrote with great dejection, "It may be the wish is father to the thought." They were running out of hope.

FOR MUNRO, MAURER, and Templeman, every day was the same as the one before, and soon all the days started running together in a long, blank, forgettable string of hunger, rain, and idleness. There was nothing to do but watch the rain and take shelter in the tent. When they could, they went hunting, but there was very little game to be found and the weather made it difficult. There was no use hunting in the rain, so on the bleakest days they stayed inside, still talking obsessively of food and the meals they wanted to devour when they were finally back home. On the days when the rain was mostly mist and the wind wasn't quite as contemptible, they trekked out to the headlands or to the spit to hunt for eggs, but there weren't many to be had. Sometimes they were lucky enough to get a few ducks, but their harvest, it seemed, was over.

The only positive aspect they could find in the strong, shifting winds and the pelting rain was that the elements would break up the ice and blow it off the coast, making it easier for a ship to get through to the harbor. For this reason, they didn't curse the rain and the winds as fiercely as they might have, and they tried to stay in a positive frame of mind, although it was a struggle. "We are all getting impatient here expecting the ice to go any minute and let in the boat," wrote Munro. "'Patience is a virtue.'"

Templeman was the only one who seemed to lack that virtue. Indeed, he had been causing a great deal of trouble lately. His constant worrying about their predicament didn't help his comrades' spirits. Munro lit into him a couple of times. It seemed to do some good, but Munro was frankly past the point of caring, worn down and disgusted by their situation, so most of the time he let Templeman grumble.

They had found some thirty-two eggs recently, but only five of these were edible. The others were rotten and nauseating, at such an advanced state of development that they could hardly be called eggs anymore. At the beginning of July, they had been lucky enough to catch two seals, which made three and a half in the larder. But since then, the seals rarely showed their faces on the ice, and Munro and the others were only able to get the eggs, and a few ducks. The ducks were scared of them by now and stayed away from the area for the most part.

The seal meat had run out on July 17. They ate every last tainted, rotten bit of it, including the hide. After that, they lived on pemmican in short rations because there wasn't much left. There was enough of the pemmican, they calculated, so that they could make it last until August 5 if they ate small portions and filled it out with blubber. The rescue ship would surely find them by August 5, Munro believed—hoped—so they would not have to worry about what would happen to them once the pemmican ran out.

On July 23, the graves dug, they buried Mamen and Malloch beneath a crude wooden cross and a border of stones. It was a solemn and grim reminder of what might lie ahead for the living, and they lowered the Canadian flag to half-mast in honor of the two. There was nothing to do but turn their thoughts heavenward and pray for relief. The gusting winds were now smashing up the ice around the beach, as they had hoped, but there was no sign of open water in the surrounding ice pack that divided the island from the world below.

Munro, Maurer, and Templeman were disheartened, but each of the three men maintained his faith in God. *He* would see them through this, they told themselves, no matter how drastic their situation. They would look to the future and expect the best.

On July 28, Munro wrote with a heavy heart, "It seems as if our luck has gone altogether. We haven't seen a seal or any living thing except ducks for weeks past. We put our trust in the good Lord who has provided for us so far and who isn't going to desert us at the last in this, our 199th day since we lost our ship."

AUGUST 1914

———— • ————

... what will be our fate, God alone knows.
—WILLIAM MCKINLAY, MAGNETICIAN

On August 9, the whaler *Herman* arrived at Herschel Island with news, at last, of the *Karluk*. The members of the Southern Party who were there listened eagerly as Captain Pedersen relayed the story. It was the first concrete news they had heard of the ship or her men since Stefansson had become separated from the Northern Party in September of 1913.

They tried to absorb it all—the ship locked in ice, the sinking of the *Karluk* in January, the struggle of Bartlett and the staff and crew to live on the ice and then to reach land, and Bartlett's journey for help with Kataktovik. Pedersen could not remember which of the scientists had accompanied Dr. Mackay when he left the main party. He thought, though, that Murray had gone, as well as one of the seaman, a big, brawny fellow. He also thought, incorrectly, that Mamen had, too.

From what the members of the Southern Party knew, Wrangel Island was reported to have plenty of driftwood and plenty of game, especially polar bears and walrus. Therefore, they concluded, their former colleagues would be in no danger of going hungry.

"WE ARE NOW ALL ANXIETY, forgetting all our ills and complaints, and thinking only of the coming of the ship," McKinlay wrote in his journal on August 4. "This all depends on the captain; if he won through, we are safe; if he was lost, we must winter here."

On August 1, he had written, "August has opened under good auspices, the sky being speckless & the sun very warm.... Altogether a promising start." Kuraluk killed an uguruk and they hoped it was a good omen for what they could expect for the rest of the month. Kuraluk had been constructing a meat rack when he spotted the creature. The rack would be used to sun-dry all of the fresh meat they obtained, so that they could then store the meat and live on it during the winter, should they—God forbid—have to remain on the island.

They dissected the great bearded seal on the cake of ice where they always cut up the animals they caught. The white of the ice had been stained red long ago and was a barbaric reminder of their crude and desperate existence. The hide and flippers were set aside to be used in the building of an umiak, the construction of which was on their list of winter preparations. They had already discussed the possibility of having to winter on the island and begun to plan ahead so that they wouldn't be unprepared by the end of the month, if a ship still hadn't come.

Other than this, life continued as usual. McKinlay picked scurvy grass while Hadley walked up to a nearby lane of water every day to watch for game. But there was no game to be found. Hadley did get off a shot at another uguruk, but it sank before he could reach it. The kayak was too far away down the beach for Kuraluk to use, so he took his nixie and tried retrieving the creature that way; but soon the ice drifted over the spot and he had to give up.

Hadley was livid. He claimed Kuraluk wouldn't have given up so soon trying to fetch the uguruk if he had killed it himself. They had enough to worry about without this kind of competition. What's more, he said, the Eskimo was becoming "unbearable" because everyone was always praising him, giving him a swelled head. Hadley declared that from now on he didn't intend to shoot anything that he couldn't get on his own—or, to be more specific, to do anything that required help from Kuraluk.

As winter approached, the game was thinning alarmingly. Their situation was grim, and quickly becoming hopeless. McKinlay had done all he could to stay well and strong, but his body was tired, weak, and suffering. He refused to lie in the tent and be sedentary, so he forced himself to get up and out and to walk around, step by painful step. It had started as influenza; at least, that is what it had felt like. As his legs and ankles began to swell to twice their normal size, he feared it was something else—the mystery disease. Auntie seemed to be suffering from it, too, and neither one of them had any feeling in their legs.

In spite of this, McKinlay and Chafe set out for the thirty-mile hike to Rodger's Harbour on August 6, taking with them some dried meat for Munro, Maurer, and Templeman. They hadn't heard from Munro since June and wanted to make sure that he and the others were surviving. McKinlay and Chafe headed along the coast, walking into a brutal wind from the southwest. They trod over rocks, moss, and mud, and from the high land near Cape Waring they had a fine view of the conditions surrounding the island. There were several miles of open water along the north coast, and a mile or more along the eastern coast. This was promising and they felt their spirits lift as they moved onward.

When they reached Hooper Cairn, a heavy fog descended, but not before they caught a glimpse of the thick ice, which seemed to grow from the southern coast and stretch out for miles, just how far they couldn't tell. They turned inland then and noted that the land here seemed more barren, with only scattered vegetation, compared to the land around Cape Waring. The hills were steep and hard to climb, and after several miles, the two men grew tired. The soles of their sealskin boots were, according to Chafe, "less than an eighth of an inch thick, and before we got half way there they had many holes in them."

They kept going anyway, until they reached a river formed by melting snow, and running down from the mountains through the center of the island. The river was too deep to walk through and at least twenty yards across, so McKinlay and Chafe turned around and headed back to Cape Waring, praying that Munro and the others were all right, and helpless to reach them if they weren't. For most of the way back, McKinlay walked on his socks because the soles of his boots were now completely worn through. They returned to camp, at last, nearly barefooted, their feet bloody and blistered, and so damaged that they had trouble walking for days afterward.

There was never enough to eat. Even Auntie's magic didn't work anymore. They skipped meals and tried not to think about being hungry.

They needed food to strengthen them, but without strength they couldn't get the food they needed. They felt as trapped on the island as they had been on the ship, and then on the ice pack at Shipwreck Camp. At every turn, the ice was their prison, surrounding them and isolating them from the rest of the world.

Despite the bitter chill in the air, Hadley spent day after day sitting by a seal hole. He would sit for six or seven hours, looking for a sign of life, but he waited in vain. It was a fruitless task and he was clearly despondent. McKinlay had never known his outlook to be so bleak. Kuraluk, for his part, managed to kill a last flock of crowbills with a throwing stick he had made. But he had not gotten many birds, and what he did get did not last long. More and more, the men felt as if they were the only living creatures on the island.

As the month wore on and no rescue ship appeared on the blank horizon, the men spent their meager energy squabbling over food—hoarding, begging, counting every crumb, some of them stealing or gorging, others sharing and rationing. Williamson, Chafe, and Clam were, as usual, out of food, "in spite of the fact," McKinlay noted, "that they had nearly half share for their tent with only three of them in it. It means now that we will have to keep them going from our portion. Something will have to be done to put an end to this, if we are destined to be here for a lengthy stay."

Just a few days later, the strangest thing happened. Williamson announced he was going to Rodger's Harbour to visit Munro and the others. McKinlay and Hadley thought, at first, that he was kidding. After all, this was a man who had been strapped to sledges and pulled for miles ever since they were thrust out onto the ice. He never exercised, even when he was healthy, and McKinlay had never known him to exert himself unnecessarily.

Yet now he wanted to make the nearly thirty-mile hike to Rodger's Harbour. Of course, he would not tell Hadley or McKinlay why he was going. They couldn't begin to understand it, particularly since Williamson and Munro had despised each other for months. The reason he gave was that he wanted to go check on Munro, to see how he was getting on. It seemed preposterous.

"What his real motives were would always remain a mystery," wrote McKinlay, "but what made his proposed trip so utterly incomprehensible was the fact that he had never walked a mile from camp, even at Icy Spit before he had become sick. To me it was the most abnormal, even fantastic event; it did not seem to make sense that a man who had for so long played sick should be capable of covering between sixty and seventy miles in that short period. I confess that it confirmed suspicions I had harboured for a long time."

Hadley was furious because his dog Molly was missing, and he was sure Williamson had either taken her with him or set her loose just to spite him. She was pregnant and had been tied to a stake so they could keep an eye on her, because on two previous instances, she had escaped from Hadley and eaten her newly born puppies. Now she was gone, stake and all, and Hadley and McKinlay scoured the area for her. She would have the puppies any day now, and Hadley needed to find her before then. He was planning to get a dog team out of her litter, counting on the fact that by the time they all set out for Siberia in the spring of 1915, the puppies would be grown enough to help their three remaining dogs pull the sledge. It was true the men were starving, and they could have killed the dogs for food, but they knew the animals would be of more use to them alive than dead. Besides, Molly was all the family Hadley had left now.

There was no sign of Molly on August 18 or 19, but on the twentieth, McKinlay walked up the hill to Breddy's grave to retrieve a snow knife that had been left there. To his astonishment, burrowed into the grave, was Molly, very much alive, with a litter of eight puppies. She had torn away the protective logs they had used to cover the ends of Breddy's grave and sheltered herself in the hole, nestled against Breddy's body. And there, beside the corpse, she had brought new life into the world. From the sight of the body, McKinlay could tell that she and the puppies had been feeding on Breddy, nourishing themselves on his flesh.

They kept the three strongest puppies and drowned the others because they knew there wouldn't be enough food for all of them. They also knew Molly wasn't strong enough to take care of them. Like the men, she was suffering the effects of a starvation diet. In spite of their hunger, it apparently never occurred to the men to eat the puppies. Or if it did occur to them, they quickly dismissed the idea.

It was growing colder now—bitterly cold. The Arctic "summer" had been so fleeting as to be practically invisible. The wind had picked up, constant and biting, and the midnight sun was gone, leaving darkening nights and frigid temperatures. All during the summer, the ice shelf surrounding the island had broken up promisingly and then reformed again and again. The snow never melted in the hills. The land was surrounded by ice for miles. Even if someone knew they were there, it would take a miracle for a ship to get through.

Still, some days—most days, really—they looked out toward sea and hoped. Once, Auntie thought she smelled the smoke of a steamship, which caused a lot of excitement, until they realized that it was, instead, the smell of the rotting entrails of their walrus. Sometimes, they thought they saw ships, but they were dreams, mirages, hallucinations. They wanted to see ships, so they did. Tall, powerful ships, cutting through the ice fields to reach them, lowering their anchors, helping them aboard, taking them away from there, taking them home. They dreamed of ships.

McKinlay wrote, "That now is our only thought in our waking moments—When will she come? Will she come? Was the captain lost? Only time will answer these questions for us. But God forbid that we should have to winter here. It's a hopeless prospect."

They had set up flags and a beacon, just in case a whaling ship might steam by the island. But winter was already upon them. They were living through their first blizzard. The birds were thinning. The seals were gone. The men were too weak to move some days, too weak to even try to find food. They spent many "blank" days, filled with "the monotony of waiting and thinking," said McKinlay. "Think, think, think! That is all we can do these days—all day and in our waking moments at night. The strain becomes more and more acute as the days pass; there is not enough for us to do to alleviate it. We pray that it may end soon."

MAURER, MUNRO, AND TEMPLEMAN had spied a polar bear near camp, just two miles off the shore of Rodger's Harbour, but the water interfered, and they couldn't reach him. All they could do was stand there, watching him longingly, and, as Maurer remarked, "savagely … with thought of devouring him. Our self preservation urged us through hunger to get and eat whatever appeared in sight and was edible."

That was on the first of August. On the seventh, Munro had shot a small duck, which they eagerly devoured. On August 13, he got another one. But that was it. Otherwise, they had been living on blubber, which they had been eating since July when the game ran out. The blubber, according to Maurer, was "spoiled and rancid, but we ate with the desperation of starving men."

They had rationed themselves, eating the smallest portions they could that would keep them alive. But when the blubber was depleted on August 9, all they would have left to eat were the decaying skins they had set aside weeks ago.

The only thing they did in the way of dressing the two ducks was to pull the feathers off. They were so desperately hungry by now that the meat needed no other preparation. When they started on the skins, they removed the hair from them, pulling it out with a knife, but that was all they had the energy to do to it. "Talk about putrid meat poisoning anyone?" wrote Maurer dryly. "We had gotten to the point where it would have no effect on us."

The winds blew high and fiercely, but seemed to do little against the ice, which remained solid and steadfast in the harbor and well out into the horizon, so far they couldn't see the end of it. They expected the ice to go at any moment, but Maurer was beginning to lose heart and so were Munro and Templeman. The mental and physical strain was beginning to show. If only they could know Bartlett had won through. "We were in entire ignorance of his fate," said Maurer, "and not knowing his were uncertain of our own."

They struggled to keep their spirits up by watching for the ship, and they promised each other that whoever sighted their rescuers first would be awarded a Bible. Maurer had with him the Bible his mother had given him, and, so eager was he for salvation, that he was willing to part with it, should Munro or Templeman see that salvation first.

"Things on the whole look very bad for us, as we can't get any game now at all," wrote Munro wearily. "We pray for a finish one way or another as the strain is great both mentally and physically and soon tells. But 'Hope springs eternal in the human breast' and so with us."

ON AUGUST 19, Williamson arrived at Rodger's Harbour. He appeared on August 19, twenty-four hours after leaving Cape Waring, and left the next day to go back. He had caught sight of the Canadian flag, flying at half-mast, before he spotted their camp, and once he reached their tent, there was no one to be seen—just the grave of poor dead Mamen and Malloch. He shouted until Munro appeared, pushing aside the tent flap and coming out, armed with his rifle.

Munro could not imagine what he was doing there.

Breddy was dead, Williamson told them. He had accidentally shot himself while cleaning his gun sometime at the end of June. Munro thanked God he was away from them all, as bleak as it was now at Rodger's Harbour. The only reason he could imagine for being back at Cape Waring, in the middle of all that mess, was that Williamson boasted that they had plenty of food. It was a lie, of course, but Munro couldn't know that. They were all fine and healthy as could be, Williamson said, with plenty of game to be had, plenty to eat, everything good. Hard words for a starving man to hear.

Williamson slept for twelve hours and then left. Munro, Maurer, and Templeman were suffering, not having had meat for some time now, and Williamson knew there was nothing he could do for them. So he bid them good bye and set out for Cape Waring, taking with him Templeman's .45 Colt revolver and some ammunition. It was, no doubt, what he had come for. And to be the first to tell Munro about Breddy's death, before McKinlay or the Eskimo or Hadley, in particular, could turn the engineer's mind against him.

As Williamson made his way up the coast and across the island, he felt his energy disappearing. He was already taxed from his recent bout with the mystery illness and the lack of food, as well as the walk to Rodger's Harbour, and now all he wanted to do was lie down to rest and sleep. He knew the dangers of this, however, and was afraid he would never wake up again if he stopped now. He pressed on, climbing over the second range of hills, which separated Cape Waring from Rodger's Harbour. His last landmark before camp was Berry Peak or, as they had come to call it, "Wine Glass Hill," because of its shape. He saw the peak of it now to his left and began to search for the ravine, which would lead him down toward camp.

The snow started to fall gently then, and then quickly gathered strength, and within minutes it had blanketed the familiar landmarks and clouded the horizon so that Williamson "wandered ankle-deep in snow in a narrow dusk-shrouded circle." He was alone and afraid of what would become of him. He was not used to going out on his own on the island. He had not been one—like McKinlay or Hadley or Chafe or Kuraluk—to wander up and down the coast, to investigate the land, to climb the nearby hills and explore the area. He was not familiar with the lay of the land. He was terrified of getting lost.

It was then he heard the voices. They were the voices of men or of women, he couldn't make them out, but he knew he must be hearing things, that there was no one there. Yet the voices persisted. They called to him, clearly, convincingly, and then, out of the fog and the mist he saw "pale faces and waving arms which beckoned me on." It made no sense; he couldn't explain it, but he followed the faces and the voices and the waving arms until he realized he was lost in the snow and the haze. He did not know east from west, north from south, or left from right. Slowly, he felt a panic rising in his heart. If he couldn't find his way back, he would die, wandering around like a blind man. Eventually, he would have no choice but to lie down and seek the rest he so badly needed, and then he really would be finished.

Thinking only of sleep, he heard another noise—not a voice, but a kind of exhaling of air, a rush of wind. He listened and there was only silence. And then it came again, closer this time, now the unmistakable hooting of an owl and the flapping of wings. The creature seemed to be waiting for Williamson—it would fly onward and then seemed to double back, calling to him.

Williamson could not see the owl, but he could hear its call and the sound of its wings, thumping slowly and distinctively as it passed over-head. "To me," he wrote, "his whisper in the overcast was the whisper of death and his wings were its shadow. I was alone, lost in a world without horizons, weak and staggering from lack of food."

But he was not alone, because on his way back from Rodger's Harbour, heading once again to Cape Waring, he believed an owl was there with him. He imagined a great, snowy creature, wild-eyed and beautiful, as it called out repeatedly, reassuringly, leading Williamson back home.

"For what reason I cannot say—except that he was another speck of life in a lonely land—I followed after him," said Williamson. "Ten times more he hooted, from the left and then from the right, truly as if he were guiding me, until finally the ground sloped down beneath my feet and, as I descended and the snow lifted, I found myself in a ravine, 30 to 40 feet wide."

It was the path to Cape Waring, and soon he was back in camp, ex-hausted but thankful. Without the cry of that benevolent, invisible owl, he would have died that day. He was sure of it.

THE FIRST THING Hadley told Williamson after Williamson returned was that "he had better not have any *more* accidents with Guns in that Tent because I wouldn't stand for any more." After what had happened to Breddy, the very notion of Williamson with a gun made Hadley sick to his stomach.

It was growing colder at Cape Waring, and on the morning Williamson returned, the ice, driven by a nasty eastern wind, crept back into the bay until the bay was filled. It was a devastating sight, but maybe, they hoped, it would bring them game. They envisioned seals basking on the ice, polar bears within reach, walrus camped nearby.

They were down to scraps now, mostly rotten flippers, filling it out with blood soup—which was now mostly water—and some roots to which the Eskimos had introduced them. McKinlay said the roots tasted like licorice sticks. They dug a sack of them daily and then cooked them up with some blubber. It was hell on their digestive systems, but it was the best they could do. Hadley's tent was saving all the meat they had dried—or "sun-cooked," as the Eskimos called it—for later, hoping they could exist on skins and blubber until a ship came. Perhaps they would not have to touch the dried meat at all.

Auntie administered a new plan one morning. Until that time, everyone in Hadley's tent had been eating what he or she wanted out of a common dish, helping themselves to what there was. But on the morning of August 22, Auntie doled out individual portions so that each man could have his own share to do with as he pleased. He could eat as much as he wanted or put it away for later. Times were excruciatingly hard, but Hadley and his tent mates knew they would probably get even harder before it was all over. Each of them set aside a portion of each meal, and it felt good to know they had a reserve, meager as it was.

On August 23, the last of their fresh meat supply was finished, and they had no choice but to delve into their dried meat stores. But the tin in which McKinlay had stowed his scraps was hanging from the meat rack, and during the night had dropped to the ground where the dogs pounced on it, devouring its contents, leaving McKinlay to beg food from his tent mates.

The men in Williamson's tent, naturally, had made no provision whatsoever for themselves and had been eating two ounces of dried seal meat with blubber every day. They had run through their stores with their usual carelessness, and now continued to beg for meat from Hadley. It was becoming a daily habit with them and, finally, sick of having to hear it time and again, Hadley and his tent mates decided to give Williamson, Chafe, and Clam one piece of meat a day. A daily ration that, as McKinlay noted, "would not be increased under any circumstances."

This time, however, Hadley and the others weren't letting them off without getting something back. Hadley's tent had exhausted their tea tablets three weeks ago, and now, in exchange for the meat ration, they asked for a share of the tea. McKinlay's own ration had been left with Mamen, and the remains of Munro's, Maurer's, and Breddy's tea rations were all left with Williamson, who had brought an additional three hundred tablets back with him from Rodger's Harbour. He gave them eighty-eight tablets grudgingly, and later that night, as they were enjoying their first mug of tea in a long time, Hadley commented cryptically that he was "as good a horse trader as the next fellow!"

The weather was worsening while the ice remained the same. The pack seemed stationary now, like thick, white plaster filling up the bay, and still no game appeared. Kuraluk was convinced he would die before a ship ever came to free them, and Mugpi's reassurances no longer calmed him. But he was determined to find game, so he headed out now and then after breakfast, rifle in hand, returning in the afternoon without having seen any signs of life. The ground, too, was covered with thick layers of snow, six feet or more, and was too frozen now to dig for roots. It snowed all day, from morning till night, without a break—a perfect blizzard. And then the rain began, freezing everything it touched until the land was covered with ice as well.

They lived inside all day, mending their socks and boots for the winter, and only venturing out to chop and carry wood for the stove. Breakfast was a cup of soup served from the "starvation tin," as they dubbed it. Lunch was a cup of tea (thank God they had some now) with walrus hide and raw blubber. Supper was cooked roots with oil.

At Rodger's Harbour they were living on one meal a day. All they had left were rotten skins, which had been their only sustenance for weeks, and these were now running out. There was a blizzard blowing from the northwest, and on August 27, the tent caved in on top of Maurer, Munro, and Templeman, who fought the wind and the sleet to set it up again and nearly froze to death in the process.

Sometimes, when they were feeling especially pessimistic, Maurer, Munro, and Templeman would discuss their deaths. They would sit together outside the tent, their eyes fixed on the crude wooden cross and the double grave of Mamen and Malloch. The sight of the grave, the cross, and the flag at half-mast cast a funereal pall over the camp that they could never shake. Doomed to live in the shadow of death, they were constantly reminded that they were but one step away from the same end. The last to die, they decided matter-of-factly, would bury the other two and then be left as food for the foxes they knew lived in the area but could never catch.

None of them knew what it was to be dying, but they felt their bodies failing every day. For five months, they had been living almost completely on meat, and that alone was far from strengthening. Their blood was thin, which meant they were constantly cold and terribly weak, so weak they could barely stand. Each of them—even the naturally thin Templeman—had lost a great deal of weight. Their strength was gone, which they noticed with every little chore or task they attempted. "In chopping wood for a little fire, three strokes of the axe was enough to wind us," said Maurer. "We staggered as we walked, and an attempt to run was almost out of the question. We slept as much as we could to save our strength."

WAR HAD BEEN DECLARED, first between Germany and France and then between Germany and England. Bartlett was aboard the *Bear*, listening to the broadcast, unable to believe what he was hearing. The news report was detached and emotionless, and it seemed a cold way to learn about such a catastrophic event in such a faraway place.

It was August 4 and the *Bear* was anchored in Kotzebue Sound. Lord Percy left them immediately, since he was an officer in the British army and needed to return to England as soon as he could.

On August 18, the *New York Times* announced that Robert A. Bartlett, captain of the ill-fated *Karluk,* had been "absolved of blame for the fate of the members of the expedition who left his party. It is too bad that Dr. Mackay, Murray, Beuchat, and Sailor Morris left the main party. But Bartlett has a paper signed by all of them, stating that they made the trip on their own initiative, and exempting him from all responsibility, and as they were not members of his crew, he had no authority to prevent them from leaving the camp."

The *Bear,* with Bartlett aboard, continued on her journey northward. She anchored at Point Hope, Alaska, where Bartlett enjoyed a moving reunion with Kataktovik. Captain Pedersen had brought him over from East Cape, Siberia, in the *Herman,* and Bartlett was pleased to see him looking well and recovered from their trying journey. The Eskimo looked wonderful, in fact, and announced that he was getting married. Bartlett paid him the wages he was owed as a member of the Canadian Arctic Expedition and then gave him an outfit of clothing provided by the Canadian government, something they were giving each man on the expedition to replace what they had lost when the ship went down.

As the *Bear* steamed up the Alaskan coast toward Point Barrow, she ran into the first sea ice they had seen so far, just off Icy Cape. Afterward, it was a struggle for the *Bear* to move, and she wrestled her way through the thickening ice, which grew more forbidding and densely packed the farther north they traveled.

A Canadian schooner called the *King and Winge* accompanied them to Point Barrow. Managed by the personable Olaf Swenson and mastered by a captain named Jochimsen, she was a walrus hunter chartered by the Hibbard-Swenson Company for trading in the Arctic and carried provisions for the mounted police at Herschel Island. As they ran up against the ice, Bartlett doubted the *King and Winge* would be able to reach Point Barrow with her overloaded deck, which kept her exceedingly low in the water. She was a light, speedy ship usually, but not at all an icebreaker. Powered only to do eleven knots at top speed, she'd not been fitted out for such work; no sheathing or stem plates had been added for extra strength and protection. However, he had to admit, she was "short for her beam" and "quick to answer the helm" and seemed to be quite successful at bucking the ice with her slender, upturned nose.

As the *Bear* charged through the ice, slicing the pack as she steamed onward, churning through the field until it was reduced to powder, Bartlett gazed longingly at the crow's nest and wished he could be up there to watch it all. As he said, "steering such a ship through the ice is not unlike driving a big automobile through a crowded thoroughfare; this time, however, I was a passenger." Somehow, they made it through the increasingly treacherous ice field and reached Point Barrow on August 21. The *King and Winge* pulled in a day behind them.

Burt McConnell had come in from the east on a small schooner and was there to greet Bartlett. The captain remembered McConnell, of course, from the *Karluk*. The last time he had seen Stefansson's ingratiating young secretary, he had been striding away from the ship with Diamond Jenness, George Wilkins, the Eskimo hunters Jimmy and Jerry, and Stefansson himself as they embarked on their fateful "hunting trip."

McConnell filled the captain in on all that had happened since leaving the *Karluk*. They had left Jenness at Cape Halkett where he was to conduct ethnological studies, while Stefansson, Wilkins, and McConnell headed for Flaxman Island. In April, Stefansson had released his supporting party and set off northward with two men, six dogs, a sled, two rifles, and supplies for forty days. Stefansson, it seemed, was planning to do what he had wanted to do all along with the *Karluk,* but which the ice had prevented them from doing—to discover new land along the 141st Meridian. He had not been heard from since.

The Canadian government had not replied to Burt McConnell's petition for a relief expedition to Wrangel Island because they were already sending the *Bear*. McConnell was disappointed, not so much for the sake of the people he was petitioning to find, but for himself. Now he needed to figure out a new plan to bolster his future polar career.

He transferred his belongings to the schooner *King and Winge,* planning to hitch a ride to Nome. There were two motion picture photographers on board from Los Angeles, and they all watched the Point Barrow shore disappear as the ship pulled up anchor and set out for Nome on August 26. They crossed Kotzebue Sound and then Cape Prince of Wales, arriving at Nome on August 30.

The *Bear,* meanwhile, delivered the mail and various provisions she was carrying, and then, on August 23, she pointed her nose northwestward, steamed out of the harbor at Point Barrow, and headed for Wrangel Island. A fresh wind blew up behind them, steering them on, and Bartlett breathed deeply and easily for the first time in months. The harder it blew, the better, and the faster they would be there. At last, after months of working toward this moment, the rescue mission was truly underway. And if they couldn't reach his men, Bartlett knew there was a good chance that someone else would get them. The Russian government, at the request of the authorities in Canada, had sent their two icebreakers, the *Taimyr* and the *Vaigatch,* toward Wrangel Island. There was also a little schooner named the *Peter J. Abler* attempting the journey, in addition to numerous privately owned vessels.

"It was getting late," he wrote, "and before many weeks the ice might close in around the island and render it inaccessible to a ship, but it was not altogether this danger alone that worried me but also the feeling that the longer the men were kept on the island the greater would be their suspense and the harder it would be for them to keep up their spirits."

As they steamed across the Arctic Ocean, fighting the ice, the thought that his men might never be rescued did not even occur to Bartlett. The only thing that he was afraid of was the possibility of thick fog or snow or ice creating an obstacle, which would delay their progress. But he pushed the thought to the back of his mind and instead focused his eyes on the horizon and watched for the first sign of Wrangel Island.

The days of waiting, he wrote, "had been nightmares to me, the more so because naturally under the circumstances I was not in a position to do anything to hasten matters. My feeling of relief at being at last on the way to the goal of all my thought and effort may be imagined."

AUGUST 27 WAS, as McKinlay observed to Hadley, the day their "mental barometer" dropped out, leaving them with the great and sudden realization that they were doomed. Bartlett was not coming. No ship was coming. Instead, they must try to survive the winter here.

Kuraluk and his family left camp and scouted the surrounding area for a good site to build a house. He went out nearly every day, sometimes alone and sometimes with his family, to climb one of the nearby hills and check on the ice conditions in the bay and beyond. At the beginning of August, he had seen nothing but water all around, which, when he told the others about it, gave them a great deal of hope. For days, they had expected a ship at any time.

But now prospects seemed dim. There was no game, even though they saw geese flying overhead now and then, probably heading south for the winter. Kuraluk had made a throwing stick out of materials he had found on the beach. He also had made a bird spear to save on ammunition, but he rarely had the chance to use either now.

If a ship didn't arrive, Kuraluk wanted them to move camp to the west—still remaining on the north coast—where they would build their house on the banks of the river. There was plenty of wood there to build a decent shelter, and he expected they might also find fish and walrus, if they were lucky. Hadley approved. He had taken a stroll over that way one day and come across a flock of molting geese, which he took as a good sign. They would begin building the house at the end of the month.

On August 29, Hadley and Kuraluk left camp after breakfast in search of birds. They didn't expect to find any. There had been no game for as long as they could remember now, and it seemed futile to even try. The ice was weak and rotten and it was dangerous going, but they reached the rookeries and somehow managed to catch thirty ducks and sixty ducklings. It was a miracle and gave them their first real meal in weeks. They knew they had been lucky, that they couldn't count on getting more, and that it was only temporary relief.

In his tattered black notebook, Hadley scrawled, "If the ship Don't show up very soon now I guess it's all up with us I guess something will have happened to the capt & the Canadian Government Don't know about us & it will be up to me & the native to get the crowd out of this the Best way we can which will be Siberia by sled if we can get grub if not the Lord Help us...."

IN THE CREWMEN'S TENT, rotten food did not harm them anymore. Their stomachs seemed able to put up with anything now. Back at home, with a well-stocked larder and a handsomely laid table, Chafe, Williamson, and Clam would have never imagined eating some of the things they were now forced to eat. But as long as it sustained life, they ate it, "and things that would poison the ordinary person had no effect on us at all," wrote Chafe.

They did anything they could to sustain themselves. Chafe, Clam, and Williamson dug up kelp from the beach, half rotten, discolored, ancient, and tried to eat it but it made them sick. They worried about winter and their lack of warm clothes, especially footgear. They had sealskins to make boots, but they needed the skins for sustenance, and besides, there was no material for making socks.

Then one of them said, "That blanket that we buried with Breddy would have come in handy for making socks."

The next morning, Williamson and Chafe opened the grave and removed the blanket along with Breddy's boots. Someone would be able to use them. Afterward, they cleaned the blanket as well as they could by covering it with snow and tramping up and down on it so that the snow would soak it through. Then they hung it up to bleach and dry.

Every day, one of the men would climb to the top of a nearby hill and scan the horizon with the field glasses, hoping to see the smoke of a ship. Williamson, Clam, and Chafe made holes in their tent, facing southeast, so that they could watch for the arrival of their rescuers. Every time one of them got up during the night, he would peer through the holes with great expectation. The expectation never seemed to die, no matter how often they looked and were disappointed. And the first thing they did when they arose in the morning was to look out the holes—or the "windows"—again.

"No, no ship yet, fellows," was always the report.

And then someone would reply with great discouragement, "I don't think there is one coming for us."

"We had been expecting a ship every day since the first of August, but now we were beginning to wonder whether there was one after us or not," wrote Chafe. "We knew that if Captain Bartlett had succeeded in his hazardous undertaking and reached civilisation, the Canadian government would spare no expense in trying to rescue us. But had Captain Bartlett succeeded? Did anyone know we were there? These were the questions we were beginning to ask ourselves. It was the uncertainty of the whole thing that worried us—for if we knew that they were trying to get us, and that ice conditions only, were preventing them, then we would be content to wait for the day that would bring us relief. The last day of August came and went, but no rescue ship. So we came to the conclusion that our faithful Captain Bartlett had met with some accident that had caused his death, and that we were doomed to stay on this desolate looking land for another winter. There was very little chance for any of us to survive another winter, and we knew it, but, nevertheless, we had made up our minds to try it, and were determined to fight to the bitter end."

THE WEATHER WAS AS DEPRESSING and dreadful as ever, and winter had clearly arrived. The blizzard had begun on August 20, bringing gusting winds, frigid cold, heavy snow, and, worst of all, hail and sleet, which sliced the air, the ground, their tent, like a thousand sharpened knives.

If a ship didn't come soon, Munro, Maurer, and Templeman would have to try for the other camp where they hoped they could beg for food. Even as low as he felt right now, Munro's pride was still intact, and the last thing he wanted to do was ask Hadley, McKinlay, and the others for something to eat. But they were starving, and if they were strong enough to make the trip, which was doubtful, they would have to be strong enough to beg. The storm was too fierce, though, for them to attempt the journey yet. They would have to pray for the weather to break, and then they would have to pray they were strong enough by that point to leave.

"Will relief ever come?" Munro did not know anymore. They had expected a ship for so long, and nothing. Nothing. "The strain is awful on our minds," he wrote. "We are still hopeful trusting in the Lord for delivery."

McKINLAY HAD, AT LAST, given up hope. Until now, he alone had clung to the belief that everything would work out.

He had revered and admired Bartlett like no other man he had ever known. But now he was faced with the hard reality that Bartlett was fallible, mortal, and human, vulnerable to the elements. In the real world, he could have survived anything. But out here, the same rules didn't apply. Out here, he was just like any of the rest of them. He was known as the greatest ice master in the world, but the ice had taken away his power. He must have died trying to reach Siberia.

There was no doubt in McKinlay's mind. Bartlett was gone and no one knew where the lost men of the Canadian Arctic Expedition were. They would have to try to survive there as best they could, until spring. Then, if they were still alive, they would try for the mainland. But McKinlay knew here was no way of surviving another winter on the island without ammunition, without game, without proper covering. They would all die here, in this cold, hostile place, thousands of miles from their homes and their families, hundreds of miles from civilization, just as Mamen had died, and Malloch, and Breddy.

THE *BEAR* WAS ENGULFED in fog so thick that it was impossible to see what lay before them. For days, it had been the same drill—the ship steaming slowly toward land before the engines were stopped at night. They had taken in the square sails on August 24, when they had first run into the fog bank. Every now and then, the haze would clear enough for Bartlett to glimpse birds circling in the distance, which suggested land. But then the mist would close in about them once again, and the *Bear* would be unable to move.

The ice was heavy and loose, but just as treacherous and hard to travel as the thicker, more tightly packed ice field through which they had already passed. As well as Bartlett could guess, they were no more than twenty miles from Wrangel Island. As soon as the fog lifted, they would be there in no time at all to bring the castaways to safety. The *Bear* was well stocked, with ninety tons of coal in her bunkers. But the fog didn't lift, and on the evening of August 25, the engines were once again silenced and the *Bear* was allowed to drift.

The next morning, the wind carried them away from Wrangel and swept the *Bear* toward the Siberian shore. For two days, they struggled to fight the wind and the ice, to regain the ground they had lost, but they only succeeded in exhausting their coal supply. On August 27, at 4:12 in the morning, Captain Cochran announced his decision. They would have to turn back to Nome for more coal. They would never make it on what they had left.

Bartlett was devastated. There was nothing he could do to change the situation, short of miraculously producing coal out of his pocket. He knew Cochran was right and that they had no choice, but he was bitterly disappointed. "The days that followed were days to try a man's soul," he said. "I spent such a wretched time as I had never had in my life."

The *Bear,* so close to her goal, now pointed her nose toward Siberia and headed away from Wrangel Island.　She stopped first at Cape Serdze, and Bartlett rushed ashore to inquire about the Russian icebreakers *Taimyr* and *Vaigatch,* which had also been sent to Wrangel, but no one seemed to know anything about their whereabouts or progress.

Afterward, the *Bear* steamed over to East Cape, and Bartlett again went ashore in search of information.　The *Vaigatch,* he was told, had managed to get within ten miles of Wrangel Island, closer than any other ship thus far.　But on August 4, she received a wireless message that Russia had gone to war, and she immediately headed south with the *Taimyr* to Anadyr, where they would join the battle and serve their country.

This was a bitter blow because, with the *Bear* delayed, Bartlett had held great hope for the Russian ships.　They were the strongest of all the possible rescue ships, and the best equipped to deal with the icy waters.　But there was nothing to be done now as the *Bear* headed once again for Nome.　Nothing to do but hope that the coaling would go as quickly as possible.　Bartlett's eye was on the sky and on the calendar.　Winter had already arrived, it seemed, and soon they would be in the thick of it.　He prayed his men had enough to eat and shelter to keep them warm.　"I could only hope," he wrote, "that when we reached Nome, we should hear that some other ship had been to the island and taken the men off."

But when they got to Nome on August 30, no such word awaited them.

SEPTEMBER 1914

————— • —————

There were twenty white men on board the 'Karluk' when she began drifting with the great ice pack north of Alaska. Nine survive to tell the story.

—ERNEST F. CHAFE,

MESS ROOM BOY

McKinlay stood atop the lookout point, scanning the horizon for a sign—of moving ice, of open water, of a ship. September had begun with sunshine, which was quickly obliterated by heavy snow, thick fog, and chilling winds. Now hunger wasn't their only problem. It was already turning bitterly cold and they weren't prepared for it. Auntie worked at repairing their clothes and creating new ones out of what scant materials she had, and the men helped when they could. But there was little they could do to improve the state of their clothing, which was filthy, thin, and tattered. Still, all hands worked at sorting boots, stockings, and skins and doing the best they could to ready their clothes for winter.

It was too cold now to dig for roots. There was too much open water to go duck hunting; the ducks were now migrating to the bigger space of water, away from the island. The men saw seals out on the ice, but were unable to reach them as well. Hadley sat for hours by holes in the ice, waiting for a seal or an uguruk, but always returned to camp empty-handed. Kuraluk set fox traps, and Williamson wasted thirteen cartridges trying to shoot the crafty little devils, which watched him with what appeared to be great amusement before disappearing unharmed. The men prayed the fox traps would work; they couldn't afford to waste any more ammunition.

Hadley, McKinlay, and the Eskimos were engaging in a healthy competition to see who could save the most food for winter. Kuraluk and his family seemed "bent on outdoing Hadley and I in the saving line," wrote McKinlay, "but Hadley swears he won't be beaten by a native, even when it comes to saving meat."

On September 2, Hadley and McKinlay walked just outside of camp to survey the game and ice conditions, neither of which looked good, although there was some open water to be seen in the distance and the ice seemed to be drifting. It was too late in the season, however, for this to inspire hope in the men. After all, they had been disappointed for too long. For two months, they had waited for a ship, expecting one to arrive any day. Now they figured there was no ship coming for them.

The people in Hadley's tent rose every morning before 8:00 to hunt, to chop and pile wood, to forage for scurvy grass, to brace themselves for another miserable winter. Even Auntie and the girls were hunting daily, fishing for tomcod in cracks along the beach. The men in Williamson's tent meanwhile slept until the afternoon, showing their faces around 2:30 P.M. or so, and spending more and more of their time in the tent. They kept to themselves even more than usual and gave little help around camp. It was worrisome, but there was nothing McKinlay or Hadley could do to change their behavior.

On September 5, Kuraluk caught a young fox in one of his traps, and Hadley's tent made a small meal of it for supper that night. The meat was tender and tasty, although Hadley told McKinlay that foxes were generally eaten only out of desperation, since the meat was so "rank." But they were desperate, and the meat tasted wonderful.

By the next morning, that meal of fresh meat was already a distant memory. On September 6, Hadley, McKinlay, and the Eskimos were forced to eat breakfast from their winter stores. All of their food was gone now except for the scraps they had saved for the coming months. Miraculously, Hadley and Kuraluk returned from the day's hunt with a seal. It was a glorious sight, and that evening they feasted on seal meat and blubber, gorging themselves on meat and blood soup. Tomorrow they would be back on short rations, trying to save every scrap of this seal for the winter. Who knew if or when they would find more meat?

They stayed up later than usual that night, discussing their situation, not that there was anything new to say. They had exhausted the game in this barren region. There was nothing left for them at Cape Waring, and no reason to stay. They decided the only thing to do was move up the north coast to a new winter site. They would build a hut out of driftwood and pray that there was still some wildlife left on the island. They would pack up camp and leave for the new location tomorrow. There, they would build their house and prepare for the winter they now thought they would have to face.

AT RODGER'S HARBOUR, Munro, Maurer, and Templeman could hear the walrus bellowing, the low, mournful cries thundering and booming like a series of foghorns. The sound was grim, disturbing, and continuous, the men helpless to do anything about the noise or the walrus.

There was heavy ice off the coast, but a cold wind had started blowing. They had been hoping for such a wind to buffet the ice and open the way for a ship to come. Still, they didn't dare let themselves dream that a ship could reach them this late in the season.

They talked at night of pies and other foods they craved, and of their friends back home. On September 2, they ran out of the sealskins they had been living on, but later that day they were lucky enough to get three foxes. The next day, by some miracle, they were able to kill three more.

They rationed the food and trusted in the Lord, who, they knew, must be providing for them and who would not see them lost. They were counting the days, hoping that each one would bring a ship. They encouraged each other as much as they could, but it was little consolation. Their minds were strained past the breaking point and their bodies were wasting away.

But as Munro said, "Every cloud has a silver lining." On September 6, he wrote in his diary, "The Lord had been good to us."

THE BEAR WAS STILL LOADING coal on September 3 when Bartlett lunched with Japhet Linderberg, a millionaire mine owner and operator who had shown him so much kindness when the *Karluk* had stopped in Nome the previous July. Bartlett was on edge, after having been forced to turn back from Wrangel Island, and now having to wait five days already while they took on more coal. The wait was agonizing, and the strain showed in his face.

Linderberg was so moved by this that he announced to Bartlett that he would send the ship *Corwin* to Wrangel Island to fetch the men. A former revenue cutter, the *Corwin* had traveled to Wrangel in the 1880s, and now Linderberg was willing to put down twenty thousand dollars of his own money to outfit and crew her and send her up there. Bartlett was greatly touched by the offer. So many people from so many parts of the world had shown a fervent interest in his band of castaways, and he was grateful to be reminded that he wasn't alone in the fight to save them.

He chanced upon Olaf Swenson, owner of the *King and Winge*, later that same day in a popular Nome meeting spot. Bartlett liked Swenson. He was a tall, personable man with a kind face. The *King and Winge* was about to embark on a walrus hunting and trading trip up the Siberian coast, and Bartlett asked Swenson—should he pass by the vicinity of Wrangel Island—to stop there if possible and search for the men of the *Karluk*. Swenson promised the captain he would.

Still, Bartlett's mind did not rest easier. Before returning to the *Bear*, he sent a wire to Ottawa to keep the Canadian government officials apprised of the situation, and to let them know that both the *Corwin* and the *King and Winge* would be looking for his men.

On Friday, September 4, the *Bear* at last left Nome. Bartlett stood at her bow, transfixed, his eyes focused on the sprawling ocean before them. On September 7, the water was smooth and calm, almost unnervingly placid. Bartlett knew that meant ice up ahead. They should run across it before too long. Indeed, by 7:45 P.M., they saw the first signs of ice, and soon they could see it stretching before them, vast and tightly packed, the whiteness of it overpowering.

They had no choice. They would have to cut the engine and stop there, on the edge of the ice pack, until daylight came. They were just 131 miles from Rodger's Harbour, but to Bartlett, they might as well have been on the other side of the world.

ON THE THIRD DAY AT SEA, the men of the *King and Winge* saw the mountains. The peaks rose up in the distance, out of the ice, sharp and malevolent. There was nothing beautiful or graceful about them. They were stark, jagged, colorless, and forbidding. It was the most isolated, barren land they had ever seen. Draped in mist, the mountains seemed encased by the mighty wind, which blew in white, translucent waves.

The most disturbing factor, though, was the ice. Immense, sprawling ice fields filled the horizon, shimmering with myriad hues of blue, green, and white. Some of the ice grew into massive pressure ridges, looming over the island, higher than the ship's mast. One hundred, two hundred feet high—they were magnificent, and daunting. These ice mountains were intimidating, making each man suddenly aware of how small and insignificant he was.

In the middle of it all, protected and remote, sat Wrangel Island. It was a lonely, unreachable fortress. And somewhere, on her shores, were one woman, two children, and twenty men. Or sixteen men. Or twelve men. Or fewer. No one could be sure. They didn't know what they would find if they ever made it through. They were almost afraid to know. Had any survived? What if no one was there to greet them when they reached the island? What if the ship broke through the ice, only to discover they had perished weeks ago waiting for help to come?

The ice pack was dense and forbidding, hugging the shoreline protectively for miles and miles. The ice was loose, the ice was thick, the ice shifted and grew around them. While that tough little schooner fought her way through the pack, there was time to reflect on what the men of the *Karluk* must have lived through these past several months.

The *King and Winge* crept along the coastline, Swenson, and the rest of the men straining their eyes for any sign of life. Swenson was a man of his word. He had promised Bartlett in Nome that he would look for his men, and that was exactly what he was doing. He had delayed his hunting and trading work and had purchased an umiak and hired fifteen

Eskimos for the journey to Wrangel Island. He ordered his engineer to get as much speed out of the little schooner as he could, and then pointed her nose northward. Burt McConnell had been hitching a ride from Point Barrow to Nome on the schooner and, at the last minute, asked to join Swenson on his mission. Now they stood on deck, staring in the direction of Wrangel Island.

Between gaps in the ice cliffs, they could see the land beyond. It was barren and still. There seemed to be nothing living on its banks, neither man nor animal. All the while, the ship pulled closer to shore, and yet they still saw nothing. They tried not to be disheartened. Bartlett had said his men would be at Rodger's Harbour, where he had instructed them to wait, but they could have been further inland, or at their original Shore Camp, on the other side of the island.

The ship pressed on. Swenson and McConnell took turns looking through the glasses. Stealthily, slowly, they drew closer to the island. Suddenly, the lookout in the crow's nest shouted out. It was a tent. Barely standing, but it was a tent. They strained for a view of it, but they had trouble seeing past the great pressure ridges of ice.

Then a break, and there it was, dilapidated and torn, a flimsy summer tent that couldn't have been sufficient shelter for anyone in this bitter cold and wind. They had hoped to find twenty-three people on this island, yet the only sign of life they saw was one four-man tent. There were no sleds, no dogs.

And then they caught sight of something jutting out of the island landscape, just beyond the tent, that made their hearts stop. A crude, wooden cross, plain and strong, was planted in the ground, and just behind it stood a flagpole. This was shocking proof of life—and death.

They were half a mile away from shore when Captain Jochimsen fired off rockets and started blowing the ship's whistle. He blew it repeatedly, at intervals, pausing while the ship's entire company watched; still, no one appeared. Their hearts sank.

Again, the captain blew the whistle, and again all waited. Finally, they saw the tent flap open and a man emerge, on his hands and knees.

They were just offshore now and Swenson dropped anchor. Aboard the *King and Winge*, they were elated. But on the island, the man showed no signs of joy or excitement. He didn't wave his arms and shout, even though they could tell by the direction of his gaze that he saw them. He didn't run up and down the beach to attract their attention. Instead, he crouched like an animal and watched. And then slowly he rose to his feet, straightening himself to his full height, and stood beside the tent, gazing in their direction. More than once, he brushed his hands across his eyes as if to clear away something that might be there, deceiving him, altering his vision.

They continued to sound the horn and all on deck began to wave to him. He did not respond and, suddenly, he turned and crawled back into the tent. His behavior was mystifying. The poor fellow was probably out of his mind.

But as quickly as he disappeared, the man returned, holding something in his hands. As they watched, he walked over to the flagpole, his gait slow and lumbering, and raised the British flag to half-mast.

The flag seemed to confirm what the cross had already suggested. Was it possible that this man was the only survivor, that there, at the foot of that cross, lay the rest of the *Karluk*'s company?

This question was quickly answered as two more men appeared from the tent. The three of them stood together and watched the ship. Still, no one waved, no one shouted, no one jumped for joy. They were clearly stunned and disbelieving. Swenson and the rest of his party expected more men to come then, but none did.

When the ship was two hundred yards from shore, the first mate and his crew launched the umiak. Swenson and McConnell climbed aboard.

When they were one hundred yards from shore, one of the men from the tent started toward them, carrying something. Finally, they thought, he knows he is saved. But their smiles disappeared as they saw the object the man was carrying. It was a rifle, and as he walked toward them, he loaded the magazine with cartridges.

The Eskimos in the umiak were terrified. One of them pointed to his forehead, shaking, and said in broken English, "That man long time not much eat. Him crazy...."

In Inuit, Swenson spoke to their fears. His words and voice were soothing and the Eskimos quieted, continuing to paddle. But they were all puzzled and alarmed by the man's behavior. What if this man was mad? What if he didn't understand that they were there to help him?

They landed the umiak and stayed close together as they started toward the castaways. They passed over the most desolate of landscapes, the earth gray and dreary, with patches of ice and snow here and there covering the otherwise empty ground. It seemed impossible that anything could live in this cold, barren place.

Time, hardship, exposure, and famine had made each of the men unrecognizable. McConnell tried to glimpse a familiar mannerism or feature in each, anything that would help him identify them. They could have been any of the men he last saw aboard the *Karluk,* nearly one year ago. They could have been strangers.

The man with the rifle met them halfway to the tent. The others stood several feet behind, waiting. The man's hair was wild and matted, and it streamed down over his eyes. His grimy face was streaked and furrowed with lines and wrinkles. He seemed to be about forty years old. His clothes, which he had lived in and slept in for the past six months, were in rags, begrimed and stinking with seal oil, blood, and dirt. His full, tangled beard hid the dark hollows of his cheeks, but his eyes shone through above, speaking of great suffering. He was ten feet from McConnell, and he was unrecognizable.

The man stepped forward to Swenson with outstretched hand. "I don't know who you are," he said, "but I'm mighty glad to see you all."

It was only after hearing his voice that McConnell knew who he was. He never would have known him otherwise—chief engineer John Munro. He wasn't yet forty, but he looked forty, and he had lost at least thirty pounds since McConnell had seen him last.

He lay down the rifle and hugged McConnell. "How did you get here and where is Mr. Stefansson? Did Captain Bartlett reach shore all right? How is he, and where?"

McConnell told him briefly that Bartlett had reached Siberia in May and that Stefansson was adrift on the ice somewhere north of the Canadian boundary.

Bartlett had won through. Munro smiled. His lips were cracked and white.

The other two men from the tent were approaching, slowly, cautiously. Munro leaned in toward Swenson. "Have you a doctor aboard?"

"You don't need a doctor," Swenson replied. "What you need is a cook, and we have a first-class one. Hurry and get your things together, and we will go aboard and have breakfast."

"Breakfast," Munro echoed. It had been such a long time.

Swenson and McConnell summoned up their courage then to ask Munro the question they were most afraid of asking, but the one they most needed to ask. How many of the expedition were left?

Twelve.

Swenson and McConnell sighed with relief that others were alive, and with grief that eleven were dead.

The remaining nine were camped at Cape Waring, about forty miles east of Rodger's Harbour. Last Munro knew, they were all well.

He pointed then to the cross that marked the nearby grave. Mamen and Malloch had died in the spring.

One of the other two men approached the rescuers now while the third man hung back. The second man was weak and emaciated. He looked as if he might lose the ability to stand or walk at any moment. McConnell didn't recognize him and it was only when Munro spoke his name that he knew who he was. Fred Maurer. Even after McConnell knew his identity, he couldn't believe it. The strong, intense young man he had known a year ago, and the frail creature standing before him now could not be the same man. Maurer smiled, but it was obvious that to talk would have been a great exertion, so they didn't press him.

The last man stepped forward then, gaunt and extremely pale. He was a little fellow, high-strung and jittery. He began babbling and it didn't take long for them to realize that the man was speaking gibberish. He was clearly on the verge of a nervous breakdown, so the men kept their conversation light and general, avoiding any discussion of the pain these men had suffered or the tragedies they had endured. McConnell recognized Templeman without Munro's guidance.

The crew from the *King and Winge* helped Munro, Maurer, and Templeman gather their few belongings. They left the tent standing as a beacon and

McConnell sat inside and wrote a message for any vessel that might come after them. It was cold in the tent and dirty, and through the holes that riddled its sides, he could glimpse the pale Arctic sky. The remains of the food supply lay just outside, within reach, so that the men could crawl to it if they had to. It was a pitiful sight—empty pemmican cans; three or four arctic fox carcasses picked clean; and a few drops of seal oil.

They had only twelve cartridges of ammunition left, Munro had told him. After that, they did not know what they would do to sustain themselves. They had given up hope of ever being rescued.

McConnell left the tent hurriedly, tying the note to the tent pole and fastening the flap so snow would not drift in.

HE HAD BEEN AWAKENED by the steam whistle. At first, Maurer lay in his bed, listening for the sound, afraid to trust his ears. And then, clearly, the drone of a ship's horn, and he was out of his bunk, crawling out of the tent on his hands and knees.

He had stood shakily and rubbed his eyes to clear them, not trusting them any more than he did his ears. Was it an illusion? Or was he really seeing a ship? It sat a quarter of a mile offshore, the American flag flying proudly from its deck.

It took a while to find his voice and then to find the words, but eventually he was able to call out to Munro and Templeman. "The ship is here."

The ship is here.

Maurer had weighed 165 pounds when he joined the Canadian Arctic Expedition and sailed from Esquimalt in June of 1913. Now, in this September of 1914, he weighed only 125 pounds. The skin was taut over his cheekbones, his piercing eyes made more intense by the shadowed lines of his face. He was all angles and bones, his flesh thin and pale underneath the layers of dirt.

There came an umiak over the side of the ship, and the men with her, and there were the men rowing toward them now. The American flag was waving, her colors brilliant against the great whiteness of that northern world. It was the first time he had seen the flag in fourteen months, and he thought it could only be described as "transcendentally resplendent."

Maurer, Chafe, and Templeman had invited their rescuers to have tea with them, but Swenson and the others wouldn't hear of it. "No, we want you to come aboard," they said, "we have better stuff than that aboard."

They ran the Canadian flag down the flagpole and took it with them. The wooden cross was left standing over the grave of Mamen and Malloch, the only mark to signify forever the "resting place of our brave comrades," said Maurer.

Leaving their camp and the island was bittersweet. Maurer had been prepared for the elation, but not for the sadness and the great hollowness he felt as well. This was a joyous occasion—the most wonderful thing that could ever have happened—the thing they had been wishing for and praying for, for so many months.

Maurer carried the Bible his mother had given him and gave thanks to God as he turned his back forever on Rodger's Harbour. But he couldn't help feeling, as he was escorted to the umiak, and then as he set foot on the deck of the *King and Winge*, that a part of him was buried out there, too.

THEY HAD GIVEN UP HOPE of being rescued long ago, Munro told them again over a meal of soft-boiled eggs, toast, cereal, and coffee. They were now aboard ship, consuming quarts of coffee, with heaping spoonfuls of sugar and condensed milk in each cup. The *King and Winge* was on her way to Cape Waring to retrieve the rest of the *Karluk's* men.

Swenson and McConnell sat with them while they ate their first meal, and afterward Munro, Maurer, and Templeman had their first baths in eight months. They were given a change of clothes, pulled from the shipboard "slop chest," and when they were clean they barely recognized themselves or each other. They ate a second meal, barely an hour later. Ham, eggs, fried potatoes, cream of wheat, toast. "There was nothing we wanted but we got," said Munro. Swenson and the rest of his men saw to it.

"Mr. Swenson, I want to ask a great favor of you," Munro finally got up the courage to say. He looked sheepish. The words came, falteringly, softly. "For several months I have been dreaming of eating a whole can of condensed milk with a spoon."

Maurer and Templeman then confessed to having the same craving. After all this time and all their suffering, the only thing they could think to ask for was a can of condensed milk.

Immediately, three cans and three spoons were brought out, one for each of the men. They ate eagerly and with great delight, relishing each mouthful, and devouring the condensed milk as if it were ice cream. Munro was barely able to finish his, it was so rich and he was so overcome.

AT FIRST LIGHT on September 7, McKinlay, Hadley, and the Eskimos started packing up camp in preparation for their move to the winter site. It was truly amazing how little it took to survive in their world.

Around 10:00 in the morning, Kuraluk slipped outside to find a piece of driftwood so that he could make for Hadley the spear he'd been promising him for weeks. Hadley was inside the tent, busy making fox traps, and McKinlay was trying to repair their stove, which had stopped working properly. It was only minutes later that McKinlay heard an excited cry. He knew it was the Eskimo, but couldn't make out what he was saying.

Hadley had heard it, too. They stopped what they were doing and listened.

"Umiakpik kunno!" It was faint, but unmistakable. And again, "Umiakpik kunno!"

Maybe a ship.

Hadley and McKinlay stumbled over each other out of the tent. "How we got out of our tent we do not yet know," said McKinlay. Kuraluk was standing there, pointing to the east. McKinlay strained, but he didn't see anything. He ducked back into the tent and came back with the field glasses. He trained them out to sea.

A ship. Their ship. A two-masted gasoline schooner, just four or five miles off to the east, at the edge of the ice that surrounded the island. From what he could tell, she was steaming northwest.

Hadley, McKinlay, and Kuraluk "raised a shout that must have scared all the seals in the Arctic Ocean," wrote McKinlay. And then McKinlay raced over to Williamson's tent. "The ship, Charlie, the ship!" he shouted, and Chafe quickly bandaged his lame foot and pulled on his boots so that he could hobble outside and join the others. Clam and Williamson had been down the beach collecting wood, but at the sound of the shouting, they rushed back to see what was happening.

They all stood there, shoulder to shoulder. It was too much to imagine that this ship was there to take them home. They had already resigned themselves to the fact that they would never be rescued, and it was easier for McKinlay to believe that she had gotten off course or been chasing walruses.

Suddenly, their hearts sank. She was hoisting her sails and seemed to be going past without stopping. Perhaps she was not a rescue ship. Instead, she might very well be up there walrus hunting. She might not even know they were there at all.

Frantically they ran toward the ship, shouting as loudly as they could. Hadley grabbed his revolver and started blazing away the precious ammunition. He aimed the gun into the air, firing at the sky, and quickly emptied the entire magazine. Kuraluk ran faster than any of them as they tried to head off the ship.

McKinlay had never run so hard in his life. He used every last ounce of his strength to run and shout. He screamed himself hoarse. The ground at Cape Waring was as thick with snow and ice as Rodger's Harbour was barren, and he stumbled over his boots, but still kept going.

Then she lowered her sail and McKinlay stopped running. He stood transfixed. Around him, his fellow castaways did the same. As they watched, a party of men disembarked from the ship and began the long walk across the ice toward their beach.

The survivors shook hands with one another and then began to dance deliriously. These were the happiest moments of their lives, said Chafe. Auntie was there by now with the little girls, having just returned from up the beach with a pot of fish.

As much as they'd dreamed of rescue, none of them was prepared for that moment. It was so much like a dream that, not knowing what to do with themselves, they went back to their tents, cooked their catch, and had a feast. For so long, they had lived on instinct, and instinct now told them to eat and to not waste the food they had been lucky enough to find. Hadley's tent traded some of the fish with Williamson's tent in exchange for tea, and soon the entire population of Cape Waring was gathered around the fire, eating.

Their rescuers arrived in the middle of the meal, having traversed the nearly five-mile stretch of ice that had kept them from sailing any closer. They must have thought everyone there crazy to be sitting down to a lunch of fish when a ship filled with provisions awaited them.

They invited their rescuers to join them in the meal, but Swenson and the others politely declined. "No, thank you … we have dinner waiting for you aboard, so you had better not eat any of that truck."

"Truck!" replied McKinlay, Hadley, Chafe, and the rest of them. "Why, if we could have had as good as that every day since we have come here, we would not have cared so much."

The campsite was now chaos, as everyone rushed about, collecting their few possessions. There were two motion picture photographers who asked if the survivors would mind posing for their cameras. "Now that we know we are safe," they said, "you can keep us here and take movies of us for a whole week."

At the request of the photographers, the survivors paraded up and down the snow-covered ground and posed for them. They held up the puppies and the black kitten, who did not like being wakened from her morning nap, even to be rescued. Auntie and her two little girls stared stoically into the camera, and Kuraluk tried to avoid it altogether. McKinlay knew how pitiful all of them must have looked, with their hollow cheeks and sunken faces and their wild hair, not to mention their miserable clothing. But he paused and smiled for the camera, unable to hold back his joy. Finally, the cameramen gathered all of the survivors together and photographed the group of them. The men were beaming, their grubby faces shining with exhilaration. Hadley puffed away contentedly on a cigarette, savoring every drag of tobacco, while beside him McKinlay grinned from ear to ear. Clam stood next to him, his reserve melting at last, unable to hold back his smile or his tears. Auntie and Helen hung back, heads bowed, while Kuraluk clutched Mugpi as the tears streamed down his cheeks. Unashamedly, he wiped his eyes with open and obvious gratitude. "We're alive now, aren't we?" Mugpi had said to him repeatedly, when he had doubted the most.

Afterward, McKinlay cleaned out his bunk, taking the few personal items that had survived shipwreck and ice and theft and hardships. He abandoned the rest, including his old clothing and furs.

They left the tents standing, and McConnell and McKinlay fixed notes to the poles in case anyone else should arrive, looking for the survivors. One by one, they did a last, thorough going-over of the tent and the camp. They were patient, calm, and meticulous. And then it was time to leave.

They were frail, but there was no reason they couldn't walk the five miles to the ship unaided. It made for better pictures, though, if each one of the survivors had assistance, so each was supported by two men from the *King and Winge*. McKinlay walked across the ice for the last time, in a daze.

He talked with Olaf Swenson as he walked, his boots crunching in the snow. He used a walking stick and stopped every now and again to point out landmarks to Swenson.

From a distance, the abandoned tents seemed particularly forlorn. It was back to civilization now and all things familiar. Yet, at 1:30 P.M. on September 7, as they ascended the wooden ladder to the ship, McKinlay knew that his life would never be the same again. He was shaking as he climbed to the deck of the *King and Winge*. His feet didn't know what it was to walk on something other than ice. He climbed, rung by rung, and someone was waiting at the top, extending a hand to pull him on board.

They were reunited with Munro and Maurer and Templeman, and McKinlay was glad to see them. The men of the *King and Winge* were euphoric. They crowded around the rescued party and slapped them on the backs and shook their hands and then wiped their own eyes. McKinlay and his comrades were taken aback. They had been so isolated from everything that was happening that they didn't understand why these strangers exhibited such emotion, such joy and elation at their rescue. They didn't know the world had been talking about them, and following their doomed journey, or that so many people cared. They had no idea that many had long ago given them up for dead.

They were told that almost all of Europe was at war: Germany, Russia, France, Belgium, Austria, Britain. This stunning news barely made an impact. As McKinlay said, "it didn't mean a thing." Compared to their rescue, war seemed to the people of the *Karluk* a small matter. Chafe wrote, "I don't think we would have cared if the whole world had been involved in war, now that we were saved from starving to death on that desolate Island."

The starving men were offered food—real food—the kind they had dreamed of and talked about for months. Time and again, they had all imagined those first mouthfuls and how they would savor them. They had talked and dreamed of little else.

They sat down together and ate. McKinlay barely tasted anything. He ate mechanically—they all did—as if they had lost the ability to taste. The first thing McKinlay ate was bread and butter. It was toast—just plain, simple toast, slathered with butter. He consumed it without tasting it. After that, he devoured cereal and soft-boiled eggs and coffee with heaping spoonfuls of sugar and condensed milk. He barely tasted those either. He ate till he was full and then he stopped. And then he could hardly remember what he had just eaten.

That first day, when the castaways were not eating, they were smoking. There was an endless supply of tobacco and they feasted on it. Afterward, McKinlay soaked in a tub, washing as much of the months of grime off his body as he could. The water was black when he was finished, and he still wasn't rid of the dirt.

Next, he had his first shave in eight months. He was startled as he looked at his reflection. He hadn't seen himself since the *Karluk* went down. His hair was wild and long and his beard was full. The bath and shave gave him the first semblance of normalcy that he had felt in a long time.

As his beard fell away, exposing the sunken flesh beneath it, he could see the toll the months of hunger and sickness had taken. His cheeks were hollow and the circles under his eyes were dark.

Early that evening, he walked up on deck and watched the Arctic wasteland disappear into the dark horizon. One of the ship's hands was standing at the rail with a pile of their sodden, tattered clothing, which he flung overboard. McKinlay watched as the threadbare shirts and trousers hit the ice and the water, and drifted away.

THEY ENJOYED ANOTHER hearty meal before going to bed and were told that the table would be left set and ready, should any of them feel like eating during the night. McKinlay and the others turned in, lying down on beds of skins, and tried to sleep, but sleep was impossible. After an hour or so, they returned to the table and spent the rest of the night drinking tea and coffee—as much as they could stand—and eating. They talked about Wrangel Island and all that had happened there, and then they began to talk about the present.

Later, it was almost impossible for any of them to remember what they talked about that night, or what they did, or what they ate, because, as McKinlay said, "my head was not my own. Everything was unreal." McKinlay lay down in the warm, clean bed again at 10:00, but was still unable to sleep. He rose once more and smoked the first pipe he had smoked in months. He lay down again, but quickly got up and smoked two cigarettes. He lay down again, but was soon back on his feet. In this way, he spent his first night aboard the rescue ship, back and forth between the chart house and the saloon, drinking coffee, eating "all sorts of indigestibles until we could hardly move," trying to sleep at intervals, but wide awake until breakfast time. And then he ate again, as much as he could.

"God bless the 7th of September!" wrote McKinlay in his journal. "God bless the *King & Winge,* her skipper & her crew!!!"

ON THE MORNING OF SEPTEMBER 8, the *King and Winge* headed toward Herald Island. After all, eight men were still unaccounted for: first mate Sandy Anderson; second mate Charles Barker; seamen John Brady, Edmund Golightly, and Stanley Morris; Dr. Alister Forbes Mackay; oceanographer James Murray; and anthropologist Henri Beuchat.

At last, the craggy mountain peaks of Herald Island could be seen through the field glasses, and then the giant ice cliffs, which circled her. All leads surrounding the island had closed, however, sealed with solid, forbidding ice. They traveled forty miles along the edge of the pack without finding a lead. There were no openings. Not even the adroit, determined *King and Winge* could subdue this ice. It formed a perfect prison around the land.

They circled the area for a good part of the morning, but the closest they could get was within forty miles. It was hard to imagine anyone breaking through to land, as vigorously protected as it was. McKinlay was horrified at the sight of that churning ice, the solid shelf behind it, the cliffs beyond that, and the rugged mountain peaks. Had Sandy and the others ever been able to reach land?

Reluctantly, Swenson gave the order, and the schooner turned to the southeast and headed for Nome. The men stood on deck, watching the jagged edges and white points of Herald Island disappear.

AT DAWN ON SEPTEMBER 8, the *Bear* steamed full speed ahead again. The ice around the ship was loose and maneuverable, although some distance away, on her port bow, they could see it was thicker and close-packed. They made fifty miles by afternoon, just seventy-five miles total from Wrangel Island. Bartlett was determined, this time, to make it through.

He had been working all morning in the chart room, and after lunch he returned to it. He was standing there looking out to sea when he saw a schooner dead ahead, running before the wind.

Bartlett grabbed a pair of field glasses and adjusted them to his eyes. It was the *King and Winge*. It was too soon for her to be coming back from her walrus trading. There could be only one of two explanations. Either she had broken her propeller and was taking advantage of the favoring wind to put for Alaska—or she had reached Wrangel Island.

After all this time, he could hardly dare to think the latter. He had tried again and again, and so had many others, but no one had been able to break through the ice mass to the island. Now, so late in the season, he could not imagine there was a chance in hell they had steamed through.

Bartlett stood, transfixed, as the little schooner drew closer. A number of men lined the deck, but it was impossible to see who they were. Finally, she hove to and he peered at the men aboard, hoping to spot a familiar face. There were one or two who looked vaguely familiar, but he couldn't recognize them as any of his men.

Then he spotted McKinlay. He was emaciated and looking like the wild man of Borneo, but it was unmistakably McKinlay.

The rest of them fell in now—Munro and Chafe, and he thought he recognized Hadley as well. They were haggard, but he could identify them. There, too, were the Eskimos, and Helen was holding the cat—

who was looking more fat and fit than the day they picked her up from the Esquimalt Naval Yard.

As the *Bear* pulled up alongside the *King and Winge* at 69 degrees 55" north longitude, latitude 175 degrees 35", Bartlett could read the emotion in the faces of his men. Nothing had prepared him for that moment—not the anguish he had suffered ever since leaving them on the island, not his fierce determination to reach them, not the months spent struggling to rescue them.

They gave Bartlett three hearty cheers when they saw him, and unable to contain their excitement, they began to shout their news to him. A boat was lowered from the *Bear,* and Bartlett was soon clambering over the side of the *King and Winge,* standing face to face with these men he had not seen since March.

In the six months since he had seen them last, there were many times when he had feared he would never lay eyes on them again. Now, as he stared at their ghastly, wasted faces, he was hit with emotion. None of these men had been given any survival training before joining this Arctic expedition. And none of them had had any experience with the Arctic. Most of them had never even been far from home.

Now here they stood, barely alive, survivors, all of them. They had endured, and it was a miracle.

As Bartlett stepped onto the deck of the tiny schooner, McKinlay, Munro, Hadley, and the rest of them rushed forward to greet him, eager to shake his hand and tell him their story. His great, horselike face was full of emotion as he shook their hands "as heartily as ever men did," according to McKinlay.

"All of you here?" were the first words out of his mouth.

McKinlay stepped forward. "No, sir," he answered. Bartlett studied the group, surveying each gaunt face. He did not see Dr. Mackay, Murray, Beuchat, or Morris. Nor did he see Sandy, Barker, Brady, and Golightly. He had prayed that they would somehow make it to the island. He had told both the Canadian government and the papers that he was confident of it. Now he wondered if he had only convinced himself because he wanted to believe it.

McKinlay took a breath and continued, "Malloch and Mamen and Breddy died on the island."

This was a bitter and unexpected blow. Bartlett fell silent. There was nothing to say when three of the men he had seen to safety on Wrangel Island "had thus reached safety only to die." It was incomprehensible, and the most brutal, tragic loss he could imagine.

AFTERWARD, BARTLETT TRANSFERRED the survivors to the *Bear*, even though they were reluctant to leave the ship that had saved their lives. But Bartlett said the move was for their own good. The *Bear* had a doctor aboard, as well as clothing and other provisions Bartlett had on hand just for them.

Aboard the *Bear*, they lived in "luxury unqualified," according to McKinlay. They were treated to bunks made up with the finest sheets, the first they had slept in for over a year.

Williamson's craggy face was permanently lined with grief, the signs of which would not fade, no matter how much distance he put between himself and the Arctic. Clam would be forever crippled. Chafe had lost his youthful spirit, and his young face, hanging above his bony neck and collarbone, had aged alarmingly. Munro's eyes were troubled, his jaw clenched, the lines of his face revealing turmoil. Templeman's stare was haunted and vacant.

The ship's doctor examined and questioned each of them extensively. The mystery illness, he said, was nephritis, an inflammatory disease of the kidneys caused by too much protein and fat in the diet. The very pemmican that had been keeping them alive had also been killing them. As long as they had had biscuits, they were fine, but without the carbohydrates in the biscuits to balance their intake of protein, they were doomed. The fresh meat had been much better for them than the pemmican, but there had not been enough of it. The pemmican, when eaten by someone suffering from hypothermia, was even quicker to damage the kidneys. It was the pure pemmican diet that had killed Mamen and Malloch, and it was the pemmican that had made the rest of them so desperately ill. Before the expedition began, Stefansson had damned the purity tests and purchased the pemmi-

can without having it analyzed. There was no way of knowing if the outcome would have been any different if he had. Years later, in a letter to
Mamen's family, McKinlay wrote, "I have clear evidence that it was he who
was responsible for the faulty pemmican that was the cause of the tragedy."

It was the first any of them had heard of the disease. They were lucky
to have survived it, and the doctor pronounced them all in remarkably
sound condition, considering all they had endured.

ON THE MORNING OF SEPTEMBER 9, the *Bear* sailed within ten
miles of the northeast point of Herald Island. As far as they could see,
there was no life onshore—no sign of Sandy and his men, no sign of Dr.
Mackay and his party. The *Bear* carried no dogs, umiaks, or sleds, but even
with these, they knew a trek to the island would be impossible, given the
wretched condition of the ice. They had no choice but to accept that
Sandy and the others were dead.

"It was as certain as anything could be that both parties had long since perished," said Bartlett, "but it was very hard for me to give them up, men with
whom I had spent so many months, men with the future still before them."

The *Bear* turned about, just as the *King and Winge* had been forced to
turn around, and headed south toward home. On deck, they stood together, side by side—the first and second engineers, the mess room boy,
the cook, the fireman, the seaman, the passenger, the Eskimos, and the scientist—and said good-bye to the Arctic.

ON SEPTEMBER 14, 1914, amid its coverage of the first major battles
of World War I, the *New York Times* devoted an entire page to the news of
the rescue. The men of the *Karluk* had been presumed dead long ago.
Almost everyone, it seemed, had given up hope, quick to write it off as yet
another Arctic tragedy. Even with the obvious prominence given to coverage of the war, international press attention was riveted on the rescue of
the survivors of the twenty-five people who had sailed out of British
Columbia on June 17, 1913, in search of an undiscovered Arctic continent.

When they reached Nome on September 13, Bartlett wanted to protect his men from the throng of people who had gathered to welcome

them home. The banks were crowded with well-wishers, newspapermen, camera teams, and everyone else who had heard of their arrival. The whole of Nome seemed to have turned out to catch a glimpse of the men of the lost ship *Karluk* and their captain who had led them to safety.

Because of their weakened immune systems, Bartlett didn't want to risk their going ashore after months of surviving on Wrangel Island; he feared they would catch the latest germ and be stricken with an illness from which they might not be strong enough to recover. Chafe and Clam were both under the doctor's care for frostbite, and Templeman was slowly being nursed back to health. Some of the other men—McKinlay, among them— were still suffering from swollen legs and feet, for which the doctor had prescribed powders and ointments that would treat the men both internally and externally. McKinlay, Munro, and Hadley also were being troubled by badly swollen throats.

They were learning to wear shoes again, after all those months of wearing mukluks, and it was a painful and awkward adjustment. Bartlett would let them leave the ship in a few days, as soon as they had the chance to gain some strength back. In the meantime, he allowed Japhet Linderberg, photographer Ralph Lomen, the editor of the Nome *Daily Nugget*, and other Nome dignitaries to board the ship and shake the hands of the twelve survivors. Bartlett appointed McKinlay spokesman of the group, so it fell to him to tell their story. "We were questioned," wrote McKinlay, "we were photographed a thousand & one times, we were offered the freedom of the town, we were invited to this, that, & the other thing; in short, we were made lions of."

In June of 1913, a similar fuss had been made over the celebrated men of the Canadian Arctic Expedition as they embarked on their journey. Then, they were heroes because of all they promised and aspired to. Now, they were heroes for simply having survived.

From the moment the castaways had set foot on the *King and Winge*, Burt McConnell had been pressing them for an interview, anxious to write the story for the press. McConnell was already trying to take credit for a rescue that he had nothing to do with, and to sell the story of it to one of the newspapers with which Stefansson had a contract. Bartlett refused to let any of his men speak with McConnell, who quickly grew miffed. There were official reports to be made first, and private words for faraway loved ones. Besides, in Bartlett's opinion, Burt McConnell only wanted to exploit these men for his own personal gain. McConnell followed them aboard the *Bear*, eager to telegraph the news of the rescue to Stefansson's newspapers. But Bartlett beat him to it, sending his wire out the night before. McConnell was livid, but Bartlett didn't care. The story belonged to his men, not to Stefansson, and certainly not to Stefansson's former secretary.

WHILE THE *BEAR* LAY IN THE HARBOR at Nome, the fields of Europe exploded in battle. While the men of the *Karluk* had struggled to stay alive in the middle of the Arctic Ocean up at the top of the globe, the rest of the world had gone to war.

Somewhere, Dr. Mackay, Murray, Beuchat, and Morris were lying, frozen or dead, lost forever. And Sandy. His letter to Bartlett on February 1 was the last his comrades had ever heard of him. He and Barker and Brady and Golightly were never seen again. They were four young sailors simply trying to follow orders, just like the rest of the men whom Stefansson chose for his grand expedition and then left behind.

But McKinlay was among the living.

> "I do not know how or where to begin; indeed I know nothing just now," began his letter home to his family. "My mind is so full and active that the result of its working is precisely the same as if it were empty. I am not going to tell you my story now, for you could only get scraps of it, and that would spoil things when I get home. You see I wish to have you all sit round me with staring eyes and mouths like to devour me, listening to my tale—how we lived, the feeds we had, and—more tragic!—those we did not have, the escapes I had, and so on, and so forth. I tell you, it's a tale in a million! The one thing I wish this letter to do for me is to show you I am alive, and how much I am alive."

He had joined the expedition with only a few weeks of meteorological training and a cursory knowledge of how to categorize Antarctic specimens. He did not know what the world held for him now. Perhaps he would go back to his job at Shawlands Academy, teaching mathematics and science, or perhaps he would join his native Scotsmen in the battle of World War I. The only thing he knew for certain was that the worst was over.

He continued his letter home in a firm, clear hand. "Just think of it all of you—I am alive. And more than alive—I am *living*. None of you know what life is, nor will you ever know until you come as near losing it as we were. Think of it again; I am alive, and not lying on the pitiless Arctic floes or buried beneath the unfriendly soil of Wrangel Island. Think again, and know that of six scientists aboard the '*Karluk*,' I alone remain. Think of it all, and thank God as I do that your son and brother has won through and will soon be among you to tell you a story the world has never heard."

THE WAKE

———— • ————

McKinlay was unconscious by the time the *Bear* reached Unalaska. Bartlett and the others had to carry him to the Jesse Lee Home Hospital. He had started feeling ill on October 1, 1914, and a day or so later his face and neck were badly swollen into blistering red patches. He had a high fever and headaches and he couldn't move. But the doctors knew instantly what it was—erysipelas, an acute, inflammatory skin disease, caused by a bacteria.

For three days, he slept. When he awoke, McKinlay looked into the eyes of a little Aleutian boy, who was sitting cross-legged in the chair beside his bed.

"Do you have Jesus in Scotland?" the boy said.

McKinlay was disoriented and confused. He couldn't remember being taken to this hospital and he did not recognize this boy.

"Do you have Jesus in Scotland?" he repeated, staring at McKinlay, frank and open, waiting.

"Yes," he finally answered. His voice was weak and sounded strange. But he could speak. "We have Jesus in Scotland."

After returning home in 1914, McKinlay spent the first months recuperating. His feet would continue to give him problems throughout the rest of his life from the frostbite he had endured, and he lost all but one of his teeth as a result of the starvation diet he had lived on in the Arctic. When he was stronger, he joined his countrymen at war, as a lieutenant in the Gordon Highlanders, eager to do his part and hoping, more than anything, that it would wipe out the memories of his Arctic nightmare. He served until 1917 when he was wounded and discharged. The memories of the Arctic were still as vivid and painful as ever. War had done nothing to change that.

Back at home, McKinlay fell in love, married, and returned to teaching. In the fall of 1917, he received a surprise visit from George Wilkins, the *Karluk's* photographer, inviting him to join an Antarctic expedition he was organizing. It was tempting. For all the hell he had suffered, there was something about the polar regions that still beckoned. There were times he still felt the chill of the ice, the bite of the wind.

But McKinlay was married now and had a new life—or rather—had resumed the old one. Besides, the war had left him with a lame knee. He would be of no use to anyone down there, so he declined.

Eventually, McKinlay would lose touch with his colleagues from Wrangel Island. "I had no contact with any of the survivors other than Bob Bartlett," wrote McKinlay years later. "After our sojourn on Wrangel Island, I had nothing in common with any of them." After all they had shared, they had remained strangers then, and they were still strangers now. Nevertheless, McKinlay did exchange letters with a few and heard news of them through the newspapers or through the letters Mrs. Rudolph Anderson wrote to him. Most of the men had retired to quiet lives, out of the public eye.

For a while, McKinlay received an occasional letter from John Munro, who had returned to Canada in late 1919, serving for a while with the Department of Marine and Fisheries. The last news McKinlay had heard of the former chief engineer of the *Karluk* was that he had married and settled in California.

Seaman Hugh Williams, better known as Clam, had been released from the hospital in Victoria, British Columbia, on January 17, 1915. After enduring further operations on his frostbitten foot, and after his foot had recovered, he returned to sea during the war. His ship was torpedoed, but he survived. He then went home to his native Wales, marrying and having three children. He died in 1937. McKinlay remembered him as one of the few "grand fellows" in the crew, with a "wonderfully attractive smile, even when things were at their grimmest."

Kuraluk, Auntie, and the children returned to Point Barrow. All of the men had spoken with great admiration for Kuraluk and Auntie, especially. "There is not a man alive from that ill-fated expedition," Chafe wrote afterward, "who does not today remember that faithful Eskimo woman with gratitude. We looked upon her as a mother."

For the rest of her life, Helen would tell her younger sister Mugpi how lucky she was that she couldn't remember much about their time in the Arctic. Mugpi grew up hearing the stories, though, and she did take away memories of riding on her father's shoulders as they hunted for eggs, and of the little black cat Nigeraurak. She is now, in the year 2000, eighty-nine years old and living in Point Barrow, the last living survivor of the *Karluk*. Mugpi is in good health, her memory is clear, and she still has a scar on her chin from the day when Nigeraurak scratched her.

John Hadley stayed for some time with Kuraluk and his family, after they all returned from Canada. He then resumed his travels, leaving his dog Molly with the family for a year while he was away. He came back to collect her and took her with him to San Francisco, where he died in 1918 during the great influenza epidemic. Four years later Stefansson, in his book *The Friendly Arctic,* printed an apparently doctored narrative, which he claimed belonged to Hadley. The narrative differed greatly in language and content from the crude diary Hadley had actually kept on Wrangel Island and was considered by many to be another one of Stefansson's fabrications.

In later years, McKinlay exchanged a handful of polite but frosty letters with second engineer Robert Williamson, who had gone on to a respectable career in the military and served with the Royal Navy and Royal Canadian Navy in World War I and World War II. But he was plagued throughout his life by the accusations in Hadley's diary, suggesting he had murdered George Breddy. In 1959, Stefansson sent him a transcription of the diary, and asked his opinion of the charges. Williamson replied: "I want to get into my mind if possible the reason of J. Hadley's silly stupid charges against me, but no, I cannot: It reads like a fairy tale; cheap heroics.... Hadley's account of the death of Breddy is another one of his hallucinations & absolutely untrue."

Williamson always remembered the bitter cold of Wrangel Island, but seldom spoke about the people or the time spent there. "Please do not think I am bitter," he wrote to Stefansson at the end of his life. "That is the main reason why I have not written a book of our trip. It does one no good raking up the past, especially when most of the men are dead. Therefore I do not care to say or write about our life on Wrangel Island or our trek across the ice from Shipwreck Camp." He died in Victoria at the age of ninety-seven in 1975.

Chafe had written to McKinlay in 1915, after he was released from the hospital in Victoria, British Columbia. He had been there for months, recovering from an operation on his foot, having had most of it amputated. He was given a discharge and three months' bonus pay and then sent home. Chafe had heard that Stefansson had helped Fred Maurer go out on the lecture circuit and wrote to McKinlay to ask for advice on how he could get in on it, too. Years later, he wrote his own account of the *Karluk* story, which seemed, in large part, to have been borrowed nearly word for word from Maurer's four articles for *The World Magazine* in 1915.

Before he returned home to Scotland in 1915, McKinlay stopped in Ottawa to visit the parents of George Malloch. They had asked that he come to see them, to tell them anything he could about the last days of their son's life. It was, he remembered, "a sad occasion, but George Malloch's parents appeared to derive some degree of comfort from having a personal account of their son's experiences, and I was glad I had gone."

No trace of Dr. Mackay's party was ever found, except for a black sailor's scarf, which his former shipmates had discovered buried in an ice floe, and which they presumed belonged to sailor Stanley Morris. Their colleagues concluded that the four men must have been crushed by the violent, raftering ice. The families of the four men were of great support to each other as they tried to deal with their loss. For years afterward, they clung to the hope that the men would reappear, alive and well, or that, at least, their bodies would be found, to offer a sense of closure. Dr. Mackay's mother wrote to the father of Stanley Morris: "I very much fear all the four are lost. I am ... little able to bear this misery."

James Murray's oceanographic studies had been the first to be carried out in the Amerasia Basin, but all of his work was lost when the *Karluk* went down. The Royal Society of Edinburgh started a fund to aid Murray's widow, but the Canadian government offered little relief. The

Canadian government stopped the salaries of Murray, Beuchat, and Dr. Mackay in 1914, with no explanation to the families. The men were never officially declared dead by the government. Finally, at the prompting of Mrs. Rudolph Anderson, McKinlay wrote to Mrs. James Murray, Mrs. Henri Beuchat, and the mother of Alister Forbes Mackay to let them know their loved ones were gone. The families still maintained the hope that the men had survived, but on July 5, 1921, Mackay, at last, was declared legally dead.

Robert Templeman emigrated to Australia, and no one ever heard from him again. Before disappearing, he smuggled Mamen's small personal notebook past the Canadian government authorities and returned it to the Mamen family as he had promised Mamen he would. In it were Mamen's last letters to his mother and his fiancée.

In the last letter he wrote home, Mamen had willed his official diary to his father. Bartlett turned the diary over to Stefansson upon his return to Canada, and Stefansson eventually sent it to the Mamen family in Norway, to be translated from Norwegian into English for the Canadian government. When the family received the journal, they noticed that the entries for March 14–April 1 were missing. Mamen wrote honestly and freely throughout his diary and was quite damning of Stefansson, who happened to read Norwegian. The Mamen brothers were certain that Stefansson had removed the missing entries from the journal. When the brothers asked the Canadian government for a fee of one hundred dollars to translate it, Stefansson accused them of holding the diary for ransom and tried to have them arrested.

In the end, Mamen's mother asked that her son's journal never be published in full, to honor his memory and to protect him from Stefansson editing and using the material for his own purposes, just as he did with material by Fred Maurer and John Hadley, after their deaths. "I will do my share in seeing that Captain Bartlett shall be exonerated from Stefansson's accusations," wrote Mamen's mother. "Bjarne wrote only good about Captain Bartlett."

One of Mamen's brothers ventured to Wrangel Island in 1926 to visit his brother's grave. He needed to see the icy, windswept shores where his brother lay. Mamen's fiancée, Ellen, remained close to the Mamen family in the years following his death. "Ellen has had a great deal to bear—poor little one," wrote Valborg Mamen, Mamen's mother. "She is a good and honest little woman whom I love very much. Yes, life is not easy. To most people it is not a dance on roses, I believe, but there is nothing to do but to take it patiently and everything will be endured...."

Given the bond they shared, it is almost certain that McKinlay confided to Bartlett his suspicions about the death of George Breddy. After reporting to the authorities in Ottawa, McKinlay never talked about it again. It *might* have been a suicide, although McKinlay didn't believe it. But the story that McKinlay and the rest of them told and stuck to was that Breddy had died of an "accidental shooting."

Although McKinlay had given his official statement regarding the death in October of 1914, he was asked by the Supreme Court of British Columbia to make an official declaration in November 1923 before a notary public, mayor, or chief magistrate of any city, regarding the death of George Breddy. In it, McKinlay stated: "The said death was caused by the accidental discharge of the deceased's revolver while he was engaged in cleaning it."

Several of the survivors and relatives of those who had been on the *Karluk* continued to speculate: "Another member of the crew, named Breddy, had been shot by another member of the crew at Cape Waring," wrote Mrs. Rudolph Anderson in a 1922 memorandum. Whatever happened to Breddy—whatever truly happened—was left on the icy shores of Wrangel Island.

Stefansson's conduct was another matter. "Over the years I have done my best to forget the whole sorry Stefansson affair, but not very successfully, I fear," wrote McKinlay in the years that followed. It was hard to forget about Vilhjalmur Stefansson. His name appeared frequently in the newspapers, and McKinlay could never seem to escape hearing of him. Stefansson had returned from the Arctic in 1918, after everyone, including the Canadian government, had given him up for dead. He returned triumphantly, having discovered the last unmapped islands of Canada: Brock Island, Borden Island, and Mackenzie King Island. Afterward, the

National Geographic Society presented him with the prestigious Hubbard Medal, and famed explorers Admiral Peary and General Greely paid Stefansson glowing tributes. At no time did Stefansson mention the *Karluk* or its crew or the men who were lost.

In 1922, he published *The Friendly Arctic,* which presented his theory that the Arctic generally was a "friendly" place where any sensible person could survive. In the book's appendix, he included the account of the *Karluk* disaster that Hadley had supposedly written, critical of Bartlett and championing Stefansson, and vastly different from the journal Hadley had kept in 1914 on Wrangel Island. Stefansson, not surprisingly, was the only person who could verify the authenticity of the account. No one else could vouch for it, and Hadley, by that time, was dead. In the book, Stefansson also accused the Southern Party of mutiny.

Stefansson's great reputation, though, did not emerge untarnished from the failure of the Canadian Arctic Expedition. The Expedition was originally designated to cost $75,000, but ultimately cost the government half a million dollars, thanks to Stefansson's extravagance and disorganization. It was embarrassing, too, when he claimed Wrangel Island for Canada, basing this solely on the fact that Munro, Maurer, and Templeman had raised the Canadian flag on the island. "Wrangel Island, claimed by the Explorer Stefansson for Canada, is in reality the property of Russia," reported Harry L. Rogers in the *Washington Times* on May 23, 1922, in an article entitled "State Department Inquiry Refutes Claim of Canada filed by Explorer."

Stefansson died in 1962 at the age of eighty-two. Long after the expedition, he continued openly and publicly to blame Bartlett for the tragedy of the *Karluk.* Bartlett, in typical dignified fashion, never responded to his criticisms, although in private, to his closest friends, he expressed his opinions of that "blankety blank liar" in his usual colorful language. Others felt similarly about Stefansson. "I think he came to believe the myths that were created about him," one observer wrote to McKinlay. "He was a ... great Arctic traveller. But he created a mythology of *The Friendly Arctic* and a lot of people died because of it."

"I want to destroy the Stefansson Myth," McKinlay wrote on January 14, 1977, "for the man was a consummate liar and cheat, who did his best to destroy not only the reputation, but also the health and happiness of anyone who dared to differ from him." He also wrote, "As far as I am personally concerned, the whole venture was a miserable, disastrous failure which I would have done much to be able to forget. But almost every other person associated with Stefansson in any position of responsibility is unstintingly traduced, and, in every case, unjustly so."

The Southern Party of the Canadian Arctic Expedition was, at least, a success. Its members had continued to map the geology and topography of the Mackenzie delta, charting hundreds of miles of Arctic coastline. Diamond Jenness spent two years studying the Eskimos, and Fritz Johansen discovered a new species of moth, which he named "Homoglaea murrayi" in tribute to James Murray. The Southern Party ceased their work when they were called home at the end of 1915 because of the war.

After the publication of *The Friendly Arctic,* members of the Southern Party, Dr. Rudolph Anderson, Kenneth Chipman, J. J. O'Neill, and Diamond Jenness, petitioned Charles Stewart, the minister of mines for the Canadian government, asking "that a commissioner be appointed to investigate the organization, conduct and events of the expedition, and to determine the truth or falsity of charges made by Mr. Stefansson. Mr. Stefansson has made statements which reflect upon the undersigned and are such serious reflections upon their personal honor that they are determined ... to clear themselves of the unjustifiable charges made against them." The request for an inquiry was ultimately declined for the reason that "no good could come of such an inquiry and much harm might be done." In response to Stefansson's charges of mutiny in his book *The Friendly Arctic,* the Canadian government made clear to Stefansson that the men of the Southern Party had simply been following the orders of the Geological Survey under which they were working.

In 1922, Stefansson organized another expedition, an attempt to colonize Wrangel Island. He sent a crew of four men and one Inuit woman, opting at the last minute not to participate himself. All four of the men perished, but the woman survived. Fred Maurer was one of the dead.

McKinlay had heard from Maurer once or twice and had sent him some Scottish shortbread in 1915. Maurer had returned to New Philadelphia,

Ohio, taking the *Karluk*'s black cat with him. With Stefansson's help, he traveled the lecture circuit, speaking about his time in the Arctic. In 1922, he was married, and only a few days later left for Wrangel Island. His three male colleagues were completely inexperienced in Arctic travel or survival. One of the men grew ill on the island and died after Maurer and the other two had set out for help, heading toward Siberia in an attempt to duplicate Bartlett's brave journey over the ice and through the wilderness. Maurer and his companions were never seen again. Maurer was twenty-nine years old. "By the time he got a chance to go on Stefansson's expedition of 1921 he considered himself sufficiently well grounded in Arctic matters to take up exploration as a career," wrote the Montreal *Daily Star* on October 24, 1923.

The black cat outlived him, surviving to a grand old age, and producing numerous litters of kittens, all black with white feet and white bibs under their chins, and all named "*Karluk*." Maurer had made presents of these to various members of the expedition, including McKinlay and Dr. Anderson.

McKinlay and the other *Karluk* survivors were stunned to hear of Maurer's return to Wrangel Island. McKinlay could not imagine what had inspired Fred Maurer to go back. Maurer himself had said that he needed to go to reclaim a part of himself that he had lost there, and to seek validation for the deaths of his friends Bjarne Mamen and George Malloch.

All of the men of the *Karluk* were lost, in one way or another. McKinlay felt this, but he never ceased thanking God for helping him survive. He believed that, more than anything else, it was his faith that sustained him.

Bartlett never married, but remained faithful to his first love—the sea. In 1938, he said of his own ship, the *Effie Morrissey,* "She's all I've got. When she stops, so do I." He led seventeen more excursions into Arctic waters, and never again lost a life. He wrote to McKinlay sometimes, his letters stamped with postmarks from exotic points around the globe. The letters were gruff, colorful, and full of exciting news. McKinlay yearned to write a biography of Bartlett someday to pay tribute to him.

In the years following the *Karluk* tragedy, the captain had faced an admiralty commission that found him guilty for putting the *Karluk* into the ice, and for allowing Dr. Mackay's party to leave, even though Mackay and the others had given him a letter absolving him of responsibility. In the eyes of the public, however, Bartlett was a hero, no matter what Stefansson or the Government of Canada claimed.

Years after the expedition, McKinlay received a copy of a letter Bartlett had written to a mutual friend, in November 1914: "McKinlay is a good boy, with a level head upon his shoulders, a true loyal friend, a good ship-mate, and a hard worker. I cannot begin to tell you of the pillar of strength he was to me and shall never be able to repay him. Strange, when we wishes [sic] each other good-bye, it was as if we both grew up together and our being together just an ordinary event.... I can truthfully say he was everything that a fellowman requires of another."

The letter meant more to McKinlay than he could say. Until the day he died, he never forgot the debt he owed Bartlett. "Speaking of heroes," McKinlay wrote, "there was for me only one real hero in the whole 1913–18 story—Bob Bartlett. Honest, fearless, reliable, loyal, everything a man should be."

"When I die," Bartlett said, "I don't want a monument. I just want some boy to say I taught him how to navigate ... and how to tell when the ice is safe." He died in 1946 at age seventy, and in 1948, a monument was built for the "Master Mariner" in Brigus, Newfoundland, just yards away from his grave.

In 1926, the Canadian government created a memorial plaque in honor of the sixteen members of the Northern and Southern Parties of the Canadian Arctic Expedition who lost their lives "for Canada and for science." The plaque was hung in the entrance of the Dominion Archives building in Ottawa, but disappeared in the 1960s when the archives moved to a different structure. No one knows where the plaque can be found now, and it lies, one imagines, in the far corners of an attic, covered in dust and cobwebs, forgotten, just as the men of the *Karluk* have been forgotten all these years.

McKinlay lived what he considered a rich and fulfilling life, and he felt blessed. He was promoted to headmaster of Shawlands Academy and spent the rest of his days collecting articles and information on Stefansson and the Canadian Arctic Expedition. In 1977, he returned to the Arctic with his daughter Nancy, visiting Calgary, Vancouver, Ottawa, and the high Arctic islands. It was an emotional visit for him, and the memories of 1913–1914 came sweeping back. At home in Scotland, his young granddaughters uncovered boxes filled with expedition-related materials hidden in his basement and encouraged him to write his own version of the story. At the age of eighty-eight he wrote his tale, published in 1976 as *Karluk: The Great Untold Story of Arctic Exploration*. In his last years, he was obsessed with his work on a more honest, revealing account of the story. "I owe that to the memory of my dead comrades," he wrote, "and to Captain Robert Bartlett, who saved my life."

He would live to be an old man, but McKinlay would never be able to make sense of the enormous loss suffered on this Canadian Arctic Expedition.

"My writing, I must confess, had reawakened all the harrowing feelings which have bedevilled my life for so many years, but I am hoping that, once I have finished, I may find some measure of peace," he wrote.

The account, in which William McKinlay planned to tell the full truth about what he had experienced in the Arctic, was still unfinished when he died in 1983 at the age of ninety-five.

EPILOGUE

———— • ————

On October 14, 1924, The Victoria *Daily Colonist* carried a report of Captain Louis Lane's gruesome discovery on Herald Island of an Arctic ghost camp, littered with artifacts—knives, pemmican, snow goggles, matches, ammunition—and human remains.

HERALD ISLAND—

Some bones, a corroded rifle, pemmican, ammunition, a sled, and other camp equipment established beyond a doubt the identity of the men.

Savage winds and polar bears have tumbled their skulls about. A few more years and there would have been nothing to tell what became of them.

It was one of our few days of sunshine, and the calm, gravelly beach was covered with a thin layer of snow, blown bare in spots, drifted in others and cris-crossed by tracks of Arctic foxes and huge polar bears. Beyond, near the foot of the islet's ridge, we could see gaunt outlines of a sled, and around about, a number of black objects which later proved to be tins of pemmican.

One of the first things we discovered was a 30-30 Winchester rifle lying on a bare patch of gravel ... cut into the wood, the initials "B.M." being distinctly to be seen. The barrel of the gun was thickly corroded with rust and the magazine partly eaten away, disclosing the cartridges inside, green with age and exposure. A loaded rifle cartridge nearby indicated that death had not come to the party, on whose camp we gazed, through shortage of ammunition. This was amply confirmed before many minutes by the discovery of whole packages of cartridges, untouched.

The beach was strewn with driftwood and a large log lay right in the middle of the camp. On the side opposite to the sled we found the remains of the party's tents. The end had collapsed upon the bed, and

those in it, for, as we scraped away the snow and carefully pulled the
frozen canvas from what was beneath, we found parts of human skele-
tons; they lay as if the men had died in their sleep.

Sandy Anderson, Charles Barker, John Brady, and Edmund Lawrence
Golightly had, at last, been found.

There were no records, no diaries, no written account of what had happened to them. But there were clues.

"I am not sure," said Captain Lane, "how long they may have been on
the island before they died. Perhaps a month or two.... The ashes of their
fire indicate they were here more than just a few days." Sandy and his men
had made it across the ice and indeed reached land.

From what Lane and his party could determine, the four men did not
die of starvation, disease, or an attack by polar bears. "All seem to have
perished about the same time. Starvation is an impossible theory because
of the great quantity of food still remaining in camp." Lane's theory was
that their vulnerable tent might have been blown away by the violent
winds that swept continually through the area, and that the men quickly
froze to death in their sleep. "I believe they died suddenly and unexpect-
edly," he said. Others, including Vilhjalmur Stefansson, later theorized that
the men died of monoxide poisoning inside their airtight tent.

The rifle turned out to belong to Burt McConnell, who had left it
aboard the *Karluk* when he departed with Stefansson in September of
1913.

Captain Louis Lane took the human remains of Sandy Anderson's party
back to San Francisco. Afterward, the bones were shipped to Ottawa for
observation and examination, and then sent back in early 1925 to Messrs.
H. Liebes and Company in San Francisco, the shipping company that employed Captain Lane. Initially, there was some question as to which *Karluk*
party the bones belonged—Sandy Anderson's or Alister Forbes Mackay's.
The relatives of the eight missing men waited for official word as to
whether their loved ones had been found. Based on the evidence discovered on the island, the Canadian government ultimately determined that
these were the bones and artifacts of the first mate's party. The remains

were never sent to the relatives, however, nor did they make it back to San Francisco. Somewhere along the way, the bones of Sandy, Barker, Brady, and Golightly disappeared.

For seventy-five years, no one knew what had happened to the bones or the artifacts discovered on Herald Island. In the summer of 1999, returning from a research trip to Scotland, I came back to an e-mail that read simply: "I found something that might be of interest to you." It was from a friend in Wales, who had enclosed a link for an auction on the Internet auction site eBay.

"*Arctic Expedition Remains from Stefansson's ill-fated expedition ....*"

Seventy-five years after they had been lost, these relics had somehow resurfaced: a rusted pocket watch now missing its hands; a tattered leather belt buckle; a pair of snow goggles, one of the lenses cracked; a long snow knife with a carved ivory handle, the blade blunt and rusted; and a human jawbone. It is, as Captain Louis Lane and his party had observed in 1924, "a firm, capable jaw, cleft as to chin and with fine, regular teeth."

The remains arrived encased in a wooden box. They are fragile and worn. The jawbone is the most haunting relic of all, a tangible link to a young man's life. There is no way to tell for certain whose jawbone it is, but it seems to be that of *Karluk* first mate Sandy Anderson. It is my intention to take him home to Scotland, to return him to his family and his homeland, just as I have hoped to bring the men of the *Karluk* home by telling their story.

NOTES

LEGEND

BC (Archives)—British Columbia Archives

BWD—Bowdoin College, Maine

CAE—Canadian Arctic Expedition

DRT—Dartmouth College

JNC—Jennifer Niven's Collection

KGC—Kenneth Gordon Chipman

MMBC—Maritime Museum, British Columbia

OJ—Official Journal of the Canadian Arctic Expedition 1913–1918

NAC—National Archives of Canada

NLS—National Library of Scotland

RAB—Robert Abram Bartlett

RMA—Dr. Rudolph Martin Anderson

WLM—William Laird McKinlay

PRIMARY SOURCES AND METHODOLOGY

This book is based on the diaries, journals, letters, unpublished manuscripts, and papers written by the members of the 1913 Canadian Arctic Expedition, and on other pertinent letters and journals, as well as on documents and public records in government archives.

Providentially, most of the scientists and crew members kept diaries and journals, wrote letters home, and composed official reports and, despite the calamities the *Karluk* endured, many of these invaluable documents have survived. Some of the diaries, as in Mamen's case, were kept up until the days just before death. Other materials, as in McKinlay's case, included writing composed by memory over the course of several decades. My objective has been to bring the reader as close as possible to these primary sources and, through them, to the actual time and experiences documented by the people who lived them.

Over the years, as I conducted my research in the Unites States, Canada, and the United Kingdom, I constructed day-by-day calendars, juxtaposing all the firsthand accounts recorded by the participants themselves. This process allowed me to weave together and compare all the accounts of each event.

In addition to relying on the primary written sources, I conducted interviews and/or carried on extensive correspondence with the following:

Nancy Scott, daughter of William Laird McKinlay

Jennifer Byrd, granddaughter of William Laird McKinlay

Mugpi, the last living survivor of the *Karluk*, and her daughter Emily Wilson

Stuart Jenness, son of anthropologist Diamond Jenness

Peter Anderson, great-nephew of Alexander "Sandy" Anderson

Sonja Carling, relative of Bjarne Mamen

Jens Anker, relative of Bjarne Mamen

Magnus and Mamie Magnusson, friends of William McKinlay

Lord George Emslie, friend of William McKinlay

GOVERNMENT DOCUMENTS

The Canadian Arctic Expedition, Agreement, Formation, and Preliminary History, NAC/MG30-B40

The Canadian Arctic Expedition, Auditor General's Report, 1912–1918, Details of Expenditures, NAC/MG30-B40

The Canadian Arctic Expedition, General Criticism and Controversy, NAC/MG30-B40

The Canadian Arctic Expedition, 1913–1918, Preliminary History, Rudolph Martin Anderson Collection/Anderson-Allstrand Collection, NAC/MG30-B40

The Canadian Arctic Expedition, Reports of Southern and Northern Divisions, MMBC

Official Journal of the Canadian Arctic Expedition, Northern Party, 1913-1918, NAC/RG42-Volume 345

Official Papers Regarding the Death of George Breddy, NLS/DEP 357

MAJOR UNPUBLISHED SOURCES

Anderson, Rudolph Martin, Papers and Documents, Rudolph Martin Anderson Collection/Anderson-Allstrand Collection, NAC/MG30-B40

Bartlett, Robert Abram, Official Journal, Ship's Log, and Personal Papers, Robert Abram Bartlett Papers 1888-1989, Special Collections & Archives, BWD

Chafe, Ernest F., *The Voyage of the Karluk and its Tragic Ending*, unpublished manuscript, MMBC.

Chipman, Kenneth Gordon, Diary and Papers, Kenneth Gordon Chipman Fonds, NAC/MG30-B66

Hadley, John, Diary, John Hadley Fonds, NAC/MG30-B2

The Karluk Chronicle, Official Newsletter of the HMCS *Karluk*, DRT

McConnell, Burt, Official Diary and Papers, Burt M. McConnell Fonds, NAC/MG30-B24

McKinlay, William L., Official diary submitted to the Canadian Government and Papers, NAC, William Laird McKinlay Fonds, NAC/MG30-B25

McKinlay, William L., Original diary (versions one and two) and Personal Papers, Correspondence and Papers of William Laird McKinlay, NLS/DEP 357

McKinlay, William L., First Draft of Manuscript *Karluk*, unpublished manuscript, William Laird McKinlay Fonds, NAC/MG30-B25. (Note: Often referred to below as "First Draft" or "First Draft of *Karluk*.")

McKinlay William L., Second Draft of Manuscript *Karluk*, unpublished manuscript, William Laird McKinlay Fonds, NAC/MG30-B25. (Note: Often referred to below as "Second Draft" or "Second Draft of *Karluk*.")

Mackay, Dr. Alister Forbes, Diary, Bio, and Petition for Death, Correspondence and Papers of William Laird McKinlay, NLS/DEP 357/3

Mamen, Bjarne, Diary of the Canadian Arctic Expedition, The Bjarne Mamen Fonds, NAC/MG30-B20

Maurer, Fred, Lecture: "A Fight for Life in the Arctic." 1914, Rudolph Martin Anderson Collection/Anderson-Allstrand Collection, NAC/MG30-B40

Munro, John, Diary, William Laird McKinlay Fonds, NAC/MG30-B25

Williamson, Robert John, Robert J. Williamson Fonds, NAC/MG30-B44

NEWSPAPER CLIPPINGS

In citing newspaper articles, many of which were contained in albums and private files, I have provided whatever data was available.

SECONDARY SOURCES CITED IN NOTES

Bartlett, Robert, *The Log of Bob Bartlett*. New York/London: G.P. Putnam's Sons, 1928.

Bartlett, Robert and Ralph T. Hale, *Northward Ho!: The Last Voyage of the Karluk*. Boston: Small, Maynard & Company, 1916.

Crich, G.E., *In Search of Heroes*. London, Ontario: Northwinds, 1990.

DeLong, Emma, ed., *The Voyage of the Jeannette: The Journals of George W. De Long* (Volumes One and Two). Boston: Houghton, Mifflin and Company, 1884.

Diubaldo, Richard J., *Stefansson and the Canadian Arctic*. Montreal: McGill-Queen's University Press, 1978.

Fitzgerald, Edward, *Rubáiyát of Omar Khayyám*. New York: Shakespeare House, 1951.

Hole, S. Reynolds, *A Book About Roses*. New York: William S. Gottsberger, 1883.

Horwood, Harold, *Bartlett: The Great Canadian Explorer*. Garden City, New York: Doubleday & Company, Inc., 1977.

Jenness, Stuart, ed., *Arctic Odyssey: The Diary of Diamond Jenness, 1913-1916*. Quebec: Canadian Museum of Civilization, 1991.

LeBourdais, D.M., *Northward on the New Frontier*. Ottawa: Graphic Publishers, 1931.

McKinlay, William Laird, *Karluk: The Great Untold Story of Arctic Exploration*. New York: St. Martin's Press, 1976.

Nansen, Fridtjof, *In Northern Mists: Arctic Exploration in Early Times* (Volumes One and Two). New York: Frederick Stokes, 1911.

Peary, Robert E., *The North Pole*. New York: Dover Publications, 1986.

Pielou, E.C., *A Naturalist's Guide to the Arctic*. Chicago/London: The University of Chicago Press, 1994.

Stefansson, Vilhjalmur, *The Friendly Arctic*. New York: Macmillan, 1921.

Thomas, Lowell, *Sir Hubert Wilkins: His World of Adventure*. New York: McGraw-Hill, 1961.

OTHER SELECTED SECONDARY SOURCES

Bartlett, Robert, *Sails Over Ice*. New York: Charles Scribner's Sons, 1934.

Brower, Charles D., *Fifty Years Below Zero: A Lifetime of Adventure in the Far North*. University of Alaska Press, 1994.

Dear, Ian and Peter Kemp, *An A-Z of Sailing Terms*. Oxford: Oxford University Press, 1987.

De Coccola, Raymond and Paul King, *The Incredible Eskimo: Life Among the Barren Land Eskimo*. Canada: Hancock House, 1989.

Falconer, William, *The Shipwreck*. London: T. Nelson and Sons, 1868.

Feeney, Robert E., *Polar Journeys: The Role of Food and Nutrition in Early Exploration*. Fairbanks, University of Alaska Press and American Chemical Society, 1997.

Hoehling, A.A., *The Jeannette Expedition: An Ill-Fated Journey to the Arctic*. London: Abelard-Schuman, 1967.

Kemp, Peter, *The Oxford Companion to Ships and the Sea*. London: Oxford University Press, 1976.

King, Dean, *A Sea of Words*. New York: Henry Holt and Company, 1995.

LeBourdais, D.M., *Stefansson: Ambassador of the North*. Montreal: Harvest House, 1963.

Lopez, Barry, *Arctic Dreams*. New York: Charles Scribner's Sons, 1986.

Mountfield, David, *A History of Polar Exploration*. New York: The Dial Press, 1974.

Mowat, Farley, *The Polar Passion*. Canada: McClelland & Stewart Inc., 1989.

Newcomb, Raymond Lee, *Our Lost Explorers: The Narrative of the Jeannette Arctic Expedition*. Hartford, Connecticut: American Publishing Company, 1883.

Putnam, George Palmer, *Mariner of the North: The Life of Captain Bob Bartlett*. New York: Duell, Sloan and Pearce, 1947.

Shackleton, Sir Ernest, *Aurora Australis*. England: Airlife Publishing Ltd., 1988.

Shackleton, Sir Ernest, *Heart of the Antarctic*. London: William Heinemann, 1910.

Stefansson, Vilhjalmur, *The Adventure of Wrangel Island*. New York: Macmillan, 1925.

Stefansson, Vilhjalmur, *The Autobiography of Vilhjalmur Stefansson*. New York: McGraw-Hill Book Company, 1964.

Stefansson, Vilhjalmur, *My Life with the Eskimo*. New York: Collier Books, 1971.

Swaney, Deanna, *The Arctic*. Oakland, California: Lonely Planet Publications, 1999.

Weems, John Edward, *Peary: The Explorer and the Man*. New York: St. Martin's Press, 1967.

Willis, Clint, *Ice: Stories of Survival from Polar Exploration*. New York: Thunders' Mouth Press/Balliett & Fitzgerald Inc., 1999.

PROLOGUE

vii "I am afraid ..." William Laird McKinlay (hereafter WLM) to Alan Cooke, September 25, 1973, NLS

vii "The two years ..." McKinlay writes in *Karluk* preface, 2nd draft, Part 1B, p. III: "A few ships did have wireless receivers then, but not the KARLUK nor the ENDURANCE." NAC

vii "Not all the horrors ..." WLM, *Karluk: The Great Untold Story of Arctic Exploration*, 1976, p. 161

ix "The greatest humbug ..." Roald Amundsen, letter to Dr. Rudolph Martin Anderson (hereafter RMA) February 16, 1928, NAC

x "If there is ... " WLM, *Karluk* preface, 2nd draft, Part 1B, p. III, NAC

SEPTEMBER 29, 1924

3 *"We did not..."* Robert Abram Bartlett (hereafter RAB), *Northward Ho!: The Last Voyage of the Karluk* (hereafter *The Last Voyage of the Karluk*), p. 1

3 Even though the ... D. M. LeBourdais, *Northward on the New Frontier*, p. 269

4 And there, on ... LeBourdais, p. 275

5 "A young man ... " LeBourdais, p. 279

5 Captain Lane and ... LeBourdais, pp. 280-281

AUGUST 1913

7 *"The Chief of ..."* Official Journal during the Canadian Arctic Expedition 1913–18, Northern Party, 1914-18, NAC

8 In fact, before ..." Extract from the Order in Council of February 22, 1914," p. 3, CAE Agreement, Formation, and Preliminary History, NAC

9 "an old coffee ..." Kenneth Gordon Chipman's diary (hereafter KGC), July 2, 1913, NAC

9 "absolutely unsuitable to ..." Quoted in Diubaldo, *Stefansson and the Canadian Arctic*, p. 71

9 But there was ... Maurer, lecture, p. 16, NAC

11 "Our parting was ..." "Captain Bob Bartlett," *New York Times*, August 27, 1937

11 "I thought Peary …" Robert Abram Bartlett (hereafter RAB), "'Greatest Of Men' Tribute to Peary," BWD

12 Without consulting the … RMA, The Canadian Arctic Expedition, 1913-1918, Preliminary History (hereafter CAEPH), p. 7, NAC

14 "exceedingly over-confident …" RMA, CAEPH, NAC, p. 10

14 "the evil influences …" RMA, CAEPH, NAC, p. 10

14 "looked … as if …" Lowell Thomas, *Sir Hubert Wilkins: His World of Adventure*, p. 64

14 "a man of …" The *Karluk* Chronicle, June 22, 1913, DRT

15 "And to think …" The *Karluk* Chronicle, June 18, 1913, DRT

16 "Snow on the …" WLM, diary, August 1, 1913, NLS

17 But he had … (Conversation with Lord George Emslie, July 7, 1999, Edinburgh, Scotland

17 While there, he … Dr. William S. Bruce to WLM, February 6, 1912, NLS

17 "Nowhere else have …" Fridtjof Nansen, *In Northern Mists: Arctic Exploration in Early Times*

18 "Best wishes" was … WLM to Mrs. Crouther Gordon, October 6, 1976, NLS

19 "Shoot now," Bartlett … Bjarne Mamen, diary, August 2, 1913, NAC

19 "He appealed to …" KCG, letter to Mr. Boyd, July 18, 1913, NAC

20 "I hope to …" Mamen, diary, October 4, 1913, NAC

20 Physically, at least … The *Karluk* Chronicle, June 29, 1913, DRT

21 He made no … WLM, *Karluk: The Great Untold Story of Arctic Exploration*, p. 12

22 "I came here …" Sandy Anderson, unaddressed letter, June 15, 1913, private collection of Peter Anderson

22 "A thirst for …" Fred Maurer, "The Life and Adventures of Fredrick Maurer," p. 1, NAC

23 "Green hands wanted …" Maurer, "The Life and Adventures of Fredrick Maurer," p. 1, NAC

23 "It was heads …" Maurer, lecture, p. 14, NAC

25 "it begins to …" Mamen, diary, August 5, 1913, NAC

25 "Our skipper has …" WLM, diary, July 3, 1913, NLS

27 "laziest man I …" Mamen, diary, August 6, 1913, NAC

29 "The Canadian Arctic …" KGC, diary, July 22, 1913, NAC

30 "at the same ..." Ernest F. Chafe (hereafter, Chafe), *The Voyage of the Karluk*, Unpublished manuscript, p. 8, MMBC

30 "Starboard—steady—Port ..." Chafe, *The Voyage of the Karluk,* p. 9

31 "absurd & suicidal ..." WLM, diary, August 8, 1913, NLS

32 He also sold ... RMA, CAEPH, p. 8

32 "seemed to resent ..." WLM, diary, July 10, 1913, NLS

32 "Certainly be crushed ..." WLM, Letter to Andrew (last name unknown), July 12, 1913, NAC

32 "V.S. in a ..." KGC, diary, July 11, 1913, NAC

33 "Capt. Bartlett says ..." KGC, diary, July 2, 1913, NAC

33 "Poor ice breaker ..." Mamen, diary, August 10, 1913, NAC

34 "do indeed not ..." *Karluk* Chronicle, June 23, 1913, DRT

35 "coarse and vulgar ..." WLM, diary, June 21, 1913, NLS

35 "Swung his head ..." WLM, diary, July 3, 1913, NLS

36 "At the earnest ..." *Karluk* Chronicle, June 23, 1913, DRT

36 "Eat when you ..." WLM, diary, July 5, 1913, NLS

36 "From now on ..." WLM, diary, August 4, 1913, NLS

38 "A man who ..." Mamen, diary, August 14, 1913, NAC

38 "We steamed along ..." RAB, *The Last Voyage of the Karluk*, 25

38 Apparently, Stefansson was ... Stuart Jenness, *Arctic Odyssey*, xli

40 "playing guitar and ..." Mamen, diary, August 14, 1913, NAC

40 "As if we ..." WLM, diary, August 15, 1913, NLS

41 "The nights are ..." WLM, diary, August 18, 1913, NLS

41 "It is distressing ..." Mamen, diary, August 18, 1913, NAC

42 "He may be ..." KGC, diary, August 16, 1913, NAC

42 "A self-seeking adventurer ..." George Phillips, Letter to G. J. Desbarats, August 19, 1913, BC

43 "That was all ..." WLM, diary, August 23, 1913, NLS

45 "How long will ..." WLM, diary, August 17, 1913, NLS

46 "When will you ..." Kataktovik, Letter to a friend, August 30, 1913, NLS

SEPTEMBER 1913

47 *"Goodbye Stefansson. We ..."* Maurer lecture: "A Fight for Life in the Arctic." 1914, p. 29, NAC

48 "Down went my ..." WLM, diary, September 27, 1913, NLS

49 "Soon we will ..." Mamen, diary, September 10, 1913, NAC

49 "Due south ..." Mamen, diary, September 17, 1913, NAC

50 "You must have ..." Mamen, diary, September 17, 1913, NAC

51 "Jerusalem's destruction; they ..." Mamen, diary, September 20, 1913, NAC

51 "If the ice ..." WLM, diary, September 20, 1913, NLS

51 "Away 20 miles ..." Maurer lecture, p. 29, NAC

52 "like the long ..." RAB, *The Last Voyage of the Karluk*, p. 41

54 "All hope of ..." WLM, diary, September 24, 1913, NLS

54 "he knows what ..." Mamen, diary, September 28, 1913, NAC

54 "There is nothing ..." Mamen, diary, September 30, 1913, NAC

55 "A nice mess ..." RAB, *The Log of Bob Bartlett*, p. 262

56 "never to see ..." WLM, diary, September 5, 1913, NLS

OCTOBER 1913

57 *"... we were drifting ..."* Chafe, p. 13, MMBC

58 "My dearest wish ..." Mamen, diary, October 4, 1913, NAC

58 *"October 28th, Friday ..."* De Long, Emma, ed., *The Voyage of the Jeannette: The Journals of George W. De Long* (Volume Two), p. 800

59 "We are lost ..." Mamen, diary, October 7, 1913, p. 28, NAC

60 "Stefansson read DeLong's ..." Mamen, diary, October 7, 1913, p. 28, NAC

60 "led to believe ..." WLM, diary, October 2, 1913, NLS

60 "The Canadian Arctic ..." Mamen, diary, October 7, 1913, p. 28, NAC

61 "as long as ..." Mamen, diary, October 7, 1913, p. 28, NAC

62 "one stares death ..." Mamen, diary, October 5, 1913, NAC

63 "I remember now ..." Maurer, lecture, p. 33, NAC

63 "We are still ..." Mamen, diary, October 10, 1913, NAC

64 "and a few ..." Mamen, diary, October 5, 1913, NAC

64 "Opposing floes which ..." WLM, diary, September 29–October 1, 1913, NLS

64 "So we are ..." Mamen, diary, October 2-12, 1913, NAC

65 "You must consider ..." Mamen, diary, October 13, 1913, NAC

67 "Dried apples ... situk ..." WLM, diary, July 16, 1913, NLS

67 "Theirs may not ..." Mamen, diary, October 8, 1913, NAC

68 "It is awful ..." Mamen, diary, October 20, 1913, NAC

69 "doesn't know anything ..." Mamen, diary, October 14, 1913, NAC

69 "a mouthful of ..." Mamen, diary, October 27, 1913, NAC

70 "I suppose the ..." Mamen, diary, October 29, 1913, NAC

70 "I for my ..." Mamen, diary, November 3, 1913, NAC

71 "There are some ..." WLM, diary, October 5-19, 1913, NLS

71 "I sense that ..." WLM, diary, October 11-13, 1913, NLS

71 "free & easy ..." WLM, diary, October 7, 1913, NLS

72 "I wish to ..." WLM, diary, October 11–13, 1913, NLS

72 "the most good-natured ..." Mamen, diary, October 5, 1913, NAC

72 "encircled by the ..." Mamen, diary, October 5, 1913, NAC

72 "We may see ..." Mamen, diary, October 6, 1913, NAC

73 "For my part ..." Mamen, diary, October 23, 1913, NAC

73 "Our large ice ..." Mamen, diary, October 8-19, 1913, NAC

74 "No human power ..." De Long, *The Voyage of the Jeannette*, Volume Two, pp. 473–474

74 "I suppose there ..." Mamen, diary, October 25, 1913, NAC

76 "By that time ..." Mamen, diary, October 30, 1913, NAC

76 "Oh my, how ..." Mamen, diary, October 30, 1913, NAC

NOVEMBER 1913

77 "*It is a dreary* ..." Mamen, diary, November 15, 1913, NAC

79 "'Captain Bartlett,' wrote ..." Mamen, diary, November 3, 1913, NAC

79 "I for my ..." Mamen, diary, November 6, 1913, NAC

80 "Ice and still ..." Mamen, diary, November 6, 1913, NAC

80 "It looks as ..." Mamen, diary, November 9, 1913, NAC

80 "Presumably Mr. Stefansson ..." Mamen, diary, November 9, 1914, NAC

80 There were 250 ... WLM, diary, November 8, 1913, NLS

81 "It surely will ..." Mamen, diary, November 4, 1913, NAC

81   "The effect of ..." Chafe, *The Voyage of the Karluk*, 15, MMBC

82   "I am sure ..." Mamen, diary, November 10, 1913, NAC

82   "People talk about ..." Mamen, diary, November 13, 1913, NAC

82   "It was difficult ..." WLM, diary, October 15, 1913, NLS

82   "Wonder and admire ..." WLM, diary, November 11, 1913, NLS

83   "A noise there ..." WLM, diary, November 14, 1913, NLS

83   "It is a pain ..." WLM, diary, November 14, 1913, NLS

83   "Just tipping the ..." WLM, diary, November 14, 1913, NLS

84   "Now he is ..." WLM, diary, November 14, 1913, NLS

84   "It blew and ..." Mamen, diary, November 20, 1913, NAC

84   Do you intend ... WLM, diary, November 15, 1913, NLS

85   "So long as ..." Chafe, *The Voyage of the Karluk*, p. 13, MMBC

85   "There is a ..." Chafe, *The Voyage of the Karluk*, p. 13, MMBC

86   "A faint, twilight ..." WLM, diary, November 20, 1913, NLS

87   "Meeting trouble half-way ..." WLM, diary, November 24, 1913, NLS

88   "It is not ..." Mamen, diary, November 2, 1913, NAC

89   "Everything that can ..." Mamen, diary, November 3, 1913, NAC

89   "I have gone ..." Mamen, diary, November 2-3, 1913, NAC

89   "There can be ..." De Long, *The Voyage of the Jeannette: The Journals of George W. De Long*, Vol. II, pp. 382-383 and 456; Background and details on the voyage of the *Jeannette* are based on De Long, 382–456, and passim.

DECEMBER 1913

90   "*We had suffered* ..." De Long, *The Voyage of the Jeannette*, p. 500

91   Another Eskimo reported ... It actually was the *Karluk*. Jenness, *Arctic Odyssey*, October 12, 1913

91   "it looks as ..." McConnell, diary, October 11, 1913, NAC

91   "A field-glass and ..." Jenness, *Arctic Odyssey*, October 25, 1913

92   "What we had ..." KGC, diary, December 14, 1913, NAC

92   "he could never ..." KGC, diary, December 16, 1913, NAC

93   "always took orders ..." Stefansson, letter to George Phillips, February 14, 1914, BC

93   "The newspapers were ..." Stefansson, *The Friendly Arctic*, p. 72

93   "What a time …" WLM, diary, December 19, 1913, NLS

95   "You would naturally …" Maurer, lecture, p. 32, NAC

96   "Gosh now, that's …" The *Christian Science Monitor*, "A Man in the News," BWD

96   "the weirdest possible …" WLM, diary, December 12, 1913, NLS

97   "'Gin ye see …" WLM, diary, December 13, 1913, NLS

97   "Yes, poor little …" Mamen, diary, December 24, 1913, NAC

100 "Because God gave …" RAB, *The Log of Bob Bartlett*, pp. 121–122

101 "Fellows … I want …" WLM, diary, December 25, 1913 (NLS)

101 "What thoughts passed …" WLM, diary, December 25, 1913, NLS

104 "We should get …" WLM, diary, December 21, 1913, NLS

104 "I hope no …" Mamen, diary, December 28, 1913, NAC

104 "I believe I …" Mamen, diary, December 29, 1913, NAC

104 "Is that land …" WLM, diary, December 29, 1913, NLS

106 "In one way …" Mamen, diary, December 11–17, 1913, NAC106

106 "The last day …" Mamen, diary, December 31, 1913, NAC

107 "raising the devil …" WLM, diary, December 31, 1913, NLS

JANUARY 1914

108 "*We must all …*" Mamen, diary, January 21, 1914, NAC

108 "extreme delicacy of …" WLM, diary, January 2, 1914, NLS

109 "God grant it …" WLM, diary, January 2, 1914, NLS

109 "Cracks and again …" Mamen, diary, January 3, 1914, NAC

111 "That time, that …" Mamen, diary, January 4, 1914, NAC

111 "it is no …" Mamen, diary, January 4-5, 1914, NAC

111 "I suppose this …" Mamen, diary, January 3, 1914, NAC

112 "Look out for …" Hadley's *Karluk* account in *The Friendly Arctic*, p. 733

113 "He who would …" Reynolds Hole, *A Book About Roses*, p. 1

114 "If we only …" Mamen, diary, January 9, 1914, NAC

115 "… we may expect …" Mamen, diary, January 9, 1914, NAC

116 "The ship was …" RAB, *The Last Voyage of the Karluk*, p. 86

116 "It was hard …" RAB, *The Last Voyage of the Karluk*, p.87

117 "I think we …" Hadley account, *The Friendly Arctic*, p. 733

117 "Then it was …" Mamen, diary, January 10, 1914, NAC

118 "On the poop ..." WLM, diary, January 10, 1914, NLS

118 "All hands abandon ..." RAB, *The Last Voyage of the Karluk*, p. 88

119 "too busy to ..." WLM, diary, January 10, 1914, NLS

120 "That is enough ..." Maurer, lecture, p. 34, NAC

120 "One cannot speak ..." WLM, diary, January 10, 1914, NAC

122 "I am sure ..." WLM, diary, January 11, 1914, NAC

122 "She's going ..." WLM, diary, January 11, 1914, NLS

123 "As we watched ..." Chafe, *The Voyage of the Karluk*, pp. 19-20, MMBC

123 "Our home was ..." Maurer, lecture, p. 34, NAC

124 "She was a ..." WLM, diary, January 11, 1914, NLS

124 "Goodbye, old girl." RAB, *The Log of Bob Bartlett*, p. 267

124 "That, and a ..." Chafe, *The Voyage of the Karluk*, p. 48, MMBC

124 "Where in hell ..." RAB, *The Log of Bob Bartlett*, pp. 6-7

125 "preparing for our ..." WLM, diary, January 11, 1914, NLS

125 "Mr. Stefansson is ..." Mamen, diary, January 11, 1914, NAC

126 "... had now only ..." Mamen, diary, January 11, 1914, NAC

126 "This has made ..." WLM, diary, January 10, 1914, NLS

127 "The ice that ..." Maurer, lecture, p. 35, NAC

127 "But I was ..." RAB, *The Log of Bob Bartlett*, p. 268

127 "Coffee!" WLM, diary, January 12, 1914, NLS

128 "tasted as sweet ..." WLM, diary, January 12, 1914, NLS

128 "We have reached ..." WLM, diary, January 15, 1914, NLS

129 "I sincerely hope ..." Mamen, diary, January 13–15, 1914, NAC

130 "She used it ..." Chafe, *The Voyage of the Karluk*, p. 21, MMBC

131 "thus, & only ..." WLM, diary, January 11, 1914, NLS

131 "They grumble if ..." WLM, diary, January 11, 1914, NLS

132 "I have decided ..." Mamen, diary, January 12, 1914, NAC

132 "Wouldn't we give ..." WLM, diary, January 15, 1914, NLS

133 "Now look here ..." WLM, diary, January 16, 1914, NLS

134 "We may thus ..." WLM, diary, January 17, 1914, NLS

136 "All the time ..." Chafe, *The Voyage of the Karluk*, p. 22, MMBC

137 "It gets on ..." Mamen, diary, January 20, 1914, NAC

138 "One must take ..." Mamen, diary, January 17, 1914, NAC

138 "Au revoir ... Good ..." WLM, diary, January 21, 1914, NLS

140 "Oh, what a ..." Mamen, diary, January 22, 1914, NAC

141 "I have not ..." Mamen, diary, January 24, 1914, NAC

142 "We came closer ..." Mamen, diary, January 25, 1914, NAC

143 "we shiver and ..." Mamen, diary, January 27, 1914, NAC

143 "wetter and wetter ..." Mamen, diary, January 28, 1914, NAC

143 "I have suffered ..." Mamen, diary, January 28, 1914, NAC

145 "You are going ..." Hadley, *Karluk* account in *The Friendly Arctic*, p. 734

146 "I reminded the ..." Hadley, *Karluk* account in *The Friendly Arctic*, p. 735

149 "throw themselves on ..." WLM, diary, January 31, 1914, NLS

150 "We are at ..." WLM, diary, January 30, 1914, NLS

151 "I have come ..." Mamen, diary, January 30, 1914, NAC

152 "It is remarkable ..." Mamen, diary, January 30, 1914, NAC

153 "hop along the ..." Mamen, diary, January 30, 1914, NAC

FEBRUARY 1914

154 *"Then to this ..." The Rubáiyát of Omar Kháyyam*, p. 76

154 "Give me a rifle ..." Hadley, quoted in *The Friendly Arctic*, p. 735

155 "They will now ..." Mamen, diary, February 1, 1914, NAC

156 "Here they're; here ..." WLM, diary, February 3, 1914, NLS

156 "Well done, Norway ..." RAB, *Northward Ho: The Last Voyage of the Karluk*, 125

157 "Oh, how nice ..." Mamen, diary, February 3, 1914, NAC

158 "There is nobody ..." Mamen, diary, February 4, 1914, NAC

160 "The temperature was ..." Chafe, *The Voyage of the Karluk*, p. 27, MMBC

161 "I do not ..." Mamen, diary, February 9, 1914, NAC

161 "If you lose ..." Chafe, *The Voyage of the Karluk*, p. 27, MMBC

162 "A night of ..." Chafe, *The Voyage of the Karluk*, p. 27, MMBC

162 "Herald Island is ..." Chafe, *The Voyage of the Karluk*, p. 28, MMBC

163 "I believe the ..." Chafe, *The Voyage of the Karluk*, p. 28, MMBC

165 "It's useless for ..." Chafe, *The Voyage of the Karluk*, p. 30, MMBC

165 "'Go on,' this ..." Chafe, *The Voyage of the Karluk*, p. 30, MMBC

166 For several days ... Interview with Emily Wilson, daughter of Mugpi, December 30, 1999

166 "Thus easily are ..." WLM, diary, February 12, 1914, NLS

167 "Mush! Mush!" ... WLM, diary, February 16, 1914, NLS

168 "Why, there is ..." Chafe, *The Voyage of the Karluk*, p. 31, MMBC

168 "You must keep ..." Mamen, diary, February 14, 1914, NAC

169 "They have a ..." Mamen, diary, February 17, 1914, NAC

170 "There is a bear ..." Chafe, *The Voyage of the Karluk*, p. 24, MMBC

172 "For the farther ..." Hadley, quoted in *The Friendly Arctic*, 737

172 "The limit of ..." RAB, *Northward Ho: The Last Voyage of the Karluk*, 147

173 "Tea! Thou soft ..." RAB, Log, 1914, BWD

175 "Canadian Arctic Expedition ..." RAB, memorandum (copy of record left at Shipwreck Camp), Bartlett Papers, BWD

176 "Wriggle your fingers ..." WLM, *Karluk: The Great Untold Story of Arctic Exploration*, 81

176 "If you can't ..." WLM, *Karluk: The Great Untold Story of Arctic Exploration*, 81

177 "'Oh boy,' Bartlett ..." WLM, *Karluk: The Great Untold Story of Arctic Exploration*, 82

177 "World in torment ..." WLM, diary, February 26, 1914, NLS

178 "The ice was ..." WLM, diary, February 26, 1914, NLS

178 "No way of ..." Mamen, diary, February 28, 1914, NAC

178 "Certainly a fine ..." Mamen, diary, February 28, 1914, NAC

MARCH 1914

180 *"It really does..."* WLM, diary, March 22, 1914, NLS

181 "That no 'relief' ..." Stefansson to RMA, March 10, 1914, NAC

181 "The front of ..." Chafe, *The Voyage of the Karluk*, pp. 39–40, MMBC

181 "To look at ..." WLM, diary, February 28–March 3, 1914, NLS

182 "Would grade a ..." Chafe, *The Voyage of the Karluk*, p. 40, MMBC

182 "Building a road ..." RAB, *Northward Ho: The Last Voyage of the Karluk*, pp. 155–156

183 "You will have ..." Mamen, diary, March 2, 1914, NAC

185 "Fantastic, mountainous formations ..." RAB, *Northward Ho: The Last Voyage of the Karluk*, pp. 155-156

185 "It was with ..." Chafe, *The Voyage of the Karluk*, p. 40, MMBC

186 "I don't give ..." Mamen, diary, March 10, 1914, NAC

187 "I have also ..." WLM, diary, March 9, 1914, NLS

187 "It don't matter ..." WLM, diary, March 11, 1914, NLS

188 "'Nuna!' he was ..." WLM, diary, March 12, 1914, NLS

188 "The most desolate ..." Chafe, *The Voyage of the Karluk*, pp. 41–42, MMBC

189 "What a sense ..." Maurer, lecture, p. 40, NAC

189 "No braver man ..." Quoted in Maurer, lecture, p. 40, NAC (Chafe gives this same account in *The Voyage of the Karluk*, p. 43. He apparently often "borrowed" Maurer's words verbatim from *World Magazine* articles Maurer wrote in 1915 and used them in his own account of the *Karluk* story.)

190 "Three polar bears ..." RAB, *Northward Ho: The Last Voyage of the Karluk*, 164

194 "'Canny Scot,' Bartlett ..." WLM, *Karluk: The Great Untold Story of Arctic Exploration* p. 95

194 "It is neither ..." WLM, diary, March 19, 1914, NAC

202 "It was a slow ..." RAB, *The Last Voyage of the Karluk*, p. 190

205 "That land? ..." RAB, *The Last Voyage of the Karluk*, p. 195

205 "We see no ..." RAB, *The Last Voyage of the Karluk*, p. 195

206 "If you 'fraid ..." RAB, *The Last Voyage of the Karluk*, p. 196

206 "Me see him ..." RAB, *The Last Voyage of the Karluk*, p. 19

APRIL 1914

208 *"It's Hell all..."* Munro, diary, April 5, 1914, NAC

210 "Work round the ..." Chafe, *The Voyage of the Karluk*, p.48, MMBC. Details of Chafe's harrowing ordeal are drawn largely from his own account.

214 "Is that you ..." Chafe, *The Voyage of the Karluk*, p. 55, MMBC

217 "I wonder when ..." WLM, diary, April 28, 1914, NLS

217 "I don't know ..." Munro, diary, April 28, 1914, NAC

217 "Everyone here swears ..." WLM, diary, April 28, 1914, NLS

217 "Another month gone ..." WLM, diary, April 30, 1914, NLS

218 "The worst going ..." Hadley, diary, April 28, 1914, NAC

218 "I could swear ..." Mamen, diary, April 15, 1914, NAC

219 "Being in poor ..." Mamen, diary, April 3, 1914, NAC

220 "Yes, I see ..." Mamen, diary, April 10, 1914, NAC

221 "Happily it wasn't ..." Mamen, diary, April 14, 1914, NAC

221 "I have you ..." Mamen, diary, April 14, 1914, NAC

221 "Malloch is certainly ..." Mamen, diary, April 15, 1914, NAC

221 "We will soon ..." Mamen, diary, April 16, 1914, NAC

222 "So that we ..." Mamen, diary, April 18, 1914, NAC

222 "It is a ..." Mamen, diary, April 22, 1914, NAC

223 "With the spring ..." Mamen, diary, April 26, 1914, NAC

224 "I don't know what ..." Mamen, diary, April 28, 1914, NAC

224 "I don't know how ..." Mamen, diary, April 30, 1914, NAC

225 "Eskimo see me ..." RAB, *The Last Voyage of the Karluk*, p. 208

225 "Which is permanently ..." RAB, *The Last Voyage of the Karluk*, p. 202

225 "Snowshoes are indispensable ..." RAB, *The Last Voyage of the Karluk*, p. 204

226 "'Ardegar,' Kataktovik said ..." RAB, *The Last Voyage of the Karluk*, p. 206

226 "Where we go? ..." RAB, *The Last Voyage of the Karluk*, p. 206

226 "It seemed pretty ..." RAB, *The Last Voyage of the Karluk*, p. 206

226 "'Eskimo igloo,' he ..." RAB, *The Last Voyage of the Karluk*, p. 208

226 "'Ardegar,' said Bartlett ..." RAB, *The Last Voyage of the Karluk*, p. 208

227 "'Maybe,' Bartlett said ..." RAB, *The Last Voyage of the Karluk*, p. 208

227 "You drive the ..." RAB, *The Last Voyage of the Karluk*, p. 209

227 "How do you ..." RAB, *The Last Voyage of the Karluk*, p. 209

228 "Eating sociably with ..." RAB, *The Last Voyage of the Karluk*, p. 210

229 "Me no savvy ..." RAB, *The Last Voyage of the Karluk*, p. 213

229 "I wondered how ..." RAB, *The Last Voyage of the Karluk*, p. 219

230 "Whisper of the ... Northeastern Siberia." Http://
umbra.gsfc.nasa.gov/elipse/970309 ... /weather-ne-siberia.htm

230 "One of the ..." RAB, *The Last Voyage of the Karluk*, p. 240

232 "Me speak 'em ..." RAB, *The Last Voyage of the Karluk*, p. 249

232 "I bring you ..." RAB, *The Last Voyage of the Karluk*, 249

232 "How much you ..." RAB, *The Last Voyage of the Karluk*, p. 250

232 "'Forty dollars,' said ..." RAB, *The Last Voyage of the Karluk*, p. 250

234 "Daredevil of northern ..." RAB, *The Last Voyage of the Karluk*, p. 262

234 "The second stage ..." RAB, *The Last Voyage of the Karluk*, p. 26

MAY 1914

238 "Tempers seem to ..." WLM, diary, May 8, 1914, NLS

238 "and dream of ..." WLM, diary, May 3, 1914, NAC

238 "What a godsend ..." WLM, diary, May 3, 1914, NAC

238 "we have sufficient ..." WLM, diary, May 3, 1914, NAC

240 "I hope some ..." WLM, diary, May 10, 1914, NAC

240 "Me no good ..." WLM, diary, May 12, 1914, NLS

241 "Munro's job is ..." WLM, diary, May 13, 1914, NAC

241 "contemptable rotter."Hadley, diary, May 21, 1914, NAC

241 "I would not ..." Hadley diary, May 14, 1914, NAC

242 "It's hard to ..." Munro, diary, May 14, 1914, NAC

243 "fed up with ..." Munro, diary, May 16, 1914, NAC

244 "It's Hell to ..." Munro, diary, May 23, 1914, NAC

244 "Me make baron ..." RAB, *The Last Voyage of the Karluk*, p. 275

247 "the worst man ..." Mamen, diary, May 5, 1914, NAC

248 "Half a pound ..." Mamen, diary, May 3, 1914, NAC

248 "I for my ..." Mamen, diary, May 6, 1914, NAC

248 "I feel weaker ..." Mamen, diary, May 6, 1914, NAC

249 "It is getting ..." Mamen, diary, May 7, 1914, NAC

250 He could only ... Mrs. RMA to McKinlay, April 25, 1915, NLS

251 "stretched his legs ..." Mamen, diary, May 17, 1914, NAC

251 "Yes, this 17th ..." Mamen, diary, May 17, 1914, NAC

251 "I don't know ..." Mamen, diary, May 18, 1914, NAC

253 "the 'scientist' was ..." WLM, diary, May 19, 1914, NAC

254 "It is a ..." WLM, diary, May 18-May 25, 1914, NAC

255 "could look down ..." RAB, *The Last Voyage of the Karluk*, pp. 277–278

255 "almost took a ..." RAB, *The Last Voyage of the Karluk*, p. 278

255 "two months had ..." RAB, *The Last Voyage of the Karluk*, p. 278

JUNE 1914

263 *"A letter from ..."* Mrs. Rudolph Martin Anderson in a letter to George Phillips, May 15, 1914, NLS

265 "Up against it ..." Hadley, diary, June 2, 1914, NAC

266 "'Underwood Pemmican again ... '" Hadley, diary, June 5, 1914, NAC

267 "A season in ..." Robert E. Peary, *The North Pole*, p. 19

268 "'I think,' Hadley ..." Hadley, diary, June 5, 1914, NAC

269   "Behold, there is …" WLM, diary, June 5, 1914, quoting *The Book of Genesis,* 42: 2 (In the verse in its entirety, Jacob said, "Behold, I have heard that there is corn in Egypt: get you down thither, and buy for us from thence; that we may live, and not die.")

269   "I take it …" WLM, diary, June 6, 1914, NAC

271   "In no very …" WLM, diary, June 7, 1914, NAC

272   "seems to be …" WLM, diary, June 13, 1914, NAC

275   "They went about …" WLM, First Draft Manuscript, *Karluk*, 242, NAC

276   "Hadley declares that …" WLM, June 13, 1914, p. 80, NAC

277   "Are we going …" Interview with Emily Wilson, daughter of Mugpi, December 30, 1999

277   "Are you sure …" Interview with Emily Wilson, daughter of Mugpi, December 30, 1999

280   "then came back …" WLM, diary, June 22, 1914, NLS

281   "fairly good for …" Munro, diary, June 18, 1914, NAC

281   "Orgy of charges …" WLM, diary, June 18, 1914, NAC

281   "This, Munro well …" WLM, diary, June 18, 1914, NLS

282   "Informing Hadley of …" WLM, diary, June 18, 1914, NLS

283   "I believe he …" Hadley, diary, June 18, 1914, NAC

285   "It was a terrible …" Burt McConnell, "The Rescue of the 'Karluk' Survivors," *Harper's Monthly Magazine*, February 1915, p. 358

286   "in that state …" Burt McConnell, "The Rescue of the 'Karluk' Survivors," *Harper's Monthly Magazine*, February 1915, p. 358

286   "We are living …" Munro, diary, June 29, 1914, NAC

287   "Clam! Call Hadley! …" WLM, diary, June 25, 1914, NLS

287   "What is the …" Hadley, diary, June 25, 1914, NAC

287   "Powder-burned and blackened …" Hadley, diary, June 25, 1914, NAC

287   "Have you another …" Hadley Appendix, Stefansson, *The Friendly Arctic*, p. 746.

288   "and there has …" WLM, diary, June 25, 1914, NLS

288   "'Of course,' he …" Chafe, *The Voyage of the Karluk*, pp. 62-63, MMBC

288   "Charlie, there has …" Chafe, *The Voyage of the Karluk*, p. 64, MMBC

289   "Breddy said he …" Chafe, *The Voyage of the Karluk*, p. 64, MMBC

289   "Wednesday last, they …" WLM, diary, June 26, 1914, 88, NLS

290   "The temptation recurred …" WLM, First Draft Manuscript, *Karluk*, p. 256, NAC

291 "And would not ..." Chafe, *The Voyage of the Karluk*, p. 65 MMBC

292 "One point I ..." WLM, diary, June 28, 1914, NLS292

292 "Our suspicions have ..." WLM, diary, June 29, 1914, NLS

293 "that Breddy's Eyes ..." Hadley, diary, June 28, 1914, NAC

293 "I think it's ..." Hadley, diary, June 30, 1914, NAC

JULY 1914

294 *"Now that time ..." WLM,* diary, July 22, 1914, NAC

296 "One good look ..." RAB, *The Log of Bob Bartlett*, p. 4

296 "could pinch them ..." Chafe, *The Voyage of the Karluk*, pp. 65–66, MMBC

298 "I am sure ..." WLM, diary, July 2, 1914, NLS

298 "made by cutting ..." WLM, diary, July 5, 1914, NLS

298 "acquired taste."WLM, diary, July 5, 1914, NAC

299 "Eight days of ..." WLM, diary, July 12, 1914, NLS

299 a seashore plant ... Pielou, *Naturalist's Guide to the Arctic*, p. 129

300 "created shocked surprise ..." WLM, diary, July 13, 1914, NAC

300 "sundry parts."WLM, diary, July 14, 1914, NAC

300 "It helps to ..." WLM, diary, July 16, 1914, NAC

301 "A few southerly ..." WLM, diary, July 13, 1914, NLS

301 "Rain, fog and ..." WLM, diary, July 17, 1914, NAC

302 "Let us pray ..." WLM, diary, July 14, 1914, NAC

302 "as a kind ..." RAB, *The Last Voyage of the Karluk*, p. 298

303 "It was a ..." RAB, *The Last Voyage of the Karluk*, p. 298

304 "SOME letter for ..." McConnell, diary, June 1, 1914, NAC

304 "At the time ..." McConnell, diary, July 1, 1914, NAC

305 "It was a ..." Maurer, lecture, p. 46, NAC

306 "little room for ..." Maurer, lecture, p. 47, NAC

306 "was enough to ..." WLM, diary, July 22, 1914, NAC

307 "would give us ..." Chafe, *The Voyage of the Karluk*, p. 67, MMBC

307 "Hey, boys! The ..." Chafe, *The Voyage of the Karluk*, p. 67, MMBC

307 "is so hard ..." Chafe, *The Voyage of the Karluk,* p. 68, MMBC

307 "both lean and ..." WLM, diary, July 20, 1914, NLS

308 "Thus does our ..." WLM, diary, July 21, 1914, NAC

308 "No more unfavourable ..." WLM, diary, July 23, 1914, NAC

309 "often on ice ..." WLM, diary, July 30, 1914, NAC

310 "It may be ..." WLM, diary, July 29, 1914, NAC

310 "We are all ..." Munro, diary, July 18, 1914, NAC

311 "It seems as ..." Munro, diary, July 24–28, 1914, NAC

AUGUST 1914

312 *"what will be ..."* WLM, diary, August 27, 1914, NAC

312 "We are now ..." WLM, diary, August 4, 1914, NAC

314 "Less than an ..." Chafe, *The Voyage of the Karluk*, p. 69, MMBC

315 "In spite of ..." WLM, diary, August 13, 1914, NAC

316 "What his real ..." WLM, First Draft, Manuscript, *Karluk*, pp. 272–273, NAC

317 "That now is ..." WLM, diary, August 10, 1914, NLS

317 "The monotony of waiting ... WLM, diary, August 12, 1914, NAC

318 "savagely, with thought ..." Maurer, lecture, p. 48, NAC

318 "Spoiled and rancid ..." Maurer, lecture, p. 48, NAC

318 "Talk about putrid ..." Maurer, lecture, p. 48, NAC

318 "We were in ..." Maurer, lecture, p. 47, NAC

319 "Things on the ..." Munro, diary, August 7, 1914, NAC

320 "Wandered ankle-deep in ..." Williamson, "The Cry of the Owl," *Victoria Daily Colonist*, Sunday, March 8, 1959

319 "Pale faces and ..." Williamson, "The Cry of the Owl"

321 "To me, he ..." Williamson, "The Cry of the Owl," *Victoria Daily Colonist*, March 1, 1959

321 "For what reason ..." Williamson, "The Cry of the Owl," March 8, 1959

321 "He had better ..." Hadley, diary, pp. 144–145, NAC

322 "Would not be ..." WLM, First Draft Manuscript, p. 274, NAC

323 "As good a horse ..." WLM, First Draft Manuscript, p. 274, NAC

324 "In chopping wood ..." Maurer, lecture, p. 49, NAC

325 Managed by the... McKinlay calls Captain Jochimsen "Joachim" in his book

325 "Steering such a ship ..." Bartlett, *The Last Voyage of the Karluk*, p. 302

327 "It was getting ..." Bartlett, *The Last Voyage of the Karluk*, p. 307

327 "Had been nightmares ..." Bartlett, *The Last Voyage of the Karluk*, p. 307

328 "If the ship ..." Hadley, diary, August 28, 1914, NAC

328 "And things that ..." Chafe, *The Voyage of the Karluk*, p. 73, MMBC

329 "That blanket that ..." Chafe, *The Voyage of the Karluk*, pp. 73-74, MMBC

329 "No, no ship ..." Chafe, *The Voyage of the Karluk*, pp. 68-69, MMBC

329 "We had been ..." Chafe, *The Voyage of the Karluk*, pp. 70-71 MMBC

330 "Will relief ever ..." Munro, diary, August 27, 1914, NAC

331 "The days that ..." Bartlett, *The Last Voyage of the Karluk*, p. 309

332 "I could only ..." Bartlett, *The Last Voyage of the Karluk*, p. 310

SEPTMBER 1914

333 *"There were twenty..."* Chafe, *The Voyage of the Karluk*, p. 79, MMBC

334 "bent on outdoing..." WLM, diary, September 3, 1914, NAC

335 "Every cloud has..." Munro, diary, September 3, 1914, NAC

335 "The Lord had..." Munro, diary, September 6, 1914, NAC

339 "That man long..." McConnell, *Harper's Monthly Magazine*, February 1915, "The Rescue of the *Karluk* Survivors," p. 356

340 "I don't know..." McConnell, *Harper's Monthly Magazine*, p. 357

340 "How did you..." McConnell, *Harper's Monthly Magazine*, p. 357

341 "Have you a... Breakfast." McConnell, *Harper's Monthly Magazine*, p. 357

342 "The ship is ..." Maurer, lecture, p. 50, NAC

342 "transcendentally resplendent." Maurer, lecture, p. 50, NAC

343 "No, we want..." Maurer, lecture, p. 50, NAC

343 "resting place of ..." Maurer, lecture, p. 47, NAC

343 "There was nothing..." Munro, diary, September 7, 1914, NAC

343 "Mr. Swenson, I..." McConnell, *Harper's Monthly Magazine*, "The Rescue of the *Karluk* Survivors," p. 359

344 "Umiakpik kunno! Umiakpik..." WLM, diary, September 7, 1914, NLS

344 "How we got..." WLM, diary, September 7, 1914, NLS

344 "raised a shout..." WLM, diary, September 7, 1914, NAC

346 "No, thank you... much." Chafe, *The Voyage of the Karluk*, pp. 76-77, MMBC

346 "Now that we ..." Chafe, *The Voyage of the Karluk*, p. 77, MMBC

346 "We're alive now..." Interview with Emily Wilson, daughter of Mugpi, December 30, 1999

347 "it didn't mean..." WLM, diary, September 7, 1914, NLS

347 "I don't think..." Chafe, *The Voyage of the Karluk*, p. 77, MMBC

349 "my head was..." WLM, diary, September 7, 1914, NLS

349 "all sorts of..." WLM, diary, September 7, 1914, NLS

349 "God bless the..." WLM, diary, September 7, 1914, NLS

351 "as heartily as..." WLM, diary, September 8, 1914, NLS

351 "All of you..." RAB, *The Last Voyage of the Karluk*, p. 314

351 "No, sir... island." RAB, *The Last Voyage of the Karluk*, p. 314

352 "had thus reached..." RAB, *The Last Voyage of the Karluk*, p. 314

352 "luxury unqualified" WLM, diary, September 8, 1914, NLS

353 "I have clear..." WLM, letter to Mr. Mamen, November 7, 1976, NCS

353 "It was as..." RAB, *The Last Voyage of the Karluk*, p. 317

354 "We were questioned..." WLM, letter to family, September 12, 1914, NLS

355 "I do not..." WLM, letter to family, September 12, 1914, NLS

356 "Just think of..." WLM, letter to family, September 12, 1914, NLS

THE WAKE

357 "Do you have..." WLM, *Karluk: The Great Untold Story of Arctic Exploration*, p. 160

358 "I had no..." WLM, undated letter fragment, "Letters re. Members of the CAE," NLS

358 "grand fellows ... grimmest." WLM, undated letter to family of Hugh "Clam" Williams, NLS

358 "There is not..." Chafe, *The Voyage of the Karluk*, p. 21, MMBC

359 "I want to..." Robert Williamson, June 1959 letter to Vilhjalmur Stefansson, NAC

359 "Please do not..." Williamson, undated letter to Stefansson, NAC

360 "a sad occasion..." Untitled fragment, WLM Collection, NLS, DEP 357, No. 38

360 "I very much..." M. Forbes Mackay, undated letter, NLS

361 The Mamen brothers... Mrs. RMA, "Re: Translation of Mamen Diary," June 19, 1930, NLS

361 "I will do ..." Valborg Mamen, letter to Mrs. RMA, November 10, 1925, NLS

362 "Ellen, has had..." Valborg Mamen, letter to Mrs. RMA, November 10, 1925, NLS

362 "The said death..." "Re. The Goods of George Breddy, Deceased," Affidavit of W.L. McKinlay, November 5, 1923, NLS

362 "Another member of..." Mrs. RMA, 1922 Memorandum, NLS

362 "Over the years..." WLM, letter to John Raffles Cox, May 3, 1975, NLS

363 "blankety blank liar" Mrs. RMA, letter to WLM, February 9, 1922, NLS

363 "I think he..." Letter from Jim Lotz to WLM, June 5, 1977, NLS

363 "I want to..." WLM, letter to Mrs. Cook, January 14, 1977, NLS

364 "As far as..." WLM, *Karluk*, 2nd draft, Part 1B, p. 363, NAC

364 "that a commissioner..." Unidentified newspaper clipping

364 "no good could..." Charles Camsell, Deputy Minister of Canada, June 8, 1923, NAC

365 "She's all I've..." The *New York Times*, "The Far Horizon," June 22, 1938

365 In the years... Horwood, *Bartlett: The Great Canadian Explorer*, p. 114

366 "McKinlay is a..." RAB, letter to Dr. W.S. Bruce, November 12, 1914

366 "Speaking of heroes..." WLM Collection, NLS, DEP 357, No. 25

366 "When I die..." *Times Herald*, "Bartlett Here for lecture," January 6, 1940

367 "I owe that..." WLM, bookflap of *Karluk: The Great Untold Story of Arctic Exploration*

367 "My writing, I..." WLM, letter to Richard Diubaldo, February 1974, NLS

EPILOGUE

369 "I am not ..." *The Daily Colonist*, October 14, 1924

369 "All seem to ..." *The Daily Colonist*, October 14, 1924

MAPS

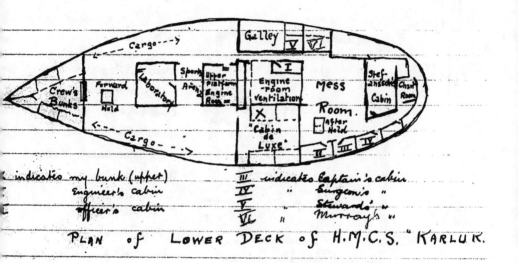

William McKinlay's plan of the lower deck of the *Karluk.*

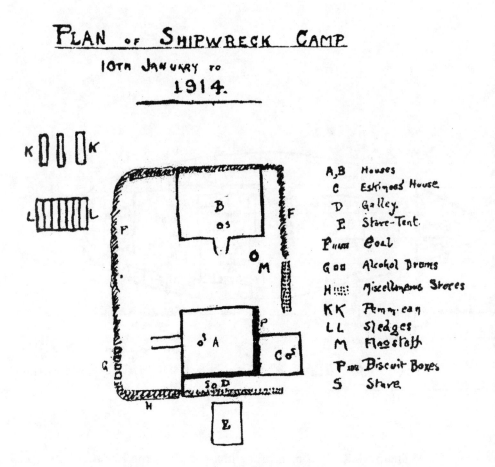

Plan of Shipwreck Camp, drawn by William McKinlay at Captain Bartlett's request.

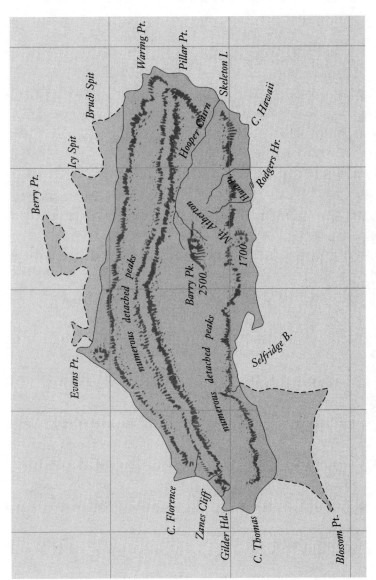

A tracing of Mamen's detailed pencil sketch of Wrangel Island.

PHOTO AND MAP CREDITS

The author makes grateful acknowledgment to the following for permission to reprint photographs:

BC Archives: D-09078 (cover photograph), 3 (G-07484)

National Archives of Canada: 1 (C-018139), 2 (PA-074063), 4 (C-086412), 5 (PA-203456), 6 (PA-203452), 7 (PA-105125), 8 (PA-074058), 9 (C-070806), 10 (PA-074053), 11 (PA-203453), 12 (PA-074047), 13 (PA-074041), 14 (C-086406), 15 (PA-203460), 16 (PA-074059), 17 (C-071058), 19 (PA-074035), 20 (C-070808), 23 (C-071039), 24 (C-071032), 25 (C-071035), 26 (C-071034), 27 (C-071050), 28 (C-071045), 29 (C-071023), 31 (C-071020), 32 (PA-074084), 33 (PA-074074), 34 (PA-203447), 36 (Lomen Bros., Nome/PA-105130), 37 (C-025961)

National Library of Scotland: 18, 21, 22, 30, 35 (Lomen Bros., Nome/NLS)

Grateful acknowledgment is also made to Bowdoin College Library (The Robert A. Bartlett Papers, Special Collections & Archives) for permission to print a tracing of Bjarne Mamen's map of Wrangel Island which appears on page 397; and to Nancy Scott and the National Library of Scotland (Correspondence and Papers of William Laird McKinlay, DEP 357) for McKinlay's plans of the Karluk and Shipwreck Camp on pages 395 and 396.

ACKNOWLEDGMENTS

I could not have written this book alone. Nor did I.

First and foremost, I want to thank Captain Robert Bartlett and the people of the *Karluk* for letting me tell their story. And I am grateful to William McKinlay for leaving me such a priceless legacy and for sharing his obsession in the materials he left behind.

There are three people without whom I could not have written this book. The journey would have been much less fulfilling had they not shared it with me. I thank my mother and fellow writer, Penelope Niven, for unconditional love, friendship, and endless support and for teaching me from childhood that anything is possible. I thank my father, Jack F. McJunkin, Jr., an artist himself, for bestowing on me a passion for truth, beauty, and all things adventurous. I thank John Hreno, III, for making the fairy tale come true every day, for being there for me in every way, and for giving me the greatest happiness.

I am lucky to have an incredible, amazing literary agent, John Ware, without whom none of this would have happened. Enormous thanks to him, as well as to my fabulous film agent, Martin Shapiro, and the splendid Carole Blake.

Tremendous gratitude goes to my superb editor Will Schwalbe, who has been absolutely wonderful to work with and who has helped make this experience such a positive one. Thanks also to Mark Chait, his top-notch assistant, and the wonderful team at Hyperion for their terrific work—Bob Miller, Martha Levin, Ellen Archer, Michael Burkin, Jane Comins, Phil Rose, April Fleming, and Breene Wesson. With them, *The Ice Master* has found a marvelous home.

The Ice Master also found a marvelous home at Macmillan of London. Thanks to my sensational editor there, Georgina Morley, who has been such a delightful force, and her sterling assistant Stef Bierwerth. And to the entire outstanding Macmillan group—Ian Chapman, Jeremy Trevathan, Katie James, Caroline Turner, and Lisa Cropman—for everything.

I was fortunate to find the last remaining survivor of the *Karluk*—Mugpi. I owe her a special tribute for all she endured in 1913–1914, and all she has contributed here. I also thank her daughter, Emily Wilson, for her patience and time, as well as the other descendants of the *Karluk*'s men, who have become a sort of family to me over the past two years—a family I am honored to be a part of. McKinlay's daughter, Nancy Scott, has been extraordinary, and endlessly generous in sharing the world of her father with me. She freely opened her home and McKinlay's life to me. And I want, too, to thank her "other Jennifer," McKinlay's granddaughter Jennifer Byrd, for sharing her own insights.

It was the wish of Bjarne Mamen's mother that his diary and personal papers never be published in full. Yet Jens Anker and Sonja Carling, both relatives of Bjarne Mamen, have been kind enough to share with me what they could, while still respecting the wishes that were expressed long ago. Sandy Anderson's great-nephew, Peter Anderson, has likewise been generous and forthcoming with his uncle's materials. And Stuart Jenness, son of Southern Party anthropologist Diamond Jenness, has been a kindred soul and supporter from the beginning of this project. He has been a great resource and has offered indispensable information.

As I embarked on my research for the book, I was warned that the work would not always go smoothly. However, I never experienced anything but the utmost support and assistance from the following institutions and their skilled personnel: The British Columbia Archives (with special thanks to Michael Carter and Kelly Nolin); the Maritime Museum of British Columbia (special thanks to Lynn Wright); the National Archives of Canada (where Marcel Barriault, Marc Bisaillon, Hector Sanscartier, Michel Poitras, Jean Matheson, Larry McNally, Jim F. Kidd, Sere St-Denis, and David Samson were particularly helpful); the National Library of Scotland (thank you Colm McLaughlin, Karen Moran, Irene Danks, and Sally Harrower); Bowdoin College in Maine (with appreciation to Richard Lindemann, Jennifer C. Fradenburgh, Kathryn B. Donahue, Susan Burroughs, and Sean Monahan); Dartmouth College Library (Philip N. Cronenwett); and the Explorer's Club (Janet E. Baldwin).

In addition, I want to thank the following close, personal friends of William McKinlay for their kindness—Magnus and Mamie Magnusson and Lord George Emslie.

I am blessed with wonderful friends and family who have been nothing but supportive during this time in my life. My soul sister, Melissa McKay, deserves numerous mentions for her constant encouragement, laughter, joy, and commiseration. My oldest friend in the world, Joe Kraemer, deserves many thanks as well for knowing me backward and forward, and for keeping me eternally young. I also give thanks to my beloved grandmother Eleanor Niven and my remarkable aunts and uncles, Lynn Duval Clark, Phil Clark, Doris Knapp, Bill Niven, and Paula and Reid Sturdivant. My cousins have always been more like siblings to me, and they are Lisa Von Sprecken, Derek and Lisa Duval, Shannon Meade, Erik Sturdivant, Evan Sturdivant, and, my other "sister," Ashley Hurley. Thanks to Patsy and Charles McGee, Frankie and Harry Gamble, and Jimmy and Polly McJunkin. Special thanks to Gayle Keller McJunkin and my little brother, John Keller. And, of course, to my loyal literary cats, Percy Shelley (who never left my side while I was writing) and George Gordon, Lord Byron (who provided much-needed comic relief).

My west coast mother, Judy Kessler, and my dear friend and partner in crime, Angelo Sourmelis, have become my second family. Scott Berenzweig has kept me laughing and has always been there for me when I needed him. And thanks to the "Brother of my Soul" (who wishes to remain anonymous) for Lord Byron and literary discussions. There are friends too numerous to name, but I must mention David Solomon, George Liggins, Phil Fitzgerald, Annie Ward, Carol Edwards, Kyri Smith, Brian Loeser, Lisa Brucker, Bobbie Jo Dombey, Any Bordy, Jill Lessard, Lori Watanabe, Robert Hamilton, Curtis Atkisson, III, Michael Hawes, Deak and Beth Reynolds, Mike and Melanie Kraemer, Jane and George Silver, Norman Corwin, Barbara Hogenson and Jeffrey Couchman, Loffie and Rob Tyson, Betsy Sulavik Gallagher, Michael Brunet, Mary Ellen Kay, Mike Bertram, and James Earl Jones.

There are others who should be thanked. I benefited greatly from James Ronald Archer's diligence and persistence. Dr. James Meade was my medical consultant on hypothermia, nephritis, and every other polar malady known to man. Craig R. Harvey, chief coroner of LA County, shared with me his professional opinion on the details of George Breddy's death. Thanks to Dr. Roger K. Wilkinson for sharing his knowledge of Alister Forbes Mackay; to Adam Hyman and MPH Entertainment for offering their material; and to Richard Diubaldo, an expert on Vilhjalmur Stefansson and the Canadian Arctic. I am also grateful to my favorite photographer, Lisa Keating, and to Peter Martin, Harold A. Pretty, Greg Schenz, Bob Higashi, Brad Wagner, Sharon Obermann, Dan and Dorothea Petrie, the Renfrewshire Taxi Company in Scotland, the American Film Institute and *Velva Jean,* and Joe Kaiser, for teaching me "pure economy of words."

I also send special thanks to my high school guidance counselor who told me I should take secretarial classes, just in case my writing career didn't work out—and who, in saying so, helped inspire me to make it happen.

And on that note, to those who have inspired me—my mother, first of all, along with Anne Brontë, George Sand, and Jane Austen.

Steve Goddard deserves a paragraph of his own for leading me to the remains of Sandy Anderson's party. It was his fortuitous e-mail that alerted me to the auction on eBay. And thanks, too, to Jerry and Vangie Lee, for selling me the artifacts and for posting them on eBay in the first place.

I want to pay tribute to McKinlay's granddaughter, Tricia Scott, who is no longer here. And to the late Lucy Kroll, who believed in me years ago, before I was old enough to understand.

Finally, there are several important people in my life whom I will always miss, and with whom I wish I could share this experience now: Jack and Cleo McJunkin, who made me feel like the center of their world; Olin Niven, for knowing instinctively when he was needed and for teaching me the true meaning of the word "gentleman"; and Dick Knapp, who should have lived to see this book, and many more.

Sinking of the *Karluk*

ARCTIC OCEAN

Karluk Trapped in Ice

Wrangel Island

Herald Island

Point Barrow

Colville River

Cape Halkett

Koluchin Bay

Point Hope

Arctic Circle

Cape Onman

East Cape

Bering Strait

Port Clarence

Yukon River

SIBERIA

Gulf of Anadyr

Nome

St. Michael

ALASKA

St. Lawrence Island

Nunivak Island

BERING SEA

Unalaska

Aleutian Islands

PACIFIC OCEAN